Essentials of Marketing

This comprehensive textbook introduces students to all the core principles of marketing practice using an employability-focused approach. *Essentials of Marketing* is underpinned by six pillars, which flow through each chapter: marketing ethics, sustainability, stakeholder engagement, globalisation, the power of new media, and measuring success. The book demystifies theory by placing it in contexts which are recognisable to a diverse readership, using real-life case studies and examples designed to engage today's technologically savvy and internationally oriented students. The book includes a comprehensive running case study in which readers are invited to adopt the roles of marketing assistant, marketing manager, and marketing director within regional markets, applying the knowledge that they have learned in each chapter into modern, realistic contexts, which simulate a marketing career. Key features to aid learning and comprehension include case studies, chapter objectives and summaries, key learning points, and key questions. With a uniquely accessible and applied approach, *Essentials of Marketing* is designed as a core text for undergraduate and postgraduate students studying introduction to marketing, marketing management, and principles of marketing modules. Digital learning resources include a comprehensive instructor's manual to guide interaction with the applied case study, PowerPoint slides, and a test bank.

David M Brown is a marketing academic and leader of the PhD programme at Newcastle Business School, Northumbria University. A qualified teacher with 18 years' industrial experience, David has led modules and programmes at all levels in the UK and overseas. As a visiting academic at Exeter University, England, he leads an executive MBA module, whilst elsewhere he acts as an external examiner of doctoral submissions, and teaches courses and programme validation events for English, Scottish, and Australian institutions.

Alexander Thompson is a senior lecturer at the University of Exeter, where he teaches marketing courses and leads the MSc in international business programme. He is passionate about marketing. His research focuses on small-firm entrepreneurship, ethnographic research, and socio-cultural approaches to marketing. In addition to his academic activities, Alex works on numerous marketing research consultancy projects that are centred on helping organisations better understand the voice of their customers. He holds a bachelor of arts degree in cultural anthropology from the College of Wooster, an MBA from Central Michigan University, and a PhD from Imperial College.

Essentials of Marketing

Theory and Practice for a Marketing Career

David M Brown and
Alexander Thompson

Routledge
Taylor & Francis Group

LONDON AND NEW YORK

Cover image: © Getty Images

First published 2023
by Routledge
4 Park Square, Milton Park, Abingdon, Oxon OX14 4RN

and by Routledge
605 Third Avenue, New York, NY 10158

Routledge is an imprint of the Taylor & Francis Group, an informa business

British Library Cataloguing-in-Publication Data
A catalogue record for this book is available from the British Library

Library of Congress Cataloging-in-Publication Data
Names: Brown, David (Writer on marketing), author. | Thompson, Alexander
    (Writer on marketing), author.
Title: Essentials of marketing : theory and practice for a marketing career / David
    Brown and Alexander Thompson.
Description: Abingdon, Oxon ; New York, NY : Routledge, 2023. | Includes
    bibliographical references and index.
Identifiers: LCCN 2022014023 | ISBN 9780367773410 (hardback) |
    ISBN 9780367773427 (paperback) | ISBN 9780367773410 (ebook)
Subjects: LCSH: Marketing.
Classification: LCC HF5415 .B698 2023 | DDC 658.8—dc23/eng/20220323
LC record available at https://lccn.loc.gov/2022014023

ISBN: 978-0-367-77341-0 (hbk)
ISBN: 978-0-367-77342-7 (pbk)
ISBN: 978-1-003-17089-1 (ebk)

DOI: 10.4324/9781003170891

Typeset in Optima
by Apex CoVantage, LLC

Access the support material https://www.routledge.com/9780367773427

Contents

Acknowledgements

Alexander's acknowledgements:

To my family. Thank you for all your support.

David's acknowledgements:

Thank you to Tannya, Lee, and Dylan (my family, not the fictionalised people in the running case study), Sophia Levine and Melissa Noke of Routledge, former editorial assistant Emmie Shand, and co-author Alexander. Special thanks to Lee Brown for creating the eye-catching icons in this book at short notice.

Introduction to
Essentials of Marketing

Welcome to *Essentials of Marketing*. This textbook provides you with the most important theories, strategies, and practices in marketing. It is concise, written in everyday language, and intended primarily for university business students. It assumes no prior knowledge of marketing, other than what we all witness in our everyday lives, and explains any concepts in simple terms. You can dip into individual chapters in any order or read through the whole book to gain a more holistic understanding. There are questions, case studies, and exercises to let you apply your new-found knowledge in real-life contexts, and there are useful online materials for both students and educators.

The Six Pillars Underpinning Essentials of Marketing

Six major considerations flow through *Essentials of Marketing*: the importance of making ethical marketing decisions; the need to trade in a manner which is environmentally and commercially sustainable; the vital role played by a diverse range of stakeholders; the global nature of many marketers' activities; the essential nature of harnessing new media; and the requirement for marketers to measure the effectiveness of their strategies through appropriate metrics. To help signpost these considerations and encourage you to reflect upon them actively, each chapter includes questions appertaining to hypothetical situations in the following areas:

- ▶ Ethics
- ▶ Sustainability
- ▶ Stakeholders
- ▶ Global marketing
- ▶ New media
- ▶ Marketing metrics

DOI: 10.4324/9781003170891-1

When tackling these questions, try to be as critical as possible, putting yourself in the position of practitioners, customers, and other stakeholders.

The Zomotor Running Case Study and Simulated Career Path

A running case study also flows through the book. Zomotor is a fictitious motor manufacturer which makes cars and vans, and we follow three marketing employees of Zomotor as they undertake tasks appertaining to each chapter's content:

▶   Tannya is an early-career marketing assistant for Zomotor. She is based in Mexico.

▶   Dylan is a more established marketing manager for Zomotor. He is based in China.

▶   Lee is the global marketing director for Zomotor. They are based in Germany.

In each chapter, you will help Tannya, then Dylan, and then Lee to undertake increasingly complicated marketing tasks. As you do this, you will gain insights into how your own career should progress, should you choose to enter marketing. Specifically, you will be charged with adopting progressively more critical and strategic positions, focusing on the 'big picture', and guiding the overall direction of Zomotor.

Additional Case Studies

Each chapter also contains an additional case study of an organisation which has recently needed to undertake major work in a specific area of marketing. These organisations represent a wide variety of industries, customers, locations, products, and services, but all are successful, market-focused, and striving to meet the quickly evolving needs of international consumers and businesses.

Structure of the Book

This book is ideal for use as an accompanying text for single-semester or full-year marketing courses, leaving space for educators to accommodate ice-breaker and revision sessions. In addition to the features already described, each chapter has clear learning objectives and outcomes, and accompanying lecture slides, multiple choice questions, and revision terms are available. Full details are given in the contents page.

It just remains for us to wish you an enjoyable learning journey!

David and Alex: co-authors of *Essentials of Marketing*

Your Rolling Case Study: Zomotor

Zomotor is a successful motor manufacturer which makes cars, vans (light commercial vehicles), other passenger vehicles, and engines for aeroplanes. Headquartered in the south of Germany, it is over a century old and known predominantly for producing smaller cars and sporty cars. As such, its main competitors have been European carmakers such as Renault, Fiat, Citroen, and Peugeot, and Japanese and South Korean rivals such as Toyota, Nissan, Kia, and Hyundai. Although it achieves around 20% market share in its home market of Germany, Zomotor has a smaller presence elsewhere, generating around 8% market share in France and the UK, 6% in Southern and Eastern Europe, 3% in North America, and 5% in South America. It has almost no presence in Africa or Central America, where larger vehicles such as sport utility vehicles (SUVs) are popular due to the rougher road surfaces. Its attempt to penetrate the Asian market, by opening a joint manufacturing facility in China with a local manufacturer, was unsuccessful as it struggled to recruit enough dealers to sell its vehicles. This reliance on European sales was very problematic during the financial crisis of 2007–2009 and afterwards, as European economies suffered depressed wages and low consumer confidence, but the situation is now becoming more buoyant. However, executives at Zomotor would like to spread risk more thinly by gaining a foothold in emerging markets.

Since the turn of the millennium, several rival motor manufacturers have disappeared (e.g. Rover and Saab) or merged. To accrue the resources necessary for survival, firms must become bigger and stronger, achieving economies of scale and reducing costs. Increasingly, carmakers are joining forces to operate shared production facilities and to use each other's components. For this reason, the Toyota Aygo, Citroen C1, and Peugeot 107 city cars are almost identical, and a Volvo estate car may have the same gearbox, engine, and chassis as a Ford family hatchback. Moreover, many rivals make light commercial vehicles collaboratively, and Zomotor's small, medium, and large van products are shared with three of its European competitors.

Zomotor's executives have noted that the firm is too reliant on small cars and city cars for several reasons. Smaller cars usually carry smaller profit margins and attract more price-sensitive customers who are less likely to be loyal to one brand. Whilst this allows Zomotor to win customers from rivals, it also makes its customer retention more difficult. It has attempted to sell more family saloon and estate cars to compete with Ford and Honda, and particularly 'junior executive' cars to compete with BMW and Lexus. However, it has struggled to overcome customer perceptions of the firm as a small car manufacturer and the lack of prestige attached to the Zomotor brand. A high proportion of its customers are young adults, who often buy smaller cars to avoid higher insurance premiums and because they are less likely to have a family to transport, and older adults who are downsizing as they retire from work or when their children leave home. Zomotor has struggled to attract middle-aged drivers and those with families.

Around half of all new cars sold in the most economically developed nations are 'company cars', provided to drivers as part of their work remuneration package. For some drivers, the car is a 'perk' – a privilege provided by their employer to reduce the chance of them leaving the firm. For others, a car is essential to their role, as they need to travel flexibly to undertake company business. Some company car drivers are given little choice of vehicle by their employer, who may operate a solus badge or dual badge policy (i.e. only buying from one or two manufacturers) to gain a heavier discount and simplify the administrative burden. Other company car drivers are 'user-choosers' who may select any vehicle they wish, within reason, in pricing bands which reflect their seniority in the company. Whilst a few cash-rich organisations buy vehicles outright for their employees, most source them through finance or contract hire companies, leasing them for three or four years. Zomotor has attempted to increase its presence in this corporate fleet sector, using a field sales force to visit organisational decision makers on their premises, but has not achieved its desired success. It has managed to sell more cars to rental companies, which has increased sales volumes and brought the brand to more people's attention. However, rental companies demand very high discounts, and in some cases Zomotor has done loss-making, high-volume deals with rental companies to chase market share and to get its products seen by potential customers.

Zomotor fares much better in the retail sector – those customers who buy their own cars. By nurturing strong relationships with leasing and contract hire companies and providing large discounts, its cars are priced attractively to people who use finance to acquire their cars, and this accounts for over half of drivers. Executives feel that Zomotor's growth in the retail sector is hindered by a mediocre dealer network. Whilst Zomotor has numerous state-of-the-art retail sites in major population centres, many of these premises are operated by franchised dealers who also represent Zomotor's rivals on-site, thereby compromising the brand and giving them the opportunity to favour one manufacturer over another. In other areas, Zomotor's network is underdeveloped, relying on 'heritage' dealerships that have not evolved sufficiently with changes in consumer behaviour and market economics. In some major cities, it has 'open points' – places where it has not yet identified, recruited, and appointed a dealership to represent the brand. Zomotor often struggles to meet its retail sales targets because many of its dealers would rather sell fewer cars at a higher profit per unit, whereas Zomotor encourages dealers to sacrifice some of the initial sales profit to achieve other revenue sources such as warranty, servicing, maintenance, repair, finance, and insurance, which present themselves later in the customer relationship. A recent mystery shop exercise revealed that many dealer-based salespeople lacked product knowledge, failed to follow-up customer interest, and some even switched customers enquiring about Zomotor into rival products. As a result, executives are seeking to replace some dealerships and are considering introducing Zomotor-owned dealerships which do not represent another brand.

Zomotor is part way through refreshing its car model range. Whilst the 'new generation' models are selling well, the outgoing models require lower prices and higher specifications to sell them, and this risks distressing the brand by making it appear cheaper. It also damages residual values – the prices for which used vehicles can be sold at predetermined ages and mileages. This is significant because finance and leasing companies base their leasing rates on three major factors: the price for which they buy the vehicle, the price for which they sell the vehicle, and the amount the customer is willing to pay. An increasing number of drivers now opt for SUVs, multi-purpose vehicles (MPVs), and smaller or crossover versions of these. Zomotor has therefore moved into these product territories, finding them extremely competitive. It has responded to governments' emissions legislation and consumers' heightened environmental awareness by producing low CO_2-emitting engines with start-stop mechanisms to reduce unnecessary idling. This enables its cars to be sold in certain very stringent markets and allows customers to enjoy low vehicle tax rates. It has also invested heavily in the development of electric and biofuel vehicles. This has been very demanding of resources and has produced few incremental sales but is necessary if the company is to meet future demands and to defend against 'non-traditional' competitors such as Tesla or, potentially, Google or Amazon.

Heavy legislation around CO_2 emissions is only one of many challenges faced. European motor manufacturers are legally responsible for the environmental footprint of their cars 'from cradle to grave'. Therefore, they must ensure that almost 100% of the new vehicle can eventually be broken down and recycled at licenced scrappage sites. Safety legislation is also increasingly stringent, not just in terms of occupant safety but also that of pedestrians and other road users, and customers demand ever-higher levels of specifications in terms of safety (e.g. the number of airbags), comfort (e.g. multidirectional adjustment of seats and steering wheel), and convenience (e.g. space-saving spare wheels and fold-flat rear seats). When attempting to enter some emerging economies, Zomotor has faced inferior quality competition which has not had to meet such stringent standards. It has also found it difficult to put long-term export plans into place due to the very uncertain political climate in many countries and the unpredictable use of government import tariffs and trade wars. Closer to home, the introduction of congestion charging zones in many large cities such as London, and car-free areas in many others, has forced many urban commuters to abandon weekday car usage in favour of public transport. As a result, some people are replacing their cars less often, as they are accruing less wear and tear, and others are avoiding car ownership completely. Many young people are deferring car ownership while they try to repay student loans and save for an apartment or house. However, car ownership is growing globally and is at an all-time high.

Like most motor manufacturers, Zomotor has split its marketing efforts roughly equally between 'traditional' print, outdoor, and broadcast media on the one hand, and 'new media' through the internet on the other. It uses billboard and bus side advertising near major dealerships and city centres to build awareness, and it also advertises in airports and shopping malls. It finds these media effective in building customer awareness of its brand and products when it launches a new model or variant or defends against a new competitor product. Likewise, it also runs advertising campaigns on national television and regional radio stations in many major markets. The intention is to drive footfall into its car dealerships, to encourage curious passers-by to visit the company's website, and to encourage those drivers who have car purchases looming to consider Zomotor. It utilises online sponsored search results, banner and skyscraper adverts on social media sites like Facebook, targeted emails to prospects identified on the company database as being aligned to the product offering, and adverts on websites which specialise in buying, selling, or reviewing cars. Zomotor realises that peer-to-peer communication is powerful, so it stimulates word-of-mouth recommendations by attempting to create 'buzz' around its product. For example, prior to one product launch it left a number of its models garishly painted by avant-garde artists in various city locations associated with hipsters and media executives, and invited passing pedestrians to play a digital branded motor racing game against each other, which was then emailed to targeted prospects and went viral.

Realising the importance of retaining loyal customers, Zomotor has developed a relationship marketing strategy which aims to deliver value to customers at the various touchpoints which they have with the brand, and to introduce new touchpoints where it tries to delight its customers. For example, it sends a birthday card to the driver on the first anniversary of the sale, with discount vouchers for accessories and products such as upholstery spray. It holds summer festivals for owners of certain models, where entertainments are provided and a sense of brand community is nurtured. It invites customer feedback and acts upon it, even including a representative range of customers in its new product development decisions. Major fleet buyers are invited to 'ride and drive' events and to corporate golf days and factory visits, where they familiarise themselves with the products and form lasting relationships with Zomotor executives and dealer representatives.

Our Contacts Within Zomotor: Tannya, Dylan, and Lee

Tannya, Marketing Assistant, Mexico

Having recently graduated in marketing, Tannya has started her career with Zomotor as a marketing assistant at their national headquarters in Mexico City. Her main duties are to help collate market intelligence and sales data for use in internal reports, to arrange sales materials and training programmes for franchised dealerships, and to liaise with external service providers such as marketing agencies and conference organisers. She also answers queries from major clients and dealerships and gets involved in any area of the company's marketing and sales operations deemed necessary by her director.

Dylan, Marketing Manager, China

Six years after graduating in marketing, Dylan has recently been promoted to marketing manager. He has already spent time in the company's German, Russian, and South African offices and is now based in Beijing. He coordinates trade exhibitions and events, manages the customer database used by the company's marketers and salespeople, orders Zomotor China's trading and demonstrator stock from Zomotor's many global manufacturing plants, works with the product manager to decide what specification and pricing the China stock should carry, collaborates with the network development manager to help run the franchised dealer network, and is responsible for Zomotor China's fleet operations (i.e. its sales and marketing to corporate and public sector organisations).

Lee, Global Marketing Director, Germany

Twelve years into their career with Zomotor, Lee is the marketing director at Zomotor's headquarters in Germany. They are responsible for the company's marketing operations and strategy not just in Germany but also globally. As such, they decide what the organisation should sell, where, and at what price. They set the global strategy based upon the international commercial objectives, manage all budgets and targets related to marketing, and make the final decision over which agencies are employed and how all marketing resources are deployed. Their role focuses on long-term strategic objectives, but they must also act to tackle more pressing issues which are often brought about by unpredictable competitor actions.

1 Marketing and Environment

1 The Meaning of Marketing

Introduction

What is marketing? You might provide a wide variety of answers that range from advertising, to selling, to social media practices, to product development and branding. While all of these answers are correct, each answer only explains one aspect of marketing. Marketing really serves four important facets of everyday business activity. These are to attract new customers, to retain current customers, to represent the voice of the customer inside an organisation, and to manage stakeholder perceptions of an organisation.

As a functional area of business, the marketing department is responsible for sales. It is the only area of the organisation that is tasked with this mission. Marketing must generate enough sales to ensure organisational survival. However, in order to generate repeat sales (and not one-time transactions), marketers must make sure that they create customer satisfaction when generating those sales. Thus, customer service and after-sales support play important roles in maintaining customer relationships. Having highly trained customer-facing personnel and offering superior products/services that exceed customer expectations are ways that organisations can create customer satisfaction and value. Without sales revenue, customer satisfaction, and value creation, businesses are unlikely to survive.

Marketing is responsible for the voice of the customer. Marketers are tasked with understanding customer wants and needs and bringing the voice of the customer inside an organisation. One way that they accomplish this goal is by conducting market research, which means that they collect information directly from customers in order to better understand their wants and needs. Marketers then take that information and disseminate it to other functional areas of the business.

For example, marketers must ensure that the accounting department takes into consideration the pricing needs of an organisation's customers. Marketers work with human resource managers to ensure that the organisation is training front-line personnel to best serve customers. Marketers also work with research and development (R&D) teams to ensure customer needs are taken into consideration when designing new products and services. One of the great things about marketing is that marketers often act as intermediaries between an organisation's customers and the organisation's internal departments. Marketers and marketing play a key role in understanding and disseminating customer needs within an organisation by putting the voice of the customer at the forefront of all organisational activities.

PHOTO 1.1
The John Lewis Partnership, which includes Peter Jones and Waitrose, is known for its positive work culture where employees are part owners in the business.

Finally, marketing tries to manage stakeholder perceptions of an organisation, which include both external and internal stakeholders. External stakeholders are an organisation's customers. Organisations often use marketing communications and customer service to build and maintain the reputation of an organisation. Internal stakeholders are employees. It is important for marketers to create and maintain internal employee satisfaction as well. Organisations can do this by creating vibrant work cultures, financial incentives, event marketing, and other activities that foster a positive working environment.

The aim of this chapter is to provide a foundation to what marketing is, how it is practiced, and what role it plays for an organisation and in society. In order to accomplish this goal, this chapter will formally define marketing and its practice. It will also highlight different business philosophies and the importance of a market orientation and the marketing concept. This chapter also stresses the importance of relationship marketing and the role that it plays in creating customer satisfaction and value. Finally, this chapter gives consideration to marketing's role in society and the prominence of marketing in people's lives.

What Is Marketing?

Marketing encapsulates a number of things to business and society. First, it is a philosophy, which means marketing refers to a particular way of thinking about business, markets, and customers. This philosophy exists at a belief level. Firms that believe in marketing as a philosophy put marketing at the core of their strategy and decision-making processes. Marketing is integrated throughout all business activities in an organisation.

Marketing is also a management orientation, which means that there are certain ways that it is practiced. At the heart, marketing as a management orientation is the ability to create, maintain, and satisfy customers. A marketing philosophy and the way it is practiced are intertwined. Organisational belief feeds into the practice of marketing and how organisations execute the strategy. Both the philosophy and management of marketing place marketing and a customer focus at the primacy of organisational strategy.

Marketing is defined as

the activity, set of institutions, and the process for creating, communicating, delivering, and exchanging offerings that have value for customers, clients, partners, and society at large.

(AMA, 2021)

The American Marketing Association definition encompasses everything that marketers do. As a practice and institution, marketing serves as a function for an organisation that enables it to produce, communicate, and deliver products and services into the marketplace. These products and serves provide utility and value in the marketplace that

PHOTO 1.2
Buying a train ticket is an example of an exchange. Customers receive the benefit of fast, reliable, and safe transit services.

satisfy external stakeholders, which include customers, clients (in business to business markets), partners, and society at large.

Marketing is rooted in the process of exchange. **Exchange** is the idea that you have something of value that you are willing to give up in order to receive something of value. In today's society, that is predominantly cash (or credit or cryptocurrency). However, exchange can also be a form of bartering, where goods or services are given up in order to receive other goods and services.

Marketing Management Philosophies

A marketing management philosophy describes the way a company does business. It is a way that a business orientates itself to the external environment. The importance of understanding different marketing management philosophies is to gain a deeper insight into how an organisation practices business and how it interacts with its internal and external stakeholders. The marketing management philosophies are known as production orientation, sales orientation, market orientation, and societal orientation. These competing philosophies shape the way that companies interact with their customers and the way that they generate profits and create value.

It is sometimes argued that marketing has undergone an evolution in marketing management philosophies. In other words, a production orientation evolved into a sales orientation, which led to a market and societal orientation. The reality is all of these orientations exist in some form in today's business environment. Some companies are production oriented, and some companies are more marketing oriented. What follows is a description of each philosophy and a brief discussion as to how they interact and influence the marketing environment.

GLOBAL MARKETING QUESTION

A UK grocery retailer is considering international expansion into the US market. A senior manager explained that one rationale for entering the US market was that British and Americans have very similar tastes. Do you agree with this statement? What questions should this retailer consider before entering into this market?

Production Orientation

A production orientation is a marketing philosophy where marketers look inward within an organisation. Companies that practice a **production orientation** focus on the internal capabilities of the firm rather than on external market needs. It is not that a production orientation completely disregards market needs; it is more about focusing in on what the organisation does best. It then leverages those capabilities to manufacture products that can be sold in the marketplace

The production orientation philosophy was born out of the industrial revolution when business began to mass produce goods. A production orientation focuses on efficiency and volume. Managers calculate what they can manufacture best, most efficiently, and at the lowest cost. The Ford Model T is the classic case study of a production orientation.

The Ford Model T was initially built in 1908 during a peak time of the industrial revolution. What made the Model T so innovative was Ford's focus on the internal efficiencies of manufacturing. Ford oversaw the creation of assembly lines, which meant worker specialisation and the use of standardised parts for every vehicle. Henry Ford once said that you can have any Model T in any colour you want as long as it is black. The reason why all Model T's were painted black was because black paint dries more quickly than pastel colours, and therefore it was quicker to produce more vehicles with quicker-drying paint (it was also cheaper to buy one colour in bulk).

It is not that customers didn't want other colours; it is just that Henry Ford never considered whether people wanted other colours. This is the problem with a production

PHOTO 1.3
The Ford Model T is an example of a production orientation where companies focus on what they can most efficiently produce over the wants and needs of customers.

orientation. It is so inwardly focused on operational efficiency, it does not value external customer needs in the same way that it privileges internal efficiency.

A production orientation is associated with what is known as a marketing myopia. In the 1960s Theodore Levitt argued that **marketing myopia** is the principle that organisations can become so focused on manufacturing products or services that they lose sight of the problems that they are solving for customers (Levitt, 2004). A myopic vision means that companies become so inwardly focused on short-term selling strategies that they lose track of what business they are in.

Levitt argued that business needed to take a bigger picture view of the marketplace. Myopic companies often define their business incorrectly. He argued that one of the reasons why Hollywood film companies lost market share to television was the inability of Hollywood executives to correctly define what business they were in. He argued, "had Hollywood been customer oriented (providing entertainment), rather than product oriented (making movies)" (Levitt, 2004, p. 1), Hollywood would not be constant under threat from outside competitors.

PHOTO 1.4
Apple might be considered a production-oriented company. It uses technological innovation to stimulate demand rather than relying upon what customers say they want.

There are organisations today that are considered to be production-oriented companies. It is sometimes argued that Apple is a production-oriented company. Apple has a long history of inwardly focused innovation that the company then brings to market to stimulate demand. The argument here is that customers often have a difficult time articulating their needs, so leading-edge Apple designers address this gap by designing products that they think their customers want. In the case of Apple, it has worked well enough for them to become one of the most successful global companies in the world by creating a market for their products. They now have many imitators who compete for the same consumer.

The problem with production orientation as a marketing-management philosophy is that it does not fully take into account what consumers want. Production-oriented companies run into trouble in markets where supply exceeds demand or where consumer tastes change rapidly. These environments mean that consumers have a variety of suppliers to choose from or consumer preferences change frequently, and production-oriented companies cannot quickly respond to changing market needs.

Sales Orientation

A **sales orientation** is a marketing philosophy that believes that consumers will not buy a product or service unless aggressive selling techniques are used to persuade customers. A central tenet to a sales orientation is that the more that you aggressively sell something, the more profitable you become. In some ways a sales orientation was born out of a production orientation. As manufacturers focused inwardly on producing goods, there was not always external demand for their products. In order to address this shortcoming, organisations hired sales teams to go out and aggressively sell this excess inventory.

An example of a sales-oriented company can be seen in financial services with short-term, personal payday loan companies. These companies pursue a sales orientation. They use aggressive sales techniques which include direct selling over the phone, a heavy use of social media, and daytime television advertising as a way to sell their service. The emphasis here is on immediacy and the short term. It feeds the consumer need for quick cash.

While these companies do provide some consumers financial resources they would not otherwise have access to, the problem with sales-oriented companies like payday loan companies is that the short-term emphasis does not focus on creating long-term customer value. These are transactional companies that primarily deal in sales volume. Payday loan companies charge high interest rates, and there is the potential for predatory practices that target vulnerable people of lower socio-economic classes who have credit problems (Barth et al., 2015). It is not surprising that many of these companies go into administration within a few years of doing business.

Not all sales-oriented companies are bad actors. In some cases adopting a sales orientation can be critical to a firm's survival. For example, some non-profit charitable organisations adopt aggressive selling techniques to make consumers aware of their social cause. Some of these organisations employ salespeople to stop and talk to people on the street. They might also place a heavy emphasis on direct marketing and aggressive telemarketing over the phone. A sales orientation can help generate much-needed money, especially during times of social or environmental crisis. A sales orientation can serve as a valuable strategy to build customer awareness.

Market Orientation

Most organisations strive to be market oriented. A **market orientation** is a customer-facing organisation that focuses on the wants and needs of its customers. **A market-oriented company** is dedicated to collecting information on the wants and needs of its customers, and it disseminates that information throughout an organisation. This means that companies disseminate customer wants and needs across different functional areas of the business, as well as actioning that information higher up within the organisation at board-level decision-making.

The importance of a market orientation is that it moves the company away from an inwardly looking focus that prioritises the internal efficiencies of an organisation towards a customer-centric view. It also orientates an organisational focus on cultivating customer relationships as opposed to transactional relationships. It is often argued that marketing is too important to leave to marketers alone, so market-oriented companies that practice a market orientation integrate all organisational members to focus on those customer wants and needs. This means all functional areas of the business are dedicated to prioritising customer wants and needs.

A market orientation centres on a marketing philosophy known as the marketing concept. The **marketing concept** is a management orientation and philosophy that directs an organisation's activities towards understanding customer needs, creating customer satisfaction, and meeting organisational objectives. The marketing concept directs organisational activities towards satisfying those customer needs in a way that is differentiated from market competitors and that is profitable. The marketing concept orientates companies into creating profitable marketplace exchanges that provide value for both the company and its customers.

A good example of a market-oriented company is Amazon, which places the customer at the centre of its business mission.

> We aim to be Earth's most customer centric company. Our mission is to continually raise the bar of the customer experience by using the internet and technology to help consumers find, discover and buy anything, and empower businesses and content creators to maximise their success.
>
> (Amazon, 2021)

What we can see with Amazon's mission statement is the enactment of a customer orientation that places primacy on a customer focus. Amazon's dedication to customer

PHOTO 1.5
Amazon puts the customer at the heart of its mission statement.

outcomes is evidenced by being a customer-centric company. Importantly, it has a long-term orientation by its efforts to 'continually raise the bar'. Finally, it seeks to empower customers to help them use Amazon as a technological platform that prioritises building competitive advantage. All of these factors have helped Amazon to become one of the most successful market-oriented companies in the world.

MARKETING ASSISTANT TASK

As a marketing assistant in Mexico, Tannya has been looking at archives from the 1950s, 1960s, and 1970s, when marketing and advertising became key functions within major worldwide organi- sations such as Zomotor. At that time, Zomotor had no internet, no smartphones or even basic mobile phones, and no email. Customer databases were not comput-erised, and product details could not be processed digitally. Letters were written on typewriters and posted in envelopes. Field-based salespeople contacted their regional and national offices each day from public telephones. Many people still smoked at their desks – even in dealership showrooms when hosting customers. Drivers were not legally required to wear seat belts, which were omitted from many cars anyway, and drink-driving legislation was significantly looser. In the early 1960s, when the Mexican government ordered sellers of cars in Mexico to have production facilities in the country and incorporate locally manufactured parts, many major overseas brands stopped trading there. Motoring also began to attract taxes; an annual car tax and a one-off car purchase tax – which were initially introduced to finance the 1968 Olympic Games and 1970 World Cup – remained thereafter.

Given your knowledge of the era, the different marketing orientations, and some of the factors impacting the motor industry in Mexico at the time, how do you think Tan-nya's job role and responsibilities would have been different to now? Jot down some ideas and think about how these differences would have made life easier or harder.

Societal Orientation

A societal marketing approach builds on the marketing concept. The focus is still on customer wants and needs, but there is an additional layer to their strategy. **Societal marketing organisations** seek to meet customer wants and needs but also seek to pre-serve an individual's or society's long-term best interest. A societal orientation places sustainability as a core ethos to its marketing philosophy.

Historically, societal orientations took root in the 1970s, where there was a growing concern about businesses' impact on the environment. Organisations created corporate social responsibility (CSR) departments, which were charged with helping organisations

PHOTO 1.6
Societally oriented companies take into consideration businesses' impact upon the environment in order to ensure their practices are environmentally friendly.

reduce waste, use more environmentally friendly products, and mitigate an organisation's carbon footprint. CSR became focused on the big Rs: reduce, reuse, repair, and recycle. These practices became the hallmark of societally oriented companies.

Today, we see organisations placing a societal orientation at the forefront of their organisational activities. A societal orientation is no longer the remit of a single department within an organisation but integrated throughout. In some cases we see organisations use a societal orientation at the heart of their business strategies to help them build competitive advantage.

A good example of a company adapting its business model to a societal orientation can be seen with Adidas. In 2021, the company launched a clothing rental business in the French market using its Terrex line, which is an outdoor adventure clothing and shoe apparel line. Adidas is tapping into a shift in consumer demand where customers want access to high-tech sports gear but do not want to pay full price for something that they may only use once. Adidas rental allows customers to rent high-tech gear for short periods of time.

Adidas' rental clothing range is geared towards those customers that have planned a special adventure holiday or only use specialised outdoor clothing equipment on an irregular basis. By using a special ozone process to sanitise the gear after use, Adidas will clean and repair its clothing so that it can be reused more than once. Adidas is hoping to address issues of sustainability by promoting a service that can be used more than once. Adidas has adapted its business strategy to tap into a societal marketing strategy that privileges the reuse of its products. In this example, we can see how an organisation can use a societal marketing strategy to create differentiation in the market and at the same time promote global sustainability.

PHOTO 1.7
Adidas' movement into rental gear is an example of a societal orientation.

SUSTAINABILITY QUESTION

As a fashion retailer, your business has a reputation for selling high-quality, fashionable denim jeans and trendy cotton T-shirts. You have built your reputation over a decade of selling clothing on the high streets and are able to charge a premium price for your clothing. This has helped to ensure your profitability over the years.

You also know that denim and cotton are resource-intensive products. It takes an average of 7,000 litres of water to produce one pair of jeans and 2,700 litres of water to grow the cotton needed for one T-shirt. You have recently identified a manufacturer that that uses less resource-intensive materials liked recycle fabric and organic cotton. However, the price of these raw materials is higher and the quality is not the equivalent as your current supplier. Would you consider switching suppliers? What impact would this have on your business? Identify and discuss the implications of this sustainability question.

Relationship Marketing

Marketing is the growth engine of every company, and a key facet to this strategy is its dedication towards attracting new customers. Relationship marketing builds upon the foundational principle of attracting new customers and integrates the principle of maintaining those relationships. The underlying principle of relationship marketing is to maintain relationships with customers in ways that meet their needs and at the same time create a stable revenue base for the organisation.

Relationship marketing starts with understanding the wants and needs within the marketplace. This can be accomplished through practices such as environmental scanning (see Chapter 2), which scans the marketplace for changing trends. Marketers segment and target (see Chapter 5) specific segments within the marketplace in order to ensure that they are able to best serve the needs of a specific group of customers. Relationship marketing builds from these foundations.

Relationship marketing is the process of cultivating and maintaining long-term customer relationships that meet the needs of customers, creating customer satisfaction, and creating value for both the customer and an organisation. Relationship marketing is not something that happens instantaneously with a sale. Marketers often rely upon customer relationship management systems to help them manage customer relationships. **Customer relationship management systems (CRM)** are tools that marketers use to collecting information on customers in order to best meet the needs of individual customers in a way that delivers value to them. CRM systems track and store individual-level consumer data in order to offer customers more personalised interactions.

STAKEHOLDER QUESTION

A core mission of a local council (i.e. – a local government organisation) is to build affordable housing throughout the borough. The council is considering a proposal to build a five-story housing project in a specific residential area within the borough, 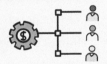 where most houses are only two stories high. What stakeholders must the council consider when deciding whether or not the building is appropriate to the area?

MARKETING MANAGER TASK

Dylan has chosen not to focus specifically on China but to analyse the global development of marketing. Dylan is particularly interested in the 1970s and 1980s, as Dylan was familiar with many movies made and set during this era, which depict sales and marketing in a very simplistic and aggressive way. Looking back through archive material of Zomotor's old brochures, adverts, and promotional materials, he feels that a key difference (apart from the strange clothes and hairstyles) is that Zomotor seemed to communicate features over benefits much more than is the case now.

continued

Dylan has also noticed that advertisers seemed to explain more things verbally rather than conveying them through creative design, music, cinematography, and mood. But the biggest difference is the lack of relationship marketing. Scouring policy documents and company handbooks, Dylan struggles to find anything about building long-term relationships with customers.

Imagine you could send Dylan back to the 1980s (not so much 'Back to the Future' as 'Forwards into the Past'). What would be the main differences in customer expectations of Zomotor, and how do you think this would impact on Dylan's role? What would you do to keep customers happy and retain their business?

Customer Satisfaction

Customer satisfaction is the goal of every market-oriented company. **Customer satisfaction** refers to a customer's overall perception of their purchase and consumption experience. When organisations are able to meet or exceed customer expectations on quality, service, or price, they are able to create customer satisfaction. It is important for marketing organisations to put into place practices that promote customer satisfaction. These include:

► Prominent brand names

► Product or service quality

► Hiring customer-oriented personnel

► After-sales service

► Warranties and product and service guarantees

By meeting or exceeding customer expectations, companies can create customer satisfaction and positive word of mouth. It is widely accepted in marketing that it is less expensive to retain your existing customer base than it is to recruit new customers, so customer satisfaction is a good indicator of customer retention. Further, research shows that 93% of customers trust the recommendations of friends and family more than marketing communications (Marketing Charts, 2020), so if you are able to create satisfied customers, they can be positive brand ambassadors for your company. Finally, studies have shown that creating satisfied customers can create greater firm profitability (Eklof et al., 2020).

On the opposite end of the spectrum, where companies might create dissatisfied customers, research shows that over 94% of customers would not patronise a business as a result of negative reviews (Review Trackers, 2020). All of these factors highlight the importance of creating a satisfied customer base.

PHOTO 1.8
Customer satisfaction is at the heart of good marketing practice.

Value

Value is a key consideration in all marketing activities and a central objective to relationship marketing. From a customer centric point of view, **customer value** is the difference between the costs associated with obtaining a product or service and the benefits that a customer receives in exchange. While this is a widely accepted definition of customer value, it has limitations. The issue here is that it assumes that customers are rational decision makers and driven to maximise their utility. It further assumes that customers are profit seeking and trying to get the best deal possible. While this might certainly be the case for some purchases, we know that many purchases are not rational decisions but decisions made on emotion or impulse.

Customers often make decisions based upon what marketers call perceived value. **Perceived value** is an overall assessment of the value that a product or service will deliver. It is a subjective opinion of the potential benefits and value that the customer perceives that they will receive in relation to the costs (Zeithaml, 1988). This perspective on value helps to capture the individual nature of many marketplace transactions that are rooted within the consumer decision-making process (see Chapter 9). While perceived value helps marketers to account for purchase decisions based on subjective consumer experience, it is still a one-dimensional perspective on marketplace value. It still conceptualises value as a trade-off between benefits and costs.

Value is an increasingly important concept in today's society, and in the domain of marketing, value has taken on a number of meanings. From a consumer perspective, value might take on the form of symbolic meaning. Symbolic meaning might be the status that owning a certain brand conveys. An owner of a Ferrari automobile might have bought the car not only for the functional value of its performance but also for the status that ownership bestows upon them.

PHOTO 1.9
Customer value is a mutually beneficial proposition, which means both the organisation and its customers benefit from exchanges.

Ethics and sustainability are important marketplace values that often drive customer perceptions of value. The origins of 'fairtrade certification' was born out of both con-sumer and producer desire to provide marketplace products that meet certain envi-ronmental, economic, and social standards. Here we see how marketplace value can be a multidimensional construct that encapsulates a number of different marketplace variables (Sánchez-Fernández & Iniesta-Bonillo, 2007).

NEW MEDIA QUESTION

Social media platforms have changed the ways that marketers communi-cate and interact with their customers. Online fashion retailers, like the Boohoo group that owns brands like PrettyLittleThing and Nasty Gal, have adapted to digital environment by partnering with social media influenc-ers on Instagram and TikTok. This has helped the group build one of the most suc-cessful online business that target 16- to 24-year-olds.

In 2021, the Boohoo group acquired the 242-year-old retailer Debenhams, a traditional department store chain, and converted it to an online retailer. What target market and social media strategy should the Boohoo group use to revive this historic brand?

MARKETING DIRECTOR TASK

As a global marketing director, Lee is most interested in people who have shaped the marketing efforts of motor manufacturers at board level, including Henry Ford of Ford Motor Company and Alfred P. Sloan of General Motors – but especially Sergio Marchionne,

continued

the great CEO of Fiat and Chrysler who rescued Fiat from the brink of extinction in 2004, refocused and rejuvenated them within two years, brought forward the development and launch of the Fiat 500 car, and absorbed Chrysler into the company before his death in 2018. Under Marchionne, Fiat rolled out extensive relationship marketing initiatives which kept their customers close, including owners' festivals, television chefs hosting dealership product launch events, elaborate personalisation of new car specifications, and branded lifestyle magazines.

Using your knowledge and experience of how organisations such as motor manufacturers build long-term relationships with their customers and prospects in the current era of marketing and using your own preferences as a guide, list five or six strategies which Lee could introduce in Zomotor to bring the brand closer to its customers and make them feel more included. How would these actions be better than the approaches used by previous generations of marketers?

Why Study Marketing?

A key focus of this chapter has been to establish a broad overview of marketing and the role that it plays within business. Throughout the chapter we have emphasised the relationship between marketing and the voice of the customer. We have also highlighted different types of marketing orientations, as well as all of the touchpoints the extending marketing mix has with the marketplace.

Now that you have a basic overview of marketing, you might be asking yourself, why should I study marketing? What makes marketing a key area of focus in business studies? There are two additional facets that highlight why marketing is an important area for study. Marketing plays an important role within society, and it is also an area that offers potential career opportunities.

Marketing's Role in Society

Marketing plays a number of key roles within our society. The omnipresence of marketing permeates social media and other forms of communication. This creates an environment where marketing has the ability to create or influence different fads and fashion trends within society.

As a social institution, marketing acts as a socialisation force that has the power to influence how we think about gender, ethnicity, and social class. Socially responsible marketers understand the power that marketing has and can use marketing to reinforce positive messages about the world we live within. Carefully crafted messages about ethnicity or the body can draw attention to and reinforce positive social changes.

Marketing also plays an important role in sustainability. While sometimes marketing is characterised as promoting overconsumption, the reality is that marketing is and will be a key player in promoting sustainable consumption. Marketing has the ability to promote positive consumption practices that emphasise the importance of economic growth and sustainable consumption practice.

ETHICS QUESTION

Critics of marketing suggest that marketers create unwanted needs within the marketplace. They see marketers and marketing as a source for resource depletion and unsustainable consumption. Proponents of marketing argue that marketing is a key tool in promoting sustainable consumption practice and that marketers are key players in raising awareness about climate change and ethical consumption practices. What do you think? Is marketing the root of environmental destruction or a pathway out of it?

Career Opportunities in Marketing

Marketing plays an important role in the economy and in the area of job growth and opportunity. As a career path, marketing provides opportunities that tap into a range of different work skill sets. Personal selling and customer service are oriented for outgoing, social people. If you are more technically oriented, marketing research and product development are good opportunities. Finally, for those that are more strategy oriented, brand management or advertising are great opportunities to grow and manage brands.

METRICS QUESTION

Marketing metrics are tools that marketers use to monitor performance. Marketers use metrics to measure the effectiveness of a marketing activity.

Non-profit organisations like Oxfam and Save the Children often deploy employees to work the high streets in urban city centres. Their job is to solicit donations from people on the high street. What metrics could Oxfam and Save the Children use to determine the effectiveness of this technique?

Key Learning Outcomes

Marketing plans an important role within an organisation as the department that generates new sales, helps to maintain existing relationships, and is responsible for diffusing the voice of the customer throughout the organisation.

There are different types of marketing philosophies. Some organisations focus inwardly on production while others focus on recruiting an aggressive sales force. Market-oriented companies are outwardly focused and integrate the voice of the customer inside of the organisation. A societal orientation builds on a market orientation and emphasises sustainability as a core objective.

Creating customer satisfaction and customer value are key objectives of market-oriented companies.

Recommended Further Reading

Eklof, J., Podkorytova, O., & Malova, A. (2020). Linking customer satisfaction with financial performance: An empirical study of Scandinavian banks. *Total Quality Management & Business Excellence*, *31*(15–16), 1684–1702.

Godin, S. (2018). *This is marketing*. Portfolio, Penguin.

Holt, D. B. (2004). *How brands become icons: The principles of cultural branding*. Harvard Business Press.

Lindstrom, M. (2012). *Buyology: How everything we believe about why we buy is wrong*. Random House.

Otto, A. S., Szymanski, D. M., & Varadarajan, R. (2020). Customer satisfaction and firm performance: Insights from over a quarter century of empirical research. *Journal of the Academy of Marketing Science*, *48*(3), 543–564.

Payne, A., Frow, P., & Eggert, A. (2017). The customer value proposition: Evolution, development, and application in marketing. *Journal of the Academy of Marketing Science*, *45*(4), 467–489.

Steinhoff, L., Arli, D., Weaven, S., & Kozlenkova, I. V. (2019). Online relationship marketing. *Journal of the Academy of Marketing Science*, *47*(3), 369–393.

References

Amazon. (2021). *Our mission: We aim to be the earth's most customer centric company*. https://www.aboutamazon.co.uk/uk-investment/our-mission

American Marketing Association. (2021). *Definitions of marketing*. https://www.ama.org/the-definition-of-marketing-what-is-marketing/

Barth, J. R., Hilliard, J., & Jahera, J. S. (2015). Banks and payday lenders: Friends or foes? *International Advances in Economic Research*, *21*(2), 139–153.

Levitt, T. (2004). Marketing myopia 1960. *Harvard Business Review*, *82*(7–8), 138–149.

Marketing Charts. (2020). *Friends and family still the most trusted sources of brand information*. https://www.marketingcharts.com/cross-media-and-traditional/word-of-mouth-113276

Review Trackers. (2020). *Stats proving the value of customer reviews*. https://www.reviewtrackers.com/reports/customer-reviews-stats/

Sánchez-Fernández, R., & Iniesta-Bonillo, M. Á. (2007). The concept of perceived value: A systematic review of the research. *Marketing Theory*, *7*(4), 427–451.

Zeithaml, V. A. (1988). Consumer perceptions of price, quality, and value: A means-end model and synthesis of evidence. *Journal of Marketing*, *52*(3), 2–22.

Glossary

Customer relation management systems (CRM): tools that marketers use to collecting information on customers in order to best meet the needs of individual customers in a way that delivers value to them

Customer satisfaction: a customer's overall perception of their purchase and consumption experience

Customer value: the difference between the costs associated with obtaining a product or service and the benefits that a customer receives in exchange

Exchange: the idea that you have something of value that you are willing to give up in order to receive something of value

Marketing: the activity, the set of institutions, and the process for creating, communicating, delivering, and exchanging offerings that have value for customers, clients, partners, and society at large

Marketing concept: a management orientation and philosophy that directs an organisation's activities towards understanding customer needs, creating customer satisfaction, and meeting organisational objectives

Marketing myopia: the principle that organisations can become so focused on manufacturing products or services that they lose sight of the problems that they are solving for customers

Market orientation: a customer facing organisation focused on the wants and needs of its customers

Perceived value: an overall assessment of the value that a product or service will deliver

Production orientation: a philosophy focused on the internal capabilities of the firm rather than on external market needs

Relationship marketing: the process of cultivating and maintaining long-term customer relationships that meet the needs of customers, create customer satisfaction, and create value for both the customer and an organisation

Sales orientation: a marketing philosophy that believes that consumers will not buy a product or service unless aggressive selling techniques are used to persuade customers

Societal marketing: seeks to meet customer wants and needs but also to preserve an individual's or society's long-term best interest

The "Return to Work" Case Study: Can Marketing Influence Employees Going Back to the Office?

The COVID-19 pandemic has caused a massive shift in the way that many people across the globe work. Coupled with advances in technology, the pandemic has created opportunities for employees to work in home-based offices. Many

continued

workers see this shift as a positive one, as it allows them to save time and money commuting and to achieve a greater work-life balance. Further, many employees have become accustomed to remote social interactions. This shift has led many workers to want to continue to work from home.

This work-at-home trend is backed by research. According to a recent study of 5,000 Americans who work in jobs that allow them to work from home, 33.3% of participants would want to work from home 5 days a week, and over 50% would prefer to work from home between 3 and 5 days per week (Barrero, Bloom and Davis, 2021).

However, many employers want employees back in the office. Some jobs require collaborative, team-based, face-to-face contact. In addition, some employers feel that employees are less distracted and more productive when working in an office environment. Getting employees back to the office also provides managers the opportunities to monitor employee workload and ensure fair distribution of tasks. Managers can also ensure that the most essential work is prioritised over less important tasks.

Can marketing play a role in connecting what are seemingly two disparate needs between employees who want to work from home and employers who want them in the office?

continued

Your Task

You work as a member of the marketing department. The senior management team has asked you to come up with an internal marketing campaign that promotes a 'return to work' campaign. The aim of the campaign is to incentivise employees to want to come to work, rather than forcing them to come to work. Your task is to come up with as many creative ideas as you can to promote the 'return to work' campaign idea.

Using what you know about marketing, what promotions and events might you hold to incentivise employee uptake?

As you write down your ideas, here are some top tips. Marketers use a range of activities to raise awareness and increase the uptake of marketing ideas. Your strategy might consider event marketing, sales promotion (i.e. short-term incentives to stimulate demand), premiums (i.e. prize giveaways), financial incentives, testimonials, and marketing communications. Compare your ideas with a friend and determine the most innovative ideas!

Bibliography

Barrero, J. M., Bloom, N., & Davis, S. J. (2021). Don't force people to come back to the office full time. *Harvard Business Review*. https://hbr.org/2021/08/dont-force-people-to-come-back-to-the-office-full-time WFH Research. (2021). https://wfhresearch.com/

2 | Strategic Planning

LEARNING OBJECTIVES

▶ To understand what strategic planning is and why is it important

▶ To establish why strategic business units have different strategic plans

▶ To discuss the importance of objective setting in strategic planning

▶ To establish the forms of competitive advantage

▶ To discuss how businesses use marketing plans in developing strategy

▶ To provide the foundations to the extended marketing mix

Introduction

Strategic plans are formal strategy documents that a company uses to guide the direction of the company. They provide an overarching vision for organisational members, they allocate resources to different areas of the business in the form of resources (i.e. money/investment, people, equipment), they monitor the ever-changing marketplace, they help to identify target markets, and they shape an organisation's position in the marketplace. In many ways, strategic plans and strategic planning encapsulate much of what the marketing function does for businesses.

Marketers use strategic planning to explore market opportunities that can create competitive advantage. For example, let us consider Uber Technologies, Inc., more commonly known as Uber. Uber has revolutionised transport services through its innovative strategic planning. What is it about Uber's strategic planning that made it unique?

Uber's strategic plan focused on a few core areas that it felt were deficient amongst existing ride hailing services (i.e. taxis).

1. Their strategic plan identified the need to invest in technology.

    a. Its technological investments enabled Uber to create sophisticated but easy-to-use GPS mapping systems that enabled less knowledgeable drivers to navigate city roads.

    b. Its app development linked drivers and consumers together, creating greater efficiencies than existing taxi booking systems. It delivered greater speed, quality of service, and driver availability.

    c. Uber's technology is transferable to other service offerings, such as food, package, and freight delivery.

2. Uber's strategic planning helped to create a more efficient business structure.

    a. Taxes: the company's tax base is in the Netherlands and Bermuda, so it pays less tax than other transport companies.

    b. Labour: Uber categorises its employees as independent contractors, which means it does not pay the same level of payroll tax or pension funding.

    c. Pricing: due to its efficient business model design, Uber can charge lower fares than competitors and still earn higher levels of profits.

    d. Equipment: Uber does not own its cars, but it provides a business collaborative sharing business model that links drivers with consumers.

PHOTO 2.1
Uber's strategic planning capabilities has helped it to create a competitive advantage over traditional taxi services.

Arguably, what is most impressive about Uber's business model is the ability to generate new demand for an existing service. Uber did not just take away existing market share from existing taxi service companies; its strategic planning helped to generate new passenger demand from people who might not have used a ride hailing service previously.

While Uber's strategic planning created an innovative business model, its future is threatened. The company has been beset with problems in recent years, which include movement by governments to categorise its drivers as employees, increasing competition, and challenges with investments in autonomous vehicles. These threats to Uber's business model stress the importance of a company continually evaluating and updating their strategic plan.

In order to use strategic planning successfully, companies are constantly updating and refocusing the core aims and objectives of their strategic plans. Uber is a great example of strategic planning. It highlights both the benefits and challenges of strategic planning and the importance of an evolving strategic plan.

The Strategic Plan

The formal articulation of marketing planning takes the form of a strategic plan. The focus of this chapter is to highlight each element of the strategic plan, which contains the business objectives, the organisational mission statement, the business portfolio, a situational analysis, environmental scanning, the marketing mix strategy, forms of competitive advantage, implementation, and evaluation and control.

The importance of the marketing plan is that it is one of the tools available to marketers in strategy creation. Much like a plumber, beautician, or medical doctor has certain tools that they use to complete a job, a strategic plan is one of the tools that marketers use. In addition to articulating strategy, strategic plans help organisations to assign tasks to specific individuals within an organisation. If you are interested in a career in marketing, a strategic plan will become an important tool for you to use as a marketer. It will act as a strategy guide for any organisation that you work within.

Objective Setting

Objective setting is a critical early step in the strategic planning process. Setting forth clear aims and objectives ensures that an organisation has quantifiable, measurable goals. These are important benchmarks to determine whether or not a strategic plan is realistic and can help an organisation achieve its goals. For example, an organisational objective that wants to achieve higher levels of customer satisfaction and customer retention is not the same as an organisational objective that wants to achieve 95% satisfaction levels and retain 85% of its current customer base in the coming year.

Specifically stated objectives allow organisations to determine where they have been successful or where they have missed their stated objectives.

It is important that marketing objectives be aligned with the organisational strategy and mission statement. This helps to ensure that all functional departments within an organisation are working towards the same set of objectives. In order to set appropriate strategic targets, SMART is a framework that can be used by organisations in objective setting. Objectives that are specific, measurable, achievable, realistic, and timely are used by organisations to help reduce business uncertainty and improve decision-making in the strategic planning process.

Specific

Each objective within the strategic plan must be tied to a specific outcome. An example of a specific objective would be a stated objective to increase sales by 6% during the next fiscal year.

Measurable

A measurable objective must be quantifiable and tracked. If the business is currently selling 1 million units and an objective is to increase sales by 6%, this means that the business would be expected to sell an additional 60,000 units in a year, or 5,000 additional units per month.

Achievable

Strategic planning helps to ensure that objectives are achievable by ensuring enough organisational resources are dedicated to achieving the strategic objective. In order to achieve a 6% sales growth, an organisation might need to recruit additional sales and customer service personnel to ensure that it can achieve the 6% sales target.

Realistic

A realistic objective is one that is aligned with the previous and future expectations of the marketplace conditions, as well as on company performance. For example, if growth within a marketplace has historically been at 1%–2% per year and is expected to remain that way in the future, an objective that seeks to increase sales by 6% is unlikely to meet the criterion of being a realistic objective without other significant strategic changes.

Timely

A strategic objective must be accomplished within a time period that is relevant to the business window of opportunity. Objectives must be coordinated to the timing of the market or the organisational resources available. Timely goals are also time specific and tied to a specific time measurement. An organisation stating it wants to increase sales by 6% the following year is an example of a timely objective.

METRICS QUESTION

A friend of yours has come up with an innovative business idea that they think will be successful. They have begun investing their own money into their business idea and have also asked friends and family to be early investors in the business. Despite your friend's enthusiasm, they have not developed a strategic plan that outlines the aims, objectives, and strategic direction of the company. Explain to your friend the importance of the strategic planning process. What do you think are some of the key variables they should consider when developing their plan and determining whether or not their idea is viable?

Business Mission

The **business mission** is a formal articulation of organisational culture. It is a set of statements that highlights the uniqueness of the organisation and its identity. A business mission is an important tool that signals what the organisation stands for with internal and external stakeholders. For internal stakeholders, the business mission aligns employees towards common organisational goals, and for external stakeholders, it can be used to enhance an organisation's image.

Effective business mission statements are clear, concise declarations about the business strategy. They specifically answer:

▶ What does the organisation do?

▶ How does the organisation accomplish its objectives?

▶ Who does the organisation serve?

▶ What values does the organisation hold?

The formal articulation of the business mission is an important strategic tool for organisations. A meta-analysis of business mission statements highlighted that customer-facing missions can lead to more customer-facing organisations, and a strategically oriented mission can lead to higher return on sales (ROS) and return on assets (ROA; Alegre et al., 2018).

SUSTAINABILITY QUESTION

Patagonia, Inc., is an American clothing manufacturer and retailer that sells products across the globe. The organisation has become renowned for putting sustainability at the forefront of its mission and strategy. While we all have a conceptual understanding of what

continued

sustainability means, what does sustainability look like in practice? Go to www.patagonia.com/our-footprint. How does Patagonia define sustainability? Are there different forms of business sustainability? How does Patagonia measure success? Does understanding Patagonia's sustainability strategy change the way you think about business and sustainability?

The Business Portfolio

Organisations are inherently resource constrained. Even large-scale organisations such as Apple, or Microsoft, or the Coca-Cola Company must make strategic decisions about where to allocate finite resources. Strategic planning helps organisations make decisions about where best to allocate their financial capital, human resources, and equipment.

One way that organisations manage their product and service portfolio is by creating strategic business units (SBUs). An **SBU** is an independently managed subgroup of products or services of a larger organisation. Each SBU operates as its own entity that has responsibility for profit and loss, resource allocation, and control over resources. An SBU might consist of a number of different product items within a broader, SBU product category.

For example, the Procter & Gamble Company, a US-based fast-moving consumer goods (FMCG) company, is organised into ten SBUs. These SBUs range from baby care to personal care. Each SBU is an autonomous unit that is independent from the other units within the organisation. Each SBU consists of a number of individual products.

For Procter & Gamble, each SBU is responsible for developing its own brand strategy, product innovations, and marketing plans (Procter & Gamble, 2021). This strategy enables Procter & Gamble to diversify its product portfolio to reach different need-based segments across the globe.

When evaluating an organisation's product portfolio, there are a number of strategic alternatives available to organisations. Marketing managers often rely upon Ansoff's opportunity matrix and the Boston Consulting Group (BCG) portfolio matrix. These models help marketing managers to manage their strategic business portfolio.

FIGURE 2.1
Procter & Gamble strategic business units and product items.

Ansoff's Opportunity Matrix

One way that companies strategically manage their business portfolio is by targeting new market opportunities with products within the existing product portfolio, or developing new product ideas. Ansoff's opportunity matrix is an SBU portfolio tool that that seeks to identify new growth opportunities. It consists of a market penetration, product development, market development, and diversification strategy. Marketing managers can use each element of the matrix to analyse business growth opportunities. Figure 2.2 highlights how Tesla might map its existing product portfolio onto the matrix.

Market Penetration Strategy

A market penetration strategy seeks to increase a product's market share amongst the existing customer base. This strategy seeks to get customers to buy more. There are a number of tools available to marketers to try to accomplish this goal.

For example, sales promotion is a short-term incentive to buy. Marketers might discount prices or offer sales incentives such as buy one, get one free. An organisation might also consider increasing its marketing communications budget to raise awareness

PHOTO 2.2
InBev acquired the rights to the Budweiser brand in its acquisition of SAB Miller. This helped InBev grow its global market share.

and stimulate purchase. Alternatively, a company may acquire another company to grow its customer base. In 2015, the multinational drinks company InBev acquired SAB Miller for $107 billion (Garcia, 2015). This market penetration strategy helped InBev acquire greater market share and helped them address competition from the growing microbrewery market.

Market Development

A market development strategy seeks to attract new customers to existing products. For many multinational organisations, market development is a globalisation strategy. This approach has been popular in the quick service food industry, where companies have successfully entered into new markets and attracted new customers to the existing product portfolio. Starbucks, Subway, and McDonald's have all pursued a market development strategy by growing their customer base and entering new markets with the same product concepts.

ETHICS QUESTION

As business expand globally, they enter into new markets where there are different laws and views of what is considered acceptable business practice. For example, there can be differences in:

▶ Child labour laws

▶ Work standards and conditions

▶ Wages

▶ Human rights issues

▶ Gifting practices and favours

▶ Environmental regulations

▶ Bribery and corruption

▶ Impacts on the environment

What set of ethical principles should guide the global expansion of multinational companies into new countries? Do you think that these companies should use the same set of ethical standards in every country of operation? What if these ethical standards put a company at a competitive disadvantage? Choose three variables and discuss.

MARKETING ASSISTANT TASK

Tannya's boss in Mexico is concerned that sales volumes are suffering due to a lack of interaction and understanding between the sales and marketing departments: salespeople are not understanding the firm's long-term commercial objectives and brand values, and marketers are unaware of the pressurised, time-bound constraints within which salespeople must operate. To help find a solution, he has asked Tannya to compile a list of factors which might cause friction between the two departments. After speaking to colleagues, her first finding is that 'domain dissensus' is an issue – this is when neither party knows exactly where their responsibilities end and the other's starts, and means that each may leave vital actions to the other, or both might duplicate each other's efforts. Moreover, staff might perceive that the other department is trying to take control of their roles.

Help Tannya by making a list of areas where misunderstandings or conflict may occur between marketing and sales. For each, explain the commercial implications of this and ways in which Zomotor may eradicate the issue.

Product Development Strategy

A product development strategy creates new products for existing markets. Apple has successfully used a product development strategy throughout the Apple ecosystem of products and services. The Apple ecosystem is a set of software and hardware that is interlinked in its performance. When Apple introduces a new product into the system, such as an Apple Watch, Siri, AirPods, or any other component, everything is interlinked into a single architecture. When new products are introduced into the system, they often have high uptake, and there are significant costs associated with trying to leave the system.

Diversification

A diversification strategy is to introduce new products to new markets. Arguably, one of the most successful companies that uses a diversification strategy is the easyGroup, which owns easyJet. The mission of the easyGroup family of brands evolved around offering customers value for money. It strips away many of the added extras in products and services and focuses on low-cost delivery. As a result the brand has diversified into a whole range of industry sectors. Examples include easyHotel, easyMoney, easyFoodstore, and easyEnergy. This diversification strategy has created a brand portfolio with over 1000 registered trademarks (easyGroup, 2021).

Ansoff's Opportunity Matrix: Tesla, Inc.		
Present Product		New Product
Present Market	*Market Penetration* Tesla sells more of its Model S, 3, X, and Y electric automobiles to its existing customer base.	*Product Development* Tesla launches its Cybertruck line of automotive vehicles.
New Market	*Market Development* Tesla opens manufacturing and sales plants in China.	*Diversification* Tesla sells solar roof panels for new home builds and existing homes.

FIGURE 2.2
Mapping Tesla's product portfolio onto Ansoff's opportunity matrix.

The BCG Portfolio Matrix

The BCG portfolio matrix is a strategic planning tool that helps organisations manage their SBU product portfolios. To use the matrix, marketers assign a product to one of the four quadrants in the portfolio according to the percentage of market share and level of profitability that the product holds within the marketplace. Cash cows, stars, question marks, and dogs are business indicators of product performance that marketing managers can manipulate. By assigning a product to a quadrant, marketing managers can make decisions about which businesses needed to be prioritised in terms of investment and resource allocation.

An underlying assumption to the BCG model is that businesses with higher market share are more likely to yield a higher rate of return. In addition, the model assumes that higher market growth rates are key performance indicators (KPIs) of where marketing managers should allocate the most resources. What follows is a breakdown of each element of the BCG portfolio matrix.

Cash cows: Cash cows are low-growth, high-market-share products that generate more cash than is needed to maintain their market share. Marketing managers should milk cash cows to provide needed resources for other areas of the business, like stars and question marks (or 'problem children').

Stars: Stars are high-growth, high-market-share products that need additional investment in order to grow the brand and maintain their market share. Marketing managers must invest in all areas of the business to improve efficiency and hold off competitors.

Question marks: A question mark show high growth opportunity but lack the profitability associated with stars and cash cows. Question marks need high levels of investment in order to grow the brand.

Dogs: Dogs have low market share and low growth. Marketing managers should harvest the remaining value associated with the brand before divesting or liquidating the brand.

The BCG Portfolio Matrix: The Coca-Cola Company	
Stars	*Question Marks*
Dasani	AdeS
One of the leading market share brands in bottled water, Dasani needs additional resources to distance itself from competitors such as Pepsi's Aquafina.	Part of Coca-Cola's plant-based portfolio (i.e. soy, coconut, almond, and flavoured milks), AdeS is a sales leader in Latin America but needs further investment to grow the brand globally.
Cash Cows	*Dog*
Coke Zero Sugar	Hi-C
One of Coke's most consistent performers that has dominant market share.	A fruit drink that is low in fruit juice but high in added sugar. A partnership deal with McDonald's might save the brand.

Market Growth Rate (vertical axis label)

Market Share Dominance

FIGURE 2.3
A proposed BCG portfolio analysis of four products in the Coca-Cola Company portfolio.

While the BCG matrix framework is still a valuable tool in strategic planning, the model does have its limitations. One issue is the speed at which products pass through the different stages of the matrix. If marketing managers do not consistently manage their product portfolio, they are unable to extract the value from areas of the portfolio and reinvest resources to grow question marks or stars. The other issue is that in today's business environment, technology and business adaptability to change are stronger indicators of performance and growth (Reeves & Moose, 2021). Despite these limitations, the BCG portfolio matrix is still a valuable tool in strategic planning and managing an organisation's SBU product portfolio.

Situational Analysis

A **situational analysis** or **situation analysis**, most commonly known as a SWOT analysis, is a tool used in the strategic planning process that identifies the internal and external factors that affect business performance. It helps organisations understand what their core competencies are, where their weakness are, and where there are opportunities and threats. SWOT stands for Strengths, Weaknesses, Opportunities, and Threats that the organisation faces within the marketplace.

Strengths

Strengths are internal to the organisation. Strengths are things an organisation does well that help to differentiate them from competitors. They are the internal capabilities that may help a company achieve the stated aims and objectives of the marketing plan. A strength might be technology, patents, or skills that the organisation possesses. Marketers use a situational analysis to convert organisational strengths into marketplace opportunities.

Weaknesses

Weaknesses are also internal to the organisation. Weaknesses are limitations or constraints that may interfere with the company's ability to achieve its stated aims and objectives. A weakness is something that an organisation lacks. This might be a lack of resources, such as financial capital or skilled workers. An organisation may lack brand recognition or a unique selling proposition within the marketplace. Strategic planning identifies organisational weaknesses and develops conversion strategies to transform weaknesses into strengths.

Opportunities

Opportunities are factors in the external environment. These are opportunities that the organisation should exploit to its advantage. Opportunities might include exploiting underserved markets, developing a proprietary technological breakthrough, or identifying new areas of growth. An external environmental scan of the micro and macro environments is a good source of marketing intelligence that feeds opportunities in the strategic planning process.

Threats

Threats are external factors that may threaten an organisation's performance and hinder the organisation from achieving its strategic objectives. Threats might take the form of changes in legislation that enact new laws or regulations that adversely affect the business. Changes might include changes in consumer tastes, the entrance of new competitors, or negative publicity. All of these are factors in the external environment that are potential organisational threats. A thorough analysis in the environmental scanning process can help organisations identify potential marketplace threats. Strategic planning helps organisations map those threats and enact contingency plans to convert those threats into opportunities.

The purpose of a SWOT is to examine critical issues in the strategic planning process that might help them to exploit marketplace opportunities that are relevant to the objectives set within the business plan. A situational analysis is most effective when it focuses in on the specific strategic objectives identified in the marketing objective-setting process. Marketers can use a SWOT analysis as part of a conversion strategy which is geared towards converting weaknesses into strengths, strengths to opportunities, and minimising threats (Piercy & Giles, 1989, see Figure 2.4).

<-------------------------------Extended Marketing Mix------------------------------->

<-----------------Marketing Mix----------------->

| Product | Price | Place | Promotion | People | Process | Physical Evidence |

FIGURE 2.4
The marketing mix and the extended marketing mix.

MARKETING MANAGER TASK

In China, Dylan is trying to decide which actions should fall within the remit of his marketing staff, which should be the domain of the sales department, and which belong to one department or the other but should be undertaken by outsourced staff. Dylan needs to balance the long- and short-term requirements of the organisation – it needs to be able to plan far into the future, as the product range is updated piecemeal over a period of around four years, but it also needs to be mobilised at short notice to capitalise upon sudden opportunities and respond to fast-moving threats. Dylan also realises that a number of the tasks are industry specific or commercially sensitive, whereas others call for marketing expertise rather than a detailed knowledge of Zomotor and the motor industry.

Help Dylan by drawing a Venn diagram consisting of three overlapping circles – one for the sales department, one for the marketing department, and one for outsourced agencies. In the diagram, enter all the major roles of marketing to show which department 'owns' that role, whether ownership is sole or joint, and if the use of an outsourced agency for that role is preferable. For each role, include one or two sentences of rationale for your allocation.

Environmental Scanning

Environmental scanning is the process through which marketing organisations collect and analyse environmental variables and action this data in their marketing strategy. The environmental variables that marketers analyse consist of both the micro and macro environments surrounding the organisation. The importance of environmental scanning is to gather key marketing intelligence that can help an organisation understand current market trends and future market opportunities.

The immediate environment surrounding an organisation is known as the micro environment. The micro environment consists of the company itself, its suppliers, marketing intermediaries, competitors, and customers. The external environment is known as the macro environment, which consists of the political, economic, socio-cultural, technological, ecological, and legal environments. Environmental scanning studies both the micro and macro environment, and this market intelligence is used within the marketing plan to guide strategy formation.

Market Segmentation, Targeting, and Positioning

As an organisation is gathering marketing intelligence on the micro and macro environment, it is using that information to feed into the market segmentation, targeting, and positioning strategy. Market segmentation, targeting, and positioning (STP) are key elements to the strategic planning process. STP involves segmenting customers into distinct groups that share similar characteristics. Targeting involves selecting specific groups within the segment that the organisation thinks it can best serve. Positioning involves tailoring the marketing mix strategy to create a value proposition for the target segment(s). For more information on the importance of STP, please consult Chapter 5.

The Marketing Mix Strategy

The marketing mix was proposed as an early framework in marketing to help capture all the activities that marketers undertake in meeting customer needs. The importance of the marketing mix is to provide students of marketing a taxonomy for understanding marketing's touchpoints with consumers in the marketplace. The original conceptualisation of the marketing mix is known as the 4 Ps: product, price, place, and promotion.

Critics of the 4 Ps approach felt that it was overly simplistic and did not fully capture the full complexity of marketing's interaction with the marketplace; they proposed a 7 Ps framework (product, price, place, promotion, people, process, and physical evidence). This framework has become known as the extended marketing mix. The extended marketing mix represents the 7 Ps, which is the framework through which marketers shape marketplace interactions in order to create customer satisfaction. Marketers manipulate each element of the marketing mix in order to create satisfactory exchanges. Each element of the extended marketing mix follows.

Product

A **product** is something that is offered in the marketplace that is used to satisfy a customer want or need in the process of exchange. A product might be something that is manufactured and is a tangible good, or it might be something that is intangible, such as a service. A haircut is an example of a service that is an intangible product offering.

Product offerings provide organisations the opportunity to create customer value and satisfaction through a number of different consumer touchpoints. The core product

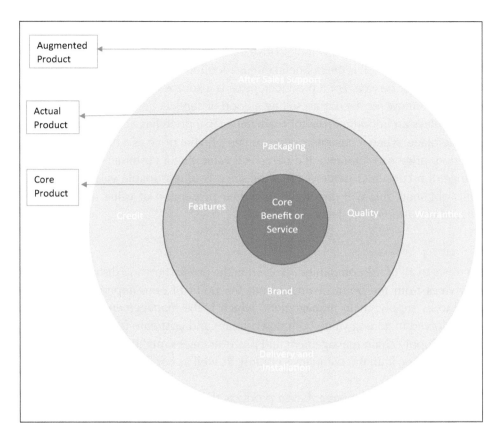

FIGURE 2.5
The many different layers to product offerings.

offers the benefits that consumers receive upon purchase. It consists of the actual product, which includes the packaging, features, and benefits, as well as the quality of the product and brand name. Marketers often augment the core and actual product offerings with the augmented product, which might include delivery, customer installation, warranty, and after-sales service.

Product offerings consist of a number of different facets, as outlined in Figure 2.5. At the core of the diagram is the core product, which is the benefit or service that a customer will receive from purchasing the product. The actual product is the tangible manifestation of the product or service, which includes the quality, features, branding, and packaging of the product. The augmented product is the value added to the core benefit or service, which might take the form of delivery and installation, warranties or guarantees, and after-sales support. Each layer of the product represents an opportunity for marketers to better meet customer needs and create customer satisfaction.

Price

Price is the amount a buyer is willing to give up in exchange for a product or service. For a buyer, price is a cost. It is the financial outlay required to obtain the benefits associated with a product or service. For a producer, price is a source of revenue. Price represents the financial inflow received from selling a good or service.

Price plays an important role for marketers. First, price has an information effect in the marketplace, where consumers often equate a higher price as a designator of quality. In addition, price can influence the perceived value that a customer obtains within an exchange. If a consumer perceives that the price is of reasonable value relative to the benefits obtained, this will directly impact their perception of value and increase the likelihood of customer satisfaction.

Place

Place refers to all of the companies involved in the production and distribution of goods and services from the point of origin until the point of consumption. Place is often referred to as supply chain management, which is the management of all of the processes involved in adding value both downstream and upstream from the point of consumption. Supply chain management and place strategies might involve those activities that are directly within the company's control, as well as companies that are external to an organisation.

For example, think of paper-based products that you might have consumed today. This might be a magazine, a newspaper, tissue, or packaging from a fast-food restaurant. The supply chain associated with these products starts in a forest where trees are grown. These are then harvested and converted into pulp, which is then used to make large paper rolls. These rolls of paper are then distributed to specialist manufacturers that convert paper into branded products. The supply chain represents the interdependent organisations that bring that product to the marketplace.

Promotion

The role of **promotion** is raise awareness about the product/service offering, provide a short-term incentive to buy, and ensure the target market has top-of-mind awareness about an organisation's offering. Promotional strategy is known as the promotional mix, which consists of advertising, sales promotion, personal selling, public relations, and social media. Marketers strategically use different elements of the promotional mix in tandem to achieve the promotional goals of the organisation.

People

People play a key role in every marketing organisation. **People** refers to the personnel of the company and how they interface with customers and within the organisation. The role that people play in creating a market-oriented company can range from providing excellent customer service, sales personnel, people who manufacture products, and people who directly interact with customers. It also includes the different functional areas of the business (e.g. accounting, R&D, human resources), which are key players in developing a customer-facing organisational strategy.

Process

Process involves all of the steps required to successfully deliver a product or service to a customer. When marketers evaluate process as part of their marketing mix, they take a holistic view in managing the customer experience. Process requires marketers to evaluate the sales funnel, the ordering procurement system, payment processes, distribution strategies, and customer service. It is important that all of these systems coordinate with each other to ensure a seamless customer experience.

Physical Evidence

Physical evidence refers to the physical and visual aesthetic of the organisation. For example, in retailing, the physical design of the store plays an important role in shaping the customer experience and their perception of the brand. Physical evidence also refers to the visual aesthetic of the brand, where companies carefully shape their logo and website and cultivate their brand image.

The marketing mix framework enables marketing managers to coordinate each touchpoint that an organisation has with customers in the marketplace. In the strategic planning process, marketers must give consideration to how each element of the 7Ps creates opportunities for customer satisfaction and customer value. The 7Ps also enable an organisation to craft its form of competitive advantage in the marketplace.

MARKETING DIRECTOR TASK

As global director of marketing, Lee is focusing on Zomotor's societal role and the firm's stance towards its stakeholders. Initial research has suggested that many consumers perceive motor man-  ufacturers as faceless corporations who drain resources, damage the environment, and exploit poorer communities to make large profits. Like other manufacturers, Zomotor has sought to reverse these perceptions by softening its image and building relationships with stakeholders. However, many prospects and customers still perceive a psychic distance between themselves and Zomotor.

Help Lee by drawing a table which shows how Zomotor can make each major stakeholder type feel included, consulted, and more trusting of the firm. Think about the values which Zomotor is trying to transmit, the messages it uses, the language it employs, and the actions it undertakes. The analysis is not confined to the marketing department but incorporates the behaviours and actions of the

continued

firm as a whole and the ways in which these impact upon its publics. The four major stakeholder groups which Lee wishes to focus on are (i) local communities; (ii) employees and trade unions; (iii) partner organisations, including dealerships; and (iv) society and the environment as a whole.

Creating Competitive Advantage

At one level, competitive advantage refers to an internal strategy that organisations develop and deploy to make their products and services unique. This refers to the managerial actions that organisations undertake that differentiate them from the competition or lower the costs associated with producing a good or service. However, external drivers can create opportunities for competitive advantage as well. Changes in consumer tastes, consumer fads, or changes in the external marketing environment can lead to marketplace changes that provide organisations new opportunities for the creation of competitive advantage.

Competitive advantage is a position that an organisation holds in the marketplace that is viewed as distinctive and superior to competitors. It is generally accepted that the two dominant forms of competitive advantage are cost leadership strategies and creating market differentiation (Porter, 2008). These two forms of advantage create economies of scale, greater buyer bargaining power, and greater brand recognition amongst buyers (Fiegenbaum & Karnani, 1991).

Marketers have come to recognise a third form of competitive advantage: niche competitive advantage. Companies with niche competitive advantage often serve the needs of smaller segments of the marketplace that larger organisations may overlook.

Cost Competitive Advantage

Cost competitive advantage is the ability to provide a product or service at a lower cost than a competitor. Organisations that build cost competitive advantage can generate greater profitability on sales by generating internal efficiencies within the organisation that it can then leverage into creating less expensive products and services. Cost is seen as a form of competitive advantage as it gives companies the potential to undercut the competition by charging less money. Companies can pass that savings onto customers, reinvest that money internally, or develop philanthropic pursuits. Companies such as Amazon, Walmart, McDonald's, and Lidl are all examples of organisations that use cost competitive advantage strategies. There are a number of sources these companies use as the source of their cost competitive advantage.

Economies of scale: The cost efficiencies that arise from scaling. Higher volume and output enable organisations to gain cost efficiencies through buying in bulk. Fixed costs per unit of output also decrease as volume increases.

PHOTO 2.3
By offering a narrow range of products, Lidl is able to build competitive advantage through economies of scale.

Experience curves: The cost of an activity decreases as organisational learning increases. As an organisation becomes more experienced, it finds new ways to produce things more efficiently.

Innovation and technology: New innovations or technological advances in industry can lead to greater cost savings.

Efficient labour: Sources of labour that are less expensive and automating routine tasks enable cost reduction.

New forms of service delivery: Finding new ways of getting products and services to customers and removing unnecessary cost overhead are methods of cost reduction.

While cost leadership is a way for companies to build competitive advantage, it is not without risk. Cost competitive advantage has the potential to be copied and replicated by competitors. New entrants in the market that are able to scale their business model quickly can threaten existing cost leaders.

Differentiation

Differential competitive advantage exists when organisations build advantages that are perceived as unique within the marketplace. Differential advantage can be built through strong dealer networks, product and service quality, and brand image. For example, marketers spend significant resources in developing marketing campaigns that help them to create unique brand identities. Brands such as Apple have spent decades cultivating a differentiated brand image around the values of innovation, creativity, and 'thinking different'.

NEW MEDIA QUESTION

What role can social media play in creating competitive advantage? Choose one company that you think has used social media to create competitive advantage. What makes their social media strategy unique? How is this strategy different from the competition?

Niche

Niche competitive advantage is built when organisations focus on smaller subsegments within a marketplace. By focusing on the wants and needs of a single market segment, an organisation can build better relationships with its customer base. Small businesses with limited resources often concentrate their marketing strategies to reach these smaller segments. Alternatively, luxury brands can concentrate their resources to target specific segments based on taste, quality, and price preferences.

PHOTO 2.4
Jomil is a haberdashery company that makes an assortment of sewing and sewing-related supplies. This is an example of a niche business.

Marketing Implementation

Marketing implementation involves the actions undertaken to implement the strategic plan. The importance of marketing implementation is to ensure the organisation is able to accomplish the stated aims and objectives of the strategic plan. Implementation assigns tasks to specific departments and personnel. It helps to ensure that each member understands their job assignments and the actions they must take in order for the organisation to achieve its goals. It also sets clear deadlines on when tasks are to be completed. From a managerial point of view, marketing implementation helps to create accountability in ensuring personnel are accomplishing their stated aims and objectives. From an employee point of view, it is a form of employee empowerment which authorises personnel to take action.

STAKEHOLDER QUESTION

You are the marketing manager of a technology company that is considering developing a new video game application service that will be available on both Apple and Android systems. The 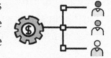 CEO of the organisation has tasked you with developing a strategic plan to explore the viability of this project. The CEO has asked you to speak with different stakeholders within the company to identify key aims and objectives that would form the basis of the plan.

  Your task is to identify which key stakeholders should be approached. What roles and responsibilities would they have? What guidance could they provide in helping you develop the strategic plan?

Evaluation and Control

The strategic planning process is only valuable to an organisation if managers are able to effectively implement the strategy developed within the strategic plan. There is little value that can be gained in an organisation where the strategic plan is a static document that sits on a marketing manager's shelf. It is important to continually evaluate the strategic plan and update the strategy. This helps to ensure that the strategic plan matches the evolving market opportunities and changes in consumer needs and preferences.

  The **marketing audit** is a systematic review of the strategic planning process that examines each element of the strategic plan that evaluates the current strategy, recommends changes, and identifies new opportunities. The audit plays a dual role in the strategic planning process. One element is retrospective and seeks to evaluate what went right and wrong in the original strategic plan. The other role is forecasting where the market opportunities will move in the future. By continually evaluating the strategic plan, audits help to ensure that the strategic planning process stays at the forefront of organisational decision-making and strategy.

In practice, a marketing audit will question the original assumptions set forth within the strategic plan by evaluating the marketing objectives. An audit can help an organisation better understand how it performed relative to those objectives. Using an organisation's performance against benchmarked objectives can provide a guide as to what other areas of the strategic plan need to be modified to achieve stated goals. For example, if gaining market share is an objective, managers might consider product modifications or price reductions to help achieve that objective. Evaluation and control are key post-audit activities that ensure the organisation is effectively able to reach its target market and create customer and organisational value.

Chapter Summary

Strategic planning encapsulates almost everything that marketers do. A strategic plan sets measurable objectives that are linked to market opportunities. It involves collecting marketing research data on both the micro and macro environments where organisations operate. It also involves collecting market data on consumers in order to segment the market as well as targeting specific segments that the organisation will serve. Finally, it involves positioning the 7Ps of the extended marketing mix to ensure an organisation is able to create customer satisfaction and value. The continuous evaluation of a strategic plan ensures that an organisation keeps a market-oriented focus.

Recommended Further Reading

Bryson, J. M., Edwards, L. H., & Van Slyke, D. M. (2018). Getting strategic about strategic planning research. *Public Management Review, 20*(3), 317–339.

Evans, V. (2015). *The FT essential guide to writing a business plan: How to win backing to start up or grow your business*. Pearson.

Freedman, L. (2015). *Strategy: A history*. Oxford University Press.

Lim, W. M. (2021). A marketing mix typology for integrated care: The 10 Ps. *Journal of Strategic Marketing, 29*(5), 453–469.

References

Alegre, I., Berbegal-Mirabent, J., Guerrero, A., & Mas-Machuca, M. (2018). The real mission of the mission statement: A systematic review of the literature. *Journal of Management & Organization, 24*(4), 456–473.

easyGroup. (2021). *About us*. https://easy.com/about-us/

Fiegenbaum, A., & Karnani, A. (1991). Output flexibility – a competitive advantage for small firms. *Strategic Management Journal, 12*(2), 101–114.

Garcia, A. (2015). *Anheuser Busch InBev strikes biggest-ever beer deal with $107B takeover of SABMiller*. https://www.forbes.com/sites/antoinegara/2015/11/11/anheuser-busch-inbev-strikes-biggest-ever-beer-deal-with-107b-sabmiller-takeover/?sh=24973ccd5348

Piercy, N., & Giles, W. (1989). Making SWOT analysis work. *Marketing Intelligence & Planning, 7*(5/6), 5–7.

Porter, M. E. (2008). *Competitive advantage: Creating and sustaining superior performance*. Simon and Schuster.

Procter & Gamble. (2021). *Structure and governance*. https://www.pg.co.uk/structure-and-governance/corporate-structure/

Reeves, M., & Moose, S. (2021). *What is the growth share matrix?* https://www.bcg.com/about/our-history/growth-share-matrix

Glossary

Business mission: a formal articulation of organisational culture

Competitive advantage: a unique market position that an organisation holds in the marketplace that is viewed as distinctive and superior to competitors

Environmental scanning: the process through which marketing organisations collect and analyse environmental variables and action this data in their marketing strategy

Marketing audit: a systematic review of the strategic planning process that examines each element of the strategic plan that evaluates current strategy, recommends changes, and identifies new opportunities

Marketing implementation: the actions are undertaken and implemented in order to accomplish the stated aims and objectives of the strategic plan

People: the personnel of the company and how they interface with customers and within the organisation

Physical evidence: the physical and visual aesthetic of the organisation

Place: all of the companies involved in the production and distribution of goods and services from the point of origin until the point of consumption

Price: the amount a buyer is willing to give up in exchange for a product or service

Process: involves all of the steps required to successfully deliver a product or service to a customer

Product: something that is offered in the marketplace that is used to satisfy a customer want or need in the process of exchange

Promotion: raises awareness about the product/service offering, provides a short-term incentive to buy, and ensures the target market has top-of-mind awareness about an organisation's offering

Situational analysis (SWOT): a tool used in the strategic planning process that identifies the internal and external factors that affect business performance

Strategic business unit (SBU): an independently managed subgroup of products or services of a larger organisation

Strategic plans: formal strategy documents that companies use to guide the strategic direction of the company

Strategic Planning, Competitive Advantage, and Forecasting the Future Case Study: The Future of Peloton Fitness

Although the pandemic took a huge toll on many families and businesses, some business benefitted from the changes it brought. One of those companies that saw its fortunes increase during the pandemic was Peloton, the manufacturer of stationary exercise equipment and livestream workouts. Peloton saw a 339% sales increase from 2019 to 2021 (see Figure One) and a 356% subscription base increase between 2019 to 2021.

Peloton exercise equipment became one of the must-have products for people in countries with government-imposed lockdowns. Many consumers were unable to work out and train at the gym but still wanted to remain fit and healthy. This led to a huge rise in demand for home-based workout equipment, as consumers were looking for new ways to work out in their home environment.

continued

Peloton positioned its exercise equipment at the high end of the market in terms of price and quality. The company's two fitness bikes are priced and $1,350 and $2,295, and its treadmill starts at £2,295. This helped to attract an affluent customer base, with over 92% of its customers earning over $50,000 and 29% of its base earning over $150,000 (Peloton, 2022a).

Their subscription-based app also provided important social connections for people who wanted to feel linked to a broader fitness community. Stay-at-home consumers were able to access fitness trainers at any time of day, every day of the week. Themed classes, which allowed users to choose different interactive workout platforms, became a big part of the company's appeal. Peloton instructors also offered high levels of personalisation by acknowledging consumer birthdays and workout milestones. All of this led to a loyal customer base with high retention rates.

Peloton's growth has not been seamless. Due to high demand, Peloton ran into supply problems in 2021, which caused delays within its supply chain. Delayed deliveries and the lack of customer service support led to consumer backlash. A number of consumer injuries while using Peloton products, and the death of a young child, led the US Consumer Protection Agency to issue consumer safety warnings (Jiménez, 2021).

Recent changes in the marketing environment have also impacted Peloton's strategic plan. The opening up of economies have led to changes in consumer behaviour. Consumers are now more willing to go back to the gym, which has led to a reduction in demand for home fitness. Consumer workarounds have enabled use of the Peloton app without purchase of the equipment. The rise of new competitors in the marketplace that also offer high-quality equipment and services, such as Mirror, FlyWheel, and SoulCycle, has also influenced demand for Peloton equipment.

Recently, John Foley, the co-founder and CEO of Peloton, issued a warning about the company's earnings statement. He indicated that Peloton was in the process of evaluating the "organizational structure and size of our team . . . and are still in the process of considering all options as part of our efforts to make our business more flexible" (Peloton, 2022b). Could this be the beginning of a downward sales trend for the company?

Your Task

Drawing from your knowledge of strategic planning, how can Peloton maintain its competitive advantage in the future? In groups, make strategic recommendations that you think the company can incorporate within its strategic plan. When

continued

considering Peloton's strategic course of action, you might give consideration to the following areas:

▶ The development of new personalised content geared towards individual users.

▶ Strategies to boost community engagement.

▶ Diversifying the product/service portfolio.

▶ Introducing new fitness products.

▶ Influencer marketing/strategic partnerships.

▶ Targeting different consumer segments.

Bibliography

Gough, C. (2021a). Peloton global revenue 2017–2021. *Statista*. https://www.statista.com/statistics/935875/peloton-revenue/

Gough, C. (2021b). Peloton global subscriptions 2018–2021. *Statista*. https://www.statista.com/statistics/1203117/peloton-subscriptions/

Jiménez, J. (2021). Peloton fights back against U.S. warnings of treadmill dangers. *NYTimes*. https://www.nytimes.com/2021/04/17/business/peloton-tread-recall-child-death.html

Peloton. (2022a). *Peloton investor and & analyst day presentation 2020*. https://investor.onepeloton.com/news-and-events/events

Peloton. (2022b). *A note from John Foley, Co-founder and CEO*. https://www.onepeloton.com/press/articles/a-note-from-john-foley-co-founder-and-ceo

3 | Marketing Research

Introduction

Marketing research is the activity used by marketers to capture the voice of the customer. It is the role of the market researcher to collect, analyse, and disseminate market research data throughout an organisation. It is important that knowledge about an organisation's customers does not exclusively sit within the marketing department but is integrated throughout all functional areas of the business. For human resources, marketing research data can help us understand what personnel decisions we need to make with staff who are customer facing. For finance and accounting, marketing research data helps us to pinpoint optimal price points that create value for a company and its customers. For R&D teams, marketing research helps us to better understand customer needs and tailor product designs or service delivery options to meet different need-based segments. Marketing research helps to integrate different functional areas of a business into a unified mission around creating customer and organisational value.

The American Marketing Association defines **marketing research** as

> the function that links the consumer, customer, and public to the marketer through information – information used to identify and define marketing

opportunities and problems; generate, refine, and evaluate marketing actions; monitor marketing performance; and improve understanding of marketing as a process. Marketing research specifies the information required to address these issues, designs the method for collecting information, manages and implements the data collection process, analyses the results, and communicates the findings and their implications.

(adopted by the AMA, 2004)

Marketing research helps to place marketing at the centre of creating value. While the core function of marketing is to generate sales, it is also the function of marketing to create satisfactory market exchanges. In order to ensure that we are able to create customer satisfaction and value, we use marketing research as the tool to understand market needs so that we can translate information into value propositions. It gives marketing a privileged position that is tasked with collecting and disseminating that information throughout an organisation.

STAKEHOLDER QUESTION

This textbook stresses the importance of the relationship between marketing and the voice of the customer. Marketing research is one of the tools that marketers use in understanding customer 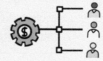 wants and needs. How do you think market research data, which represents the voice of the customer, can help different functional areas of the business create customer satisfaction? How might market research help the human resource department, the accounting department, the marketing department, or the R&D department better meet customer needs? Be specific in your answer.

The Role of Marketing Intelligence Systems Within Organisations

The ability of an organisation to collect, analyse, and disseminate marketing research information is a key source of competitive advantage. This holistic perspective on marketing research is known as a marketing information system. **Marketing information systems** consist of the "people, equipment, processes and procedures to gather, sort analyse, evaluate and distribute needed, timely and accurate information" (Kotler et al., 2008, p. 325). While Kotler's definition provides important insights, we opt for the term **marketing intelligence systems** in order to capture the dynamic capabilities of marketing research that include the increasing sophistication of big data, data analytics, and artificial intelligence (AI). Marketing intelligence systems have the added capability of being able to learn from marketing research without being programmed. Thus, marketing

PHOTO 3.1
Marketers are increasingly using marketing intelligence systems which capture large volumes of data that can be processed and then tailored to individual customers.

research is not something that is collected and archived; it represents an active system where data can be collected in real time and has the potential to learn independently and predict. New technologies have enabled marketing researchers to make predictions to a greater level of accuracy than ever before.

We are entering an age in marketing research where we have access to large amounts of data and where we can make hundreds of marketing decisions in a single day. Marketing research data can help us to determine what internet search terms we need to buy, where and when to place our advertising, what content we should deliver to our target audiences, and what platform we should use to deliver this content. The sheer number of variables and activities that marketers must consider has grown exponentially with technology, and marketers have put into place marketing intelligence systems to help capture that data, action that data, and intuitively learn from its decision-making. The term that we use to describe this process of data collection, dissemination, and action is a marketing intelligence system.

The Marketing Research Process

The **marketing research process** is a framework that marketers use to identify evolving market opportunities. It sets forth a series of steps that marketers follow when planning marketing research design. It involves setting aims and objectives for research, evaluating different research approaches, sampling strategies, analysis and report interpretation, and report dissemination. In many organisations, the marketing research process is articulated in a formal strategy document known as a marketing plan. A **marketing plan** is a formal strategy document that marketers use to articulate organisational aims and objectives, resource allocation, and short- and long-term planning objectives that can achieve organisational milestones. The marketing plan helps organisations make

PHOTO 3.2
A marketing plan is a document that marketers use to develop marketing strategy.

data-driven decisions that are integral to the marketing research process. What follows is a step-by-step explanation for each stage in the marketing research process.

Setting Research Aims and Objectives

Aim and objective setting help an organisation to articulate information needs and problem statements. Research objectives are formally articulated questions or statements that specify a course of action for marketing researchers to follow. The importance of research objectives is that they provide managers alternatives to choose from and allow managers to make data-driven decisions rather than relying upon intuition or instinct. The advantage of meeting research objectives is that they help managers to make choices about resource allocation, target marketing strategies, and product decisions.

Most organisations set forth the research objectives in a strategy document known as a research proposal. A marketing **research proposal** is a formal document that outlines the research objectives of a study, the type of sample that will be studied, the research design, the budget necessary to undertake the research, and the deliverables of the research. Research deliverables are what managers can expect to receive from the marketing research team. They specify the type, format, and structure of the final report generated from the marketing research proposal.

When developing the marketing research proposal, there are three types of research designs that marketing researchers can incorporate: exploratory, descriptive, and causal.

Exploratory research is an informal, unstructured approach used in order to generate more information about research objectives. The aim of exploratory research is to help marketing researchers better understand the research problem at hand and to generate some initial data and findings that can aid in further research collection. It helps marketing researchers clarify problems that may not be fully understood and can provide insights that allow for more targeted research approaches. A good example of an exploratory study might be to use secondary data to help guide researchers to develop their own research objectives.

Descriptive research is used to describe the characteristics of a population. It helps marketers answer questions of "who, what, where, when, and how" (Burns & Bush, 2010, p. 149). Marketing researchers might use descriptive research to uncover how respondents make meaning of certain behaviours. It is also used describe current behaviour or, in other cases, the frequency of that behaviour. We might use descriptive research at a single point in time, known as cross-sectional data, or over a period of time, known as longitudinal data.

Causal research seeks to establish the relationship between cause and effect. This method can be used to understand causality through the experimental method, which uses random assignment and planned intervention. Planned intervention is the process through which marketers create a disturbance in the environment and track the resulting change. Experiments randomize different variables in a study in order to measure the effect of these changes.

Depending upon the type of research objective identified, marketing researchers might use one approach or a combination of different approaches in order to answer the research objectives. The ways in which marketing researchers operationalise their research design is through different marketing research approaches.

Marketing Research Approaches

After an organisation has clearly identified its information needs and objectives, **secondary data sources** are often a starting point for market intelligence gathering. Secondary data is any data that has been collected by another researcher or data that has been previously collected for purposes that are outside of the current research objectives. Secondary data sources include trade industry data, competitive intelligence, governmental agency reports, news media information, internal corporate information, or information collected by market research firms.

For example, the US Homeland Security Research branch collects global market data looking at the use of big data and data analytics (see Figure 3.1). This report, which

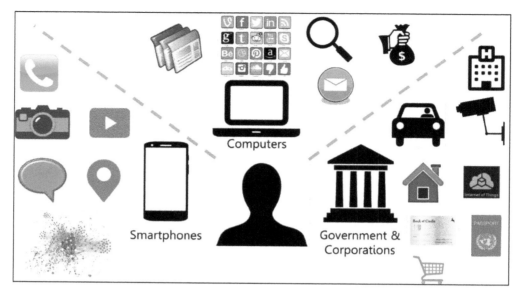

FIGURE 3.1
Homeland security and public safety main data sources for intelligence (Homeland Security Research, 2019).

is available for purchase, highlights trends in big data technologies used by governments and security organisations. It provides insights into market size, types of big data technologies, technology use by country, and investment allocation across both country and technology. This secondary data information source would be of interest to big data companies looking to benchmark and forecast growth potential by data intelligence type and country. It would also be of interest to investors of big data, intelligence agencies, and firms developing new data analytic capabilities.

The advantage of this data is that it can quickly provide companies with an overview of market trends and forecasts. It can save a company time and money by buying this data source readily off the shelf rather than having to collect this data first-hand, which would be time-consuming and expensive. Secondary data can also help pinpoint areas needed for future research, serve as a benchmark for the comparison of other data, and help an organisation refine the aims and objectives of existing research projects.

The disadvantage of using secondary data is it is publicly available data, which means competitors also have access to this information. Another issue with secondary data is that the aims and objectives of the research might not align with the strategic aims or research questions of a company looking to collect marketing research information. It is also important to know the quality of secondary data and for what purposes the data was collected. While there are both advantages and disadvantages to using secondary data, companies would not use it exclusively and often use it as the platform for conducting primary research.

SUSTAINABILITY QUESTION

Sustainability is a key issue for consumers. Many consumers make their purchase decisions based on the environmental performance of an organisation and whether or not that organisation is perceived as environmentally friendly. Can secondary data help organisations improve their environmental performance? How?

Primary research involves collecting first-hand. It uses an organisation's in-house marketing research team or an independent market research firm to actively collect data that addresses a specific business problem or information need. The advantage of primary data is it is proprietary information that is exclusive to the organisation conducting the research. It also has the advantage of being current information that is readily known to an organisation. The disadvantages of primary data collection are that it is expensive to collect and it can be a time-consuming process where the data is not immediately available.

The most common form of primary research is survey research. **Survey research** is any research approach which includes both qualitative and quantitative approaches that seek to evaluate the opinions of other people through interaction, where we are interested in understanding opinions, attitudes, beliefs, and practices. Primary research can be broadly characterised as qualitative research and quantitative research. **Qualitative research** refers to a range of different methods of data collection that are focused on eliciting verbal, textual, visual, and observational data. This method places primacy on individual data points, smaller sample sizes, and understanding potential data outliers in a study. **Quantitative research** refers to a range of different methods of data collection that are primarily focused on statistical measurements or establishing causality. This method is used to develop representative sampling, generalizability, and hypothesis testing. In the context of marketing research, both approaches are valuable and are often used together in order to understand and yield insights in behaviour. Each approach consists of a number of different methods that can yield different types of marketing research intelligence.

METRICS QUESTION

You are a recent graduate of university and have been shortlisted to interview for a marketing research position at a company you are interested in. During the interview process, the interviewer asks you about the importance of data-driven decision-making. What does data-driven decision-making mean? Why is it important for organisations? What can data-driven decision-making tell an organisation about its customers?

Qualitative Research Approaches

Focus group research is one of the most popular forms of qualitative market research. A focus group is an interactive discussion group led by a moderator for the purposes of uncovering information about a specific business problem. Focus group participants are paid for their time, and a typical focus group will often consist of 7 to 10 people and last for approximately 2 hours. Focus groups can be conducted in a studio setting, where participants travel to a research centre to take part, or they can occur online.

During a focus group, participants can collectively build upon ideas through group dialogue and group dynamics. This technique, known as group effects, is designed to enhance group creativity. Focus groups help to overcome some of the limitations associated with one-to-one interviewing by encouraging participants to collectively brainstorm ideas through moderated discussion.

Moderators play a key role in determining the success of focus group research. Moderators are highly trained researchers that help to facilitate but also to control group discussions and group dynamics. Good moderators are able to mitigate the downsides to group effects by avoiding the trap of building group consensus or allowing single individuals to dominate a group discussion. The ability to capture multiple perspectives within a focus group session can add to richness of the data.

PHOTO 3.3
Focus groups are moderated discussions where marketers can better understand customer preferences and test concept ideas.

Another advantage of focus groups is they enable companies to observe participant interactions first-hand. Face-to-face focus groups occur in controlled settings where participants are invited to studios and clients can observe group interactions behind a screened glass. This helps brand managers better understand customer needs by witnessing the dialogue as it unfolds in real time. This research method is most often used to gauge reactions to different product variations, marketing communication messaging, and new product ideas.

A famous example of the power of focus groups was Mattel's use of focus groups in the 1950s, where focus group data with young girls led to the development on one of the first adult dolls on the toy market. Barbie represented the aspirations of young girls who idealised becoming adults. While Mattel and Barbie have long been criticised for creating an unrealistic body type, it was focus group research that led the company into reconfiguring the doll in 2014 to represent a diversity in body types and skin colours (Stromberg, 2019). The repositioning of Barbie as an empowered woman has helped to revitalise the brand.

The disadvantage of focus groups is that they represent a small fraction of the overall customer base and are non-representative samples. The data generated from focus groups are highly subjective and are based upon the strength of the research team tasked with analysing the data. As a result, the information gathered from focus group data is non-generalizable and is often best used in conjunction with research data collected from other research approaches.

PHOTO 3.4
Focus group research has been instrumental in creating and maintaining Mattel's Barbie competitive advantage.

Interviews are a qualitative research technique where marketing researchers ask respondents a series of questions in an attempt to understand a respondent's point of view. A **structured interview** is used when a marketing researcher wants to ask a number of different respondents the same question. An **unstructured interview** is a blend of structured questions, but it also allows for a marketing researcher to probe a respondent in different areas. Interview probes are an important part of interviewing, as they enable marketing researchers to ask follow-up questions in areas where respondents might have strong feelings about a subject or have a particular area of expertise. An example of a probe might be to ask a respondent what they meant by something or asking them to elaborate more in their response.

There is no one single technique associated with interviews, and interviewing consists of a number of different approaches. Some researchers prefer the long interview process, whereby a researcher spends a longer period of time with a respondent in order to build rapport and elicit a clearer picture of their beliefs and the experiences of participants (McCracken, 1988). In other cases, marketing researchers may not have the time or resources to spend long periods with respondents and instead might prefer a high street intercept interview. **Intercept interviews** allow marketing researchers to approach larger numbers of people quickly. They can do so on the high street of a city or through online channels. Another approach is an **executive interview**, which involves targeting

PHOTO 3.5
High street intercept interviews allow marketers to approach a large number of research participants quickly.

professionals in their place of work or recruiting them to an interview studio. For example, a drug manufacturer of diabetes medication might be interested in recruiting and interviewing doctors in order to better understand prescribing behaviour.

Ethnography is a research method, born out of the disciplines of anthropology and sociology, which seeks to gain a better understanding of behaviour through participant observation techniques that place a researcher within the context of the everyday lives of the people they are studying. A central aim to ethnographic research is to convey the culture of the people they are studying in order to understand their beliefs, practices, norms of behaviour, relationships, and meaning.

Marketing researchers who study consumer and business behaviour must always be aware of the degree to which participants are able to accurately recall their behaviour (Elliot & Jankel-Elliot, 2003) and account for the fact that people do not always do what they say (Wirth-Fellman, 1999). It is not that participants are actively trying to deceive researchers; it just might be the case of where they cannot recall their behaviour to the level of detail that is of interest to a market researcher. Ethnography helps researchers to prioritise what people do over what they might say.

In order to leverage ethnography to generate new insights, market research organisations have uniquely adapted ethnography to fit the needs of commercial business practice. **Commercial ethnography** represents a movement away from the study of 'native cultures' and a movement towards the study of consumer cultures. While the underlying principles are the same, the research procedure is quite different. Instead of traveling to faraway lands, commercial ethnographers study people within their homes and workplaces. Due to both consumer and business pressures, commercial ethnographers spend shorter periods with people. Commercial ethnographers also work with more targeted research objectives due to the nature of the research design process, but their aim is still to directly participate in people's lives. They then take this understanding into the realm of business practice in order to meet the needs of an organisation's target market.

There has also been a movement towards conducting ethnographic research in online environments. **Netnography** represents the adaptation of ethnographic research methodologies to study the cultures and communities emerging through computer-mediated communication (Kozinets, 2015). Netnographers can observe or participate in online interactions through online forums, message boards, Instagram, Facebook, blogs, Twitter, and YouTube. The advantage to netnographic research is the speed and convenience of online interactions and the ability to readily capture textual and visual data. Many ethnographers will supplement traditional commercial ethnography with netnographic approaches.

While there is no one way to conduct a commercial ethnographic study, some of the attributes that are unique to commercial ethnographic practice are (i) a methodology that is bought and sold in the marketplace, (ii) a narrow focus of a commissioned study, (iii) the incorporation of rapid assessment procedures, (iv) a greater potential for what has become known as the 'observer effect', and (v) a special set of ethical concerns that are unique to its practice.

PHOTO 3.6
Commercial ethnographers spend time with research participants in their homes in the hope that they can better understand the lifestyles, values, preferences, and beliefs of their target market.

MARKETING ASSISTANT TASK

In Mexico, the major problem facing Zomotor has been a declin- ing sales conversion rate amongst dealer salespeople. In each of the previous two years, the rate of success has dropped by around 5%. Whilst Zomotor has attempted to address the shortfall by providing larger numbers of sales leads and introducing sales promotions aimed at driving dealer footfall (i.e. the number of prospects visiting the dealership), this is costly and frustrating when the net result in terms of sales volumes and profitability remains the same. The issue seems most serious in the larger city dealerships, and especially those which operate other manufacturer's franchises alongside Zomotor.

Tannya has been asked to design a research process which will investigate this issue, gain new customer insights, and identify the causes. Initially, she must decide which techniques to use in tandem to gain a comprehensive and reliable picture. Help Tannya by drawing a table which compares the advantages and limitations of the different research techniques available, but ensure your comments are in the context of Zomotor and the challenges which it is currently facing.

Quantitative Approaches

As an industry, global marketing research generates almost $47 billion in annual turn-over (ESOMAR, 2019). The dominant methodological approach, in terms of use and organisational expenditure, is the questionnaire. A **questionnaire** is a set of standardised questions that follows a fixed sequence and is used to collect information from a participant. Questionnaires govern the type and nature of responses due to their formal structure.

Questionnaires rely upon three different types of survey questions: closed questions, scaled response questions, and open-ended questions. **Closed questions** are mutually exclusive questions that require respondents to choose from a limited set of responses. An example of a closed question is a **dichotomous response question**, which requires a yes or no answer.

Do you own an automobile?

Yes 1
No 2

Scaled response questions are closed questions that require respondents to choose from a set of pre-coded answers. In some cases, these questions might measure frequency:

In the last week, how often have you driven your automobile?

Everyday 1
Four to six days 2
Two to three days 3
One day 4
Not at all 5

In other cases, we might use scaling techniques to measure the intensity of a respondent's answer:

How satisfied are you with the current performance of your automobile?

Completely satisfied 1
Somewhat satisfied 2
Neutral 3
Somewhat dissatisfied 4
Completely dissatisfied 5

Open-ended questions give respondents the freedom to express their opinions using their own words. A question that asks a respondent, 'What do you like most about your car?' is likely to give respondents an opportunity to express a range of different opinions that would not be captured in a more structured question.

One of the key challenges in developing a questionnaire is ensuring that marketing researchers "maximize the relationship between the answers recorded and what the researcher is trying to measure" (Fowler, 1993, p. 69). In order to achieve this, marketing researchers must take the time to carefully craft questions and avoid the use of jargon or ambiguous language. When questionnaires are clearly developed, there are a number of advantages to using this approach.

Speed and technology are key factors in using questionnaires. Marketing researchers can develop and administer a questionnaire more quickly than other forms of survey research. Most questionnaires are now administered through websites such as Survey-Monkey, which can be used to reach large numbers of people quickly. Online questionnaires also have the added advantage of automating responses so the data can also be analysed quickly. While questionnaires represent one of the dominant forms of quantitative marketing research, there are other approaches available.

The **experimental method** is the only research approach that helps marketers to understand causality. Experiments help us to measure cause and effect. They do so through the manipulation of independent variables and measuring their effect on a dependent variable. For example, let's say we are interested in measuring marketing comprehension amongst business school students. Marketing comprehension, or teaching the ability to understand marketing, would be the dependent variable. Marketing comprehension would be dependent upon a number of different independent variables, which might include the number of students within the class, the experience of the teacher, the method of teaching delivery, or the ages of the participants. The manipulation of one of these independent variables, while holding the others constant, can help us understand how each independent variable might influence our dependent variable, which is the ability to understand marketing.

A good example of how the experimental method can help us understand consumer behaviour was the seminal work on brand exposure by Fitzsimons et al. (2008). In their study, they used the experimental method to subliminally prime participants with brand logos to see if there was a resulting effect on their behaviour. Their work looked at brands such as Apple, which has a distinctive brand personality. In the case of Apple, we often associate the brand with personality characteristics such as nonconformity, innovation, and creativity. Does subliminal exposure to the Apple brand logo actually trigger behaviour that leads people to be more creative? Their experiment highlighted that brand exposures can trigger goal-oriented behaviour that leads people to be more creative. The importance of this research helps us to better understand how everyday brand exposure might influence how people behave.

The advantage of the experimental method is that it allows marketing researchers to establish causality through the manipulation of variables. Another advantage to the method is that experiments are easily replicable due to the structural characteristics of the method. The disadvantage of the method is that it is often artificial, as most experiments occur in controlled laboratories, they may use university students who are non-representative of broader populations, and they often elicit a narrow behavioural range due to artificial nature of the laboratory setting.

GLOBAL MARKETING QUESTION

MM Lafleur is an upscale women's clothing boutique based in the US. The company targets affluent, middle-aged, professional career women who are looking for clothing that is suitable for office environments. MM Lafleur is considering expanding their operations to the European market. What type of market research do you think MM LaFleur should conduct in order to help them decide whether or not Europe is a viable market?

Sampling Procedures

Sampling is the process of selecting participants to actively participate in a market research study. In order to determine what participants will be potential candidates for a marketing research study, researchers must identify a **universe**. A universe represents the total population from which a sample will be drawn. A **sample** represents a subset of this population and the actual number of participants taking part in a study.

For example, let's say we are interested in understanding students' perception of university fees. We could identify our universe as all of the students registered at a university. We could then select every 50th student within that population list to obtain our sample. This approach to sampling applies to both qualitative and quantitative research approaches (Given, 2008). However, sampling procedures can be very different according to the methodological approach we want to take, the type of information we want to collect, the speed in which we need that information, and the degree to which we want to rely upon the results of a study.

A **probability sample** is a sampling procedure that uses random selection, where every member of the universe has an equal chance of being selected. The advantage of using a probability sample is that, due to its objectivity, a researcher can make inferences about the larger population studied. Using the previous example, we can see that by choosing every 50th student registered at a university, there is a greater chance that the sample will be representative of the overall population that is attending that university. We are more likely to have an even distribution based on gender, ethnicity, age, and income level. This enables a marketing researcher to make overall statements about students' perception of university fees at that university with levels of confidence. While our example here highlights what is known as a systematic sampling technique, there

TABLE 3.1

Types of probability samples.

Simple random sample	A sampling procedure where every member of a population has an equal chance of being selected for a study.
Stratified random sample	A procedure where a marketing researcher might split a population into different education levels and then draw a random sample.
Systematic sample	A procedure where every nth participant is drawn from the population.
Cluster sample	A procedure in which researchers work with very large populations where it is difficult to obtain the entire universe. Researchers split the population into mutually exclusive groups and then draw a random sample. For example, it would be difficult to obtain a list of participants from an entire country, but we are likely to obtain a representative population from individual postcodes (i.e. clusters) within that country.

TABLE 3.2

Types of non-probability samples.

Convenience sample	A sampling procedure where a researcher recruits participants who are readily available and accessible to the researcher. Interviewing participants on a city high street would be a convenience sample.
Judgement sample	A researcher uses their judgement when selecting the sample. A researcher might target specific individuals that they feel offer particular expertise about a subject.
Snowball sample	A type of judgement sampling technique where research participants within a study help a researcher to identify other research participants.
Quota sample	A sample where a researcher will target specific quotas that are representative of an overall population. When conducting research about student opinions at university, research might target a representative number of first, second, third, or fourth year students.

are a number of different approaches marketing researchers can take when developing a probability sample (see Table 3.1).

A **non-probability** sample is a sampling approach where a marketing researcher makes no attempt to obtain a representative cross section of a population they are trying to study. Going back to the university fees example, a non-probability sample could be asking students in an introductory marketing course about their perception of university fees. Introductory marketing students are not likely to be representative of a university's overall student population, because marketing (or any subject) might draw people from a narrower range of backgrounds that differ from the overall university population.

TABLE 3.3

Types of errors.

Measurement error	A result in which there is a difference between the information desired and the information provided. A respondent might mislead a researcher into thinking that they consume less alcohol than actually do in order to avoid potential embarrassment.
Sampling error	When the sample selected does not represent the target or overall population. Sampling error can frequently result from non-response.
Frame error	The wrong sub-population is selected that is not representative of the overall population. Drawing from a university register of students that live on campus would miss distance learners, students who live off-campus, study abroad students, industrial placement students, etc.
Random error	When measurements differ due to variability or unpredictability. For example, if brand loyalty was measured at 15% one day and 30% the next day, the variation might be due to random factors.

No matter how well a marketing researcher designs the marketing research process, there is always the potential that this approach contains some type of error that might potentially bias the findings.

Data Analysis and Implementation

The final stage in the marketing research process is to analyse the data and disseminate this information throughout an organisation. When it comes to data analysis, marketing researchers interpret data through the process of coding. In **coding**, data is "broken down into discrete parts, closely examined, and compared for similarities and differences" (Strauss & Corbin, 1998, p. 102). Coding is about data reduction and trying to make meaning of different patterns contained within the data. While coding is commonplace in both qualitative and quantitative research, there is no one way to analyse data, and different research approaches will require different types of data analysis techniques. Here are a few dominant approaches used:

Thematic analysis is used in qualitative research as a technique that looks for patterns of meaning that exist across a data set. Themes can take the form of word or pattern association or more robust narratives within the data. Thematic analysis as a form of analysis helps a researcher understand commonalities that exist in the data in the form of shared experiences.

Frequency analysis is used in both qualitative and quantitative research approaches. It involves counting the number of times a data point appears in a category. In qualitative research, it can take the form of conversational analysis, where researchers might track the frequency of patterns, sequences, and the number of instances in a data set. In quantitative research, frequency analysis can provide summary statistics and histograms.

Descriptive statistics provide the distribution of participant responses for a given variable and include measures of central tendency, which include the mean, median, and mode.

Cross tabulation is one of the most common data analysis approaches in quantitative research, as it helps a researcher to explore the relationship between two or more variables within a study. For example, a cross tabulation might look at age or gender and the frequency of purchase of different brands within a product category.

These are just a few of many types of data analysis approaches available to marketing researchers when analysing data. In most cases, marketing researchers will use computer software to help them analyse data due to the sheer volume of information collected. Qualitative researchers can utilise NVivo software to help them manage their data, whereas many quantitative researchers might utilise SPSS or STAT. The advantage of these software tools is that they help marketing researchers to organise data and present findings in ways that help to improve the readability of a marketing research report.

The final step in the marketing research process is the presentation of the final results. While it sounds cliché to indicate that the final report is just as important a step as the research design, it is a critical final step in the process. The final presentation of results takes the form of a written report and is often accompanied by a final presentation. An important consideration to managing the dissemination of the final report is for marketing researchers to find ways to make the data come to life and to be actionable. What we want to avoid is the final report being filed away and forgotten. Good marketing research design links the final report to the overall strategy of the organisation.

MARKETING MANAGER TASK

In China, Zomotor has recently undertaken a large research exercise on the issue of declining sales conversion rates in dealerships. This invited responses from customers, prospects, dealer salespeople, and dealer managers. The research comprised questionnaires, interviews, and focus groups. Some of the results were rather alarming. It is important that Dylan crystallises the key findings into a report which is concise and intuitive and enables his directors to make well-informed commercial decisions. In particular, the key information needs to be clear and not obscured by details which may be irrelevant. The 'big picture' information which seems most pertinent falls into the following outcome categories of sales appointments: 'sale achieved', 'test drive', 'quotation provided', 'further information requested', 'additional appointment diarised', and 'no further contact diarised'. For each of these categories, Dylan thinks it would be useful for his directors to see performance against target, this year's performance against the previous year's performance, and three or four bullet points for

continued

each category offering explanation of the main comments emerging from research participants.

Assist Dylan by designing a dashboard – an eye-catching and user-friendly panel of graphics – which conveys the relevant findings in these six categories in a way which helps directors make their strategic decisions. It may be useful to include some sort of 'traffic light' system, in which red signifies the need for immediate action, amber demands scrutiny, and green indicates a satisfactory performance.

Understanding the Impact of Big Data, Data Analytics, and Artificial Intelligence on Marketing Research

As we stated at the beginning of this chapter, marketing research has been transformed by technology. It is possible to know more about target markets than ever before. In fact, large organisations often suffer from data overload, where it becomes difficult to action the sheer volume of data collected. Large companies rarely lack enough data, but they do often lack the capability to develop marketing strategy from the data that they have collected. Big data, data analytics, and AI represent new marketing research approaches that are helping organisations grapple with the volume of data they are able to collect. In order to get a grasp of how technology has impacted marketing research, it is important to understand the basic terminology in order to know what it can do and how marketers utilise technology in marketing research.

Let's start with big data and data analytics. **Big data** refers to the data set, or database, that marketing researchers have collected. Researchers call it 'big data' due to the large volume of data points marketing researchers have collected. Big data can come in the form of social media data, email, point-of-purchase data, governmental records, behavioural data collected from the interconnection of IT devices, and data collected from cloud platforms. All of these different data sources can be rolled up into databases that marketing researchers can manipulate. Scholars have characterised big data as having three defining characteristics (McAfee et al., 2012):

Volume refers to the amount of information collected. Volume can be characterised as the number of individual data points that make up a big data source, or the technological storage associated with that data measured in petabytes and exabytes (a petabyte equals 1 million gigabytes and one exabyte equals 1 billion gigabytes).

Velocity refers to the instantaneous nature of the data being created, collected, and analysed. Big data can be collected in real time as it unfolds. Big data represents an unprecedented speed of marketing research data.

Variety refers to the different sources of data that are available to be collected. Marketing researchers can triangulate from different data sources to gain a richer set of data that captures different types of behaviour.

The process through which technology converts raw data, in the form of big data, into forecasts and predictions through the use of algorithms is known as data analytics. **Data analytics** is the "*extraction* of hidden insights about consumer behaviour from big data and the *exploitation* of that insight through advantageous interpretation" (Erevelles, 2016, p. 897). The algorithms used within data analytics are developed through AI software. The sheer volume, velocity, and variety of big data go beyond the comprehension of marketing research analysts. Marketing researchers use computer algorithms to help them better manage all of the different variables in big data and to analyse patterns in the data. **Artificial intelligence** (AI) is the technology that underpins big data and data analytics. In marketing research, AI is the engine used in data analytics, where computer software uses machine learning techniques to make intelligent decisions about large sets of data. AI is able to process, analyse, and predict behaviour.

SUSTAINABILITY QUESTION

Social media has become one of the dominant forms of communication for consumers. At the same time, social media is in a constant state of change. The ways in which we interact on social media are different today than they were two or three years ago. New social media platforms have arisen that offer consumers new ways of communicating and sharing information. How do you see social media changing in the future? How do you think marketers might benefit from these changes?

Artificial Intelligence

We are on the cusp of different eras within AI, which is likely to come in overlapping waves. The first wave of AI can be characterised as leveraging existing technological platforms and marketing research information to increase firm efficiency. A good example of this is how AI can be used to create these efficiencies can be seen with the use of automated and web-based 'robo-advisors' or 'conversational bots'. These robo-technologies represent new ways in which companies interact with their customers. Robo-technologies are able to access large marketing research databases of stored transactions, previous customer interactions, and social media data. They are able to draw upon these resources to provide interactive service exchanges with customers. One application is to use them in call centres or in online settings where scripted interactions with customers predominate.

Charles Schwab, the financial investment management company, uses robo-technologies to guide investors through a series of choices to calculate risk tolerance, age, salary, and financial goals to create a financial portfolio that adjusts a client's portfolio as the investor ages (Collins & Stein, 2016). Conversational bots draw from existing marketing research data to guide customers into choosing relevant products/services that fit their demographic and psychographic profile, search history, or customer query type. The advantage of using these conversational bots is that they can deliver information instantly, interactively, proactively, and personally.

A second wave will involve AI technology's ability to leverage deep learning capabilities, where computer software will no longer need a human programmer to function. This means that AI systems have the ability to learn intuitively by processing large data sets. This area, which has also become known as predictive analytics, means that instead of requiring a computer programmer to program the parameters of an AI system, AI has the capability to learn through the processing of marketing data itself. The importance of this capability is that an AI system can train itself to search an infinite number of documents, photographs, purchases, e-profiles, email, web pages, and social media exchanges to either locate or retrieve these documents, or to suggest automated responses to complex marketing activities with high levels of accuracy. An unsupervised learning system will recognise patterns in the data and create clusters of shared examples which can then be used for prediction. Deep learning systems have the ability to reveal patterned clusters of behaviour that humans may or may not be cognitively aware of due to the sheer volume of examples the system is able to process.

PHOTO 3.7
Chatbots are increasingly being used by companies where customer interactions are often standardised.

This is an important shift in how we use marketing research data. Deep learning systems and predictive analytics mean that AI systems can leverage multiple data sources to make predictions about future behaviour to a much higher degree of accuracy than ever before. For example, many car insurance companies are willing to offer customers discounts if they place black boxes in their cars to record driving behaviour. A black box can record acceleration, braking systems, car positioning, engine revolutions, cornering speeds, and severity of an accident. With predictive analytics, car insurance companies can make accurate predictions as to the type of driver that you are and the likelihood that you will get into an accident. An insurance company can assign a predictive score, which then determines what premium you are charged (Ralph, 2017).

An additional wave of technology will be the development of digital personal assistants. Companies such as Amazon, Apple, Google, Alibaba, and Microsoft are building technologies that move away from traditional, static, PC-based website interactions towards more interactive personal assistants. While many of these embedded technologies exist today (think Apple's Siri, Amazon's Alexa, or Microsoft's Cortana), AI will link all of this marketing research data into a singular data umbrella managed by digital personal assistants. New interactions will be built, where consumers may interact with multiple platforms within different social contexts. So, one technology may feature predominantly in the home, another on the phone, and potentially a third when people are out and about. Digital assistants will have the ability to bridge all of this information to create a holistic understanding of human behaviour through marketing research information. What is so transformative about this information is that this marketing intelligence does not exist as an aggregate data set (i.e. a collection of many data points) but as a set of individual data points that provide targeted marketing research information on specific individuals. If the current trajectory of AI assistants comes to fruition, predictive purchases of items such as food, clothing, or the use of services could be conducted through your AI personal assistant. This would have the computational power and the marketing research intelligence to interpret and manage the task.

An important compliment to digital assistance is the simultaneous rise of the internet of things (IOT), where microchips are being embedded in everyday household goods that can not only record marketing research intelligence but also use that data to proactively interact with humans. In other words, our phones, smart watches, personal computers, tablets, refrigerators, automobiles, and more will have the ability to all link together into a singular marketing research intelligence system. A good example of how this might work is Procter & Gamble's use of microchips that can be clipped to disposable diapers. The company is currently piloting a project, known as Lumi, which places an activity sensor within a diaper that can track when your baby needs to be changed, the child's sleep patterns, feeding routines, and important growth milestones (Procter & Gamble, 2019). The sensor is then linked to an app which can help a parent make informed decisions based upon the marketing intelligence collected. All of this marketing research information can be captured by Procter & Gamble (with informed

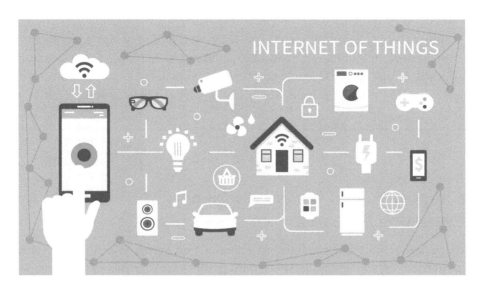

PHOTO 3.8
The internet of things (IOT) refers to the interconnectivity of everyday products into an integrated system that can be easily controlled.

consent), which can then feed into other product offerings, such as baby food, formula, and complementary products and services that adapt to the changing age of the child.

It is clear that marketing research is on the cusp of a new era with artificial intelligence systems, big data, and data analytics. Many of these technologies will transform society in positive ways by delivering an unprecedented amount of information to both consumers and businesses. It will help businesses to become more profitable, and it will help consumers to make better informed choices. However, the ushering in of this new wave of marketing research intelligence will also bring ethical concerns that are paramount to both marketing researchers and consumers.

MARKETING DIRECTOR TASK

Having delegated the research on declining sales conversion rates to Zomotor's national offices, Lee's global concern is Zomotor's relatively static performance in the compact car sector against Nissan's new model. Using questionnaires and interviews, they plan to approach a very large sample of prospects and customers in the following six categories: 'bought the Nissan product', 'bought the Zomotor product', 'considered the Zomotor product but did not buy', 'used to drive the Zomotor product but has replaced it with something else', 'saw Zomotor advertising campaign', and 'saw Nissan advertising campaign'.

continued

> Help Lee by compiling questions which you would ask to each category of research participants. For each one, explain the rationale for your choice of question. You may ask each question either within a questionnaire (perhaps allocating graded responses in a Likert scale) or in an interview or focus group.

The Importance of Ethical Protocols in Marketing Research

Marketing researchers are expected to conduct themselves with the highest order of research ethics and integrity. The nature of the research process and marketing research means that marketing professionals are collecting information that is sensitive and could potentially leave respondents vulnerable. This is why marketers often represent anonymous data to protect the identity and integrity of the respondents who are generous in collaborating on marketing research projects. Associations such as the American Marketing Association prescribe a set of ethical norms, which call attention to not doing harm to respondents, fostering trust by avoiding deceit, and embracing ethical values of honesty, integrity, transparency, and respect (AMA, 2019). These moral principles are used to guide marketing researchers in how they conduct their practice.

While moral principles in research are important, there are also formal legal protections written in law. The EU General Data Protection Regulation (GDPR) prescribes formal rules and regulations on how businesses are able to use marketing research information and also provide legal protections for consumers' personal data. GDPR applies to any organisation that collects and holds personal information of EU residents no matter where the organisation resides. The guiding principles to the GDPR include but are not limited to requiring organisations to process data legally and transparently, collect data for specific purposes, limit the amount of personal data for a given research situation, be accurate, and limit participant traceability.

Despite these guiding principles to marketing research practice, there are still a number of ethical issues within marketing research that still warrant attention. The advent of big data alone has raised serious concerns about breaches in consumer privacy, targeting consumers with unwanted products, and the use of discriminatory pricing practices (Martin, 2015). In fact, there is a tendency to view big data as a marketing research panacea where any of the costs associated with its practice are outweighed by the benefits that it delivers.

ETHICS QUESTION

Many of us spend part of our day interacting over social media channels such as Facebook, Twitter, Instagram, WeChat, Weibo, Snapchat, TikTok, and others. Knowing that marketers can track your social media preferences and networks, what kind of information do you think marketers would know about you? Do you think that this information can be of benefit to you?

There are no easy answers when looking at marketing research ethics. However, the greater awareness that is generated about research ethics can provide an important pathway for ethical practice. Here are few that warrant extra attention that are pertinent to both online and offline marketing research practice.

1. **Intrusions of privacy**: The proliferation of independent marketing research firms, organisations that collect their own internal data, and the rise of technology linked to marketing intelligence gathering means the amount of data being collected on individuals is growing exponentially. Marketers are collecting massive databases of marketing intelligence that contain personal and sensitive data about individual consumers. This information can be used to potentially manipulate purchasing decisions or restrict consumer choice based upon previous history. This personal data is also being packaged and resold by data aggregators and brokers to other companies without consumers' full awareness.

2. **Ubiquitous surveillance**: We live in an age where data is being collected and consumers are not always aware that they are being watched. Closed circuit television, facial recognition software, social media data mining, and household goods embedded with chip technology that monitors our behaviour mean that marketers are able to collect marketing intelligence without consumers always fully aware that they are being watched. Data collection and dissemination requires informed consent, but many consumers overlook the fine print and in other cases, such as facial recognition, they are not aware their data is being collected. This raises a series of unanswered questions about informed consent, transparency, data surveillance, and security.

3. **Data ownership**: The amount of detailed information marketing researchers can collect on single individuals or groups of people leads to questions on data ownership. For example, should data collected from a smart device such as your refrigerator or should a fitness tracker be used to determine your health insurance premiums? As a

consumer, are you entitled to ownership of or access to this data to help you make appropriate life choices? Who owns data and how that data is used are important ethical issues in marketing research. There is a fuzzy boundary here between consumer ownership of data and marketing researchers' ability to collect and disseminate this information.

4. **Misuse of research findings** The potential for organisations to exploit patterns in data can lead to the misuse of data. An early example was the retail giant Target using data analytics with customer loyalty data. Target was looking for changing patterns in shopping behaviour that might tell the company something about their customers that they would not normally and openly disclose to the company. In this specific case, Target was looking for shopper patterns that might help the company determine if a shopper was pregnant. The goal was to look for purchasing changes that might signal a customer who was pregnant so that they could target that person with marketing information by the end of their second trimester. By targeting women early before they had their child, Target hoped to establish routine shopping behaviour patterns that facilitated repeat purchases (Duhigg, 2012).

5. **Data security**: It is of paramount importance for organisations to put into place data security protocols that prevent security breaches. Because most data is stored and archived in electronic form, it is important for organisation to invest in the proper firewalls, anti-malware protection, and data encryption software. Even the most well-intentioned companies can be vulnerable, and it is not uncommon to find examples of where the lack of security can lead to security breaches. One extreme case saw the data of almost the entire population of Ecuador leaked online. This security breach revealed names, birthdates, home and email addresses, national identification numbers, tax identification numbers, and a treasure trove of additional personal information. Over 20 million data points were leaked, which included almost the entire population of Ecuador, including 7 million children and deceased people (Yeung, 2019). Criminals can use this information to create false identities and exploit vulnerable people.

Chapter Summary

The aim of this chapter was to familiarise students with some of the basic tools available to marketing researchers when developing a marketing research plan. We highlighted the nuances of the research design process and the components that are part of its make-up. We have also drawn special attention to the roles that big data, data analytics, and AI have played in transforming marketing research. We are no longer on the cusp of massive technological change; we are immersed in it. Importantly, we must pay special consideration to marketing ethics to ensure that we adhere to the tenet of doing no harm to our respondents.

Recommended Further Reading

Duhigg, C. (2012). How companies learn your secrets. *The New York Times*, p. 16.

Fitzsimons, G. M., Tanya, L. C., & Fitzsimons, G. J. (2008). Automatic effects of brand exposure on motivated behaviour: How Apple makes you 'think different'. *Journal of Consumer Research*, *35*, 21–35.

Sterne, J. (2017). *Artificial intelligence for marketing: Practical applications*. John Wiley & Sons.

Sunderland, P. L., & Denny, R. M. (2016). *Doing anthropology in consumer research*. Routledge.

Thompson, A., Stringfellow, L., Maclean, M., & Nazzal, A. (2021). Ethical considerations and challenges for using digital ethnography to research vulnerable populations. *Journal of Business Research*, *124*, 676–683.

References

AMA. (2004). https://www.ama.org/the-definition-of-marketing/

AMA. (2019). *Codes of conduct/AMA statement of ethics*. https://www.ama.org/codes-of-conduct/

Burns, A., & Bush, R. (2010). *Marketing research* (6th ed.). Pearson.

Collins, M., & Stein, C. (2016, March 28–April 3). The Vanguard Cyborg takeover. *Bloomberg Business Week*.

Elliott, R., & Jankel-Elliott, N. (2003). Using ethnography in strategic consumer research. *Qualitative Market Research: An International Journal*, *6*(4), 215–223.

Erevelles, S., Fukawa, N., & Swayne, L. (2016). Big data consumer analytics and the transformation of marketing. *Journal of Business Research*, *69*(2), 897–904.

ESOMAR. (2019). *Global market research 2018: An ESOMAR industry report*. Retrieved September 5, 2019, from https://www.esomar.org/knowledge-center/reports-publications

Fellman, M. W. (1999). Breaking tradition. *Marketing Research*, *11*(3), 20.

Fitzsimons, G. M., Tanya, L. C., & Fitzsimons, G. J. (2008). Automatic effects of brand exposure on motivated behaviour: How Apple makes you 'think different'. *Journal of Consumer Research*, *35*, 21–35.

Fowler, F. J. (1993). *Survey methods*. Sage.

Given, L. M. (2008). Respondent. In *The Sage encyclopedia of qualitative research methods*. Sage.

Homeland Security Research. (2019). *Big data & data analytics – hardware, software & services market in national security & law enforcement: 2019–2022*. Retrieved September 5, 2019, from https://homelandsecurityresearch.com/reports/big-data-data-analytics-homeland-security-public-safety-global-market/?gclid=CjwKCAjwnrjrBRAMEiwAXsCc47BoD66l_V5kqSf-wLKaFVg419fi1e5MTvm6ZXug3KH-B-A9Y3JA5RBoCfZsQAvD_BwE

Kotler, P., Armstrong, G., Saunders, J., & Wong, V. (2008). *Principles of marketing* (5th European ed.). Prentice Hall.

Kozinets, R. V. (2015). *Netnography: Redefined*. Sage.

Martin, K. E. (2015). Ethical issues in the big data industry. *MIS Quarterly Executive*, *14*, 2.

McAfee, A., Brynjolfsson, E., Davenport, T. H., Patil, D. J., & Barton, D. (2012). Big data: The management revolution. *Harvard Business Review*, *90*(10), 60–68.

McCracken, G. (1988). *The long interview* (Vol. 13). Sage.

Procter & Gamble. (2019). *Lumi by pampers*. Retrieved September 16, 2019, from https://www.pampers.com/lumibypampers

Ralph, O. (2017). Drivers put the brakes on car insurance with a black box. *Financial Times*. https://www.ft.com/content/894c3f5e-786c-11e7-a3e8-60495fe6ca71

Strauss, A., & Corbin, J. (1998). *Basics of qualitative research*. London: Sage.

Stromberg, J. (2019). *Focus groups shape what we buy: But how much do they really say about us?* Retrieved September 5, 2019, from https://www.vox.com/the-goods/2019/1/22/18187443/focus-groups-brand-market-research

Yeung, J. (2019). *Almost entire population of Ecuador has data leaked*. Retrieved September 17, 2019, from https://edition.cnn.com/2019/09/17/americas/ecuador-data-leak-intl-hnk-scli/index.html

Glossary

Causal research: seeks to establish the relationship between cause and effect

Cross tabulation: helps a researcher to explore the relationship between two or more variables within a study

Descriptive research: used to describe the characteristics of a population

Descriptive statistics: provide the distribution of participant responses for a given variable; includes measures of central tendency, which include the mean, median, and mode

Ethnography: a research technique that places a researcher within the context of the everyday lives of the people they are studying

Experiments: a research technique that seeks to measure cause and effect

Exploratory research: an informal, unstructured research approach used in order to generate more information about research objectives

Focus group: an interactive discussion group led by a moderator for the purposes of uncovering information about a specific business problem

Frequency analysis: involves counting the number of instances a data point appears in a category

Interviews: a research technique where marketing researchers ask respondents a series of questions in an attempt to understand a respondent's point of view

Marketing intelligence systems: capture the dynamic capabilities of marketing research that includes the increasing sophistication of big data, data analytics, and AI

Marketing research process: a framework that marketers use to identify evolving market opportunities

Netnography: represents the adaptation of ethnographic research methodologies to study the cultures and communities emerging through computer-mediated communication

Non-probability sample: a sampling approach where a marketing researcher makes no attempt to obtain a representative cross section of a population they are trying to study

Primary research: involves collecting data first-hand

Probability sample: a sampling procedure that uses random selection, where every member of the universe has an equal chance of being selected

Qualitative research: refers to a range of different methods of data collection that are focused on eliciting verbal, textual, visual, and observational data

Quantitative research: refers to a range of different methods of data collection that are primarily focused on statistical measurements or establishing causality

Questionnaire: a set of standardised questions that follows a fixed sequence and is used to collect information from a participant

Sampling: the process of selecting participants to actively participate in a market research study

Secondary data: data that has been collected by another researcher

Thematic analysis: a technique that looks for patterns of meaning that exist across a data set

Universe: represents the total population from which a sample will be drawn

Food Choices on Campus Case Study: Using Market Research to Improve Catering Facilities at University Campuses

Attending university is a unique time in the life of young adults, especially when it comes to diet and health. One of the challenges amongst university students is adhering to a healthy dietary lifestyle. Evidence of these challenges are backed by research. A meta-analysis of dietary health of first-year students highlights that

continued

85

TABLE 3.4

Summary of dietary patterns of 795 university students.

Cluster Name	Rank*	Purchasing Pattern: Most Frequent Purchases	Cluster Size (%)
Vegetarian	1	Salads, yogurts, breakfast cereals, fromage frais	14.2
Omnivores	2	Ice cream, dessert, and cakes; breakfast cereals; fish	14.7
Dieters	3	Soups, rice, pasta, noodles, salads	15.3
Dish of the day	4	Meat and meat products; Indian, Chinese, or Thai food	15.8
Grab-and-go	5	Sandwiches, crisps, nuts, snacks, cheese and egg dishes, pizza	13.8
Carb lovers	6	Bread, cheese, and egg dishes; pizza; ice cream, desserts, and cakes	9.7
Snackers	7	Confectionary, biscuits, crisps, nuts, snacks	16.4

* Rank: 1 = most healthy; 7 = least healthy.
Source: Taken from Morris et al. (2020).

almost two-thirds of US university students gain weight during their first year at university (Vadeboncoeur et al., 2015). Similar studies in the UK show that UK students are also susceptible to weight gain (Finlayson et al., 2012; Nikolau et al., 2015). One of the concerns here is that the behaviours developed during university will carry over into adulthood and could potentially lead to a further rise in adult obesity and unhealthy eating choices.

The vice chancellor and the senior executive team at your university are concerned about the dietary choices available to student on campus. The team wants to ensure that the university is meeting the needs of their students and promoting healthy lifestyle choices. The executive group is interested in understanding what students eat while on campus, where they go to buy this food, what they think about this food, and what food choices students would want more of when eating on campus.

They recently read a report from the University of Leeds Institute for Data Analytics, which categorised the dietary habits of "795 students, who collectively conducted 107,723 transactions, spending £457,369 on 303,714 items during one semester" (Moris et al., 2020, p. 1408). The study categorised students into seven distinctive groups (see Table 3.4).

continued

Your Task

Your job is to form a team of market researchers and help the vice chancellor and the executive group understand student perceptions of food choices on your campus. Using the full range of quantitative (questionnaires) and qualitative (interviews, focus groups, and ethnography) approaches, design a market research study that surveys the opinions of fellow students on their feelings of food offerings on campus. When designing your approach, you might give consideration to the following questions:

- ▶ Where do they shop for food on campus?
- ▶ What types of foods to they eat on campus?
- ▶ Do these foods differ from what they eat at home/halls of residence?
- ▶ What do they think about the types of food available?
- ▶ Are they satisfied with existing choices?
- ▶ What do they like about the existing availability of food choices on campus?
- ▶ What would they like to see more of when shopping for food on campus?

When you have completed your research, put together a three to five page PowerPoint presentation that summarises your findings. When analysing your data, did you notice different behavioural clusters in your data? Did your data find new clusters? What recommendations would you provide to the vice chancellor and the executive group at the university?

Bibliography

Finlayson, G., Cecil, J., Higgs, S., Hill, A., & Hetherington, M. (2012). Susceptibility to weight gain: Eating behaviour traits and physical activity as predictors of weight gain during the first year of university. *Appetite*, *58*(3), 1091–1098.

Morris, M. A., Wilkins, E. L., Galazoula, M., Clark, S. D., & Birkin, M. (2020). Assessing diet in a university student population: A longitudinal food card transaction data approach. *British Journal of Nutrition*, *123*(12), 1406–1414.

Nikolaou, C. K., Hankey, C. R., & Lean, M. E. (2015). Weight changes in young adults: A mixed-methods study. *International Journal of Obesity*, *39*(3), 508–513.

Vadeboncoeur, C., Townsend, N., & Foster, C. (2015). A meta-analysis of weight gain in first year university students: Is freshman 15 a myth? *BMC Obesity*, *2*(1), 1–9.

The Marketing Environment

Introduction

The **marketing environment** consists of factors that are both internal and external to an organisation that impact its ability to build relationships with its customers and create competitive advantage. Internal factors are known as the micro environment, which consists of actors that are within the firm's immediate operating environment. **The micro environment** comprises the company itself, suppliers, intermediaries, competitors, and customers. The **macro environment** comprises the political, economic, social, technological, ecological, and legal forces that shape the external environment. The macro environment consists of external marketplace factors that impact both an organisation and its customers. Both the micro environment and the macro environment are in a constant state of change.

The marketing environment is a key consideration for marketing managers, and it is the way in which marketers build relationships with their customers. For example, think about the development of COVID-19 and the impact that it had upon businesses,

DOI: 10.4324/9781003170891-5

business supply chains, and consumers. Within a period of weeks, the marketing environment had been completely transformed. Whole industries were forced to shut down, many workers were furloughed or laid off, and governments were forced to take on enormous debt loads to keep industries from collapsing. This macro factor's impact continues today. While disruptive exogenous shocks are difficult to accurately predict, what is clear is that in order for a marketing organisation to succeed, it must adapt to existing changes and anticipate future changes to the external environmental. Adapting and anticipating environmental change is formally done through environmental scanning.

Environmental scanning is the process through which marketing organisations collect and analyse environmental variables and action this data in their marketing strategy. The importance of environmental scanning is linked to the marketing research function (see Chapter 3), where marketers collect and analyse both internal and external data in order to better understand the voice of the customer. Environmental scanning takes both a micro and macro perspective in the environment by trying to understand how changes might impact the marketing environment and ultimately a target market. The process of environmental scanning is seen as a key marketing strategy in creating competitive advantage through market knowledge. Those companies that are able to anticipate and adapt to environmental changes can better meet the needs of their customers and create value in ways that their competitors cannot.

For example, suppose a legal firm was interested in commissioning a study on the future of legal services. An environmental scan would be a key element in that analysis. It would highlight a fundamental shift in the ways in which consumers consume legal services. These changes are driven by both internal and external factors associated with an environmental analysis. External factors in the technological environment would highlight the rise of chatbots or robo-advisors that can give automated, standardised legal advice at low costs. This emphasis on technology will lead to increasingly scripted interactions with customers for basic legal needs and the development of more 'customised' interactions through the use of artificial intelligence (AI) that requires little to no human interaction. An environmental scan would also highlight social changes where customers want access to legal information outside of traditional business hours and a preference for web-based service interactions. This fundamentally changes the work week of legal service firms and the demand for their services. Internal factors in the environment would highlight the proliferation of global web-based legal companies offering legal advice in markets across the globe, which creates new competitive pressures for legal firms. This is an example of how environmental scanning can help businesses understand the changing dynamics of their marketplace.

From an employability perspective, environmental scanning represents a key strategic tool in company strategy. Organisations often have in-house staff or hire independent market research firms that conduct research and monitor both the internal and external environments. These personnel work in coordination with other functional areas of the business, such as R&D, human resources, and finance, in order to provide them with key information needed for decision-making. For example, technological changes in the external environment help R&D better understand new product and service design. Changes in the competitive environment directly impact an organisation's pricing strategy. Finally, changes in the socio-cultural environment directly feed into human resource management strategy by providing organisational understanding of what employee skills training and hiring practices are needed to deploy amongst staff.

As mentioned in Chapter 1, one of the key functions of the marketing department is understanding the voice of the customer. Customer-focused organisations know that customer wants and needs are not static but are in a constant state of change. These changes are often driven by the marketing environment, which shapes consumer behaviour and consumer choice. This chapter is about better understanding the environment where organisations operate, and the influence this environment has upon target markets. The external environment must be monitored to be understood.

The Elements of the Micro Environment

The micro environment is driven by the premise that organisations exist within a network of organisations that are interlinked in their ability to meet customer needs and create customer satisfaction. This network can consist of elements found within the business itself or factors that are within the immediate operating environment of the business.

The micro environment comprises the company, suppliers, intermediaries, competitors, and customers. Many organisations are dependent upon elements within the micro environment to provide raw materials or market information that help a company manufacture products or deliver services. For example, suppliers might be marketing research companies that provide us information data on customers or raw materials needed in the manufacture of goods. Intermediaries help us to sell products and services on the market. Information on competitors is a key element of formulating a marketing strategy and how we differentiate our products from the competition. Customers are at the core of all marketing activities and the practice of the marketing concept.

The micro environment is measured by environmental scanning, as it helps an organisation to understand those critical factors within the immediate operating environment. Organisations are concerned with how each of the elements of the micro environment work individually, as well as understanding how these variables act in coordination with each other. The micro environmental scan is compiled with an understanding of the macro environment, and this helps to inform operational strategy. What follows is a breakdown of each element within the micro environment.

The Company

The **company** consists of key stakeholders within an organisation, which include the management executive team and the different functional areas of the business. The executive team is responsible for setting business objectives, strategy, and the overall mission of the organisation (see Chapter 2). This is a key element to building the culture of an organisation and how people interact. In some cases, organisations have charismatic founders whose leadership style shapes how members define their role and how the organisation addresses both internal and external problems that face the company (Schein, 1983). Elon Musk, a co-founder of Tesla, Inc., is often credited as a visionary leader who is willing to take risks. His charismatic leadership style is embodied with Tesla's business practices and its organisational culture. In other cases, organisations have less hierarchical structures and prefer a more shared leadership style that is decentralised and where decision-making happens at different levels of the organisation.

Another important element to the company environment is the different operational departments that work within an organisation. These operational environments include accounting, purchasing, information technology, R&D, human resources, finance sales, marketing, and manufacturing. Each one of these departments plays key roles in helping an organisation meet its aims and objectives. Successful companies integrate information across these different functional areas of the business to ensure they are able to create customer value.

Marketing is a very dynamic department in the company since they interface with all the other departments. It is the role of the marketing department to bring the voice of the customer inside the organisation and disseminate that information to key stakeholders within the organisation. For example, marketing works with accounting to provide information on competitive pricing and the pricing needs of different target segments. This interaction between different functional areas of the business helps the accounting

PHOTO 4.1
Elon Musk has a charismatic leadership style that has helped to create a unique corporate culture at Tesla.

department to better understand customer wants and needs, including pricing alternatives. The marketing function liaises with different departments collecting and sharing information and therefore is a central determinant in organisation decision-making. This creates customer value and satisfaction.

STAKEHOLDER QUESTION

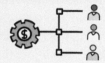

In February of 2021, Harley-Davidson Motorcycles, Inc., unveiled its five-year strategic plan and called it 'The Hardwire'. The Hardwire articulated Harley-Davidson's vision that would take the company forward through the years 2021–2025. A key element to that plan was what the company called 'Inclusive Stakeholder Management', which identified three key stakeholders: people, planet, and profit (Davidson, 2021). Who do you think are the key stakeholders in each of these categories? Why do you think Harley-Davidson has prioritised these three areas?

Suppliers

Suppliers are companies that provide goods or services to other companies. Suppliers work as a set of interdependent organisations that facilitate the movement of products or services from their point of origin to their point of consumption. Most organisations do not produce and source all of the raw materials necessary for the manufacturer of goods, or employ all of the people necessary in the delivery of a service. This interlinked network of companies is known as a marketing channel (see Chapter 15). Marketing channels operate as a coordinated network of interdependent organisations that facilitate the movement of raw materials to finished goods. Suppliers form a close relationship with organisations in meeting the needs of customers.

An important attribute of supplier relationships is the specialisation and division of labour. Suppliers often concentrate on one specific aspect of the marketing channel. This enables them to become focused on meeting the wants and needs of smaller segments of the market rather than trying to satisfy the needs of the entire market. This narrow focus enables a firm to develop expertise within a particular area of the market. For example, many companies work with advertising agencies to help them with marketing communication and promotion. These advertising agencies provide a number of specialised services ranging from marketing research to brand positioning, media buying, and advertising development.

The benefit of working with an advertising agency is that it offers specialised expertise in creative development. It means that an organisation does not have to staff an entire department of employees with expertise in marketing research or creative design. Advertising agencies often work with an extensive list of media providers, which means an organisation can also benefit from cost savings that agencies can provide through their bulk purchasing and discounting associated with large media buys. Suppliers can play key roles in helping an organisation deliver a service without having to develop in-house expertise.

Marketing Intermediaries

Marketing intermediaries, sometimes referred to as distributors, are companies that help an organisation sell, promote, and distribute goods and services to a target market. Intermediaries represent a number of different business types in the marketplace that play a number of different roles.

▶ Agent/brokers do not own a product but represent their client companies in helping to sell goods or services. They play an important role in bringing buyers and sellers together. Agent/brokers charge a commission for their services. An example of an agent/broker might be someone who sells property or travel services. Another example is brokers who represent several different non-competing product lines to the same customer, and provide their client companies lower cost and expertise than hiring individual sales representatives.

▶ Wholesalers buy products in bulk and then resell products to retailers. Large bulk purchases enable wholesalers to buy products at lower prices. They then leverage their extension distribution network to pass this cost savings onto retailers while

PHOTO 4.2
Estate agents are examples of agents/brokers whose primary purpose is to bring buyers and sellers together.

making a profit. The restaurant industry is a heavy user of wholesalers for the purchase of fish, meat, beverages, and produce.

▶ Retailers help organisations promote and sell products directly to consumers. They range from large online retailers such as Alibaba or Amazon, to small, independent, privately owned shops.

The role of marketing intermediaries is to help streamline the transfer of ownership of goods in services within a marketing channel. A common misperception is that marketing intermediaries add additional costs to products or services. In reality, their market specialisation helps consumers save money through the efficiency of the distribution systems. If an intermediary were to add additional costs to the system, marketers would seek out those intermediaries that could provide the same level of service and quality at lower prices. This helps to ensure that consumers are not paying more than they should for a product or service.

MARKETING ASSISTANT TASK

Zomotor Mexico has a significant problem. All of its 12 dealerships in the Mexico City metropolitan area are operated by one dealer group, and this company is having financial difficulties. For several months its share price has been spiralling downwards and, despite rumours that it was going to be refinanced (i.e. receive a substantial cash injection), this has not transpired. In recent weeks, Zomotor Mexico's regional managers have been unsuccessful in getting the dealer group to adhere to the franchise agreement – it has repeatedly refused to take new display and demonstrator vehicles. Mystery shopping has revealed that staff have been switch selling prospects from profitable Zomotor vehicles, which would need to be built to custom or ordered from central manufacturer stock, into less profitable vehicles which the dealer has in their own local stock and which can be sold immediately. Clearly, this is a channel partner which is breaking the rules to reduce its stock liability and generate income hurriedly.

If the dealer group goes into liquidation, Zomotor will be without any representation in North America's most populous city and use massive sales volumes and profits. Even if the dealer group staggers on, the brand is being undermined and the dealer group does not constitute a suitable partner. Tannya's boss must make a contingency plan to ensure that Zomotor is damaged as little as possible, whatever the outcome, and to take steps towards finding a suitable replacement for the dealer company. Help Tannya by making a list of what actions Zomotor should take, when, and how. Explain the possible consequences of undertaking these actions, and of doing nothing.

Competitors

A **competitor** is an organisation that competes against another organisation. Michael Porter, a famous strategist from the Harvard Business School, argued that it is the role of a marketing strategist to understand and react to competitors in the marketplace (Porter, 2008). In order to accomplish this goal, a competitive analysis is a key element of an environmental analysis. A micro environmental scan of competitors seeks answers to the following questions:

▶ Who are our competitors? How large are they (i.e. market share or sales volume)?

▶ What is the range of products and services they offer? What markets do they serve?

▶ What are their strengths and weaknesses?

▶ What do customers value about them?

▶ How do their products and services differ from the ones the company offers?

These questions are key data points collected in an environmental analysis that help to inform overall strategic objectives as a company.

In many ways, understanding competition in the micro environment is really a story about profitability. The degree of competition an organisation faces in the marketplace is a factor in determining the overall organisational profitability. The number of competitors within a marketplace and the degree of competitive rivalry amongst those companies helps to determine a company's profitability. Most industries face stiff competition that affects price strategies and profit margins. The grocery industry is an example of high degrees of competitive rivalry, which often means grocers must pursue low cost and high sales volume market strategies in order to be profitable. In other cases, markets might have a few dominant players that impact choice. For example, Apple, Amazon, Google, Facebook, and Microsoft dominate technology markets, which can develop into new profit centres over time. When there is restricted competition, consumer choice is often restricted.

Marketers use competitive information as the basis for creating competitive advantage. We can use a competitive analysis as the basis for understanding the market positioning of competitors within a market that can become the basis for creating a differential advantage or pursuing niche markets (see Chapter 5). Alternatively, understanding the cost structure of a company's competitors and suppliers can become the basis for building cost-competitive advantage. A competitive analysis represents yet another important analysis tool in the micro environment that shapes strategy.

MARKETING MANAGER TASK

Zomotor has a less precarious situation in China than in Mexico, but one that still requires plenty of planning. One of its major competitors is to stop selling its best-selling compact car in Mexico after a disagreement with the Mexican government over the terms and conditions of some state funding resulted in a high-profile court case. At a superficial level, this seems like good news for Zomotor: if it can absorb just 10% of its competitor's lost customers, it will achieve a significant number of incremental sales, plenty of additional profit, a greater market share, and the chance to build long-term relationships with these new customers.

However, the vacuum caused by the disappearance of a major player from a high-volume car sector could seriously destabilise the Mexican market, attracting other competitors to attempt to fill the void, and produce a new set of supplier dynamics. Assist Dylan in his contingency planning by drawing up a poster showing different scenarios which could emerge from the current situation, and for each, suggest Zomotor's best line of action, with rationale and projected outcomes.

Customers

Customers are the current or future buyers of products or services. Customers represent the lifeblood of an organisation, and it is the role of marketing to ensure that we have a clear understanding of a customer's needs and wants. Marketing's quest to understand consumers and their needs is a thread that runs throughout this textbook and informs our understanding of the marketing concept.

It is rare for an organisation to look at customers as a universal whole. Organisations often have many different types of customers with different needs. In consumer markets, organisations use the process of consumer segmentation (see Chapter 5), which is the process of dividing a market up into different need-based segments. A marketer might segment the market by age, income, lifestyle, geographic location, or usage rate. This enables an organisation to target specific groups of consumers in order to meet their tastes, preferences, and consumption requirements. For example, the Coca-Cola Company owns over 500 global beverage brands to target different need-based segments across the globe. Each brand represents a different customer segment within the marketplace.

In business markets, organisations purchase goods and services that are used to meet the needs of business customers. There are three broad market characteristics

PHOTO 4.3
Coca-Cola uses a number of different flavourings in its flagship Coca-Cola brand to appeal to consumers that have a variety of tastes and preferences.

associated with business customers: industrial customers, resellers, and governments (see Chapter 11 on B2B markets). Industrial markets are organisations that buy raw materials, machinery, or component parts used in the transformation of a final good. Reseller markets buy goods and services to resell them to other customers further down the marketing channel. Finally, governmental customers are agencies that buy goods or services in the delivery of public services, which range from healthcare to defence.

MARKETING DIRECTOR TASK

Lee, as global marketing director, has a much more conceptual and long-term task to undertake. They are aware that indirect competi- tors may one day emerge which can sell products very dissimilar to current cars but which fulfil the transportation requirements of customers through disruptive innovation. Alternatively, they may offer services which make cars less necessary or provide cars to customers through supply arrangements which have not yet been anticipated.

Help Lee by describing what one or more of these indirect competitors may look like, what Zomotor should do to plan for their arrival, and how it can compete effectively in this new environment of the future.

The Elements of the Macro Environment

The macro environment consists of factors that exist within the marketing environment that are outside of the immediate domain of a company. There are a number of acronyms that marketers use when conducting a macro environmental scan, including STEEP (sociological, technological, economic, ecological, political) and PEST (political, economic, social, technological). While these are equally important tools to understand the macro environment, we have chosen to use PESTEL analysis, which includes the political, economic, social, technological, ecological, and legal environments. The importance of using the PESTEL acronym is to account for the legal and ecological variables, which are not fully captured in the STEEP and PEST acronyms. PESTEL does account for sociological factors in the external environment through understanding the social environment.

A **PESTEL** analysis is a market information tool that helps marketers to understand key trends that are happening in the external environment. It helps companies to understand emergent opportunities as well as potential threats. The importance of understanding the macro environment is that the factors within the external environment not only impact a company but they also exert strong pressures on target markets, which are equally impacted by change. A company must monitor the external environment as closely as it does the micro environment. In the remaining sections of this chapter, we unpack each of the variables associated with a PESTEL.

Political Environment

The **political environment** refers to governmental policy and its impact on an organisation or an industry. It includes tax and fiscal policy, legislative structures, employment legislation, governmental orientation, and type. The political environment also extends to broader forces in the external environment which exert influence on governmental policy and decision-making. These influence groups include industry trade groups and political pressure groups, such as MADD, a non-profit group in North America that seeks to stop drunk driving. Political lobbyists and special interest groups might try to exert pressure on governments in the hopes of influencing policy before it becomes law. In countries such as the US, political lobbying is an influential element to the political environment where the total expenditure on lobbying is over $3 billion annually (Statista, 2020).

The political environment also extends to the political orientation of different countries. Recently we have seen the rise of political nationalism, an ideological orientation towards the interests of one's own country, as a variable in the external environment. Countries such as the UK, the US, and Hungary have seen rises in nationalist parties. This influence in the external environment led to Donald Trump's 'America First' policies in the US, the UK leaving the European Union, and Hungary centralising political power.

MARKETING DIRECTOR TASK

Lee is trying to understand how the effects of national elections throughout Europe might affect Zomotor's trading position there. Whilst uncertainty surrounding the European Union membership of the UK (and other countries) and the content of trade deals between international trading blocs poses perhaps the biggest challenge in the motor industry, changes in national governments threaten similar levels of instability given the political polarisation emerging in many countries between 'left' and 'right'. In particular, one of Europe's major economies is experiencing frequent leadership changes, deadlock within their government, and a move away from centrist party politics. It is possible that, within the next year, it could have a right-wing government which believes in pushing a capitalist, conservative agenda via (i) low corporate taxation; (ii) few wage controls and employment regulations; (iii) limited health and safety legislation; (iv) low trade tariffs; (v) a weaker home currency; and (vi) a smaller public sector. On the other hand, it could have a left-wing government which believes in pushing a socialist agenda through (i) higher corporate taxation; (ii) higher wages, more wage controls, and employment regulations; (iii) more comprehensive health and safety legislation; (iv) an uncertain stance of trade tariffs; (v) a stronger home currency, and (vi) a larger public sector.

For Lee, analyse each of the six factors listed above, and suggest how first a right-wing government and then a left-wing government might affect Zomotor's ability to manufacture and sell vehicles profitably in that country.

While the political environment has historically been cast as an environmental constraint on companies (DiMaggio & Powell, 1983), it also offers marketers unique opportunities for 'strategic political management', value creation, and competitive advantage (Oliver & Holzinger, 2008). A good example of strategic political management can been seen with the Nike Corporation. For the 30th anniversary of Nike's iconic 'Just Do It' campaign featuring Michael Jordan, Nike partnered with former National Football League star and political activist Colin Kaepernick. In addition to being an elite football quarterback, Kaepernick garnered attention for kneeling during the playing of the American national anthem as a form of protest to raise awareness for the Black Lives Matter movement. Nike's partnership with Kaepernick led to the re-creation of the 'Just Do It' marketing campaign that centred on the political message of 'Believe in something. Even if it means sacrificing everything'.

PHOTO 4.4
Nike is adept in using the political environment in its marketing campaigns to gain brand recognition.

Nike's advertising campaign invoked a strong political reaction amongst the American public due to Kaepernick's political activism and kneeling before the American flag. Many people called for boycotting Nike, and a number of people took to social media and posted imagery of burning their Nike products. The hashtag #JustBurnIt began trending on Twitter. Despite the political backlash, Nike found that the message resonated with its core demographic of 14- to 22-year-old male 'sneakerheads'. Sales figures immediately rose after the launch of the campaign, and one year after the campaign, Nike attributed the campaign to $163 million in earned media – a $6 billion increase in brand value and a 31% increase in sales. According to Nike co-founder Phil Knight:

> It doesn't matter how many people hate your brand as long as enough people love it. . . . And as long as you have that attitude, you can't be afraid of offending people. You can't try and go down the middle of the road. You have to take a stand on something, which is ultimately I think why the Kaepernick ad worked.
>
> (Beer, 2019)

For Nike, the Kaepernick campaign was successful because it enabled Nike to take a political stand that resonated with its target audience. Here we can see how the success of a campaign can be attributed to strategic political management.

METRICS QUESTION

Marketers use a number of metrics to determine the effectiveness of an advertising campaign. These include the return on investment that the campaign brings. Marketers also measure brand recognition, brand recall, and brand consideration (whether consumers intend to purchase). What do you think makes an advertising campaign effective? What marketing measurements do you think are missing? Identify one of your favourite ads and list the attributes that you think make it effective.

Economic Environment

The **economic environment** refers to the external factors that impact both consumers and businesses through the effect of supply and demand. Economic factors help marketers to determine the overall health and viability of different markets. There are a number of different economic factors that exert influence in a market. These include purchasing power, unemployment, income distribution, interest and exchange rates, tariffs, and economic growth rates of different economies. When marketers conduct their economic environmental scan, they must choose those factors that are most relevant to the business. In this section we will focus on two economic factors: inflation and recession. We conclude our discussion with some of the economic considerations necessary for environmentally sustainable companies.

Inflation is the percentage rate at which prices for goods and services increase. It is an important economic indicator as it determines the overall purchasing power of buyers in a market. The higher the rate of inflation, the fewer goods and services consumers can buy. If inflation is measured to be a 5% annual increase for the cost of a good or a service, consumers must have a corresponding wage increase in order to buy the same amount of goods or services, or else they must buy less. If the cost of petrol rises by 5%, then consumers must earn 5% more, or either travel less or make purchasing sacrifices elsewhere in their budget. If the consumer is an airline buying petrol, they might pass those extra costs on to their consumers or risk being less profitable.

During times of inflation, marketers must take appropriate strategies to minimise the risk associated with inflationary periods and maintain an appropriate level of profitability. Inflationary periods often mean that consumers seek out the lowest-cost providers or seek discounts on purchases. Marketers can leverage their promotional strategies by offering 2-for-1 deals or emphasising value packages. Alternatively, marketers might focus on their supply chain to cut costs or find new ways of working that increase productivity. For marketers that compete in highly price-sensitive markets, they might unbundle packs and sell smaller packs or individual items at appropriate pricing points.

PHOTO 4.5
Basic consumer goods such as food are vulnerable to inflationary pressure, which increases the cost of living for consumers.

Highly price-sensitive consumers might focus more on price than on quantity. If marketers simply pass inflationary costs onto their consumers, they risk losing sales volume or customer satisfaction.

While inflation is often seen as a difficult period for marketers and consumers, are there instances where inflation can be good for an economy? Why do central banks, which regulate monetary policy in an economy, target a 2% annual inflation rate? There is an important balance that must be struck when looking at inflation in the economic environment.

The answer is that economies are equally at risk during deflationary periods, where the inflation rate drops below 2%. During deflationary periods, consumers might lack the incentive to buy new goods or services, thinking that the price will remain the same or become cheaper later. During the 1990s, Japan faced deflation when consumers purchased fewer goods and services. The period 1995–2003 saw the Japanese GDP shrink 1.2% annually (Morana, 2005). Companies were fearful of raising prices and losing out on a shrinking market characterised by reduced demand. The Japanese economy provides an important example as to why central banks often view 2% annual inflation as a healthy economic indicator. Some levels of moderate inflation can provide consumers incentives to buy goods and services before they become more expensive and prevent economies from running into a recession.

A **recession** in an economy is two consecutive quarters of negative GDP growth. This means that the economy is contracting. Both consumers and businesses are buying less, fewer goods and services are being produced, unemployment rises due to the lack of demand, and consumer purchasing power decreases. The financial crisis of 2007–2009 is an example of a recessionary period.

The period before the financial crisis can be characterised as a period of strong economic growth, low inflation, and low interest rates. Within the banking sector, low interest rates triggered investors to look for investments with higher returns. One sector that generated higher but riskier returns was the mortgage industry. Banks lent money to less wealthy consumers with poor credit histories in order to create a bigger loan market. In order to increase the value of these mortgages, banks packaged these higher risk mortgages with more secure, wealthy mortgage borrowers. Banks then resold these mortgage packages to other banks, which spread the risk. When house prices fell, high-risk borrowers could no longer afford the interest rates on their homes, which created a 'subprime' market. Consumers defaulted on their loans and financial institutions defaulted on their financial obligations, which brought down economies in North America and Europe and ultimately led to the financial collapse of Lehman Brothers.

Recessionary periods are characterised by periods of uncertainty and volatility for both consumer and business markets. Recessionary periods are difficult for any marketer to predict. The COVID-19 outbreak has had an even greater initial recessionary impact than the financial crisis. It led to restrictions on global factory production, suspension of entire industries such as the restaurant, pub, tourism and leisure industries, and forced people to stay at home. Governments across the globe were forced to borrow huge sums of money to keep economies afloat. We also saw huge rises in unemployment figures, decreases in consumer incomes, and significant drops in global GDP. Unlike the financial crisis, where factors built over time, COVID-19 demonstrates the suddenness of volatility that can be injected into markets that no environmental scanner can forecast.

A final point to make about the economic environment is the unique challenges marketers face when tackling the relationship between the economic environment and environmental sustainability. Marketers must balance the need for short- and long-term growth opportunities with environmental stewardship. From a macro perspective we see some markets where consumerism and overconsumption are the norm. In other markets, we see where consumers do not consume enough, and basic needs and resources need to be fulfilled to pull people out of poverty. Marketers play a dual role here that can be both positive and negative.

When marketers conduct their economic environmental scan, they must consider the role of the natural environment and its impact on local economies. Economic considerations focus a marketer's attention on production and distribution of resources in an economy that can be a positive force for improving consumer incomes, purchasing power, and market stability. Market development strategies must strike the balance in

PHOTO 4.6
Recessionary periods are when economies contract, which causes business and consumer uncertainty.

their ability to "meet the needs of the present without compromising the ability of future generations to meet their own needs" (World Commission on Environment and Development, 1987, p. 25). Marketers concerned about the natural environment play a key role in maintaining that balance.

Socio-cultural Environment

The **socio-cultural environment** is the beliefs, attitudes, and values of people within a society that are shaped by institutional forces within a marketplace. Religion, marriage, families, gender, and education are all examples of institutional forces that shape meaning and behaviour within a society. They shape what people believe is right or wrong, or how they should behave. These institutional forces are of interest to marketers, as they influence the type of products consumers buy, their perception of different brands and brand categories, the types of relationships that they want to have with business organisations, and their consumer behaviour.

There are a number of socio-cultural variables that are of interest to marketers, which include aged-based generational differences within a population. Generational differences are of interest to marketers, as different age groups hold different values and belief systems. Marketers can further refine generational differences by analysing smaller segments within a specific age group by income, gender, ethnicity, and educational levels. Understanding the characteristics of these different segments forms the basis for demographic segmentation, which can be found in Chapter 5.

ETHICS QUESTION

Do you think it is ethical to segment a market by age, gender, or ethnicity? Are there examples where this might be considered an unethical practice?

To illustrate how a socio-cultural environmental scan can yield important insights for marketers and demonstrate how marketplace activities can shape or reflect belief systems, attitudes, and values, the focus is on the Generation Z market. Generation Z is the name given to a demographic group born between 1995 and 2010. Some of the broad characteristics of this group are that they are technologically savvy, independent, open-minded, financially and professionally focused, concerned about the environment, and risk averse. One market activity that embodies these characteristics is a movement towards access-based consumption.

Access-based consumption activities are forms of exchange where consumers pay to temporarily access a good, but there is no transfer in ownership (Bardhi & Eckhardt, 2012). It is the idea that goods or services can be purchased and consumed without being owned. The rise in popularity of these businesses can be attributed to the proliferation of digitally based companies on the internet as well as Generation Z's preference for app-based service providers like Uber. The global value of this industry was estimated at $15 billion in 2014 and is projected to grow to $335 billion by 2025 (Mazareanu, 2019).

Zipcar allows consumers to access a fleet of automobiles for a monthly service charge. Airbnb allows consumers to access premium properties in strategic places at prices that are lower than hotels. FrontRow, the Philippines-based retailer, allows consumers to rent luxury clothing, shoes, accessories, and handbags. Many cities across the globe offer bike-sharing schemes that enable access to bicycles without the burdens of storage. Access-based consumption practices enable consumers access to materials that they either could not afford or prefer not to own (Bardhi & Eckhardt, 2012). While access-based consumption is not limited to Generation Z, the model does hold special appeal for this group.

Access-based consumption taps into Generation Z's risk averse nature. It enables consumers to minimise financial risk due to the temporal nature of ownership. Consumers can try a number of different brands rather than having to commit to a single brand. This interchangeability of brands allows for experimentation and has the added benefit of minimising social risk. For example, the social consequences of wearing fashionable designer clothes or carrying a designer handbag are lessened if there is not transfer of ownership. This gives consumers the opportunity to try a much wider array of products and services without having to incur large financial outlays or social risks to trying experimental designs. It is also a consumption more aligned with Generation Z's belief in sustainability due to the reusability of products that lessens its disposability or perishability.

PHOTO 4.7
Spotify is an example of an access-based service that has changed the ways consumers view ownership.

There are important implications for marketers when considering the impacts of access-based consumption. Studies have shown that access-based consumption prioritises price and convenience while de-emphasising brand relationships (Eckhardt & Bardhi, 2015). This is a fundamental shift away from marketing perspectives on brand communities or brands as symbolic aspirations of consumer identity. This perspective argues that brands and brand meaning play central roles in consumer's lives.

Access-based consumption highlights the plug-and-play nature of consumption practices. Companies that are able to tap into the temporal nature to ownership and understand Generation Z's emphasis on price and convenience are well positioned to create competitive advantage within the marketplace. The process of understanding socio-cultural variables within the marketplace can help marketers better position their product and service offerings, as well as the messaging that they are using, to specific groups of target consumers.

NEW MEDIA QUESTION

Influencer marketing over social media has transformed the way that marketers communicate with target market groups, such as Generation Z. Marketing analysts suggest that almost half of Generation Z has made a purchase based on an influencer recommendation and that 70% of Generation Z follow at least one influencer (Williams, 2020). Discuss what has led to the rise of influencer marketing in the Generation Z demographic? What influencers do you follow, and why?

Technological Environment

The **technological environment** consists of the innovative technologies that foster service, product, and process innovations, as well as a firm's ability to respond to these changes. The technological environment represents one of the most transformative forces in the external environment. It has the ability to dramatically shift the ways that marketers manage their product and service offerings, as well as to influence the ways in which consumers interact and consume product and services. We can see the impact that product technology has had in the automotive sector with the rise of the electric automobile. In travel, we have seen how digital technologies have led to service innovation, with Expedia and Travelocity replacing the need for human travel agents. Uber has led process innovations that have fundamentally shifted car ownership and travel. The ability to forecast, integrate, and action information from the technological environment represents a key variable in strategy formulation.

Ecological Environmental

The **ecological environment** is the natural resources required to develop and sustain marketing activities, those natural resources that are affected by marketing activities, and the stewardship associated with protecting those resources. Some have argued that marketing and the natural environment are inherently at odds with each other, with marketing about promoting consumption and sustainability about reducing consumption (Bond & Seeley, 2004; Jones et al., 2008). These critics point to unstable levels of consumption and environmental destruction across the globe. While a tension exists between marketing and the natural environment, there are a number of factors that have led marketers to think differently about the natural environment. Three core factors that are of concern to marketers are the rise of environmental pollution, increasing consumer awareness for environmental protection, and the potential for sustainability to become a form of competitive advantage.

MARKETING DIRECTOR TASK

As the Chinese government attempts to tackle the problem of air pollution in its major cities, it is considering a number of measures which have been used around the world – with varying degrees of success. Examples include imposing a toll on drivers of the most-polluting vehicles in order to enter cities; allowing each car to enter a city only on alternate weeks; providing carpool lanes for vehicles with two or more occupants; giving tax incentives to firms who allow employees flexible working hours; installing recharging points and other infrastructure to encourage adoption

continued

107

of electric vehicles; and investing heavily in trams, monorails, and other public transport initiatives.

Dylan suspects that, if these changes happen, they will not just present Zomotor China with threats but also opportunities, and he wished to present a positive picture to his superiors. Help Dylan by making a poster which shows both the threats and opportunities, showing the potential commercial consequences and the strategies which Zomotor may adopt to address them.

Environmental pollution is the contamination of the earth to the extent that what would be the normal environmental processes are disrupted due to human-led activities. The rise of environmental pollution can largely be traced back to the industrial revolution, which began in the 18th century. The transition from handcrafting goods towards mechanised, machine-based production methods meant that economies could produce a large number of materials in a short period of time at low cost. The abundance of natural resources and the industrialisation of the production of goods transformed human society as we know it. It ushered in a new era of production and consumption that ultimately led to the globalisation of society. While this era is credited with great wealth creation, unfortunately it has also led to natural resource depletion, industrial levels of pollution, and waste.

In today's business environment, companies are increasingly looking at environmental sustainability as a form of competitive advantage. Sustainable marketing is an organisational focus on environmental issues with an objective to minimise environmental damage. Marketers that practice sustainability focus on "creating, producing and delivering sustainable solutions with higher net sustainable value whilst continuously satisfying customers and other stakeholders" (Charter et al., 2002, p. 13). Cast in this light, marketing becomes the organisational epicentre for creating sustainability rather than the source of environmental destruction. Some scholars argue that sustainable marketing has emerged as a new marketing paradigm for creating competitive advantage (Baldassarre & Campo, 2016).

SUSTAINABILITY QUESTION

There has been substantial growth in products that promote 'green' or 'sustainable' marketing. Consider what you have consumed over the last couple of days. Are some of these products that you consider more green or sustainable? What is it about those choices that make them more or less so?

Legal Environment

The **legal environment** is the laws and regulations that govern marketing practice. It is used to promote economic commerce, protect the development of new technologies, promote fair competition, and provide consumer protections for the society as a whole. Legal factors effectively regulate economies, ways of doing business, and the way in which people behave within societies. Given the fact that multinational companies compete in many different countries, a challenge for marketers is that companies must adhere to the legal environment in countries with widening different rules and regulations. While there are no universal laws that business can use to navigate the complexity of different legal systems, most countries and trading zones create degrees of standardisation when it comes to human rights laws, product safety, transparency in packaging, labelling, and pricing.

The legal system works in conjunction with the political environment and different elements of society. For example, the formation of laws and legal frameworks will take into consideration issues such as public health. The inter-relationship between public health and the legal system helps to ensure that laws protect the general well-being of a population. Because the external environment is in a constant state of change, we can look at how the relationship between the external environment and the legal environment has changed over time. A good example of this can be seen with governmental regulation of the tobacco industry and the impacts that it has upon legal frameworks in packaging and labelling, advertising, and taxation, which are key institutions in the legal environment.

PHOTO 4.8
The vaping industry has been the focus of recent legislation.

MARKETING DIRECTOR TASK

One of Zomotor's rival manufacturers in Mexico has recently been prosecuted by the government for breaking a state investment agreement which stipulates the proportion of Mexican-built components to be used in one of its vehicles. The manufacturer argued that it had abided by the agreement and that the disagreement was a misunderstanding surrounding the nationality of a component which had been manufactured in one country and amended in another, whereas the Mexican government said the manufacturer had taken the full investment but knowingly not used enough local components, thereby breaking both the spirit and the letter of the contract. The resulting fine amounted to around $100 million.

Whilst Zomotor has not yet entered into a similar state-funding agreement in Mexico, it plans to. Design a checklist for Tannya showing the list of legal threats which may arise from any such agreement, so that Tannya is able to brief colleagues.

The functional role of **packaging and labelling** in marketing are used to contain and protect products, promote products, and facilitate their use and re-use in the form of recycling (see Chapter 9). Packaging and labelling are governed by the legal environment of the country in which the product is sold. In countries such as the UK, the legal framework for product packaging and labelling must ensure that packaging does not mislead consumers in regard to quantity and size, price, contents, where it is made, and what it can do. It also requires manufacturers to disclose health warnings associated with the use of their products.

The final element regarding the legal environment is taxation. **Taxation** is a legal framework that requires corporations to pay tax on profits, transactions that involve the transfer of ownership of goods and services (value added tax), and make contributions towards employee pension schemes. Taxation can also be used as a form of governmental policy to stimulate or suppress demand. For example, taxation on tobacco, reflected in higher consumer prices, is the most effective measure the legal system can use to suppress demand for cigarettes. Studies by the World Health Organization (WHO) have demonstrated that a 10% increase in price reduces demand in high-income countries by 4%. Demand is reduced by 5% in mid- to low-income countries (WHO, 2020). Effectively, tax acts as a cessation tool that helps to prevent people from smoking in the first place. The WHO recommends a benchmark tax of 75% to help keep smoking rates low, and in the UK and US, national smoking rates are approximately 14% of the adult population.

One of the challenges that large tobacco companies have faced is the decline of smoking in places such as Russia, China, Europe, and the US. These declines are attributed to legal frameworks that restrict tobacco advertising and higher excise taxes

TABLE 4.1

Smoking rates and tax rates in five African countries.

Country	Smokers as Percentage of Population (Aged 15+)	Taxation Rate (in %)
Algeria	19.7	16.55
Botswana	28.7	39.16
Congo	31.6	21.24
Mozambique	25.3	14
Tunisia	39.1	42.66

Source: The Tobacco Atlas.

that encourage quitting. One continent where this trend has not held true is in Africa. According to WHO reports, in the last 15 years smoking rates have only increased in 27 countries; 15 of these are African countries. The rise of smoking rates in some countries in Africa can be attributed to weak smoking regulations and low taxation rates.

Tobacco companies have insisted that they are not specifically targeting African countries and have argued that it is a myth perpetuated by anti-tobacco lobbyists (Wild, 2018). However, it is clear that the legal system, in the form of low taxation, has allowed tobacco companies to exploit market opportunities in new markets.

GLOBAL MARKETING QUESTION

Nestle Purina Petcare is a global multinational company that specialises in pet foods of all types. The company recently decided that it would invest resources to make inroads into the growing Chinese pet food market. There are projected to be 136 million dog owners in China by 2022 (Ma, 2020), and Nestle wants to ensure that is able to capitalise on the rising popularity of dog ownership.

You are the brand manager for Purina's Complete Health Pet Nutrition dog food. Your manager has asked you to conduct a PESTEL analysis of the Chinese market. Using the PESTEL framework, map out two or three key considerations for each element of the PESTEL analysis that Purina should consider before entering into this market.

Chapter Summary

The marketing environment forms one of the foundations to a marketing plan. Marketers use the marketing environment and the process of environmental scanning as a strategic tool to better understand environmental factors that might affect a business. The importance of environmental scanning is to ensure that an organisation has up-to-date information on its immediate operating environment as well as the factors that are external to the company. This information must be updated regularly to ensure its accuracy and relevance.

Marketers use the marketing environment and the information collected as the basis for strategic planning and forecasting. It helps them anticipate trends within the marketplace. The quality of the data collected within the environmental scanning process is a key determinant in the accuracy of a company's forecasts, competitive intelligence, and market knowledge. Marketers can use the information gained in an environmental scan to conduct additional market research studies more narrowly targeted towards the wants and needs of its target markets.

The marketing environment and environmental scanning provide a portrait of the factors that affect target markets. A company's consumers are equally affected by changes in technology or the economic environment. Equally, changes in the cost of components within a marketing channel or new entrants will also affect consumer behaviour. The marketing environment represents a key strategy element in formulating the marketing plan in the quest to build competitive advantage, position their products, and understand changing customer wants and needs.

Discussion Questions

▶ Discuss the marketing environment and how it affects an organisation.

▶ Explain the role of environmental scanning.

▶ Discuss the elements associated with the micro and macro marketing environments. How are they different? What roles do they play in organisational strategy?

▶ Explain how companies can respond to the marketing environment.

Recommended Further Reading

Gbadamosi, A. (2020). The entrepreneurship marketing environment. In *Entrepreneurship marketing* (pp. 46–71). Routledge.

Hambrick, D. C. (1982). Environmental scanning and organisational strategy. *Strategic Management Journal, 3*(2), 159–174.

Kelly, P., & Ashwin, A. (2013). *The business environment.* Cengage Learning.

Lamberton, C. P., & Rose, R. L. (2012). When is ours better than mine? A framework for understanding and altering participation in commercial sharing systems. *Journal of Marketing, 76*(4), 109–125.

Porter, M. E. (2008). The five competitive forces that shape strategy. *Harvard Business Review, 86*(1), 25–40.

Schwab, K. (2017). *The fourth industrial revolution.* Currency.

References

Baldassarre, F., & Campo, R. (2016). Sustainability as a marketing tool: To be or to appear to be? *Business Horizons, 59*(4), 421–429.

Bardhi, F., & Eckhardt, G. M. (2012). Access-based consumption: The case of car sharing. *Journal of Consumer Research, 39*(4), 881–898.

Beer, J. (2019). *One year later, what did we learn from Nike's blockbuster Colin Kaepernick ad?* https://www.fastcompany.com/90399316/one-year-later-what-did-we-learn-from-nikes-blockbuster-colin-kaepernick-ad

Bond, C., & Seeley, C. (2004). Paradox in marketing: An inquiry into sustainability, ethics and marketing. In *Towards an environment research agenda* (pp. 256–282). Palgrave Macmillan.

Charter, M., Peattie, K., Ottman, J., & Polonsky, M. (2002). Marketing and sustainability. In *Centre for Business Relationships, Accountability, & Sustainability* (pp. 1–34).

Currás-Pérez, R., Bigné-Alcañiz, E., & Alvarado-Herrera, A. (2009). The role of self-definitional principles in consumer identification with a socially responsible company. *Journal of Business Ethics, 89*(4), 547.

Davidson, H. (2021). *Investor relations.* http://investor.harley-davidson.com/news-releases/news-release-details/harley-davidson-unveils-hardwire-five-year-strategic-plan

DiMaggio, P. J., & Powell, W. W. (1983). The iron cage revisited: Institutional isomorphism and collective rationality in organisational fields. *American Sociological Review*, 147–160.

Drope, J., & Schluger, N. (2018). *The tobacco atlas* (6th ed.). The American Cancer Society.

Eckhardt, G. M., & Bardhi, F. (2015). The sharing economy isn't about sharing at all. *Harvard Business Review, 28*(1).

Jones, P., Clarke-Hill, C., Comfort, D., & Hillier, D. (2008). Marketing and sustainability. *Marketing Intelligence & Planning, 26*(2), 123–130.

Kugel, S. (2020, March 24). The case against frequent flyer programs. *The New York Times International Edition*, 16.

Ma, Y. (2020). Number of pets in China, 2017–2022, by type. *Statista.* https://www.statista.com/statistics/992300/china-number-of-pets-by-type/

Mazareanu, E. (2019). Value of the global sharing economy 2014–2025. *Statista.* https://www.statista.com/statistics/830986/value-of-the-global-sharing-economy/

Morana, C. (2005). The Japanese deflation: Has it had real effects? Could it have been avoided? *Applied Economics, 37*(12), 1337–1352.

Oliver, C., & Holzinger, I. (2008). The effectiveness of strategic political management: A dynamic capabilities framework. *Academy of Management Review, 33*(2), 496–520.

Porter, M. E. (2008). The five competitive forces that shape strategy. *Harvard Business Review, 86*(1), 25–40.

Schaefers, T., Lawson, S. J., & Kukar-Kinney, M. (2016). How the burdens of ownership promote consumer usage of access-based services. *Marketing Letters, 27*(3), 569–577.

Schein, E. H. (1983). The role of the founder in creating organisational culture. *Organisational Dynamics, 12*(1), 13–28.

Statista. (2020). Total lobbying spending in the United States from 1998 to 2019. *Statista.* https://www.statista.com/statistics/257337/total-lobbying-spending-in-the-us/.

Wild, S. (2018). Smoking has risen 50% in Africa in thirty-five years even as it drops in high income regions. *QuartzAfrica*. https://qz.com/africa/1228845/africas-smoking-is-up-50-even-as-it-drops-in-wealthy-continents/

Williams, R. (2020). *Gen Z relies on influencers for purchase decisions*. https://www.marketing-dive.com/news/gen-z-relies-on-influencers-for-purchase-decisions-kantar-says/582890/

World Commission on Environment and Development. (1987). *Our common future*. http://www.un-documents.net/our-common-future.pdf

World Health Organization. (2020). *Tobacco free initiative*. https://www.who.int/tobacco/economics/taxation/en/

Glossary

Company: key stakeholders within an organisation, which includes the management executive team and the different functional areas of the business

Competitor: an organisation that competes against another organisation

Customer: the current or future buyers of products or services

Ecological environment: the natural resources required to develop and sustain marketing activities, those natural resources that are affected by marketing activities, and the stewardship associated with protecting those resources

Economic environment: the external factors that impact both consumers and businesses through the effect of supply and demand

Environmental scanning: the process through which marketing organisations collect and analyse environmental variables and action this data in their marketing strategy

Inflation: the percentage rate at which prices for goods and services increase

Legal environment: the laws and regulations that govern marketing practice

Macro environment: the political, economic, social, technological, ecological, and legal forces that shape our external environment

Marketing environment: factors that are both internal and external to an organisation that impact its ability to build relationships with its customers and create competitive advantage

Marketing intermediaries: companies that help an organisation sell, promote, and distribute goods and services to their target market

Micro environment: the company itself, suppliers, intermediaries, competitors, and customers

PESTEL: a market information tool that helps marketers to understand key trends that are happening in the external environment

Political environment: governmental policy and its impact on an organisation or an industry

Recession: two consecutive quarters of negative GDP growth

Socio-cultural environment: the beliefs, attitudes, and values of people within a society that are shaped by institutional forces within a marketplace

Suppliers: companies that provide goods or services to other companies

Taxation: a legal framework that requires corporations to pay taxation on profits, transactions that involve the transfer of ownership of goods and services (value added tax), and make contributions towards employee pension schemes

Technological environment: the innovative technologies that foster service, product, and process innovations, as well as a firm's ability to respond to these changes

The Role of the Technological Environment Case Study: The Impact of Artificial Intelligence, Big Data, and Machine Learning

A good example of how the technological environment can change an industry and how an organisation can manage technological change can be seen in fast food and the McDonald's Corporation. In 2019, McDonald's initiated a series of investments in AI and data mining software capabilities to reposition the company to become the Amazon.com of fast food. These investments, totalling hundreds of millions of dollars, are seen as key strategic initiatives to move McDonald's away from being just a fast-food company and towards a more data-driven, marketing-intelligent enterprise. According to Daniel Henry, chief information officer, "we don't think that food should be any different than what you buy on Amazon"

continued

(Locker, 2019). The analogy here is that when ordering from Amazon, you are prompted with 'those who bought . . . also bought'.

The fundamental problems that McDonald's has been facing are that same store sales are declining and it is facing increasing competition. Faced with the difficulties of continually trying to grow the company through new store openings, they decided to use the technological environment to increase growth strategies. McDonald's went through a series of partnerships and acquisitions, which have helped to create a digital ecosystem. They acquired Dynamic Yield, an AI company; Apprente, a voice recognition company; and a stake in Plexure, a mobile application developer.

Voice recognition software enables the company to take orders from people in multiple languages and regional dialects. It also provides the potential to streamline the ordering process. AI enables McDonald's to read license plates and gives it the potential to customise its drive-through ordering board and self-ordering kiosks. These ordering boards can tailor food offerings based on previous order history, time of day, popularity of food items, weather, and length of time to make an order. It can also recommend upgrades to your meal or recommend 'those who ordered . . . also ordered'.

Recently, McDonald's sold off ownership of Dynamic Yield to Mastercard but continues to use the company as a vendor to help manage its technology strategy. McDonald's has implemented its digital menu boards across the globe, and same store sales had increased by 12.3% by the end of 2021 (Haddon, 2022). While this increase in sales is attributed to a number of factors and not to the use of technology alone, McDonald's and the fast-food industry as a whole offer examples of how changes in the technological environment are being harnessed to generate sales growth and better meet customer needs.

Your Task

Choose one of the following industries:

- ▶ Retail clothing
- ▶ Personal fitness
- ▶ Healthcare
- ▶ Banking, finance, or insurance
- ▶ Marketing

continued

Do you think these industries will be impacted by changes in the technological environment? What impact do you think AI, big data, and machine learning will have on any one of these industries? How do you think that companies in these industries can leverage technology to create a better customer experience?

Bibliography

Haddon, H. (2022). *McDonald's*. https://www.wsj.com/articles/mcdonalds-sales-lifted-by-higher-prices-sandwich-campaigns-11643284802

Locker, M. (2019). McDonald's is spending $300 million to be more like Amazon. *Fast Company*. https://www.fastcompany.com/90325388/mcdonalds-tries-to-be-more-like-amazon-with-300-million-ai-bet?partner=feedburner

5 | Segmentation, Target Marketing, and Positioning

LEARNING OBJECTIVES

▶ To understand the concepts of market segmentation, target marketing, and positioning

▶ To identify the criterion necessary for successful market segmentation

▶ To discuss how marketers segment consumer markets

▶ To discuss how marketers segment business markets

▶ To understand the interrelationship between market segmentation strategies, target marketing, and positioning

Introduction

Market segmentation strategies are rooted in marketers' attempts to understand complex and diverse marketplaces. Market segmentation brings a semblance of order, whereby marketers take the heterogeneous demand characteristics of a market and assign them to a number of smaller groups that share similar characteristics (Smith, 1956). It is a recognition that while markets are diverse, there are subgroups within a market that share the same wants and needs. Segmentation is an important step in the marketer's ability to meet these different needs in the marketplace.

Market segmentation is a process in marketing strategy where marketers differentiate customers that share similar characteristics into unique target market groups within a marketplace. Rather than treat a market as an undifferentiated whole, marketers use market segmentation to identify different need-based segments within a market. After marketers select viable market segments, the next step in the process is to identify a **target market**, which is a group of customers that have specific wants and needs and also a willingness to buy. **Target marketing** is a strategic process whereby marketers evaluate

DOI: 10.4324/9781003170891-6

119

the attractiveness of different target market segments. This process helps organisations to determine what segments it can serve best.

Positioning is the managerial activity that marketers use to influence product or service characteristics within the marketplace. Positioning is the final step in the segmentation and targeting process. Once markets have been segmented and a target market has been identified, marketing uses positioning to tailor a unique marketing mix strategy that can communicate the value of the offering to the consumer.

Market segmentation, target marketing, and positioning (STP) are interlinked strategies. Each segment represents a unique, aggregated group of customers that share similar wants and needs. The way in which marketers segment consumer markets is through demographic, psychographic, and behavioural approaches to segmentation. In business markets, marketers segment the market through demographic, operation type, and purchasing criteria. Whether marketers are segmenting consumer or business markets, each market segment will have a targeted product, price, place, and promotional strategy uniquely developed for that segment.

Segmentation is important for four reasons. First, it identifies specific groups of people. By quantifying the attributes associated with specific groups of customers, marketers are able to meet the needs of specific market segments. Second, it helps marketers gain important marketing research insights on target markets and how they behave. By tracking and monitoring segmentation groups, marketers can ensure that their marketing strategy stays relevant to the target market. Third, market segmentation is a form of organisational resource allocation. Segmentation helps organisations determine segments that are most profitable and enables the organisation to allocate resources that best target those segments. Finally, marketers can build economies of scale, which are cost savings associated with purchasing things in larger quantities. By grouping individuals into segmentation groups, marketers can lower their transaction costs and reach larger groups of consumers more efficiently.

STAKEHOLDER QUESTION

Think of a product or service that you have purchased in the last few weeks. This could be a major expenditure in terms of time or money, or a routine purchase from the supermarket. Who do you think the target market is for this product? What consumer attributes are marketers trying to appeal to in terms of age, gender, location, lifestyle, or personality? Do you think that the product or service is successful in appealing to those consumer characteristics? How and why?

Important issues marketing managers must consider when segmenting a market include how to determine if the approach is successful and what happens if the market has been over-segmented. To address these issues and ensure an organisation pursues a successful segmentation strategy, marketers use four criteria when evaluating the success of their market segmentation and target marketing strategy. These criteria include whether the segment is measurable, substantial, accessible, and actionable.

Measurable: The size of a market segment must be quantifiable. This means managers must be able to determine the size, purchasing power, and profitability of a market segment. In order to meet this criterion, marketing managers work closely with their market research department to estimate the segment's size and profitability.

Substantial: A market segment must be large enough to warrant a customised marketing mix. An example of a product that did not meet the criterion of substantiality was Coca-Cola Life. The soft drink was launched in the UK in 2014 and was positioned to 35- to 55-year-olds as having 45% less sugar than original Coke. However, there was never a market substantive enough for the soft drink. While Coke Life had fewer calories than original Coke (Coke Life had 89 calories while Coke has 139), it still had more calories than the zero-calorie Coke Zero and Diet Coke. This middle-of-the-road position was never substantive enough to generate enough sales volume for the Coca-Cola Company. By the time Coca-Cola discontinued the brand in most countries in 2017, it garnered less than 1% of total Coke sales (Roderick, 2017). Coca-Cola Life failed to meet the segmentation criterion of substantiality.

Accessible: Accessibility relates to a company's ability to reach a target segment with a customised marketing message. In the early 2010s, Procter & Gamble's Old Spice body wash brand was losing sales to competitive rivals. The advertising agency in charge of the Old Spice brand, Widen and Kennedy, found that 60% of all body wash purchases for men were made by women (Widen & Kennedy, 2020). It created an iconic campaign targeted to women using the actor Isaiah Mustafa in the 'Man Your Man Could Smell Like' campaign. This campaign helped Old Spice become the number-one body wash brand. In order to reach its product's target market, Widen and Kennedy needed to reach women who purchased male body wash.

Actionable: Actionability is the ability of an organisation to attract, persuade, and serve a market segment. While target markets can be segmented according to a number of different variables, unless a new market segment has measurably different wants and needs from existing segments, there is no need to create additional market segments. Additionally, organisations must have the resources to effectively serve their target markets. One of the lasting effects of the COVID-19 pandemic was the pressure it put on organisations and their ability to serve their target markets. Companies like Virgin Atlantic filed for bankruptcy protection in order to reorganise and keep the airline running.

Once these four criterion have been meet, then it is possible for marketers to tailor their marketing mix to reach their target markets. This chapter will explore how marketers go about segmenting both consumer and business markets, as well as developing targeting strategies that identify the needs of market segments.

PHOTO 5.1
Market research indicated that many Old Spice purchases were being made by women. Old Spice changed its marketing communications to reach women, which improved its accessibility.

NEW MEDIA QUESTION

Market segmentation is based upon the principle of grouping like-minded customers into similar groups where people share the same tastes and preferences. The advent of new technology in the areas of artificial intelligence and machine learning is transforming market segmentation from targeting groups of customers to more personalised targeting strategies.

For your next online purchase, take note of the personalised targeting strategies marketers are using to inform or persuade your purchase. Make note of the type of pop-up ads in your web browser, product recommendations made in your web basket, recommended news articles, infomercials, or sponsored content. What recommendations are being made, and how is the information influenced by your purchase?

Segmenting Consumer Markets

Segmenting consumer markets seeks to identify and group consumers through tangible characteristics, such as geography, demography, and psychographics. Consumers living in specific geographic locations may share similar wants and needs. It is also possible to group people according to demographic characteristics, such as age or income. Psychographic characteristics are an attempt to group people according to their lifestyle and values.

Consumer segmentation also involves grouping people according to behavioural characteristics. This form of segmentation groups people according to their actual purchase behaviour. Marketers can tease out subgroups of people according to the amount of expenditure they spend with a company or the benefits that they seek. The purpose of this section is to explore the ways in which marketing managers segment consumer markets in order to better serve their wants and needs.

Geographic Segmentation

Geographic segmentation is the process of segmenting a market that targets customers by neighbourhood, city, region, country, or international region. Other geographic segmentation approaches might include segmenting the market by population density or climate. Segmenting by population density would differentiate rural areas, suburban centres, or urban inter-city populations. Climate considerations dictate where marketers might target ski equipment, snow blowers, and winter clothing apparel. Geographic segmentation represents both a micro and macro targeting strategy.

Micro targeting geographical segments can enable marketers to target specific groups of people down to the level of a neighbourhood. The principle here is that people of the same socio-economic class may live in geographic clusters where it is relatively easy to target them. For example, the postal zip code 90210 in Beverly Hills, California, is synonymous with educated, affluent, suburban Americans. This means marketers can geographically segment customers in this area knowing that customers have similar characteristics.

A micro targeting strategy might also include cities or regions where consumers share certain tastes that are unique to that area. Restaurants often incorporate this micro targeting strategy by tailoring their menu to feature locally sourced foods that are indigenous to that region. This form of geographic segmentation helps to differentiate their offering to meet local tastes.

Marketers can also use geographical segmentation as a macro segmentation strategy where companies might target countries or international regions. This is a particularly effective segmentation strategy for large multinational companies. For example the KFC Corporation, a large US multinational fast-food company, uses geographic segmentation throughout sub-Saharan Africa.

PHOTO 5.2
Country Living magazine uses geographic segmentation to reach its target markets.

The importance of geographic segmentation for KFC in countries such as Ghana is that it represents new growth opportunities for a company that competes in saturated Western markets that are crowded with many competitors. With fewer Western fast-food competitors in Ghana, KFC is able to stand out as a unique offering. There is also a uniqueness associated with KFC in Ghana, where eating fast food is seen as a special treat and can confer an elevated 'social status' amongst local people (Searcey & Richtel, 2017). Here we can see how segmentation and target strategies work in conjunction with marketing positioning, which is a focus of Chapter 7. KFC holds a certain level of prestige in Ghana that it does not have in Western markets. While this geographical segmentation strategy is clearly beneficial to the KFC Corporation, there are significant ethical concerns with introducing processed foods that are high in saturated fats to new

PHOTO 5.3
KFC uses geographic segmentation strategies.

markets that have fewer governmental health regulations and lower consumer awareness about the link between obesity and fast food.

Demographic Segmentation

Demographic segmentation is the process of dividing the market by age, family life cycle, income, gender, ethnicity, occupation, education levels, and nationality. Demographic segmentation represents one of the most commonly used segmentation approaches. When using demographic variables, marketers often combine them when segmenting a market. For example, successful companies such as Nike use demographic segmentation variables that target people by age, gender, marital status, nationality, and income. It is the combination of these different variables, in coordination with their marketing mix, which allows Nike to reach different need-based segments.

Age segmentation categorises a market by different age groupings. The rationale to grouping people by age is that many people within the same age groups will share many of the same cultural reference points that shape their values and belief systems. Referring to groups of people by their birth years is something that is not only common in marketing segmentation but also a key reference point in popular culture. Different age groups have become synonymous with different labels, which have become key identifiers for people who are born in different generations. For example:

Baby boomers: People in the Baby Boom generation were born between 1946 and 1964. The group is characterised by a post-WWII 'baby boom' that marked an

125

age of prosperity associated with rising incomes, growth in employment, and a more leisure-oriented society. At the time, baby boomers represented the largest demographic segment in the Western world.

Generation X: This generation was born between 1965 and 1978. It is often dubbed the 'MTV generation' in reference to the creation of the MTV channel, the rise of music videos, and the popularisation of video gaming culture. Children born in this generation grew up in a time characterised by family change where many mothers entered the workforce.

Generation Y: This generation was born between 1979 and 1994. This group is often referred to as the 'Millennial' generation, as many people from this generation came of age during the millennium. The term 'millennial' is used to characterise a forward way of thinking and a special consideration for the future. It is also the first generation shaped by the rise of the internet.

Generation Z: Generation Z was born between the years of 1995 to 2010. Generation Z has grown up in an age of unprecedented consumer technology and social media that shapes the way that they communicate and how marketers communicate to them. This group is arguably the most marketed to group in the history of the world.

Generation Alpha: Marketers have coined the generation after Generation Z as the alpha generation, those born in 2011 and after. While people in this segment are obviously young, they are tech savvy and know how to use mobile and tablet devices. The amount of screen time this generation spends has led to a disproportionate influence on family purchasing habits (Pasquarelli & Schultz, 2019).

MARKETING ASSISTANT TASK

Zomotor's Mexican marketers believe that they have been unsuccessful so far in reaching young adults, as they have relied on a profile segmentation strategy which has focused on prospects' age, location, marital status, number of children, occupation, and socio-economic classification. Whilst they believe it makes good sense to retain some of these factors – especially 'number of children' – they think that by having a larger emphasis on behavioural characteristics, they could segment the market in a more effective manner which is more meaningful to consumers.

Tannya has been asked to use the main criteria of behavioural segmentation to write a pen portrait of the typical family which Zomotor should be trying to reach. Although it may seem rather essentialist, patronising, and even stereotyping to reduce an entire customer segment to a description of one 'representative' couple, it is nonetheless useful in helping marketers to visualise their target and to empathise with their needs and wants. Help Tannya by providing the following details about the target couple, plus any others which you might think of: (i) what competitor models they consider; (ii) how often they change their vehicle; (iii) what time of year they change their vehicle; (iv) how many alternative manufacturers' products they consider; (v) how many dealerships they visit; (vi) how they collect information on new cars; (vii) how long they take between deciding they need a new vehicle and placing an order; (viii) whether they pay cash or take a lease; (ix) which features they find the most important; (x) what major benefits they seek from their vehicle.

Another common demographic variable used in segmenting markets is gender segmentation. **Gender segmentation** is a segmentation approach that targets consumers on the basis of their gender, sexual orientation, or gender identity. This definition of gender segmentation takes into account gender as an identity and not predetermined by biological sex.

An example of how marketers use gender segmentation, in combination with age segmentation, can be found in the children's toy category. Marketers have a complex history in marketing to young children by gender. It is not uncommon to walk down the aisle of a toy store or a retail department where children's toys are sold and see gender segmentation. Boys' toys are often associated with the colour blue, superheroes, and trucks. Girls' toys are packaged in pink and often involve dolls or make-up. These create contrasts in boys' toys that feature play activities for boys that involve excitement, competition, and danger. Girls' toys facilitate forms of play that emphasise physical attractiveness, caregiving, and domestic skills (Blakemore & Centers, 2005).

This form of gender segmentation can reinforce unhealthy stereotypes that encourage boys to pursue more aggressive, active, and competitive forms of play and for girls to be more passive, nurturing, and emphasising aesthetical beauty. A study of how marketers segment LEGO City, which targets boys, and LEGO Friends, which targets girls, found that the messaging associated with this segmentation strategy promotes gendered stereotypes that "encourage boys to enact various skilled professions, heroism, and expertise, whereas girls are encouraged to focus on having hobbies, being domestic, caring for others, socialising, being amateurs, and appreciating and striving for beauty" (Reich et al., 2018).

While there are concerns about how some marketers use gender segmentation in unethical ways, some toy manufacturers and retailers have become increasingly sensitive to negative stereotypes. Companies such as Amazon no longer use gender-based categories for toys, and the Disney Store stopped using gender designations in its retail

PHOTOS 5.4 and 5.5
Examples of gender-based marketing in toys.

stores. A number of other companies have turned to gender segmentation to promote more diversified messages of gender. Mattel, the maker of Barbie, introduced a series of gender neutral dolls and introduced Jazz Jennings, a LGBTQ+ rights activist and the first transgendered doll. These forms of marketing highlight gender as an identity rather than gender as a determinant of biological sex (Bussey & Bandura, 1999). Here we can see how gender segmentation can also be used to promote more diversified messages about gender, marketing, and targeting.

The final demographic segmentation variable that we will look at in detail is family life cycle segmentation. **Family life cycle segmentation** acknowledges the changing demographic nature to consumers whose income, marital status, age, employment status, and the presence and absence of raising children changes over time. For example, the way that marketers target a 21-year-old, single university student is different than the way that they would target a 21-year-old, fully employed married person with two children. These changes in the life cycle mean that target markets have different needs and wants at different stages of their lives. In order to create customer satisfaction and build customer loyalty, marketers must be in tune with these different subgroups. Family life cycle segmentation helps marketers to tease out and differentiate different need-based segments using family life cycle analysis.

METRICS QUESTION

One way that marketers build market segments is through collecting consumer data on customers who frequent a website. Companies such as Google provide analytical data on customer visits and their level on interaction on a company website. This service, known as Google Analytics, provides organisations detailed metrics on customer behaviour.

Choose a website that you frequent on a daily basis. Make note, or estimate, the following variables:

▶ *Sessions*: how many times did you visit that site in a day?

▶ *Average session duration*: how long do you spend on the site each time you browse?

▶ *Device type*: what type of desktop, mobile device, or tablet did you use?

▶ *Page depth*: to what depth did you explore each page?

▶ *Visitor interaction*: did you blog, comment, purchase, or forward content contained on the page?

Using market segmentation variables outlined in this chapter, what do you think your segmentation profile would look like?

Psychographic Segmentation

Psychographic segmentation involves segmenting the market by personality, lifestyle, motives, attitudes, and belief systems. This segmentation strategy groups people according to how they live and what they value. Psychographic segmentation can provide marketers with insights into the type of brands that that consumers buy and how these choices can become distinctive expressions of their consumer identity. Marketers use psychographic variables in combination with other segmentation strategies, such as demographic or behavioural segmentation. This helps to add layers of complexity and greater accuracy in targeting different subgroups of people.

Values is a psychographic variable that represents the importance of something to someone. For example, environmental sustainability is an important consumer value in today's society. This value is rooted in consumer concern for the planet and manifests itself in a consumer desire to purchase goods and services that reflect this concern and commitment to the environment. Marketers are able to tap into the psychographic variable of sustainability by targeting consumers with specific messages about environmental sustainability.

Personality is a psychographic characteristic that represents one's personal characteristics, attitudes, and identity. These personal characteristics are reflected in the choices that consumers make about different brands. Consumers often make consumption choices about brands that are reflective of a consumer's sense of self or self-concept. These connections can become so strong that we see consumers form personal links with brands where the brand becomes a key component in a consumer's expression of self-identity.

For example, the Harley-Davidson Motorcycles Company has spent decades cultivating a brand identity that is rooted in values associated with freedom, patriotism, rebellion, and masculinity (Schouten & McAlexander, 1995). Harley-Davidson's brand identity is targeted to speak to consumers that value these brand personality

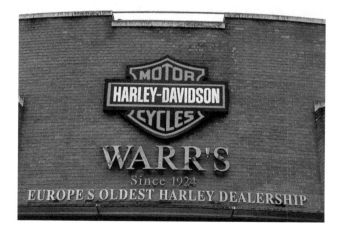

PHOTO 5.6
Harley-Davidson has created a unique brand identity that inspires the followers of its brand.

characteristics. Consumers who purchase these brands discharge the embedded brand identity into their own sense of self-identity (Black & Veloutsou, 2017). Brand identity and consumer identity are interlinked in a co-created meaning system.

The use of psychographic segmentation helps marketers to create what are known as marketing personas. **Marketing personas** represent the segmentation characteristics of 'aggregate consumers'. These aggregate consumers are fictional representations of what a certain type of customer looks like based on demographic, behavioural, and psychographic segmentation variables.

In the marketing research process, marketing organisations collect consumer data as individual data points as well as large-scale surveys, representing thousands or tens of thousands of data points. When this large-scale data is analysed, marketers can tease out aggregate segmentation traits, which are characteristics shared by groups of people. These segmented groups are called marketing personas, as they help marketers to understand different target markets within the data set.

For example, marketing personas can be used to understand global consumer types. Euromonitor International is a market research firm that collects consumer data using psychographic, behavioural, and demographic data to create global consumer types that can help marketers to understand global consumer trends.

Euromonitor's ten consumer types are examples of marketing personas. Each individual persona has certain behavioural characteristics that help marketers to better understand global consumers. According to Euromonitor, the 'undaunted striver' represents up to 17% of the total global population. This persona is characterised as an individual who is willing to spend their disposable income in order to maintain their social status. They "prioritise experiences and leisure activities as well as name-brand and luxury products" (Shridhar, 2021, p. 6). In the case of undaunted strivers, marketers might consider emphasising brand image, brand heritage, quality, exclusivity, and prestige. Because undaunted strivers value status, these messages will resonate with this group of consumers.

On the other end of the consumption spectrum, we can see the 'empowered activist', who represents 15% of the global population. According to Euromonitor, the empowered activist is someone who is environmentally conscious and technologically driven. When making purchasing decisions this group prioritises sustainability and considers the impact their purchases may have upon the planet. In the case of the empowered activist, marketers might position their message around features that emphasise quality, durability, use of renewable components, and sustainability.

The importance for understanding these global consumer personas from a segmentation and targeting perspective is that once marketers are able to identify like-minded consumers, it allows marketers to better target their message to specific groups of people. In these examples we can see how segmentation strategies can be used to create marketing personas that allow marketers to better target their message to the aggregate characteristics associated with large groups of consumers.

Global Distribution of 2021 Consumer Types

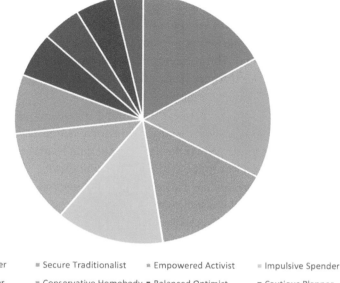

- Undaunted Striver
- Secure Traditionalist
- Empowered Activist
- Impulsive Spender
- Minimalist Seeker
- Conservative Homebody
- Balanced Optimist
- Cautious Planner
- Self-Care Aficionado
- Inspired Adventurer

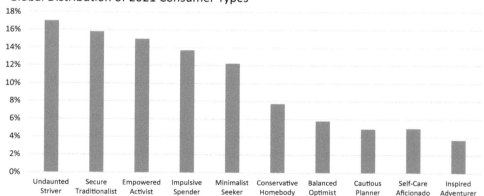

Global Distribution of 2021 Consumer Types

FIGURES 5.1 and 5.1A
Euromonitor's global consumer types.

Sources: Shridhar (2021); *Euromonitor International, Voice of the Consumer: Lifestyles Survey 2021.*

MARKETING MANAGER TASK

In China, Dylan's team have come to a conclusion that their previous reliance on profile segmentation techniques has been unsuccessful in reaching a sufficient number of young families. However, rather than changing the segmentation strategy to one which focuses on behavioural traits, Dylan has decided to segment the market psychographically, figuring that people who are grouped together by their values rather than their actions are likely to have more in common at a deeper emotional level. By tapping into this and reflecting their values, Dylan hopes that Zomotor can build a closer bond with the segment, leading to greater levels of customer recall, recognition, and loyalty. Dylan has considered the lifestyles, social statuses, personality traits, interests, hobbies, opinions, attitudes, and values of his target audience and, after some initial market research, he is beginning to develop an understanding of what might attract their attention, fuel their desire, and drive them to action.

Dylan's pen portrait depicts a couple who are happy, loyal and outgoing, with a fairly large circle of friends. Probably educated to degree level, and eight years into a professional career in finance, engineering or technology, the family take two holidays each year – one abroad by plane and another within their home region in China. Politically moderate or progressive, they are interested in literature, music, and the arts. They watch around ten hours of broadcast programmes each week (by television and via the internet), read 12 fictional novels per year, try to recycle as much as possible, and dislike people who are selfish in their actions. They hope to achieve promotions at work within the next three years, valuing hard work, determination, and honesty, and in their free time they play the violin or piano, racquet sports, or snooker, and enjoy hiking in the countryside.

Using Dylan's pen portrait, design a poster which would appeal to this preferred customer segment and present the ZoFamilia in a way which they would find persuasive. You may use some text, but not enough to detract from the visual design.

Behavioural Segmentation

Behavioural segmentation is a form of segmentation that looks at patterns of behaviour that customers exhibit when they interact with different brands or services provided, or when they purchase products. Behavioural segmentation divides the market by benefits sought by customers, customer usage rate, and purchase occasion. Whereas demographic and psychographic segmentation seek to map out the descriptive attributes associated with segments, behavioural segmentation seeks to understand how these segments behave.

Benefits sought segmentation is a demand-side characteristic that identifies customers by the benefits they seek when purchasing different products and services. These benefits might be functional, self-expressive, or emotional benefits. Functional benefits could be the quality of a picture in a high-definition television. The benefits sought here are based on performance, technical engineering, and quality. Self-expressive benefits might lead consumers to purchase a brand of television that is closely aligned with their self-identity. Consumers seek out those brands that have distinctive brand identities that are closely aligned with their own sense of self. Finally, emotional benefits are where consumers seek out those brands that give them the greatest emotional feeling. This might be an aspirational benefit where a consumer has an idealised television that they have always wanted to purchase.

The importance of a benefits sought segmentation approach recognises that consumers share similar purchasing characteristics when evaluating different products and services. For example, the Colgate-Palmolive company segments the category of toothpaste according to the benefits that consumers seek.

Each product category of Colgate-Palmolive toothpaste is focused on the benefits that customers seek in protecting, maintaining, or repairing healthy teeth. A focus on the benefits sought by consumers enables marketers to group people according to the needs they have in the market. Marketers then target these benefit-seeking consumers with specific products and marketing communication messages that deliver those benefits. A strength of benefit segmentation is that it helps marketers to focus on the attributes

TABLE 5.1

Examples of Colgate-Palmolive's benefit segmentation strategy.

Benefits Sought	Toothpaste Product	Benefit Segment Description
Whiteness of teeth	Colgate Max White	People looking for whiter teeth and freshness of breath.
Prevention	Colgate Total Whole Mouth Health	People looking to prevent gum disease, bacteria, tartar, cavities, and bad breath.
Sensitive teeth	Colgate Pro-relief Enamel Repair	People seeking pain relief and to repair damaged tooth enamel.
Flavour/appearance	Colgate Natural Extracts – Ultimate Fresh	Emphasising taste and refreshment with Asian lemon oil and aloe extracts.
Developing teeth	Colgate Maximum Cavity Protection –Kids	No artificial flavours, preservatives, sweeteners, or colours. This product strengths enamel and prevents cavities in children's teeth.

associated with a product offering that are linked to the specific cut-off criteria consumers use when making purchasing decisions (see Chapter 9).

(see Chapter 9)

ETHICS QUESTION

Vaping uses a battery-powered smoking device that heats tobacco, flavourings, and other chemicals. Many vaping companies use benefit segmentation in their marketing approach. This segmentation strategy involves producing different flavours of nicotine products and nicotine strengths to target people with different tastes. The flavourings include menthol, cinnamon, citrus, mango, and cotton candy. When adding demographic segmentation, in addition to benefits sought, who do you think the target market would be for some of these products? Discuss the ethics of this segmentation and targeting approach.

Usage rate segmentation divides the marketing according to the amount of a product or service that is purchased. Organisations group customers that are high, medium, or light sales volume consumers. Usage rate segmentation taps into what is known as the Pareto principle, which states that 80% of results stem from 20% of their causes (Koch, 2011). Taken in reverse, this principle highlights that a small percentage of causes will have a disproportional effect on the outcome. In marketing, we take this principle to mean that 80% of our revenue can come from 20% of the customer base. While the Pareto principle is not an exact science, and there can be some variability in these percentages, it helps to orientate an organisation's focus on those customers that deliver the most value to a company.

Usage rate is a key segmentation variable that marketers use in targeting the different financial expenditures generated by each customer group. It helps to ensure that marketers reward those customers at the highest end of the spectrum, but also ensures that they do not miss out on lower-volume transactional customers. Targeting through usage rate segmentation ensures marketers capture the full spectrum of their customer base. A good example of this strategy in practice is the American Express card. American Express uses different cards and reward levels that tap into usage rate segmentation.

The importance of usage rate segmentation to the American Express Company is that it allows the company to tailor different products, levels of service, and customer rewards to different usage segments. It ensures that those customers at the highest end of the consumption spectrum receive the highest levels of customer service. At the lower end of the consumption spectrum, American Express does not ignore its lighter volume customers. It targets them with a special card that captures the full value of its usage

TABLE 5.2

The American Express tiered approach to usage rate segmentation.

Card Type	Product	Usage Rate Segmentation Description
Green Card		Launched in 1958 for business travellers, it is the original American Express corporate card. While iconic, it is now targeted towards entry-level, lower-volume purchasers. The card has an annual membership fee of $150.
Gold Card		The Gold Card was launched in 1966 as an attempt to capture the elite, frequent business traveller. The card has an annual membership fee of $250. The Gold Card was the company's first exclusive prestige card.
Platinum Card		Launched in 1984 as a step up from the gold card, the Platinum Card offers members additional membership rewards upon joining and for purchases. The card has an annual membership fee of $550. Platinum members are eligible for upgrades and higher levels of customer service.
Centurion Card		The Centurion Card (often referred to as the Black Card) was launched in 1999 by invitation only. This card is segmented for the global elite with a $10,000 initial registration fee and an annual membership fee of $5,000. It provides 24/7 concierge services and elite upgrades at hotels, airlines, car rentals, and a host of other services.

segmentation base by capturing lower volume customers other companies may overlook. This example highlights how usage rate segmentation and targeting work in coordination with each other to market to different need-based usage segments.

Purchase occasion segmentation divides the market by the timing of the purchase during the year. Customer wants and needs greatly vary by the day, over the course of the year, and throughout their lifetime. Think about a really hot day in the summer. The weather can influence a consumer's purchase occasion by triggering a desire for ice cream or a cold drink. This segmentation strategy enables marketers to take into account different times of the year, different purchasing occasions, and different stages of the consumer family life cycle. For example, the Starbucks Corporation successfully uses purchase occasions that are linked to different times of the year. For example, the autumn season features pumpkin spiced drinks and the summer months feature cold frappes. By tapping into product occasion segmentation, Starbucks is hoping to stimulate demand for seasonal drinks.

Segmenting Business Markets

Marketers approach business segmentation in much the same way that they approach consumer segmentation. Business segmentation requires an organisation to identify different need-based segments which share similar characteristics and to customise a marketing mix targeted to reach those segments. While business markets are smaller than consumer markets in terms of the number of buyers, business buyers require a higher degree of customisation.

The buyers that exist within business-to-business (B2B) markets consist of producers of goods and services, resellers, governmental agencies, and institutional buyers. Institutional buyers are often large-scale organisations such as hospitals, schools, or universities (see buyer types in Chapter 12). These organisations employ purchasing departments, which help businesses to procure goods and services. Purchasing agents are highly specialised buyers who work inside a buying organisation that procures goods and services.

The importance of B2B segmentation is that it helps organisations understand market needs. The process of segmentation helps organisations to differentiate various organisational buyers. This helps to ensure that a marketing organisation has the necessary capabilities to serve market segments. There might be cases where a marketer might not be able to meet market demand in some areas of business, so B2B segmentation strategies ensure a best fit between an organisation and its buying segments. B2B segmentation strategies also provide important areas for new market growth. Segmentation helps an organisation to identify opportunities to diversify its segmentation base and provide new opportunities for profitability or diversification.

B2B segmentation takes a two-stage approach in the form of macro segmentation and micro segmentation (Wind & Cardozo, 1974). This helps to ensure that marketers are able to capture the full financial potential of the market by segmenting both broad-based variables and highly targeted segmentation variables. **Macro segmentation** strategies are the demographic characteristics of B2B segmentation. Macro segmentation strategies segment the market by geographical location, organisational size, and industry type. **Micro segmentation** strategies segment the market by purchasing criteria, buying situation, decision-making unit, and purchasing organisation.

Micro Segmentation

Geographic segmentation strategies divides the market by business location. This is one of the most common B2B approaches, as it allows an organisation to narrow down to a specific area that can be serviced. Geographic segmentation is often reflected in a business phenomenon known as clustering. In clustering, organisations in the same industry will often band together geographically. These geographic clusters offer organisations a number of efficiencies through the concentration of similar buyers and sellers in a targeted location. For example, the Bangalore area has become known as the Silicon Valley of India, with a large concentration of software, biotechnology, aeronautics, and defence companies. This geographic concentration of industries is a form of geographic segmentation, as these industries draw from the same labour markets, specialised components, and complementary products that enable marketers to serve these markets more efficiently (Rao & Balasubrahmanya, 2017).

Organisational size segmentation strategies divide the market based on size, volume, and throughput. Organisational size is determined through high, medium, and low volume buyers of a company's product or services. Some industries are reliant upon high volume, bulk purchases in order to lower costs and generate economies of scale. For example, the Brazilian JBS Corporation is the largest food processor of beef, chicken, and pork in the world. Farmers looking to sell their animal products to JBS must meet minimum standards in terms of size, volume, infrastructure, and regulatory compliance. Farmers that cannot meet those requirements must find smaller market segments to target for their products.

On the other end of the spectrum, small firm segmentation offers organisations the opportunity to target smaller firms that are sometimes overlooked by larger organisations. The market research industry is a good example where independent research firms are able to offer bespoke services to smaller clients. This enables them to conduct research on behalf of smaller firms that take into account these firms' market needs, budget, geographical area, and data requirements.

Industry type segmentation divides the market according to the business category where a customer operates. Organisations that operate within a business category will share the same wants and needs as other businesses within that category. Electrolux AB is a Swedish multinational company that uses industry type segmentation strategies for its business products. One division of the company manufacturers industrial kitchen equipment. The company tailors its marketing mix according to industry types.

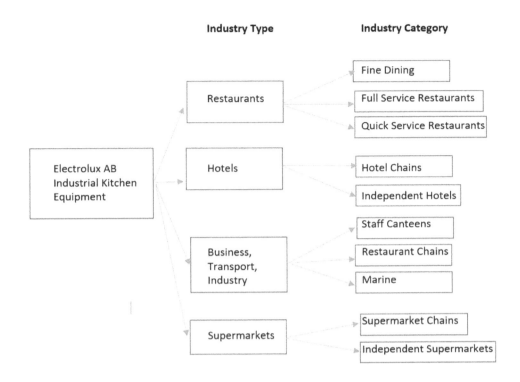

Industry Type

Industry Category

Restaurants
- Fine Dining
- Full Service Restaurants
- Quick Service Restaurants

Electrolux AB Industrial Kitchen Equipment

Hotels
- Hotel Chains
- Independent Hotels

Business, Transport, Industry
- Staff Canteens
- Restaurant Chains
- Marine

Supermarkets
- Supermarket Chains
- Independent Supermarkets

FIGURE 5.2
Electrolux segmentation strategy by industry type.

Figure 5.2 illustrates how Electrolux segments the market by industry type and then further segments the market by industry category. Rather than treating the market as an undifferentiated universal whole, this segmentation strategy enables Electrolux to differentiate different types of restaurants, hotels, businesses, and supermarkets. It then further segments the market by targeting specific businesses to differentiate the needs between fine dining, full service, and quick service restaurants.

GLOBAL MARKETING QUESTION

McDonald's is one of the largest and most successful fast-food franchises in the world. It operates in over 100 countries across the globe. The success of McDonald's has often been attributed to a universal appeal of quick service, low-cost food. At the same time, McDonald's uses different marketing strategies in different parts of the world.

How do McDonald's STP strategies differ in Japan, India, and the US?

Micro Segmentation

Purchasing criteria segmentation divides the market according to the choice criteria buyers use when purchasing different products and services. This segmentation approach mirrors the benefit segmentation approach used in consumer markets (Bonoma & Shapiro, 1984), where marketers segment markets based upon the benefits that customers seek. In business markets, there are a number of different benefit segmentation variables an organisation might choose when segmenting the market. They might target segments based on price, service levels, quality, levels of compliance, environmental sustainability, reputation, or lead time. These purchasing criteria are key considerations an organisation gives when selecting target segments for purchase.

The Apple Corporation uses purchasing criteria segmentation as a key component of its business strategy. It chooses its suppliers based upon their performance within the areas of labour and human rights, health and safety, and environmental sustainability. The company only selects those partner organisations that meet Apple's high standards of performance, which forms its supplier code of conduct. Each year it ranks its suppliers on a 100-point scale based upon their performance.

Apple's purchasing criteria of labour and human rights segments vendors based on factors that include anti-discrimination, prevention of involuntary labour, working hours, wages, and benefits. Its health and safety criteria segment based on occupational health, safety practices, and working conditions. Its environmental criteria selects vendors by environmental permits, hazardous waste and wastewater management, and resource consumption (Apple, 2020). It uses a combination of these purchasing criteria segmentation variables to determine organisations with which they will do business.

While there are a number of other factors that go into Apple's purchasing criteria segmentation strategy, these three segmentation variables help to guide Apple as an environmentally and socially responsible company. In this case, purchasing criteria helps the company to benchmark its performance on an annual basis to make a determination as to which customers are performing or underperforming. It can then make adjustments in segmentation strategy to improve year-on-year performance.

Buying situation segmentation groups the market according to the buying situation associated with an organisation's target markets. Generally, there are three types of customer buying situations: a straight rebuy, a modified rebuy, or a new buy. Each of these purchasing decisions is influenced by the experiences of target customers and whether they are repeat customers or new customers. From a segmentation perspective, the buying situation influences not only how an organisation clusters these buyers together into segments, but also how organisations can then tailor their market mix to target these customers.

The straight rebuy is often associated with existing business customers who reorder existing product or service inventories. An example of the straight rebuy would be to reorder items on an existing purchase order or from a catalogue. This type of business routine response behaviour can be serviced with customer service representatives trained to help customers reordering products and services.

A second buying situation category is the modified rebuy. In a modified rebuy, a business customer requires a modification to existing product, purchase order, or service inventory. This type of buying situation might require additional sales support or input from R&D in order to service this segment.

The final buying situation category is the new buy. New buys might be new customers or existing customers looking to purchase new products or services. Due to their lack of familiarity with an organisation or the risk associated with an existing customer purchasing a new product, these segments require intensive servicing. An organisation would need to utilise its sales team, upper management, and R&D department in order to meet the needs of this segment.

Decision-making segmentation is an approach that clusters organisations according to the buying process associated with procurement of goods and services. B2B decisions are collective decisions made by a number of different people within an organisation on behalf of the whole organisation. Studies have shown that, on average, 6.8 people are involved in making a high-involvement business purchase (Toman et al., 2017). Decision-making segmentation seeks to group buyers according to the internal organisational structure of buyers. This form of segmentation takes into account the influence of different decision makers within an organisation, as well as the decision-making process that buyers undergo when evaluating different suppliers of goods and services.

The decision-making unit structure of an organisation groups customers by the influence that different decision makers have within an organisation when making a purchasing choice. These include users, buyers, influencers, deciders, and gatekeepers (Webster & Wind, 1972). Scholars later added an additional user segment, the initiator (Kotler & Armstrong, 2020). This segmentation strategy can help marketers understand the different influences each of these six constituencies has on the decision-making process. Marketers can then tailor the information each group needs to ensure they have the necessary data and criteria to make a buying decision (Webster & Wind, 1972). By targeting subgroups within the decision-making unit structure, marketers can help to expedite the decision-making process.

The final micro segmentation variable to explore is the type of purchasing organisation. **Purchasing organisation segmentation** differentiates buyers based upon the degree to which they are centralised or decentralised. These two systems require different targeting approaches.

Centralised organisations have a central purchasing department that tightly controls the purchasing decisions for all of the different divisions within a company. These purchasing agents are highly specialised business buyers who deal with all organisational purchases. They have a great deal of experience in dealing with different suppliers and will be more familiar with different product and service offerings.

In a centralised system, category managers must seek monetary approval from the purchasing agents who control all expenditures. This centralised system means that buyers will purchase in high volumes, which require bulk discounts. Centralised buyers look for suppliers that can handle large demand at lower cost. Marketers must target their marketing mix to highly skilled, informed, and professional buyers who are familiar with different marketing offerings. Marketers must be able to sell products across different functional areas of the business. There will be instances where different departments in an organisation will have similar needs. A marketing organisation must be able to fulfil those needs that may cut across different functional areas of the business. In this case, total organisational knowledge of the buyers' needs must be serviced.

Decentralised organisations devolve purchasing decisions down the organisational hierarchy to category or line managers. This means that there are high levels of autonomy when making important buying decisions. The rationale for decentralising purchasing decisions is to improve the efficiency associated with decision-making. Purchasing decisions are integrated into managerial roles, so there is no extra overhead associated with a specialised purchasing department. Additionally, category or line managers are often more aligned with the needs of their department, and purchases can be made more quickly.

From a segmentation perspective, decentralised organisations require highly targeted and specialised marketing mixes. Marketers must constantly monitor decentralised organisations for employee turnover or job progress. Each new category manager, or line manager, might require up-to-date messaging on the products and services being offered by marketers.

Target Marketing

After the process of market segmentation, marketing organisations must determine which market segments they want to serve. Target marketing is the process identifying the specific marketing segments that an organisation wants to serve in the marketplace and then tailoring its marketing mix to reach those segments. This process involves evaluating different market segments on the basis of the sustainability, measurability, accessibility, and responsiveness of each segment, as mentioned in the introduction to this chapter. Targeting enables an organisation to concentrate its organisational resources by customising its marketing mix towards the wants and needs of specific segmented target groups. The general strategies marketers take when selecting target markets are undifferentiated, differentiated, and concentrated target marketing.

An **undifferentiated targeting** strategy is an approach where marketers view the market as a universal whole and do not differentiate segmentation characteristics. Undifferentiated targeting is a mass marketing approach that seeks to target consumers according to the similarities they share. The advantage of this approach is that it allows companies to appeal to a mass audience. It also enables marketers to tap into economies of scale by developing the same marketing mix for mass audiences. The same message, product, communications, and price can be used throughout. An undifferentiated approach can often be used in governmental health campaigns that raise public awareness about key issues.

While there are clear advantages to developing a single targeting approach to reach large segments, critics argue that an undifferentiated approach is not a viable marketing strategy, beyond public health campaigns. The issue here is that markets are so fragmented with different consumer demands, and it is unusual for a brand to appeal to a universal category of consumers. For example, take a basic commodity such as dairy milk. Even this category is benefit segmented and targeted towards different demand characteristics, such as whole milk, skimmed milk, and semi-skimmed milk. An undifferentiated approached is criticised for its lack of creativity, simplicity, and differentiation.

A **differentiated targeting** strategy identifies multiple segments from the segmentation process and tailors the marketing mix to reach those different segments. A good example of a differentiated targeted strategy is the Campbell Soup Company. The company produces a number of soup varieties that enable the company to reach different need-based segments. It produces soups that cater to vegetarians, meat eaters, low-sodium seekers, low fat, organic, and a healthy requests line. It also produces portable soups that can be sipped on the go. The company is using benefits sought and usage occasion segmentation as a targeting approach to reach multiple segments within the market.

There are a number of advantages to using a differentiated targeting strategy. One advantage to differentiated targeting is what is known as a brand halo effect. The brand halo is a type of brand equity where different items or product lines under an organisational umbrella are perceived as similar. In other words, consumers often equate similar functional and symbolic attributes to all of the products offered by the brand (Vázquez et al., 2002). Functional attributes are the needs that the product or service fulfils, and symbolic attributes involve the meaning of the brand and its brand identity. Once a consumer becomes brand loyal, they often equate functional and symbolic attributes to all of the organisation's products.

Another benefit to a differentiated strategy is the ability to serve a wide range of market needs. In the Campbell's Soup Company example, because Campbell's is able to meet so many diverse needs within the soup category, it is able to generate greater levels of sales, market share, and profit. This enables Campbell's to tap into economies of scale through similar marketing communication strategies and lower manufacturing and distribution costs.

While there are many benefits associated with a differentiated targeting strategy, there are drawbacks. One downside to this targeting approach is the potential for a lack of differentiation between products. A lack of differentiation between products means that a marketer has over-segmented the market and has not met the target marketing criteria of substantiality. This process is known as cannibalisation. In cannibalisation, the introduction of new products takes away market share from existing products. As highlighted earlier in this chapter, Coca-Cola Life represented an over-segmentation of the market, as it took away market share from Diet Coke and Coke Zero rather than generate new sales for the business.

A **concentrated targeting strategy** is when marketers target one specific segment of the market. This strategy, often referred to as focused or niche marketing, enables companies to concentrate their marketing resources on the wants and needs of smaller segments in the marketplace. These segments are sometimes overlooked by larger organisations. Concentrated marketing is a targeting strategy often used by organisations with limited resources, specialist categories, or in the luxury segment where business seek to target specific clientele.

An example of a concentrated targeting strategy can be seen with Lefty's: The Left Hand Store. Left-handed people make up 10% of the world's population (Searing, 2019). Lefty's is a store that caters exclusively to this concentrated segment by offering a tailored marketing mix focused on left-handed people. Its product offering ranges from office and school supplies to cooking equipment to gardening.

Another example of a concentrated targeting strategy that can be seen in the luxury segment is the German-based Marchi Mobile. Marchi Mobile manufactures luxury travel vehicles that are targeted towards affluent seniors. The vehicles are often referred to as 'houses on wheels' and are exclusive luxury recreational vehicles equipped with many of the traditional features of a home. The eleMMent version comes equipped with a bedroom and a king-sized bed, a shower, sky roof, and satellite TV. With a production run of fewer than ten vehicles per year and an asking price of $3 million, Marchi Mobile is pursuing a concentrated niche strategy that enables it to serve the market needs of a specific target market.

While there are advantages to targeting the needs of narrow segments, marketers must ensure that these segments are substantive enough to warrant a tailored marketing mix. In some cases, companies may choose market niches that are too small. In 1989, the Pepsi Corporation introduced Pepsi AM, a cola drink with 28% more caffeine than regular Pepsi. The drink was targeted towards people who did not like to drink tea or coffee in the morning. Pepsi AM used a concentrated targeting strategy geared towards the breakfast cola drinker and a specific usage occasion. The problem with this strategy was that Pepsi had so narrowly defined its benefit segmentation approach that consumers did not want to drink something different in the morning than they did the rest of the day. In this case, Pepsi too narrowly defined their targeting approach and withdrew the product due to poor sales. This example highlights the potential risks of too narrowly defining your targeting strategy.

MARKETING ASSISTANT TASK

Lee, in tackling the issue of the missing ZoFamilia customers both in Germany and worldwide, has come to very similar conclusions to Tannya and Dylan, and also has a mind's eye picture of the target couple which closely resembles Dylan's pen portrait description of the Chinese consumers he wishes to attract. As such, Lee is confident about understanding the desired segmentation strategy and is using this to decide how targeting should be done.

Suggest to Lee which mix of marketing communications media should be used to best reach the target audience for the ZoFamilia and the messages which Zomotor should transmit through each of them for optimal effect. For instance, perhaps you think that Lee should build the initial customer awareness of the product by advertising on national television channels between 6pm and 8pm on weekdays and convey a message which focuses on the safety of one's children. Perhaps you think Lee should convert early interest into dealership visits by communicating discounted lease offers via banner and skyscraper advertisements on social media sites. Or perhaps you think Lee should do something which focuses more closely on the desired segment rather than the mass market, to be more meaningful and less wasteful. Make six recommendations and explain your rationale for each.

Positioning

A market **position** is the way that consumers perceive a product or service relative to the competition. Position is a consumer-driven metric. Organisations conduct market research to understand how consumers perceive and value competing brand positions in the marketplace. The advantage of understanding a market position is that it represents a consumer point of view of competing marketplace offerings. Understanding a product's position helps organisations to overcome potential internal managerial biases about what an organisation thinks about its own market position, by deferring to consumer-driven perceptions. External consumer perceptions about different products or services are used to determine where different brands are positioned relative to each other.

Positioning is the managerial activity that marketers use to influence product or service characteristics within the marketplace. Positioning helps to influence how consumers perceive the different attributes associated with products or services. After marketers segment the market and narrow in on their target market, they use positioning as a way to make the product more appealing to the wants and needs of its target consumers. For example, marketers might leverage market R&D teams to improve product quality or perceived value. Marketing communication can help to shape brand identity and differentiate a brand from its competitors. Different price strategies can influence perceptions of marketplace prestige or value. Positioning is a key tool in how a product or service is positioned in the mind of a consumer. Consumer perceptions of a product or service offering are determined by different positioning bases.

A **positioning base** is a product or service attribute. It represents the characteristics that consumers might value or associate with a particular brand, group of brands, or product category. Consumers use different positioning bases to form their opinion of different products in a given industry. While there are a number of different positioning bases marketers might use that may vary by industry, here are some examples of positioning bases that are often universal across different product and service categories:

Price: Price is often an indicator of quality or value. A higher price denotes quality, whereas a lower price denotes value. Marketers can use price positioning to influence consumer perceptions about luxury, prestige, value, or savings.

Quality: While quality and price are interlinked, quality is its own positioning base. Marketers can use quality to denote value or savings when coupled with a low price strategy. Alternatively, high quality, durability, or luxury can be used on a positioning basis to charge a price premium.

Personality type: Personality type refers to a brand's identity and personality. Consumers identify with some brands as having certain personality types that marketing managers can cultivate. For example, Red Bull Energy drink has cultivated a brand personality type around thrill seeking, risk, and adventure.

End user: A product or service can be positioned for a particular end user, which might be based on psychographic or demographic characteristics. Psychographic characteristics allow marketers to position products based on lifestyle characteristics or consumer values. Demographic characteristics might appeal to specific genders or may use a unisex appeal desired by all genders.

Attribute: Attributes are the directly observable features a customer will receive from a product or service. These can be tangible or intangible.

A tangible attribute is a concrete, functional, or measurable attribute to a product. A tangible attribute for a personal computer might be the processing speed, the type of graphics card, or the RAM (random access memory). These are quantifiable product attributes consumers use to compare one product or brand with another.

Alternatively, attributes might be intangible or symbolic. For example, consumers may perceive certain products as more creative, innovative, or groundbreaking than other products. Apple has built competitive differentiation based upon consumer perceptions of the intangible characteristics of the brand. Consumers perceive Apple as a more innovative and creative brand than its rivals.

MARKETING DIRECTOR TASK

Tannya has been given the task of ascertaining how Zomotor owners and prospects perceive the brand in relation to the competition. Rather than attempting to compare Zomotor with every manufacturer selling cars in Mexico, Tannya will focus on Zomotor's 'competitor set' in the small car market – Citroen, Peugeot, Fiat, Nissan, and Toyota – because previous research found that buyers of small Zomotor cars also had these brands in their evoked sets (i.e. their unconscious shortlist of suppliers from which they select a winner).

Tannya recently read Al Ries and Jack Trout's (2001) seminal book, *Positioning*, to get some ideas on how to undertake consumer research on their perceptions of the Zomotor brand. As a result, Tannya has decided to use 'semantic differential' to map the prospects' minds by giving them a set of attributes and asking them to rank Zomotor and each competitor on a Likert scale of 1–10, giving a direct comparison. 'Price' and 'size' could be two useful but basic attributes to use. Help Tannya by suggesting another eight to ten attributes which can be used, and explain the commercial relevance of each to the task of positioning the brand.

The positioning bases outlined above are just a few examples of how marketers use positioning strategy to influence consumer perception of a product's position. One of the aims and objectives of a good positioning strategy is to help the organisation create a **unique selling proposition (USP)**. A USP is a value proposition that sets a product offer apart from that of its competition. It represents all of the primary benefits offered to the selected target market. It is the full mix of benefits received from the positioning bases and influences how consumers perceive an organisation's unique market position.

Repositioning

There are times when a brand's position within the marketplace can become stagnant. Consumers may not perceive a brand as offering a unique and differentiated brand position. **Repositioning** is the managerial activity where marketers try to change consumer perceptions of a brand by changing the product's positioning basis. Perhaps one of the most famous brand repositionings can be seen with Marlboro cigarettes. Marlboro was originally targeted towards women using a positioning base, known as the 'Mild as May' campaign, that appealed to the sophisticated, well-travelled woman.

By the 1950s Marlboro held less than 1% market share in the tobacco industry. It was at this time they turned to the Leo Burnett advertising agency, which shifted the product's positioning base towards men. It used imagery of ruggedness, masculinity, the outdoors, and the cowboy to reposition the brand towards a different target market. The result was the creation of the Marlboro man, which became one of the most successful brand repositioning strategies in the history of marketing.

MARKETING MANAGER TASK

Dylan is focusing on millennial consumers, as he believes there is potential to sell more small city cars to them. To do this effectively, Dylan needs to create some space between Zomotor and competitor brands in consumers' minds and differentiate the brand from the competition. This will prevent the products from becoming commoditised and enable him to charge a premium for the added value which customers perceive in Zomotor's products and the equity in the brand – or at least to defend the product's position in the marketplace without resorting to discounts or price reductions.

However, before Dylan can differentiate Zomotor's products through marketing, it must be decided in which category the company will differentiate from the following: product, service, channel, relationship, and reputation. (Dylan has ruled out price.) Suggest to Dylan in which category you think Zomotor is best equipped to differentiate against the competition, explaining why this is the case and the possible commercial benefits of doing so.

Chapter Summary

The objective of this chapter was to identify some of the basic tools available to marketers when segmenting and targeting the market. We highlighted the approach that marketers take when segmenting both consumer and business markets. We also discussed the importance of segmentation as a tool for marketers to better understand marketplace needs and wants. After marketers have segmented the market, we discussed the importance of consumer targeting, which is tailoring the marketing mix to reach specific segments. Targeting approaches range from broad, macro approaches to highlighting concentrated targeting strategies. After a marketer segments and target markets, the next step in the process is the ability to influence a target market, which is a process called positioning.

MARKETING DIRECTOR TASK

Lee is helping to plan a global television advertising campaign for Zomotor's small (B sector) car. It competes against models such as the Renault Clio, Volkswagen Polo, Ford Fiesta, Citroen C3, and Toyota Yaris, and is priced similarly. The television adverts will build the brand, convey the personality of the brand and the car, express some of the product benefits – although in an often implicit manner – and attempt to generate website traffic and dealer footfall. It is vital that the advertising agency creates some 'open space' between the new model and competitor products in the minds of consumers.

Using a storyboard technique which shows the most important scenes during the advert, suggest to Lee how this 'open space' might be achieved. Explain what visual content may set Zomotor apart from competitors, how the adverts may be presented to create maximum impact, what messages should be conveyed to create distinctiveness, and why your ideas are likely to be of particular appeal to the target audience.

Recommended Further Reading

Brotspies, H., & Weinstein, A. (2019). Rethinking business segmentation: A conceptual model and strategic insights. *Journal of Strategic Marketing, 27*(2), 164–176.

Dolnicar, S., Grün, B., & Leisch, F. (2018). *Market segmentation analysis: Understanding it, doing it, and making it useful* (p. 324). Springer Nature.

Wedel, M., & Kamakura, W. A. (2012). *Market segmentation: Conceptual and methodological foundations* (Vol. 8). Springer Science & Business Media.

Weinstein, A. (2013). *Handbook of market segmentation: Strategic targeting for business and technology firms* (3rd ed.). Routledge.

References

Apple. (2020). *Supplier responsibility: 2020 progress rep   ort.* https://www.apple.com/uk/supplier-responsibility/pdf/Apple_SR_2020_Progress_Report_EN.pdf

Black, I., & Veloutsou, C. (2017). Working consumers: Co-creation of brand identity, consumer identity and brand community identity. *Journal of Business Research, 70*, 416–429.

Blakemore, J. E. O., & Centers, R. E. (2005). Characteristics of boys' and girls' toys. *Sex Roles, 53* (9–10), 619–633.

Bonoma, T. V., & Shapiro, B. P. (1984). How to segment industrial markets. *Harvard Business Review, 64*, 104–110.

Bussey, K., & Bandura, A. (1999). Social cognitive theory of gender development and differentiation. *Psychological Review, 106*(4), 676.

Koch, R. (2011). *The 80/20 principle: The secret of achieving more with less: Updated 20th anniversary edition of the productivity and business classic*. Hachette.

Kotler, P., & Armstrong, G. (2020). *Principles of marketing* (global ed.). Pearson Education, Ltd.

Pasquarelli, A., & Schultz, E. J. (2019). Move over generation Z, generation alpha is the one to watch. *Advertising Age*. Retrieved July 4, from https://adage.com/article/cmo-strategy/move-gen-z-generation-alpha-watch/316314

Rao, P. M., & Balasubrahmanya, M. H. (2017). The rise of IT services clusters in India: A case of growth by replication. *Telecommunications Policy*, *41*(2), 90–105.

Reich, S. M., Black, R. W., & Foliaki, T. (2018). Constructing difference: LEGO® set narratives promote stereotypic gender roles and play. *Sex Roles*, *79*(5–6), 285–298.

Ries, A., & Trout, J. (2001). *Positioning: The battle for your mind*. McGraw Hill.

Roderick, L. (2017). Coca-Cola's Life's demise always felt inevitable. *Marketing Week*. https://www.marketingweek.com/coke-lifes-demise/

Searcey, D., & Richtel, M. (2017). Obesity was rising as Ghana embraced fast food: Then came KFC. *The New York Times*, p. 2.

Schouten, J. W., & McAlexander, J. H. (1995). Subcultures of consumption: An ethnography of the new bikers. *Journal of Consumer Research*, *22*(1), 43–61.

Searing, L. (2019). The big number: Lefties make up about 10% of the world. *Washington Post*. https://www.washingtonpost.com/health/the-big-number-lefties-make-up-about-10-percent-of-the-world/2019/08/09/69978100-b9e2-11e9-bad6-609f75bfd97f_story.html

Shridhar, A. (2021). *Understanding the path to purchase: 2021 global consumer types*. Euromonitor International. https://go.euromonitor.com/white-paper-consumers-210518-global-consumer-types.html

Smith, W. R. (1956). Product differentiation and market segmentation as alternative marketing strategies. *Journal of Marketing*, *21*(1), 3–8.

Toman, N., Adamson, B., & Gomez, C. (2017). The new sales imperative. *Harvard Business Review*, *95*(2), 118–125.

Vázquez, R., Del Rio, A. B., & Iglesias, V. (2002). Consumer-based brand equity: Development and validation of a measurement instrument. *Journal of Marketing Management*, *18*(1–2), 27–48.

Webster Jr, F. E., & Wind, Y. (1972). A general model for understanding organizational buying behavior. *Journal of Marketing*, *36*(2), 12–19.

Widen and Kennedy. (2020). *Old spice: Smell like a man, man*. https://www.wk.com/work/old-spice-smell-like-a-man-man/

Wind, Y., & Cardozo, R. N. (1974). Industrial market segmentation. *Industrial Marketing Management*, *3*(3), 153–165.

Glossary

Age segmentation: categorises a market by different age groupings

Behavioural segmentation: looks at patterns of behaviour that customers exhibit when they interact with different brands or services provided or when they purchase products

Benefits sought: a demand-side characteristic that identifies customers by the benefits they seek when purchasing different products and services

Buying situation: groups the market according to the buying situation associated with an organisation's target markets

Concentrated targeting: marketers target one specific segment of the market

Decision-making segmentation: an approach that clusters organizations according to the buying process associated with procurement of goods and services

Demographic segmentation: the process of dividing the market by age, family life cycle, income, gender, ethnicity, occupation, education level, and nationality

Differentiated targeting: identifies multiple segments from the segmentation process and tailors the marketing mix to reach those different segments

Family life cycle: targeting acknowledges the changing demographic nature to consumers whose income, marital status, age, employment status, and the presence and absence of raising children changes over time

Gender segmentation: a segmentation approach that targets consumers on the basis of their gender, sexual orientation, or gender identity

Geographic segmentation: the process of segmenting a market that targets customers by neighbourhood, city, region, country, or international region

Industry type segmentation: divides the market according to the business category where a customer operates

Macro segmentation: segments the market by geographical location, organisational size, and industry type

Market segmentation: a process where marketers differentiate customers, who share similar characteristics, into unique target market groups within a marketplace

Micro segmentation: divides the market by purchasing criteria, buying situation, decision-making unit, and purchasing organisation

Personality: a psychographic characteristic that represents one's personal characteristics, attitudes, and identity

Position: the way that consumers perceive a product or service relative to the competition

Positioning: the managerial activity that marketers use to influence product or service characteristics within the marketplace

Psychographic segmentation: divides the market by personality, lifestyle, motives, attitudes, and belief systems

Purchase occasion: divides the market by the timing of purchases during the year

Purchasing criteria: divides the market according to the choice criteria buyers use when purchasing different products and services

Repositioning: the managerial activity where marketers try to change consumer perceptions of a brand by changing a product's positioning basis

Target market: a group of customers that have specific wants and needs and also a willingness to buy

Target marketing: a process whereby marketers evaluate the attractiveness of different target market segments

Undifferentiated targeting: an approach where marketers view the market as a universal whole and do not differentiate segmentation characteristics

Unique selling proposition (USP): a value proposition that sets a product offer apart from that of its competition

Usage rate: divides the marketing according to the amount of a product or service that is purchased

Values: a psychographic variable that represents the importance of something to someone

---

Packaging, Positioning, Market Segmentation, and the Regulatory Environment Case Study: The Challenges Posed by Juul Cigarettes

Historically, tobacco companies used packaging, labelling, and marketing communications not only to designate size, quantity, and price but also as a key brand differentiation strategy to better position their products in the marketplace. The brand imagery, colour, and design of tobacco packaging worked in conjunction with advertising imagery in order to reinforce a distinctive brand identity. Tobacco's use of imagery reinforced notions of glamour, sophistication, heritage, and masculinity or femininity, and these became effective marketing tools in positioning different tobacco brands. Early evidence demonstrated how effective tobacco packaging and marketing positioning was in targeting specific segments of the population (Wakefield et al., 2002). Further studies showed that attractive packaging also undermines health warnings about the harmful effects of products (WHO, 2014).

In recent years, the tobacco industry has faced legal regulation of branding on their packaging and positioning strategies. Canada and Australia were early movers in creating legally mandated warning labels on cigarette labelling. In 2012, Australia enforced plain packaging and labelling that stripped tobacco companies of the ability to brand their packaging. Today, there are legal restrictions on tobacco packaging and labelling that require tobacco companies to feature large graphic packaging warnings in both imagery and text in 91 countries, affecting 3.9 billion people (WHO, 2019). While it might seem like a logical approach to use the legal environment to protect public health, countries like the US, which has large political pressure groups that exert influence on the legal environment, have not changed their tobacco packaging since 1984.

The legal environment extends to legal codes of practice within the advertising industry. In the UK and the US, the government gives legal authority to

continued

the Advertising Standards Authority and Food and Drug Administration, respectively, where legal codes of advertising practice enforce government regulations on advertising to children, taste, decency, product placement, political advertising, and causing offense. In the case of tobacco advertising, tobacco companies have been banned from advertising on TV and radio for over 50 years. However, because the legal environment interacts with other elements of the external environment where the pace of change differs, we can see changes in the technological environment of tobacco can outpace changes in the legal environment.

An inherent challenge in the external environment is a marketer's ability to manage a single variable in the external environment to match the changes that are occurring in other areas. For example, the rise of e-cigarettes and changes in social media are examples of rapid technological changes in the external environment that have important effects within the legal environment. The rise of the e-cigarette brand Juul is a good example of how marketers can sometimes take advantage of the slow pace of legal change, with questionable ethics. This can enable marketers to target vulnerable market segments.

The Juul cigarette is a battery-operated vaping device that heats pods of liquid which vaporise, delivering nicotine. Juul's liquid product line includes traditional tobacco flavours as well as fruit, mango, mint, and cucumber flavours, which helps to broaden its appeal. Because e-cigarettes had positioned themselves as smoking cessation products and as 'safer' alternatives to traditional cigarettes, they escaped initial scrutiny from governing bodies such as the US Food and Drug Administration (FDA). Juul's core advertising slogan encouraged consumers to 'Make the Switch'.

The core of Juul's advertising campaign was to use young influencers as spokespersons for the company coupled with a heavy use of Instagram, Twitter, Facebook, and hashtag extensions as advertising tools. The use of social media gave Juul greater license to market its products than traditional broadcast media, where there are tighter regulatory controls. While most e-cigarettes have positioned themselves as smoking cessation products to help people quit smoking, Juul took an advertising approach that specifically targeted teens and young adults. The term 'juuling' became synonymous with teens' use of e-cigarettes.

Researchers at Stanford University collected thousands of social media posts from the inception of Juul's marketing campaign and found that the brand used advertising strategies that were specifically targeted towards teens and young adults. Researchers found Juul's advertising approach to be "patently youth oriented" (Jackler et al., 2019, p. 1). It depicted smoking as pleasurable, youthful, social, and fun. As youth smoking rates in the US began to grow exponentially, especially among children aged 15–17, Juul faced increased public scrutiny from the FDA, which

continued

PHOTO 5.7
A JUUL point of purchase display.

included a federal raid that seized thousands of documents related to its marketing practice. Facing the potential of an outright ban, the company suspended all media advertising, withdrew its flavoured pods, and forced the resignation of its CEO.

Building upon your previous knowledge of the marketing environment and your knowledge of STP, what do you think about Juul's approach? What do you think about the relationship between the legal environment and market STP?

Bibliography

Jackler, R. K., Chau, C., Getachew, B. D., Whitcomb, M., Lee-Heidenreich, J., Bhatt, A., & Rama-murthi, D. (2019). *JUUL advertising over its first three years on the market.* SRITA White Paper. https://tobacco-img.stanford.edu/wp-content/uploads/2021/07/21231836/JUUL_Marketing_Stanford.pdf

Wakefield, M., Morley, C., Horan, J. K., & Cummings, K. M. (2002). The cigarette pack as image: New evidence from tobacco industry documents. *Tobacco Control, 11*(suppl 1), i73–i80.

World Health Organization. (2014). *Evidence brief: Plain packaging of tobacco products: Measures to decrease smoking initiation and increase smoking cessat ion.* http://www.euro.who.int/__data/assets/pdf_file/0011/268796/Plain-packaging-of-tobacco-products,-Evidence-Brief-Eng.pdf?ua=1

World Health Organization. (2019). *WHO report on the global tobacco epide mic.* https://apps.who.int/iris/bitstream/handle/10665/325968/WHO-NMH-PND-2019.5-eng.pdf?ua=1

Introduction

Products are objects, items, and goods which may be bought or sold. They may be as small as a pin or screw or as large as a building or supertanker. Some are used to undertake specific functions and others for more enjoyable, hedonic purposes. They are usually visible and tangible, but not always. For instance, a steel manufacturer may buy oxygen.

Although customers often believe that their product purchasers are determined overwhelmingly by the core product itself, those decisions are usually heavily influenced by other factors or characteristics surrounding the core product (Singh, 2012). Some products, such as salt or petrol, are commoditised. Others, such as consumer electronic goods, are extremely differentiated from competitors' offerings, necessitating fastidious planning, manufacturing, and marketing (Araujo & Spring, 2006). The main custodian of a product within its organisation is usually a product manager, or perhaps a brand manager. However, numerous stakeholders, especially within the marketing function of a firm, contribute to the success or failure of a product within the marketplace. It is crucial for these people to research and understand the needs and wants of potential customers, to design their products to deliver value to those customers, and to ensure that those customers perceive the value which they have received. In this chapter we will define some of the key characteristics of products and examine the changes through

PHOTO 6.1
A hedonic product. This ice cream sundae is not simply for sustenance but for indulgent pleasure.

which products pass during their life span. We will discuss the importance of marketers nuancing their strategies to conditions within the external environment and explore how different types of customers affect the success of products over time.

What Is a Product?

Although we often think of products as visible, tangible objects, they are more correctly a collection of benefits which are conveyed by the seller to the buyer. For example, when we buy an Apple iPhone, we also receive the packaging, the box, the instruction booklet, the brand artwork, and perhaps a charger or SIM card. The **primary characteristics** of a product are those which are shared by all competing goods within a specific product category. Using the example of our iPhone, its primary characteristics – which it shares with the Samsung Galaxy and other rival products – are that it has a touch screen which enables users to make phone calls, send texts and emails, access the internet, and watch visual content. However, **auxiliary characteristics** are those features and benefits which differentiate it physically from its competitors and may provide Apple with a competitive advantage or unique selling proposition (USP), which entices consumers to buy from Apple. When brand and product managers are managing their product portfolios, they are careful to understand the points of parity (POP), and – respectively, the characteristics of their products which are shared with competitors (POP) or unique (POD; Keller et al., 2002).

NEW MEDIA QUESTION

Look through your social media platforms to see what products are advertised by the selling brand, promoted by social media influencers, or even
discussed by your friends. Ask yourself the following questions: How are
these products relevant to your needs? How are they presented on social
media? How are the consumers and users of the product portrayed? How has seeing these products on social media changed your feelings towards them? Has it
influenced your intention to buy any of them? This is a 'netnographic' approach
(Kozinets, 2019) to understanding products and their audience members, as it uses
the internet to gather data and insights. Now, ask yourself: How have I presented
products online? When and how have I shown photos of products, discussed them,
or reacted to others' content about products? This is 'autonetnographic' research
(Kozinets, 2019), using the internet to research your own interactions with products.

Features and Benefits

Perhaps you noticed in the description above that auxiliary characteristics often include benefits, whereas primary characteristics do not. It is crucial for the marketer to understand the differences between a feature and a benefit.

A **feature** is an attribute with which we can judge a product against its competitors. For example, if you were selling a printer or photocopier to an office manager, the features which you might explain could include its size, how many decibels it produces during operation, and how many standard sheets of paper it can print in a minute. These characteristics may also be meaningful and important to the customer, enabling them to eliminate unsuitable products from their decision-making process. However, what customers really seek are benefits. The **benefit** of a small printer is that it takes up less office space and does not get in the way of colleagues. The benefit of a quieter printer is that it does not disturb people's concentration. And the benefit of a faster printer is that it does not interrupt colleagues' productivity to the same extent as a slower one. For this reason, it is important that products not only carry features which make them attractive, but that these translate into benefits which are readily recognised and valued by the customer. If the customer does not recognise that the printer is small, quiet, and fast, they will be

PHOTO 6.2
A high-quality product. Doc Martens footwear is manufactured and tested to the most rigorous standards.

TABLE 6.1

Examples of customer benefits from different product types.

Benefit	Example Product
saves you time/effort	vacuum cleaner/food blender
saves you money	solar panel
saves you space	sofa bed
keeps you safe	crash helmet
keeps you comfortable	waterproof coat
saves you expertise/training	'just-add-water' concrete mix
confers status upon you	expensive wristwatch
makes you feel good about yourself	expensive shoes
supports your relationships	house 'granny annexe'
delivers gratification	chocolate bar

no more likely to buy it than a competitor's larger, noisier, and slower printer. Likewise, even if the customer is aware of these product advantages, if they do not consider the advantages to be important to them, the printer manufacturer is still unlikely to instil in the customer a commitment to purchase. When simplified, there are only a handful of benefits, but they are very powerful, as we can see in Table 6.1.

Types of Product

Products are categorised in several ways:

1. By who will use the product

   Consumer products for private individuals

   Business-to-business (B2B) products for organisations

2. By when and how consumers buy the product

   Convenience products (e.g. soap, coffee) are bought routinely and inexpensively to satisfy a basic need, so the consumer spends little time deciding

   Shopping products (e.g. smartphones, sofas) are bought infrequently and are more expensive, so the consumer has a much longer decision-making process

   Speciality products (e.g. guitar effect pedals) involve carefully planned, infrequent purchases where no substitute product would be suitable

   Unsought products (e.g. central heating boilers) are usually bought without planning, due either to a sudden need or as a favourable reaction to marketing

3. By when and how businesses buy the product

   Core products or **generic products** (e.g. photocopiers and printers) are the 'main' products which organisations plan to buy

   Expected products (e.g. photocopiers and printers plus toner cartridge and paper) are the core products plus the expected, necessary extras

   Augmented products (e.g. automatic, built-in print-out binder) are the differentiating features which persuade the buyer to select one particular supplier's product

   Potential products (e.g. photocopier/printer with built-in scanner, print-out binder, postal scales, and franking machine) are what the customer would wish to buy if it was made, available, and affordable

4. By what businesses will do with the product

   Raw materials are processed into something else to be sold (e.g. wool into knitwear)

   Component parts are assembled into something to be sold (e.g. brake pads into cars)

   Major equipment is used to undertake the firm's core business (e.g. industrial knitting machine)

   Accessory equipment is used to undertake the form's non-core functions (e.g. fire alarms)

   Process materials are specialised materials or parts which will enable manufacture of a product to be sold (e.g. platinum thread for catalytic converters)

   Consumable supplies do not become part of the firm's sold products (e.g. gravel for their car park)

   B2B services are intangibles (e.g. consultancy, insurance, or cleaning)

5. By the newness of the product – the Booz Allen Hamilton (1982) typology

   New-to-the-world products are totally new

   New-to-the-firm products have only previously been made by other firms

   Product line additions expand upon the firm's current offerings (e.g. if Heinz started selling Caribbean refried beans)

   Amendments to existing products (e.g. laundry detergent 'with a powerful new formula')

   Repositionings take products into a different market, or give them a different position within the same market (e.g. Lucozade redesigning its offering to sell it as a sports drink rather than a health tonic)

   Cost reductions (e.g. a slight decrease in the size of a chocolate bar) reduce a firm's expenditure whilst attempting to preserve profitability

---

STAKEHOLDER QUESTION

What consumable supplies do you think a motor vehicle dealership might need to purchase if it is to be successful in attracting visitors and persuading them to buy a car? Make a list of the ten most important things and prepare to explain their significance.

If you get stuck, try remembering what the inside and outside of a car dealership looks like; what objects does it have, and why?

New Product Development

Designing, testing, manufacturing, and marketing a new product represents a significant investment of time and money. If a firm gets it wrong – perhaps by making something which its target market does not like or need – it can lose money, market share, and reputation, and may even go out of business. Before embarking upon the process, a firm must ensure that it has adequate time, money, information, and staff resources to complete it successfully. It must also draw upon analyses of its external environments to ascertain if the new product satisfies a current or future customer need at a price they will pay, and if this brings a competitive advantage which will translate into increased profitability or business stability (Cooper, 2019).

Firms may undertake **proactive new product development (NPD)**, in which they try to add customer value to attain a competitive advantage, or **reactive NPD**, in which they seek to defend against a proactive competitor, changing customer demand, or an obsolescent product line-up. NPD project teams should be drawn from all disciplines within the business (e.g. production, sales, marketing, legal, finance, R&D) and should include other stakeholders such as retailers, customers, and prospects wherever possible. This provides a variety of perspectives and avoids 'silo thinking' (Ernst et al., 2010).

The New Product Development Process

Although numerous suggested variations of the NPD process exist, what follows are the most important stages:

Product strategy: The firm ascertains how a new product might serve its overall business objectives and customer needs by complementing its other products.

Conceptualisation and ideation: The NPD team brainstorms ideas which may fulfil the brief. At this stage, staff should be encouraged not to filter their own ideas but to raise even outlandish suggestions (Schemmann et al., 2016).

Idea screening: The team then narrows down those ideas to remove any which do not fit the brief, which cannot be made, or which could not be marketed effectively.

Product viability testing: The chosen ideas are presented to participating internal and external stakeholders for their input.

Business scrutiny: The potential contribution of the product to the firm's finances is evaluated, along with the impact which it might have upon the product range and upon competitor responses.

Product refinement: R&D, production, and engineering staff refine the design to produce prototypes.

- Product strategy
- Conceptualisation & ideation
- Idea screening
- Product viability testing
- Business scrutiny
- Product refinement
- Market feasibility
- Commercialisation

FIGURE 6.1
Stages in the new product development process (adapted from Cooper & Kleinschmidt, 1988).

> **Market feasibility**: Market researchers collect data from potential customers to ascertain how many would buy the product and for what price.

> **Commercialisation**: A product idea which makes it this far is put into production, and the marketing function prepares to launch the product.

In addition to these stages in the NPD progress, firms may also source new product ideas, or be stimulated into seeking them, for the following reasons:

1. A competitor is having great success with a product which the firm can replicate profitably.
2. The firm can make a product which is superior to its predecessor due to technological advances.
3. It is commercially sustainable to design and market variations of existing products.
4. There is a gap in the market presented by an unfulfilled customer need or want.
5. Socio-economic conditions have evolved, demanding new solutions to new issues.
6. A business partner, such as a consultancy or even a channel intermediary, has generated a viable new product idea.

SUSTAINABILITY QUESTION

Imagine that you are a marketer working in a consumer electronics firm's NPD team tasked with introducing a new smartphone. How would you ensure that the smartphone is as environmentally sound as possible? What steps could you take to embed and promote the sustainability agenda throughout the NPD process? Who might you wish to include in the process, and for what purpose? Make a bullet point list of your ideas and consider why each suggestion may be effective.

Age and Obsolescence in Products

With time, even well-considered products usually become dated, unfashionable, or technologically obsolete. Even when ageing products continue to sell in sufficient volumes and at profitable levels, it may still be wise to update them or remove them for a number of reasons: (i) they may undermine the freshness of the firm's brand and taint customers' brand perceptions (Burns, 2016); (ii) they may soak up marketing budget for a minimal return on investment; (iii) it may be cumbersome for a firm to focus on many different products; and (iv) it may be impossible to manufacture many different products at one time due to factory capacity.

The Boston Consulting Group (BCG) Matrix

The Boston Consulting Group developed a matrix to help practitioners to analyse what their products contribute to their companies. Although it is rather simplistic (like many models that use a 2 × 2 matrix), it nonetheless encourages managers to be critical (Madsen, 2017). In the BCG matrix, a **star** enjoys a high growth rate and market share. Whilst the current marketing costs outstrip sales revenue, it is expected that once the product has become established against the competition, marketing spend can be decreased and the product will generate a healthy product. Therefore, firms should invest in their stars. A **cash cow** is a mature product with a large market share. It used to be a star but is now well established and selling in as much volume as is ever likely to be achievable. The firm should therefore 'milk' it to fund its stars. A **dog** has a low market share and low prospects for growth. Whilst the product may be profitable, it may be wise for the firm to redeploy its resources to fund a new product with the potential to generate better sales volume and profit. The **question mark** (or **problem child**) presents the marketing team with a great deal of uncertainty – with investment and direction, it may become a star and very profitable, but it may also fall by the wayside. Therefore, the firm should analyse it in more detail to establish its viability.

MARKETING ASSISTANT TASK

Zomotor would like to develop a new product which is not a car or van but which takes advantage of their engine technology. Zomotor Mexico has been invited to provide possible ideas, and Tannya has been tasked with making sure that the idea generation process runs smoothly. Help Tannya by suggesting who she should invite to take part, what types of products they may wish to consider, and any other operational issues which she might encounter.

The Product Life Cycle

Have you noticed that a car, smartphone, or television set which seemed modern five or ten years ago now seems completely out of date? Perhaps it lacks the recent innovations which are widely expected in current products, such as blind-spot cameras on cars. Perhaps it includes features which have been made superfluous to requirements by newer technology, such as a car's compact disc player. Or perhaps it just looks old-fashioned, unstylish, awkward, and clumsy. This is largely because most products – apart from more commoditised products such as salt or petrol – have a life cycle. As each new competitor product is launched, it changes customers' expectations of that product category and what to demand. Over time, the cumulative effect of technological change and repeated competitor product launches chip away at a product's freshness until it must be modernised or replaced (Stark, 2016). Failing to do this would result in dwindling sales volumes and profits and damage to the brand through an association with substandard products. The product life cycle (PLC) model is a popular marketing model which suggests that products pass through five stages in their life cycle, each with its own characteristics and significance (Table 6.2).

TABLE 6.2

The product life cycle model.

PLC Stage	Characteristics and Their Significance
Pre-launch	R&D and planning takes place
	Heavy marketing spend on pre-launch and launch activities – especially to build awareness of the product amongst the target market
	No income yet from sales
	The product does not face any competition yet
Introduction	The product is launched, and it may also be tweaked to overcome any teething problems
	Marketers encourage target audience members to try the product
	Marketing still needs to raise market awareness but also to provide important information about product features and benefits
	Sales income grows quickly but is usually insufficient to cover heavy marketing spend
	The product faces low competition
Growth	Sales increase rapidly
	Marketers aim to increase sales, encourage retailers to be productive, and amend prices and specifications to raise profitability
	Profits increase rapidly and peak
	The market share grows
	The product faces moderate competition

continued

TABLE 6.2 (CONTINUED)

PLC Stage	Characteristics and Their Significance
Maturity	Sales plateau and begin a gradual decline
	Marketers aim to remind customers of the product and its appeal
	Customer retention is especially important, often through relationship marketing
	The product faces intense competition
Decline	Sales of the product, and often sales within the product category more broadly, decrease
	Profits decline
	Marketers may wish to improve the product or introduce a product line extension, but may prefer for the product to be withdrawn from the market and replaced
	The product faces moderate competition

METRICS QUESTION

Product managers use many metrics to ascertain the success of their products, and to decide what actions to make to improve their performance. If you were the product manager for a global athleisure brand, what metrics would you use to measure the commercial performance of your leggings and gym tanks? List four or five metrics and make a note of your reasons for choosing them. Remember: you may choose marketing or more general business metrics, and even suggest your own – just as long as there is a viable commercial rationale for doing so.

Many organisations sell multiple products. If this is the case, they should ensure that the products are at different stages of the PLC whenever possible. If not, each product will pass through the resource-intensive, loss-making pre-launch and introduction stages at the same time, putting the firm under severe financial and logistical pressures. Moreover, it would also mean that each product will enter the decline stage simultaneously, damaging the brand image and reputation.

MARKETING MANAGER TASK

In China, Zomotor's mid-sized car is continuing to sell well four years after its initial release, but newer competitor products are beginning to take market share and undermine its appeal to the mass market. As Zomotor aims to replace each model within its range every 6–7 years, the Zomotor China marketing manager, Dylan, has been asked to draw up a list of possible actions which the marketing team could take to slow its decline in sales volumes and remind customers of its attractiveness. Help Dylan by suggesting eight actions which the marketing team might consider. For each, give bullet points assessing its benefits and limitations to the brand and to its customers.

Diffusion of Innovations (Rogers, 1962)

A major reason for the PLC is that customers are not one homogenous group but differ greatly in their expectations of newness, prestige, and price. This is particularly pronounced in product categories like consumer electronics (e.g. smartphones), in which constant technological innovation can result in significant product improvements from one year to the next. To analyse which customers are likely to buy at each stage of the PLC, marketers use the diffusion of innovations (Rogers, 1962) model. This is closely related to the PLC model, as it shows sales volumes as a bell curve, rising and falling as the product ages. The model identifies five categories of consumer. Although the proportions of customers in each category may differ a little between product categories (Vargo et al., 2020), the model is broadly applicable to products which use a high degree of innovation (e.g. smartphones, electric cars). The consumer categories and their characteristics are shown in Table 6.3.

These findings are very significant to marketers. As we will explore in Chapter 8, firms often structure their prices to cater to the cost-consciousness of consumers in each of the five categories, dropping prices as they run out of customers in one category and move on to the next. Firms also need to communicate the product and its brand differently to each of the five consumer types. To appeal to innovators, firms may advertise in specialist publications such as *Electronics Weekly* or *Diesel World*, provide them with

TABLE 6.3

The diffusion of innovations model consumer categories and characteristics.

Consumer Category	Characteristics
Innovators	Approximately 2.5% of the market
	Highly motivated to try the very latest technology
	Often work in technologically oriented jobs
	Extremely knowledgeable in their preferred product category
	Willing to pay very high prices for new, untried products
	Willing to tolerate a high risk of the product failing or experiencing teething problems
	Are likely to give comprehensive feedback to the manufacturer

continued

TABLE 6.3 (CONTINUED)

Consumer Category	Characteristics
Early adopters	Approximately 13.5% of the market
	Like to have recently launched products and to keep up with (or ahead of) their peers
	Often work in managerial roles
	Willing to pay high prices and tolerate some risk, but much less than the innovators
	Usually relatively affluent – either wealthy or earning comfortably more than the national average wage
	Likely to be well-respected amongst their extensive peer group
	Very influential in trying the product and communicating their opinions to others; they act as a bridge between the innovators and manufacturer on one side and the mass market on the other
Early majority	Approximately 34% of the market
	Like to have relatively fresh products but are not competitive about discovering the latest trend
	May pay a little above the average price for a good-quality product
	Accepts that product failures sometimes occur, but would not accept a high risk of failure
	Careful with their money
	The nearest to an 'average' consumer
Late majority	Approximately 34% of the market
	Very similar to the early majority, but a little more price conscious and risk averse
	Very careful with their money
	Willing to wait until a product is very well established before buying
Laggards	Approximately 16% of the market
	Very risk-averse and price-conscious customers
	Likely to deliberate over purchase decisions and have a very long decision-making process
	Often fearful or suspicious of new technology or lack confidence in their ability to use it
	Willing to wait until a product is ageing to get the cheapest possible price

demonstrator products, invite them to pre-launch events, and seek their opinion. However, when marketing to laggards much later in the PLC, firms are likely to rely more on retailer displays, mass media advertising (if any), and low pricing. Some people may belong to one consumer type when buying in one product category (e.g. surfboards) but another consumer type in another product category (e.g. kitchenware), due to their

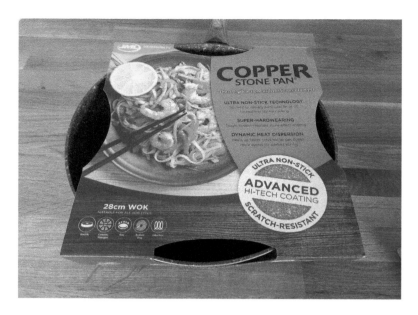

PHOTO 6.3
A product with a powerful benefit. As this is an ultra-non-stick wok that requires no oil, users can enjoy crispier stir fries and less calorific food.

personal interests and hobbies. This further complicates the marketer's task, especially in terms of market segmentation and their choice of marketing communications.

MARKETING DIRECTOR TASK

As Zomotor's global marketing director, Lee has noticed that the approaches taken by the firm towards early adopter and early majority customers – particularly in Zomotor's marketing communications – are very similar and fail to account for the psychographic differences between the two market segments. Write a brief report (500–1,000 words) for Lee, suggesting ways in which Zomotor might more meaningfully differentiate between early adopters and early majority audiences through its marketing communications. Think about aspects such as the messages conveyed, the tone used, the benefits presented, and the promotions offered.

Ansoff's (1957) Matrix

Ansoff's (1957) matrix (Figure 6.2) is one of many quadrant models beloved by marketers. Whilst it is similarly oversimplistic to the BCG matrix (De Waal, 2016), it nevertheless

	Existing Product	New Product
Existing Market	**Market Penetration**	**Product Development**
New Market	**Market Development**	**Diversification**

FIGURE 6.2
Ansoff's (1957) matrix.

offers a generalised insight into what product strategy firms may wish to take, based upon a product's age and the age of the market in which it competes.

Market penetration is considered the most appropriate product strategy for a firm whose well-established product competes in a well-established market. Penetration means steadily increasing market share through aggressive marketing which encourages consumers to switch from rival products to theirs.

Market development is usually favoured by firms whose existing, established product is competing in a new market. In this case, the focus would not be on making changes to the product but on pushing the current product into new segments – perhaps based on geographical location, consumer lifestyle, customer age, and so forth.

Product development is usually pursued when the product is new (or recently improved or modified), but the market is not. Marketers will be familiar with the people to whom they need to sell but must strive to sell new products to them.

Diversification is resource intensive and also entails a high degree of risk, as the firm would need to sell new, unfamiliar products to new, unfamiliar customers, thereby compounding the unfamiliarity. Such a strategy can online be pursued if the organisation is strong financially and well resourced.

GLOBAL MARKETING QUESTION

Imagine you are the commercial director (in charge of sales and marketing) for an international chain of mid-range burger restaurants. Although your UK locations remain popular with diners, your sites in mainland Europe struggle badly. Therefore, you have decided to close loss-making sites in France and Germany whilst opening sites in Ireland and the US, where you plan to develop and sell dishes specific to those markets. What are the main challenges and risks the new restaurants will face? How might they mitigate these issues? What sort of information might they need when deciding what products to offer, and to whom? Make a mind map to express your ideas.

PHOTO 6.4
A simple, inexpensive product which is extremely useful and environmentally sound.
This IKEA smartphone stand has just one component.

Chapter Summary

In this chapter, we have explored the major concepts which shape the products we know and love. Products that are usually visible and tangible, which we can take away from the place of purchase to use later, should convey and fulfil one or more customer benefits to be differentiated from the competition. Marketers categorise products in several ways – by newness, user, use, purchase method, and consumer type – and should be important stakeholders in a multidisciplinary new product development process rather than simply being charged with producing sales. However, the passage of time, evolution of customer demands, and competitive actions age products, reducing demand for them and often making them obsolete. Therefore, marketers must continuously nuance their strategies to fit the needs and expectations of different market segments and product competences.

Key Learning Outcomes

▶ Products may be categorised by who uses them, when, how, and for what purpose.

▶ The product life cycle (PLC) demands that products are marketed according to their age.

▶ Successful products require a well-structured new product development process.

▶ The diffusion of innovations model dictates which customer types buy a product at various stages of the PLC.

Recommended Further Reading

Cooper, R. G. (2019). The drivers of success in new-product development. *Industrial Marketing Management, 76,* 36–47.

Madsen, D. O. (2017). Not dead yet: The rise, fall and persistence of the BCG matrix. *Problems and Perspectives in Management, 15*(1), 19–34.

Vargo, S. L., Akaka, M. A., & Wieland, H. (2020). Rethinking the process of diffusion in innovation: A service-ecosystems and institutional perspective. *Journal of Business Research, 116,* 526–534.

References

Ansoff, H. I. (1957). Strategies for diversification. *Harvard Business Review, 35*(5), 113–124.

Araujo, L., & Spring, M. (2006). Services, products, and the institutional structure of production. *Industrial Marketing Management, 35*(7), 797–805.

Booz, E. G., Allen, J. L., & Hamilton, C. L. (1982). *New products management for the 1980s.* Phase II.

Burns, B. (2016). Re-evaluating obsolescence and planning for it. In *Longer lasting products* (pp. 65–86). Routledge.

Cooper, R. G., & Kleinschmidt, E. J. (1988). Resource allocation in the new product process. *Industrial Marketing Management, 17*(3), 249–262.

De Waal, G. A. (2016). An extended conceptual framework for product-market innovation. *International Journal of Innovation Management, 20*(5), 1640008.

Ernst, H., Hoyer, W. D., & Rübsaamen, C. (2010). Sales, marketing, and research-and-development cooperation across new product development stages: Implications for success. *Journal of Marketing, 74*(5), 80–92.

Keller, K. L., Sternthal, B., & Tybout, A. (2002). Three questions you need to ask about your brand. *Harvard Business Review, 80*(9), 80–89.

Kozinets, R. V. (2019). *Netnography: The essential guide to qualitative social media research.* Sage.

Rogers, E. M. (1962). *Diffusions of innovations.* Free Press of Glencoe.

Schemmann, B., Herrmann, A. M., Chappin, M. M., & Heimeriks, G. J. (2016). Crowdsourcing ideas: Involving ordinary users in the ideation phase of new product development. *Research Policy, 45*(6), 1145–1154.

Singh, M. (2012). Marketing mix of 4P's for competitive advantage. *IOSR Journal of Business and Management, 3*(6), 40–45.

Stark, J. (2016). Product lifecycle management. *Product Lifecycle Management, 2*, 1–35.

Glossary

Amendments to existing products: changes made to products which are already sold

Augmented product: the product and differentiating features which customers value

Auxiliary characteristics: the characteristics that differentiate a product from its competitors

B2B product: a product normally sold to a business

Consumer product: a product normally sold to private individuals

Convenience product: a product bought routinely to address a consumer's basic need

Core product: the main product which the buyer plans to buy

Expected product: the core product, plus any additional items which the buyer expects to buy with it

Generic product: see *core product*

New-to-the-firm product: a product only previously sold by other firms

New-to-the-world product: an entirely new product

Points of difference (PODs): ways in which a product is different from its competitors

Points of parity (POPs): ways in which a product is the same as its competitors

Potential product: what the customer would buy if it were attainable

Primary characteristics: product characteristics shared with competing goods

Product line addition: a product which expands the firm's offerings

Repositionings: amendments designed to take the product into a different market position

Shopping product: a product bought infrequently by consumers, usually after deliberation

Speciality product: a product bought infrequently by consumers that has no substitutes

Unsought product: a product bought without planning due to a sudden need or a reaction to marketing

---

Product Management Case Study: IKEA Smartphone Stands

Swedish furniture and homeware retailer, IKEA, is a much-loved and well-recognised brand throughout Europe and beyond. Its brand is conveyed not just through its products but also through its distinctive blue and yellow store exteriors (which represent the colours of Sweden's national flag), its IKEA Family loyalty cards, its inexpensive but high-quality store restaurants (especially its famed meatballs and lingonberry sauce), and the leisurely browsing

continued

experience which it offers shoppers. Consumers do not only visit IKEA stores to service a specific product requirement and leave. Many visit with family members to be inspired and entertained by IKEA's product displays, which enable customers to imagine how they could transform their homes into an ideal.

Whilst IKEA is famous for its flat-pack furniture, which is robust yet easy to assemble by even the least technically minded customers, it also sells a broad range of simple, low-priced items which are designed to solve consumers' day-to-day issues. Sometimes these are issues which consumers may find irksome, but they have unconsciously accepted them and do not actively seek a solution to them – such as holding or propping up a smartphone whilst watching a video. An example is the BERGENES 'holder for mobile phone/tablet', currently priced at £1.50 in the UK. The product is simplicity itself: a tile of wood approximately 128 mm × 80 mm × 18 mm with a narrow, angled, half-depth slot (just wider than a smartphone) cut across the width of each of the larger two faces. It is a single-component block of wood, smoothed and rounded at the edges and presented in a light colour, natural wood finish. On its website, IKEA introduces the BERGENES, and its closely related products, with these words: "Whether you're double-checking a recipe while elbows deep in dough or watching a series while commuting on the train, life throws up lots of reasons to need easy hands-free tablet and mobile viewing. With our range of mobile and tablet stands, you're all set to get the most out of your device". The BERGENES may have few features but can deliver a variety of rudimentary yet valuable consumer benefits.

Imagine you work for IKEA, developing new products which are simple, low cost, and intended to solve those small, barely perceivable issues which consumers face in their everyday lives. You need to work within IKEA's brand ethos, using recyclable and regenerative materials such as wood. You should keep your products simple and functional yet elegant. Your aim is to instil in customers a sense of surprised delight when they first encounter your products. Imagine a customer seeing BERGENES for the first time, and saying to their family, 'Oh, look at that! What a clever idea! That would make watching YouTube videos so much more comfortable and enjoyable. And at that price, we should just get one each for the family'. That is the kind of reaction which you want to recreate.

Your task is to identify one everyday consumer need or a situation which would benefit from a simple solution. Using Cooper and Kleinschmidt's (1988) New Product Development Process as a foundation, make a Gantt chart to show what actions you will undertake/oversee, in which sequence, and when. Then

continued

173

make bullet point lists to indicate (i) which stakeholders you will involve and how, (ii) the benefits which the product must provide, and (iii) your broad strategy for promoting and launching the product, which will be sold in IKEA's stores and on their website.

Source

IKEA. (2022). Retrieved January 27, 2022, from https://www.ikea.com/gb/en/cat/mobile-tablet-stands-41068/

7 | Brands and Brand Management

Introduction to Brands and Brand Management

A brand was traditionally an indelible mark burnt onto something – a barrel, a cow, or even an imprisoned slave – to display ownership and discourage theft. As brands evolved from these crude beginnings, they became symbols to differentiate one company's products from those of competitors and imitators. In the 19th-century UK, Bass Brewers printed a red triangle trademark on their casks, to enable customers to distinguish their premium product from a cheaper but inferior, generic alternative. In doing this, Bass could charge a higher price, building profit and customer loyalty, and customers could be assured that they were choosing a tasty, reliable product.

Brand management is caring for, measuring, and understanding others' perception of your organisation, and adapting your approaches to account for those considerations (Barwise et al., 1990). This emphasises the need to build and nourish a relationship, to explore stakeholders' perceptions, to act accordingly, and to monitor success. French brand managers sometimes comment that they must *chercher le créneau* – literally, seek a gap in a fortification – and a brand is indeed a mechanism used to enter someone's mind. Ries & and Ries (2001) considered brands "a singular idea or concept that you own inside the mind of the prospect". However, can an organisation truly own something conceptual in a customer's mind? Perhaps the most satisfying definition was provided by Neumeier (2005): "a brand is a person's gut feeling about a product. It's not what you say it is. It is what they say it is". This seems to acknowledge the power of audiences and the scope for individuals to apply their own interpretations to the messages which they receive from organisations.

What May Be Branded?

We may think of brands as 'makes' of clothes, cars, or other products, but many other entities may be branded, as Table 7.1 demonstrates.

Sometimes brands are not created and financed by identifiable individuals and organisations but may grow organically within the media and society – one example being 'Brexit'. We even brand ourselves through what we wear, who we accompany, where we are seen, what we stand for, our accents, our hairstyles, our belongings, our physiques, and even our skin. Nowhere is this more apparent than on social media.

MARKETING ASSISTANT TASK

As a marketing assistant, Tannya needs to collect relevant information on prospects, customers, and competitors for her manager so that strategic branding decisions can be made for the Mexi- can market. One of the tasks she has been set is to list words which represent the brand values currently associated with Zomotor. After undertaking some preliminary market research, she has compiled the following words: 'fun', 'sporty', 'city', 'youthful', 'leisure', and 'freedom'. Consumers and corporate managers use these words more than any others when asked to describe Zomotor. However, Tannya realises that, whilst these words represent a brand personality which is very attractive to younger existing customers, they could be less appealing to the target segment of 35- to 55-year-olds. For each of these six words, briefly explain what negative connotations they might carry for older customers.

TABLE 7.1

Examples of branded entities.

Branded Entity	Examples
Product	BMW Mini car, Sony television, Dormeo mattress, Hershey's chocolate bar
Service	National Health Service (UK), Skyscanner flight comparison site, Virgin Money
Organisation	Harvard University, North Atlantic Treaty Organization (NATO), The Green Party
Place	Route 66, French Riviera, Midtown Manhattan, Italian Lake District
Person	Muhammad Ali, Cristiano Ronaldo, Greta Thunberg, Beyonce
Event	Glastonbury Festival, FIFA World Cup, London Pride, NFL Super Bowl

PHOTO 7.1
Changing 'HMV' to 'The HMV Shop' suggests that many of its activities lie elsewhere – online.

The Role and Remit of Brands

To build a successful brand is usually time-consuming and costly, so they must provide important benefits to organisations, customers, and other stakeholders. Brands are essential commercially as they do the following:

▶ Constitute a "lens through which the consumers view the product and the firm" (Blythe, 2007), and are intended to improve the favourability of customer perceptions

▶ Tell who the organisation is and what it does (Keller & Richey, 2006)

▶ Differentiate the firm's products and services from those of competitors (Keller et al., 2011)

▶ Promise delivery of things which consumers desire (Kotler & Pfoertsch, 2006)

▶ Provide quality assurance

▶ Prevent customer relationship from being purely transactional (Moore & Reid, 2008)

▶ Convey 'brand knowledge' through information (i.e. awareness, attributes, and benefits) and through image (i.e. images, attitudes, experiences, thoughts, and feelings; Dutta, 2012)

Customer-Specific Benefits of Brands

Without brands, consumers would struggle to eliminate unsuitable goods, services, and sellers when deciding what to buy. In effect, brands help customers to formulate a 'short list' or 'evoked set' of choices which are acceptable to them, and then assist in making final purchasing decisions. Brands give customers the following:

▶ Easy identification of a preferred manufacturer or supplier

▶ A heuristic (a decision-making shortcut or 'rule of thumb') and a proxy for quality

▶ A mechanism through which worth may be perceived – an instinctive, intuitive resource for evaluating alternatives

▶ The buyer comfort which arises from buying from an organisation which shares one's own values

▶ Tools with which to express one's self-image, and to state one's position and status, to others

▶ Reduction of risks associated with purchase

There are five main categories of risk to customers, all of which may be reduced by brands (Table 7.2).

TABLE 7.2

Types of customer risks which brands help to reduce.

Risk type	Description
Financial risk	The purchase may cost too much relative to its merits. The purchase price, associated costs, and potential expense of replacing an unsuitable purchase may be financially damaging to the customer.
Performance risk	The purchase may not perform as intended, expected, or required. This may prove damaging to the customer. For example, an unreliable car might make the customer late for work and hinder their career, and an unreliable truck might incur late-delivery penalties to a freight company.
Time risk	The decision-making process may be so lengthy that it prevents the customer from addressing more important issues. For consumers, this may be their family, friends, and job. For organisational customers, it may be their firm's core commercial activity.
Social risk	By purchasing poor quality, unpopular, or unethically produced items, a customer may undermine their reputation amongst friends and associates.
Psychological risk	By making a poor decision, the customer risks suffering from the 'buyer's remorse' or cognitive dissonance (Festinger, 1957) – an uncomfortable psychological state in which the emerging reality fails to match prior expectations, leaving them feeling foolish and duped.

Organisation-Specific Benefits of Brands

By creating strong brands which resonate with audiences, organisations enjoy numerous immediate and deferred benefits. Brands may give organisations the following:

▶ Identity within a crowded marketplace – a uniqueness and advantage

▶ Certain legal protections (e.g. trademarks, product details)

▶ The ability to convey much information and meaning in few or no words

▶ The opportunity to charge a price premium

▶ Increased customer loyalty

▶ Enhanced market share

▶ Reduced price elasticity (i.e. a reduction in loyal customers' price sensitivity)

▶ A barrier to potential competitors and new market entrants

▶ An asset which may be sold to, or shared with, other organisations

▶ Easier commercial forecasting and strategic planning, and more consistent cash flow

Organisations have many other stakeholders – including employees, suppliers, and channel intermediaries, local communities, governments, and unions. By being associated with a strong, ethical brand, these stakeholders may benefit through feeling pride, peace of mind, and a firm understanding of their partner.

MARKETING MANAGER TASK

As a marketing manager, Dylan has been tasked with ensuring that the brand-supporting activities of Zomotor's franchised dealers in China are consistent with the activities of Zomotor itself. The manufacturer intends to take responsibility for communicating the brand through broadcast, print, outdoor, and digital advertising, generating leads which it passes to dealerships. Dealers will look after local advertising, following up local leads, providing demonstrator test drives and quotations, and selling to retail customers. To ensure that the efforts of manufacturer and dealers complement each other, design a table for Dylan which identifies (in the left-hand column) around six or seven dealer activities where there is a risk that the brand will not be reflected consistently with Zomotor's intentions, and (in the right-hand column) actions which he can take on behalf of Zomotor to prevent or mitigate these risks.

What Brands Should Convey

As we found in the last chapter, people often buy not just the **core product** (e.g. photo-copier), but the **actual product** (e.g. Bluetooth inkjet printer with scanner and copier), basing their decision upon factors such as the features, design, packaging, and brand name. However, they also choose **augmented products** (e.g. printer with scanner and copier, which comes with manual, warranty, and after-sales support). This is because they seek benefits rather than features. Brands should therefore convey the benefits which are most meaningful to their target audiences.

Functional benefits are the basic ways in which the item fulfils its purpose, such as a ski suit keeping out the cold. These benefits should be delivered before the organisation turns to more sophisticated benefits. **Functional brands** cater most to customers seeking functional benefits.

Self-expressive benefits are ways in which the item enables the customer to express who they are, their values, their priorities in life, and their social status. For instance, Moncler ski suits convey prestige and quality, whilst Fendi are particularly chic. **Image brands** usually serve customers seeking self-expressive benefits.

Emotional benefits include entertainment, belonging, and a sense of community. A skier may prefer to buy Canada Goose ski wear if that is the brand most revered by their ski club members or by their favourite professional skiers. **Experiential brands** are

PHOTO 7.2
LEGO and Star Wars co-branding is part of a strategic alliance in which each benefits from association with the other.

most closely aligned with customers seeking emotional benefits. Organisations should decide which category of brand they belong to, which types of benefit are most important to their target customers, and how to convey those benefits clearly.

Brand Challenges

Brand managers have always faced complex challenges and address them by asking probing questions. They fall into three main domains: questions appertaining to brand management strategies, to customers and competitors, and to employees and stakeholders. Figure 7.1 shows some of the key questions within each domain.

Additionally, whilst today's brands have many more routes to their audiences than before – chiefly presented by the internet and interactive digital technology – they also face a number of growing challenges:

Customers are increasingly market savvy, well informed, and can communicate their experiences with each other (e.g. on consumer websites).

Brand proliferation can fatigue customers. Successful brands have to find a way to stand out from the crowd.

Trade power can inhibit manufacturer brands. Supermarkets, for example, squeeze manufacturer profit margins and increasingly perceive themselves as their customers' manufacturer-agents rather than their suppliers' customer-agents.

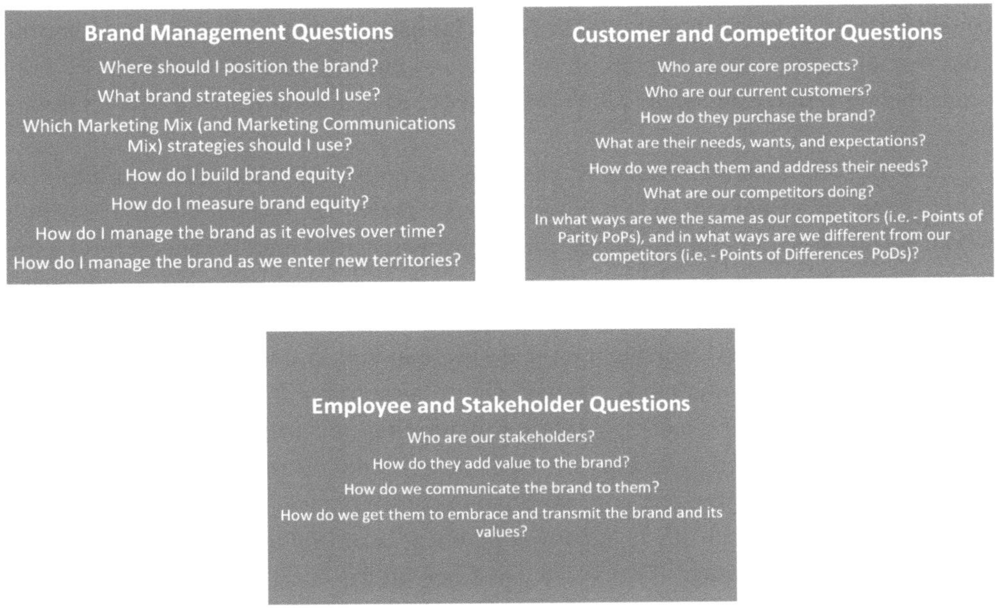

Brand Management Questions

Where should I position the brand?

What brand strategies should I use?

Which Marketing Mix (and Marketing Communications Mix) strategies should I use?

How do I build brand equity?

How do I measure brand equity?

How do I manage the brand as it evolves over time?

How do I manage the brand as we enter new territories?

Customer and Competitor Questions

Who are our core prospects?

Who are our current customers?

How do they purchase the brand?

What are their needs, wants, and expectations?

How do we reach them and address their needs?

What are our competitors doing?

In what ways are we the same as our competitors (i.e. - Points of Parity PoPs), and in what ways are we different from our competitors (i.e. - Points of Differences PoDs)?

Employee and Stakeholder Questions

Who are our stakeholders?

How do they add value to the brand?

How do we communicate the brand to them?

How do we get them to embrace and transmit the brand and its values?

FIGURE 7.1
Questions commonly asked by brand managers.

Media fragmentation and the rise of new media means that customers are spread across a broader media landscape. A generation ago, a brand using a motion advert could reach almost all prospective viewers through terrestrial television channels, cinemas, and movie videos. Subscription broadcasters and web-based outlets have greatly dispersed those viewers.

Private labels (e.g. the George clothing label in the UK's Asda supermarket) produce increasingly attractive, low-cost offerings which challenge more budget-conscious customers. They purchase product from undisclosed manufacturers and brand it as their own.

Product introduction and **customer support** are more complex and costly now as a result of the above factors.

Overcoming Brand Challenges by Building Brand Equity

Firms must strive to build **brand equity**. This is the commercial value derived from the customer's brand-related perceptions rather than from the product or service itself. If a firm has a strong reputation or an aspirational brand, customers will pay more for its products or services than if they were unbranded. The additional value is brand equity (Verma, 2021). However, if a firm has a poor reputation, its brand may damage sales, and this is known as **negative brand equity**. It means that it could sell product in greater volume, or more profitably, if unencumbered by its brand. For this reason, brand equity is sometimes considered the sum of a brand's intangible assets and liabilities as perceived by its audiences (Aaker, 2009). **Financial-based brand equity** derives from the commercial stability and strength of the firm, and **customer-based brand equity** from the perceptions of customers and their responses to its actions and characteristics (Keller et al., 2011).

Aaker's (2009) seminal model of customer brand loyalty levels demonstrates how careful brand management may reduce customer churn (i.e. the number of customers who then buy from a competitor) and price sensitivity whilst increasing purchasing frequency and peer recommendations (i.e. positive word-of-mouth communications when customers recommend the brand to their contacts).

Marketers and brand managers must ensure that employees 'live the brand', or at least support its values and ethos, as they will be responsible for conveying it to stakeholders through their interactions. **Internal marketing** and **internal branding** are the two major concepts used to do this, and both are explored elsewhere in this book. They entail communicating frequent, consistent, and positive brand-related messages to staff, involving them democratically in the development of brand values, and guarding against any sign of **brand sabotage** (Wallace & De Chernatony, 2008), in which employees' cynicism or alienation may lead them to undermine the brand.

A brand is distinguished from an unbranded commodity and reflects customer perceptions about its attributes and performance. **Brand equity** is so important that Warren

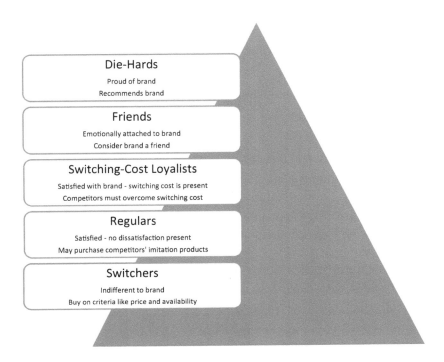

FIGURE 7.2
Types and characteristics of customers.

Buffett, one of the world's most successful investors, attaches more importance to a firm's brand when investing than to its product range or management staff – both of which can be changed more easily than the brand. Coca-Cola is worth several times more than the value of all its tangible assets precisely because of its brand equity – if all of its factories, machines, infrastructure and personnel were to disappear, it could still be resurrected very quickly due to the position of strength which it holds in consumers' minds. Brand equity is therefore closely linked to the future earning potential of the brand (Moran, 1991), and the differential effect which the brand has on consumers' responses to its marketing (Keller, 2010).

Measuring Brand Equity

Measuring brand equity may be difficult due to its qualitative nature, so marketers use a combination of secondary and primary research for this purpose. To have strategic value, the research must clarify the strength and nature of the brand's equity by asking questions such as these:

▶ Which brands do consumers consider to be the strongest?
▶ How readily do consumers recognise and recall our brand when buying?

▶ How do consumers understand our brand differently from those of competitors?

▶ What dimensions do they associate with our brand and appreciate?

▶ What benefits do customers value in a brand?

▶ How important are each of these benefits?

▶ How positively do they perceive our brand in relation to these benefits, and compared with our competitors?

▶ How loyal, committed, and price sensitive are our customers towards our brand?

▶ Can our brand be extended, and if so, how?

Naturally, these are only the major questions, and a researcher would need to drill down deeper to obtain more detail upon which to base strategic branding decisions.

METRICS QUESTION

As the community relationship manager of a professional football club, you wish to ascertain how supporters and other local people perceive the club's brand so that you can compare it with results a year from now, after a major community initiative. Design a questionnaire which can be distributed to participants by email which collects all the necessary information to make strategic brand decisions.

Brand Values

The three key aspects of brand planning are arguably (i) establishing and maintaining the core values, (ii) positioning the brand against competitors, and (iii) managing the brand's life cycles. We will consider the final two later in this chapter, but it is essential from the outset to place appropriate values at the heart of the brand. Brands are often thought to embrace three clusters of values (Urde, 2009):

1. Values appertaining to the organisation (e.g. habits, norms, and practices)

2. Values which represent the brand's essence (e.g. empowerment, simplicity, or convenience)

3. Values perceived by the customer (e.g. honesty, openness, or warmth)

These values should 'speak' to the customer through brand communications and contact with the brand's employees (De Chernatony et al., 2004). They must be enduring and consistent, permeating everything which the brand says and does, defining the corporate brand identity, and supporting the brand promise (Urde, 2009). When customers understand the core values, it shapes their expectations of the brand's performance, and these expectations must be met – this is the role of brand management.

Creating a Brand

To create and sustain a successful brand, Olins (2004) suggested that marketers would need to manage product, environment, communication, and behaviour – which he collectively termed the **Four Vectors**: the **brand architecture**, the **changes to the brand** as it ages, and the **clarity, coherence**, and **congruence** of the brand.

Almost all brands are a combination of the Four Vectors, through which they manifest themselves:

1. **Product**: the entity which is created to be sold

2. **Environment**: the place where the entity is sold

3. **Communication**: how the firm tells people about the brand

4. **Behaviour**: how the firm, and everyone in it, behaves

The first three vectors constitute the driving force of a brand. **Product-led brands** (e.g. Ronseal, Bosch) *must* have a highly effective product. **Environmentally led brands** (e.g. Hilton Hotels, Nandos, House of Fraser) rely heavily upon excellent brand experiences. **Communication-led brands** (e.g. Budweiser, M&Ms, Kellogg's) tend to leverage more heavily upon advertising and other marketing communications to sell. Whilst behaviour is important to all brands, many service providers are **behaviourally led brands** (e.g. Virgin Airlines, Prudential Life Assurance) which emphasise the importance of intangibles – aspects which cannot be seen or touched.

Brand architecture is the structure and relationships between a firm's brands. Some organisations (e.g. Procter & Gamble, Unilever, Reckitt Benckiser) own numerous brands which may be related to each other in different ways, or not at all. A **corporate brand** (or **monolith brand**) is a single brand name presented to the consumer to convey the firm's brand (e.g. IKEA, Kawasaki). An **endorsed brand** occurs where the parent company applies its name or identity to sub-brands or associated brands (e.g. Cadbury's Dairy Milk, Tesco Extra). **Branded companies** are those which have their own publicly recognised brand which is separate from that of their parent company (e.g. Stella Artois' hidden relationship to Anheuser-Busch, or Smirnoff's to Diageo).

Brands may be reinvented or changed gradually over time to ensure that they remain relevant to customers' expectations. Alternatively, they may undergo a major noticeable change due to a merger, acquisition, or a co-branding agreement where compatible brands work together to synergise their marketing and provide mutual customers – as Taco Bell and Doritos did to great effect. Firms may sometimes reposition their brands. Lucozade, previously marketed as a health tonic, was relaunched as a sports drink, reaching a younger and more profitable audience. Brand managers achieve clarity, coherence, and congruence by ensuring that any customer touchpoint – when a customer interacts with the brand – reinforces the same meanings and feelings. This entails communicating **intangibles** such as behaviour, attitude, and values with a unified voice, and reinforcing this with visually unifying tangibles such as graphics, typefaces, and colour schemes.

Brand Elements

The essential elements making up a brand are its brand **name, symbols, logos, characters, jingles and slogans, packaging**, and **signage** (Keller, 2010). McDonald's, for instance, has 'McDonald's' and its 'Mc' product prefix, its 'golden arches' symbol, Ronald McDonald, the 'I'm Lovin' It' jingle, its distinctive cartons of fries, and its predominantly yellow colour scheme and signage. Six key criteria for brand elements appear in Table 7.3.

Brand Positioning

Although positioning was explored in Chapter 5, it is worth considering some implications for the brand here. Since Ries and Trout's (2001) highly influential discussion of positioning, it has been at the heart of marketing. It does not simply entail moving or placing a product or brand somewhere but also influencing the way in which it is perceived by the audience. A brand's position is how it is perceived relative to its competitors. Aaker and Shansby (1982) suggested a choice of strategies for positioning a brand:

1. *On price or quality*: Customer perceptions of product superiority enable brands to charge a higher price. Undercutting competitors' prices can 'buy' market share but also distress the brand by undermining the respect which customers have for it.

TABLE 7.3

Six criteria for brand elements.

Criteria	Characteristic
Unforgettable	Audiences can recall and recognise it easily
Consequential	It describes something and persuades customers to purchase
Engaging	It is interesting, enjoyable, and fun
Interchangeable	It can be used in different product categories and/or cultures and markets
Malleable	It is capable of being updated and refreshed
Defensible	It can be protected against imitation and intellectual property infringement

Source: Adapted from Keller (2013).

2. *On attributes*: Even a basic pasta product could be positioned by whether it is quick boil, microwaveable, or simply needs adding hot water for two minutes. Branders should consider how a product is delivered or used.

3. *On use or application*: Fast-moving consumer goods (FMCGs), such as orange drinks, may be intended for home-based or on-the-go usage, for mixing in cocktails, or drinking at breakfast time.

4. *By product user*: A cereal bar brand may be targeted at parents who pack their children's school lunchboxes, hikers who carry a picnic, or commuters who eat breakfast on the train.

5. *By comparing with a competitor*: A car brand may be positioned as the safest for occupants, the most reliable, or the most fuel efficient.

6. *By product class*: A consumer electronics brand may be perceived as the strongest for cordless, rechargeable, or solar-powered products.

In addition to these, a brand may be positively positioned against its competitors due to the strengths of its service, its channel intermediaries (such as its network of retailers), its staff, symbols, its stance towards corporate social responsibility (CSR), and its image.

STAKEHOLDER QUESTION

If you were a brand manager for a prestigious cosmetics and perfume brand, how would you ensure brand consistency from the retailers which sell your products to consumers? Remember that they are also selling rival manufacturer products. Draw a mind map to ideate some potential solutions, and consider the pros and cons of each within the context of brand performance.

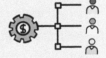

Even when a brand must fight directly against competitors for the same customers using the same product for the same purpose (and so on), it can be positioned against competitors based upon customer perceptions of the attributes which influence their purchase decision. For example, Brand A may be perceived as more ethical, environmentally friendly, and caring, but Brand B may be considered more reliable, a better value for the money, and more practical. The brand managers should try to quantify such customer perceptions, gauge their relevance to their target audiences, and consider how to influence those perceptions to their advantage. To understand how differentiated their brand is from competitors against selected criteria, they may use a positioning map or perceptual map – a diagrammatical technique which plots the brand and competitors along the *x*- and *y*-axes of a graph. An example is provided in Figure 8.4 in the next chapter on pricing.

Positioning Statements

Successful brands often use positioning statements (Moore & Reid, 2008), which identify their underlying objectives. The fundamental questions which they answer appear in Table 7.4.

The key to positioning is to differentiate the brand from rivals, as this prevents the products from becoming commoditised and the firm from descending into a profit-damaging price war. Sometimes it may be necessary to reposition a brand because one of the following scenarios has occurred:

▶ The brand is currently occupying an undesired market position

▶ It is intended for the brand to penetrate the market (i.e. gain market share)

▶ The brand is slightly incongruous with customer preferences

▶ The brand has become slightly outdated/the market conditions and characteristics have evolved

▶ The brand needs to overcome new or evolving competition

When these scenarios occur, there are four main choices of repositioning strategy:

1. Image repositioning: improve the brand image to improve current target customers' perceptions of the brand

2. Product repositioning: sell new products to the same market to improve customers' brand perceptions

TABLE 7.4
Brand positioning statement.

Question	Example Answer
Who is our brand for?	Young adults and families
What do they need from the brand?	Value, style, ease of use, clear information
How do our products address their need?	Save space, easy to assemble, inexpensive
What major benefit do we provide?	Help customers create a modern, practical home
Which competitor(s) are we very different from?	Traditional furniture retailers such as DFS
How are we different?	We sell modern, stylish, affordable, space-saving solutions for all rooms

Source: Applied to IKEA by the authors.

3. Intangible repositioning: sell the same products to an additional or amended target market

4. Tangible repositioning: sell new products to a different target market

Extending, Stretching, and Retrenching Brands

Marketers may choose to undertake a **brand extension** by using an existing brand to sell products or services in a related category, such as a life assurance brand being extended to sell car and house insurance (Yuen et al., 2021). Where an existing brand is used to sell products in an unrelated category, this is called **brand stretching** (e.g. if a motorcycle manufacturer used its brand to sell lawnmowers). Ries and Trout (2001) warned that stretching or extending a brand too far – into a product category where customers seek different attributes – can weaken or even break the brand in its core market. It may be necessary or advantageous to pursue a **brand retrenchment** strategy, in which a less competitive brand, or one which is incapable of being extended or stretched, is denied the resources necessary to broaden its remit beyond its original category.

Branding Online

The principles of traditional offline branding apply to online branding; consistency, coherence, and clarity are equally important in either location. Whilst the subject will be explored in much greater depth in Chapter 16, there are some key points about online branding communications to consider here: online media enables communication which is **synchronous** (i.e. with no delay between partners' comments), **dialogical** (i.e. two-way) or **multidirectional** (e.g. between numerous community members), and may be viewed both instantly and for a long period by **very large audiences**. The proliferation of online media means that audiences often split into many smaller groups with a common interest rather than in larger, heterogenous groups which are more reflective of society and easier to reach. Online audiences experience the brand through a **range of devices**, such as laptops, tablets, smartphones, and digital televisions. They may also experience the brand in a **variety of settings**: in bed, whilst commuting, at work, in a restaurant, and even in the bathroom. Their brand interaction may be **deliberate or accidental, welcome or intrusive**. They may **act instantly** and favourably by **following** a brand, **liking** or **forwarding** a comment, **subscribing** to an email list, **following** a content provider, interacting with a **chatbot**, or even **placing a customer purchase order** and **paying online**. They may be lured to a new brand through a fun online experience, or the **gamification** of the relationship (e.g. if the site includes a branded digital game). Conversely, they may act unfavourably by **blocking or unfollowing** a sender, **replying negatively**, seeking **comparisons with alternative suppliers**, or simply liking the brand less than before. So, whilst online brand management principles are the same as offline, brands are experienced differently online, in more divergent environmental contexts. Moreover, brand value is co-created more collaboratively between organisations and customers in online spaces due to the interactivity and synchronicity of digital technology, and power is shared more evenly between the brand and its audience. Branders must consider the implications of this in their strategies.

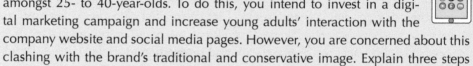

NEW MEDIA QUESTION

The upmarket furniture brand which you manage has a loyal following amongst affluent 40- to 65-year-olds but wishes to increase its sales amongst 25- to 40-year-olds. To do this, you intend to invest in a digital marketing campaign and increase young adults' interaction with the company website and social media pages. However, you are concerned about this clashing with the brand's traditional and conservative image. Explain three steps which you might take to minimise this risk.

Brand Archetypes and Personality

In today's world, many consumers live a 'postmodern' existence very different from how life would have been a century ago. They often leave their families and their hometown to go to university or to seek work in large, distant cities, living alone or sharing accommodation with near strangers. Partially as a result of this, they seek brands which may feel like living entities – family members – and which reflect their values and help them to express their identities. Although most brands, including large ones, have a surprisingly short life span before they merge, are acquired, or are discontinued or rebranded, major brands often provide a welcome feeling of permanence. However, consumers are naturally attracted to certain brands and repelled by others, depending on how congruent the brand personality is with their own. Mark and Pearson (2001) explained this by adapting the 'archetype' theories of the seminal social psychology theorist Carl Jung. He stated nearly a century earlier that humans lack the time or motivation to assess thoroughly the characteristics of every new person they meet, so they make a quick judgment using heuristics – decision-making shortcuts – to decide what category of personality that person has. Mark and Pearson (2001) argued that consumers use the same process when deciding which brands to follow and adopt, suggesting 12 main categories.

As archetypes are interpreted by the individual, you may disagree with some of the examples. However, the strongest brands tend to belong unambiguously in one category, and everything which they say and do – messages, tone of voice, web content, packaging – reflects that personality. The personalities of each archetype are shown in Table 7.5.

TABLE 7.5

Archetypes and their traits.

Archetype	Personality Traits
Sage	Wise, erudite, thoughtful, considered, analytical
Explorer	Independent, resourceful, adventurous, free
Hero	High-achieving, competitive, strong, athletic
Magician	Transformative, surprising, catalytic
Outlaw/rebel	Challenging, critical, naughty, anti-authoritarian
Jester	Humorous, entertaining, witty, performative
Lover	Romantic, sensuous, indulgent, classy
Every person	Universal, neutral, inclusive, moderate
Caregiver	Soothing, caring, nurturing, helping
Ruler	Dominant, powerful, leading, omnipotent
Creator	Artistic, empowering, creative, cultured
Innocent	Pure, benevolent, uncritical, vulnerable

PHOTO 7.3

LEGO is a strong brand known worldwide. It conforms to the 'creator' brand archetype.

Have you noticed anything about the table? Not only do many major brands conform very clearly to one specific archetype, but so do many people who we meet in everyday life, and so do many memorable movie and literary characters. For instance, Forrest Gump, and Dorothy from *The Wizard of Oz*, are innocents, lacking worldly knowledge or cynicism, and trusting others. On the other hand, Jim Stark, James Dean's character in *Rebel Without a Cause*, is (of course) a rebel who challenges traditions, conventions, and authority.

Which movie and literary characters do you like the most? Which brands do you prefer? What sort of people are you drawn to? The chances are that if you conform to one archetype, you will be attracted to characters, people, and brands which represent the same archetype. For example, if you are an expedition hiker and have an 'explorer' personality, it is likely that you will like brands such as Jeep, North Face, and Patagonia and characters such as Indiana Jones or Phileas Fogg in Jules Verne's *Around the World in Eighty Days*. Likewise, you may find that you are naturally averse to personalities, characters, and brands which embrace an archetype very dissimilar to your own.

But what does this mean for brands? Not only should brands be consistent in their membership of one archetype, but they must understand that they are likely to appeal strongly to consumers who share that archetype, appeal moderately to consumers who have similar archetypes, and not appeal to consumers from very dissimilar archetypes. More importantly, brands should remember what motivates and demotivates people from one archetype and design their brands and messages accordingly. For this purpose, we can group archetypes into four related groups of three (Table 7.6).

TABLE 7.6

Motivations and fears of people belonging to different archetypes.

	Creators, Caregivers, and Rulers	Jesters, Every Persons, and Lovers	Heroes, Outlaws/ Rebels, and Magicians	Innocents, Explorers, and Sages
Are motivated by . . .	control stability influence improvements	enjoyment belonging friends and family partnership	mastery risk excitement unpredictability	fulfilment independence freedom variety
Are afraid of . . .	disorder financial instability illness	abandonment isolation engulfment	powerlessness impotence ineffectiveness	entrapment routine meaninglessness
Like brands which help people to . . .	feel safe and secure	be close to others	achieve	be happy

Source: Adapted from Mark and Pearson (2001).

Therefore, an 'explorer' brand such as Fjällräven should emphasise freedom, adventure, and fulfilment, whilst avoiding any allusion to routine, mechanisation, and 'selling out'. Failure to do so would undermine their brand personality and alienate their core customers. As archetypes are deep within our psyches and we understand them unconsciously, it is likely that segmenting the market by archetype (i.e. psychographic segmentation) may help brands to form stronger customer bonds than if they had used profile segmentation (e.g. grouping people by age, gender, location, income) or behavioural segmentation (e.g. by what people do and how/when/where they do it).

ETHICS QUESTION

Brands can become almost surrogate family members to modern consumers who often live postmodern lives, far from their hometown and families; such can be the depth of the emotional connection. Make a list of potential ethical concerns which may arise from this phenomenon and, for each, briefly say what approaches a brand could put into place to ensure responsible brand management.

Adding Value to a Brand

We have already discussed brand values (plural) – the defining practices, beliefs, and ethos of the brand. Now we turn to value (singular). In the context of products, **perceived value is product quality divided by product price**. That is, customers judge the standard of the product (quality), then consider the money exchanged for something of that standard (price), and in doing so, they judge whether the quality merits the price (value). Therefore, customers are tolerant of poorer product quality if the price is lower, and tolerant of higher prices if the product quality is better.

Value is at the heart of all marketing activities, but the concept of value has evolved from its earlier focus on delivering superior performance, to its current focus on providing certainty and peace of mind and reducing anxiety and post-purchase cognitive dissonance (Festinger, 1957). Put simply, value has become less about outperforming competitors' products and more about truthfully reflecting the merits of the firm's products and services. Moreover, this understanding increasingly occurs at a brand level – rather than judging individual products, consumers are nowadays more likely to judge the brand responsible for those products.

PHOTO 7.4
The Metrocentre shopping centre in Northeast England nurtures brand affinity by expanding visitors' experience from shopping into leisure – for example, by providing a mini train to entertain children.

Added Value Offerings

Compared to non-brands, brands are noticeably differentiated by offering additional or better attributes which customers welcome (De Chernatony, 2010). Brands do not simply offer a core product but also functional and emotional benefits within an augmented product. They communicate this value to their target audiences and satisfy their needs at an acceptable or attractive price. Jones (2005) suggested that added value could be derived from the following:

▶ Experience of, or familiarity with, the product
▶ The types of people using the brand
▶ The brand appearance or packaging

For example, Marks & Spencer provides added value, because shoppers have gained trust in its product and service quality over a lifetime's experience, because they see other shoppers there who are usually 'respectable' in their appearance and behaviour, and because the brand appearance and packaging consistently reflects an aspirational brand.

Customers usually perceive value for one of four reasons: (i) a low price, (ii) a product which entirely satisfies their needs, (iii) good quality in relation to the price paid, or (iv) altruistic sentiment, such as that gained through goodwill, donating, or engaging with an ethical organisation.

More recently, many theorists have understood that value can be derived from consumer participation. **Co-creation of value** (Prahalad & Ramaswamy, 2004) occurs when firms, customers, and other stakeholders collaborate to build value which would not be achievable by the firm alone. For example, if a sportswear manufacturer invites its web-based community to film themselves using the brand's clothing in unusual situations so that footage may be incorporated into a televised advert, this can reduce the firm's production costs but can also help customers feel more visible, involved, empowered, and appreciated. This phenomenon has contributed towards the adoption by marketers of **service-dominant logic** (S-D logic; Vargo & Lusch, 2004), in which value is derived at numerous points along the customer journey through experience rather than simply at the time of transaction. The rise of digital, interactive technology, and the internet, and the resulting opportunities for sophisticated relationship marketing, have significantly amplified the importance of value co-creation and S-D logic.

MARKETING DIRECTOR TASK

As marketing director, Lee has overall responsibility for ensuring that Zomotor's new SUVs and MPVs are a success in Germany and globally. As such, they need to make sure that every brand element

continued

> for each vehicle is consistent with Zomotor's brand. The SUV will have a model sub-brand embracing the 'explorer' archetype, and the MPV will have a model sub-brand embracing the 'every person' archetype. Help Lee by listing the brand elements in a table and then explaining how each can be made consistent with the brand archetype.

International Brands

Brands may choose to expand internationally for a variety of reasons: (i) due to increased competition, saturation, or slow growth in their home market; (ii) to pursue more profitable opportunities, or to take advantage of tax incentives or more favourable economic conditions in new markets; (iii) to expand by selling to an existing customer segment in a new market rather than a new customer segment in an existing market; or (iv) to diversify their risk across multiple countries.

Foreign expansion presents several brand-specific opportunities and risks (Table 7.7).

TABLE 7.7

Advantages/opportunities and disadvantages/risks faced by brands when expanding internationally.

Advantages/Opportunities	Disadvantages/Risks
Economies of scale (i.e. manufacturing in larger quantities to achieve a lower cost per item, or dividing total marketing cost across a larger audience)	Foreign customers may have different needs, wants, and usage patterns
Increased brand life cycle (i.e. by selling ageing products into less sensitive markets)	They may respond differently to marketing and branding
Leveraging foreign consumers' perceptions of brand superiority/prestige/status	They may prefer home (local) brands
Increased strategic flexibility (e.g. if Europe experiences a recession, trade more heavily in Asia instead)	The firm would face unfamiliar political, socio-economic, legal, technical, and cultural factors
Opportunity to benefit from good product availability	It might need to appoint channel intermediaries who represent the brand properly

Source: Adapted from Hollensen (2020).

GLOBAL MARKETING QUESTION

Imagine you are the brand manager for a classic motorcycle manufacturer based in the UK. You have already exported product successfully to the US, and now the firm will begin exporting to Denmark and Sweden. Your brand has a strong 'rebel' archetype. However, your market research tells you that Danes and Swedes tend to be less individualistic, nonconformist, and confrontational in their attitudes than the British and Americans. List possible complications which this may pose for your brand in the new markets and, for each, explain what (if anything) you may do to combat these.

Service Brands

Although products and services are marketed, and often branded, along the same principles, there are some differences to be considered. Services are defined by four characteristics:

1. **Intangibility**: Unlike products, you cannot see or touch a service.

2. **Heterogeneity**: Services cannot be replicated exactly like products, but are infinitely variable.

3. **Inseparability**: The service cannot be taken away from the producer to be consumed at another time or in another place.

4. **Perishability**: The service cannot be stored, saved, returned, or resold at a later date after delivery.

In practice, few brands sell only products or only services. Almost all brands occupy a position on a **product-service continuum**. For example, iPhones may be products, but Apple provides warranties and after-sales support with them. For this reason, Berry (2000) argued that **service branding** varies from product branding only in the additional emphasis which is placed on human performance (in the delivery of the service) rather than machine performance (in the manufacture of a product). He also suggested that this renders brand management even more important to service consumers than product consumers.

Chapter Summary

In this chapter, we have explored how brands have evolved from simply identifying a manufacturer or supplier for customers to instilling customer goodwill, peace of mind, and willingness to collaborate. At the heart of brand management, like all marketing, is a focus on the deliverables. If a brand manager allocates resources to a particular strategy, they must be clear about what they wish to achieve and how it might be measured. The main function of brand management is to create customer loyalty, which in turn makes customers less price sensitive, less likely to buy from the competition, and more open to increasing the frequency and value of their purchases. However, brands also provide numerous benefits to customers themselves, such as simplifying the decision-making process, reducing risks, and creating an enjoyable interactive experience.

Key Learning Outcomes

▶ Brands are important in meaningfully differentiating products and services from those of competitors, to the benefit both of organisations and their stakeholders.

▶ Successful brands employ a variety of constantly evolving strategies to address ever-changing environments.

▶ Brands build value and equity for a variety of stakeholders.

▶ Evaluate the characteristics and properties of powerful brands.

Recommended Further Reading

Verma, P. (2021). The effect of brand engagement and brand love upon overall brand equity and purchase intention: A moderated – mediated model. *Journal of Promotion Management, 27*(1), 103–132.

Yadav, A., Ling, P., & Glantz, S. (2020). Smokeless tobacco industry's brand stretching in India. *Tobacco Control, 29*(e1), e147–e149.

Yuen, T. W., Nieroda, M., He, H., & Park, Y. (2021). Can dissimilarity in product category be an opportunity for cross-gender brand extension? *Journal of Business Research, 135*, 348–357.

References

Aaker, D. A. (2009). *Managing brand equity*. Simon and Schuster.

Aaker, D. A., & Shansby, J. G. (1982). Positioning your product. *Business Horizons, 25*(3), 56–62.

Barwise, P., Higson, C., Likierman, A., & Marsh, P. (1990). Brands as 'separable assets'. *Business Strategy Review, 1*(2), 43–59.

Berry, L. L. (2000). Cultivating service brand equity. *Journal of the Academy of Marketing Science, 28*(1), 128–137.

Blythe, J. (2007). Advertising creatives and brand personality: A grounded theory perspective. *Journal of Brand Management, 14*(4), 284–294.

De Chernatony, L. (2010). *Creating powerful brands*. Routledge.

De Chernatony, L., Drury, S., & Segal-Horn, S. (2004). Identifying and sustaining services brands' values. *Journal of Marketing Communications, 10*(2), 73–93.

Dutta, K. (2012). *Brand management: Principles and practices*. Oxford University Press.

Festinger, L. (1957). *A theory of cognitive dissonance* (Vol. 2). Stanford University Press.

Hollensen, S. (2020). *Global marketing* (5th ed.). Pearson.

Jones, R. (2005). Finding sources of brand value: Developing a stakeholder model of brand equity. *Journal of Brand Management, 13*(1), 10–32.

Keller, K. L. (2010). Brand equity management in a multichannel, multimedia retail environment. *Journal of Interactive Marketing, 24*(2), 58–70.

Keller, K. L. (2013). Building strong brands in a modern marketing communications environment. In *The Evolution of Integrated Marketing Communications* (pp. 73–90). Routledge.

Keller, K. L., Parameswaran, M. G., & Jacob, I. (2011). *Strategic brand management: Building, measuring, and managing brand equity*. Pearson Education India.

Keller, K. L., & Richey, K. (2006). The importance of corporate brand personality traits to a successful 21st century business. *Journal of Brand Management, 14*(1), 74–81.

Kotler, P., & Pfoertsch, W. (2006). *B2B brand management*. Springer Science & Business Media.

Mark, M., & Pearson, C. S. (2001). *The hero and the outlaw: Building extraordinary brands through the power of archetypes*. McGraw Hill.

Moore, K., & Reid, S. (2008). The birth of brand: 4000 years of branding. *Business History, 50*(4), 419–432.

Moran, W. T. (1991, February). *The search for the Golden Fleece: Actionable brand equity measurement* (pp. 5–6). ARF 3rd Annual Advertising and Promotion Workshop.

Neumeier, M. (2005). *The brand gap* (revised ed.). Peachpit Press.

Olins, W. (2004). *Wally Olins on brand*. Thames & Hudson.

Prahalad, C. K., & Ramaswamy, V. (2004). Co-creation experiences: The next practice in value creation. *Journal of Interactive Marketing, 18*(3), 5–14.

Ries, A., & Ries, L. (2002). *The fall of advertising and the rise of PR*. HarperBusiness.

Ries, A., & Trout, J. (2001). *Positioning: The battle for your mind*. McGraw Hill.

Urde, M. (2009). Uncovering the corporate brand's core values. *Management Decision, 47*(4), 616–638.

Vargo, S. L., & Lusch, R. F. (2004). Evolving to a new dominant logic for marketing. *Journal of Marketing, 68*(1), 1–17.

Wallace, E., & De Chernatony, L. (2008). Classifying, identifying and managing the service brand saboteur. *The Service Industries Journal, 28*(2), 151–165.

Glossary

Brand architecture: the structure of a firm's brands and the relationships between them

Brand elements: brand ingredients such as names, logos, symbols, slogans, signage, and jingles

Brand equity: commercial value derived from the brand rather than the firm's tangible assets

Brand extension: using an existing brand to sell products in a related category

Brand retrenchment: restricting investment to a brand which has low developmental potential

Brand sabotage: the purposeful undermining of a brand by alienated employees

Brand stretching: using an existing brand to sell products in an unrelated category

Co-creation of value: collaboration between brands and customers or other stakeholders

Emotional benefits: how products and brands make customers feel happy and fulfilled

Functional benefits: how products and brands fulfil their main purpose

Heuristic: a decision-making shortcut

Monolith brand: a single brand presented to convey the firm's brand

Private label: a brands which sells products manufactured by an undisclosed third-party brand

Self-expressive benefits: how products and brands enable customers to express their personalities

Service-dominant logic: the idea that service delivers more value than the product it accompanies

---

Brands and Brand Management Case Study: Hoka One One

Hoka One One (pronounced 'Hoka On-Ay On-Ay') is a California-based athletic footwear brand founded in 2009. It has a very broad range of footwear, predominantly running shoes and 'lifestyle' trainers/sneakers. Its products are sold as men's, women's, and all gender, and most feature bright colours and prominent Hoka branding. The brand has built a strong reputation amongst trail runners and road runners, as the shoes offer previously unknown levels of cushioning and comfort by using a very thick sole and supportive insoles. This enables runners to complete longer distances; reduce the risk of injury to their ankles, shins, knees, hips, and backs; and enjoy their hobby more.

Despite its very strong reputation amongst 'serious' users, Hoka has also garnered cult fashion status amongst more casual users. Hollywood actors Reese Witherspoon and Gwyneth Paltrow have been spotted wearing Hoka trainers to jog in the park and go shopping, whilst Chelsea Football Club manager, Thomas Tuchel, was seen celebrating from the dugout in his Hokas. Furthermore, a large proportion of its range appears to be intended as streetwear rather than sportswear, boasting rainbow, leopard skin, and other eye-catching designs.

Hoka's range does not end there. Some products use wool in the upper, others are vegan, and the brand also manufactures recovery shoes and hiking boots. Many customers purchase their products online from a user-friendly but comprehensive website and may narrow down their product choices by multiple criteria, including whether they are overpronators (having flat feet which roll inwards) or supinators (having high-arched feet which roll outwards) when running and walking. Hoka therefore combines the 'seriousness' of a technical brand with the

continued

hedonism of a fashion brand. This is rather remarkable when we note other 'serious' outdoor clothing and footwear brands which have lost their core audience when they were adopted by casual wearers (e.g. Timberland), and those which deliberately avoid marketing to casual users to preserve their core market of technically minded, committed outdoors enthusiasts (e.g. Fjällräven).

Hoka's recent success is noteworthy for another reason. There has been a trend in recent years towards minimalist footwear. The underlying belief behind the minimalist movement is that by wearing hiking boots or running shoes with thin soles and little cushioning, the lower body is strengthened and encouraged to adopt a more natural and independent position during exercise – although the supposed benefits are contested by many podiatrists, physiotherapists, runners, and walkers. Hoka's extra-thick, ultra-cushioned soles – some of which protrude markedly from the rear of the heel – are in direct contrast to the minimalist shoe movement and constitute not a neutral stance towards the issue but an overtly maximalist approach.

Your task is simple to describe but undoubtedly very difficult to achieve. There are no definite right or wrong answers, but you should be prepared to explain the rationale for your strategic choices, analysing the ways in which you wish to exploit the potential of the brand without damaging its longevity.

Imagine you are the digital marketing director for Hoka One One. You report to Hoka's global head of marketing. You have been advised that Hoka expects its sales volumes to at least double in the next five years, due to the power of word-of-mouth communications and the buzz factor generated by celebrities and sportspeople wearing their product. Hoka would like to penetrate the lucrative fashion and lifestyle footwear market, especially amongst young urban professionals, but is totally committed to maintaining its credibility and market share amongst committed runners and athletes. Prepare a brief plan, possibly in table form, outlining the changes of approach which you intend to make online. Consider how you will use the Hoka website, third-party website, social media, and other online locations to convey a brand which will appeal to both your 'young urban professional' and 'committed athlete' target markets without alienating either. Explain the potential risk areas and the ways in which you will mitigate those risks to your brand.

8 | Pricing

LEARNING OBJECTIVES

▶ To identify the main pricing strategies and their characteristics

▶ To assess their suitability for different commercial contexts

▶ To consider the advantages and limitations of pricing strategies to different stakeholders

▶ To analyse the interconnectedness of pricing, commercial performance, and stakeholder needs

Introduction to Pricing

Pricing is the only element of the marketing mix to produce a profit. Pricing too low generates losses, insufficient profit margins, and brand damage, but pricing too high undermines sales volumes and total profits (Nagle & Müller, 2017). Pricing is therefore a pragmatic balancing act requiring constant research and great awareness of one's product, customers, and competitors. Prices are usually set by senior management with input from marketing, sales, and finance colleagues. Some multinationals have pricing departments if prices constantly fluctuate in a dynamic market (e.g. petrochemicals). Many consider **stock turn** rates (i.e. the number of times annually that the entire stock is sold and replaced), **return on sales (ROS)** (net profit generated by all sales) and **return on capital employed (ROCE),** or ROS multiplied by stock turn; some industries have benchmark figures considered acceptable. In B2B sales markets, companies may give salespeople negotiating leeway. Price should be consistent with the other extended marketing mix elements (Hanna & Dodge, 2017) to avoid undermining the brand.

Getting the Price Right

Total costs dictate the minimum price – at least in the long term. If it costs £25 to buy materials to make a television, £25 for design and manufacture, £25 for transport and

DOI: 10.4324/9781003170891-9

PHOTO 8.1
Newcastle-based bakery chain, Greggs, has said that prices at the till may need to increase due to rapidly increasingly energy prices and a shortage of retail job applicants.

logistics, and £25 for marketing, the manufacturer has a break-even point of £100, assuming costs like wages, taxes, and rent have been accounted for. This is the minimum price of each television to avoid a loss. The maximum price is decided by customer perceptions of the product and their willingness and ability to pay for it. Therefore, pricing must stay within these economic parameters. Firms should not cut prices unnecessarily. This risks distressing the brand – undermining customer perceptions of prestige and quality – and making customers price sensitive. It is preferable to justify charging more by conveying the product's value. Owning or using the product may confer social status, make them feel good, or save money, space, time, effort, or risk. Emphasising these helps differentiate the product from competitors rather than competing on prices. Even tiny price cuts may deliver a major reduction in profit, so underpricing carries risks. Ultimately, customers decide if a product or service is appropriately priced and indicate it through their purchase activity (Diallo et al., 2015). A product may sell badly for reasons other than price (e.g. poor design or underpromotion), but by comparing sales levels with customer feedback, the firm can check for mispricing and take corrective measures.

Markets and Pricing

Firms' pricing choices are influenced by the market conditions in which they trade, which can be summarised as follows:

PURE MONOPOLIES

▶ In pure monopolies, there are no competitors, and firms can price as high as customers will tolerate.

▶ The more essential the product (e.g. tap water), the more likely customers would continue buying at unfairly high prices.

▶ However, basing prices on the product's cost and worth avoids consumer unrest, government regulation, and attracting new, cheaper competitors.

▶ Where monopolies are regulated or state owned, governments may set pricing to encourage certain usage behaviours, safeguard resources against high demand, or protect poorer customers.

OLIGOPOLIES

▶ There are few sellers, as it is difficult for competitors to enter the market.

▶ Each supplier reacts quickly to competitor pricing.

▶ This may involve cutting prices or providing extra value in lieu of discount.

▶ The small number of competitors creates high customer awareness of alternative suppliers, encouraging product comparisons (e.g. motor manufacturers).

▶ Therefore, sellers must work hard to retain customers and protect market share.

MONOPOLISTIC COMPETITION AND PURE COMPETITION

▶ Goods are highly differentiated, and prices vary greatly.

▶ Firms encourage customer loyalty by adding value through marketing and product and service design.

▶ In pure competition markets, many suppliers and customers prevent one seller from dictating price trends.

GLOBALISATION AND PRICING

▶ Firms may sell identical products in multiple markets simultaneously.

▶ The different market characteristics may necessitate bespoke pricing strategies (e.g. Fiat sold its inexpensive and basic Palio 'world car' to Brazil's less wealthy drivers, but not in more economically advanced Europe, where Fiat's brand would have been undermined by basic product offerings).

▶ Firms may have several pricing strategies across international or cultural borders due to varying support infrastructure (e.g. retailers and brokers) and because certain countries represent a higher priority to them.

▶ Certain companies may sell to secondary markets within one territory (e.g. a restaurant serving formal evening and weekend diners but also informal weekday diners) by adopting two pricing strategies.

GLOBAL MARKETING QUESTION

Globally there are nearly 3 billion 'bottom of pyramid' consumers who survive on under $2.50 per day. Recent theory suggests that they are not simply a social cause to be served but a viable commercial segment. If the Sri Lankan government wished to tackle food waste from shops and restaurants by developing an app to match this surplus to poorer consumers, what pricing strategies do you think they should embed in the app to ensure that it addresses food poverty and wastage whilst ensuring that businesses are protected from 'cannibalising' trade from their wealthier customers? Write 100 words on each of three options.

Economics in Pricing Decisions

Assuming all other things being equal, increasing price should, by increasing profit margins, make products more attractive to downstream channel partners, attracting more retailers but deterring more customers. Inversely, reducing price should deter more retailers due to perceptions of a smaller profit opportunity but should attract more customers, who perceive greater value for money. However, rarely are all other things equal. The idea of 'economic man' (or 'economic woman'; Albanese, 2015) is idealistic. When purchasing, people rarely have complete information on alternative choices and, if they did, they would lack the time, patience, and skills to compare accurately. Indeed, suppliers may offer alternatives which are difficult to compare, as with phone tariffs or utilities contracts. Even if desired, consumers may not be able to choose cheaper options, like cartridges which are incompatible with their printers. They may be influenced by factors like retailer size and location, convenience, peer recommendations, a desire to impress others, misinformation, misassumptions, and self-esteem. In short, humans are irrational. Of course, we sometimes conform to economic factors, too.

Price Elasticity

If something is **price elastic**, a small change in its price would significantly affect sales volumes. Price-elastic products usually have viable alternatives available to consumers (e.g. printers) or the decision carries risk to the customer (e.g. a mortgage). Other things are **price inelastic** if a large price change would barely influence demand. This often happens if customers are unable to discontinue or defer purchases, as is the case with car fuel (Coglianese et al., 2017). As we shall explore later in the chapter, some consumers are prepared to pay much more than others for certain products which offer a significant technical improvement over the competition and previous products (Lee et al., 2016). Conversely, when consumers share purchase costs with others, they may be less price sensitive. For example, someone sharing a taxi ride with ten friends may worry less about the price, because the premium is divided ten ways. If a transaction cost represents a small proportion of a consumer's overall wealth, they may value the convenience of a quick decision more than saving money. Product quality also influences price elasticity. Some products carry greater utility – they are more useful and necessary – in certain conditions. For instance, sun cream has more utility during a heatwave and will become more price inelastic. If the product has a unique selling proposition (USP) – a benefit making it unique to consumers – then the lack of close alternatives will create price inelasticity by desensitising customers to higher prices (Payne et al., 2017). If, as with Rolex watches or Fjällräven backpacks, customers perceive the product quality more favourably than rivals, they are less likely to shop around.

Customers, Competitors, Costs, and Pricing

Prices are largely determined by production and marketing costs and what customers wish to pay – although these are determined by other considerations, including competitor actions. Therefore, pricing strategies must please customers, generate profit, and position against the competition (Figure 8.1).

Although successful pricing strategies must generate adequate profit per unit, position the brand against the competition, and entice sufficient customers, many organisations favour one of these factors whilst considering them all. This entails adopting strategies which may be customer-based, competitor-based, or cost-based.

PHOTO 8.2
When choosing food from a menu on a special occasion, such as a wedding anniversary, price is likely to be less a factor in the decision-making process than at other times.

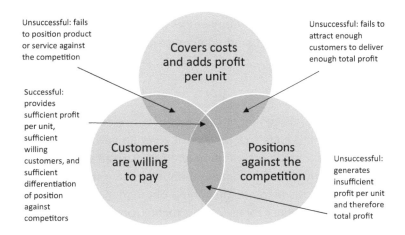

FIGURE 8.1
Major considerations when setting prices.

Customer-Based Pricing

Customer-based pricing focuses on the pricing requirements of the customer base and target audiences, taking an 'outside-in' approach to setting prices. It scrutinises customers' value perceptions, needs and wants, their price sensitivity, and the elasticity of demand before using this information to ascertain the economic parameters within which it must manufacture and supply a product. The organisation's costs are managed to deliver the value specified by customers at prices acceptable to them. Implementing customer-based pricing strategies depends upon market research and analysis.

Competitor-Based Pricing

Competitor-based pricing observes the influence of competitor products and actions. It is often used in industries with many competing firms and price-sensitive customers. An organisation may adopt a **meet-the-competition** strategy by offering prices mirroring rivals' prices, or an **undercut-the-competition** strategy, which usually deprioritises product differentiation, instead enticing customers with cheaper offerings, perhaps through reducing production costs (Fisher et al., 2017). This can distress the brand (i.e. undermine customers' value perceptions) and trigger a price war between competitors, which damages profit opportunities. Occasionally, an established supplier may stifle a new competitor's growth aspirations by undercutting the competition. Occasionally, this constitutes anticompetitive practice, which is illegal in many countries and may attract the unwanted intervention of government regulators; monopolistic organisations may be forced to sell parts of their businesses. Established suppliers may sell cheaper due to economies of scale, by having production plants in low-wage economies, or by negotiating tax discounts with national governments. They may even price products higher than they desire to avoid wiping out competitors and entering an externally regulated monopoly, or because their high brand equity encourages customers to pay more for their products (Bös, 2015).

Cost-Based Pricing

Cost-based pricing takes less account of customer needs or competitor actions, instead focusing on the costs of products and services. It takes an inside-out approach, basing prices on information within the organisation and its upstream suppliers of raw materials, resources, and components. The organisation then determines the minimum price required to cover these costs before adding the profit margin. Organisations using this approach may be more product focused than market oriented. This is only possible where there is little competition and few consumer alternatives.

The main forms of customer-based, competitor-based, and cost-based pricing strategies are shown in Table 8.1 and discussed in detail next.

TABLE 8.1

Main forms of customer-based, competitor-based, and cost-based pricing strategies.

Customer-based	Competitor-based	Cost-based
Value-added pricing	Penetration pricing	Cost-plus pricing
Everyday low pricing (EDLP)	Predatory pricing	Mark-up pricing
Good-value pricing	Meet-the-competition pricing	Target profit pricing
Demand pricing	Undercut-the-competition	
Price skimming	pricing	
Psychological pricing		
Customary pricing		
Second market pricing		

Types of Customer-Based Pricing

Customer-based pricing, or **value-based pricing**, adds customer value without reducing the price. Marketers and salespeople should avoid bamboozling customers with features – superfluous technical specifications and hard data – instead translating features into benefits. For example, when selling a barbecue, rather than conveying the product dimensions, it is better to explain how they contribute towards a convivial summer's gathering. There are relatively few types of value and benefits: products or services may save a customer money, time, space, or effort; they may be more sustainable, convenient, durable, usable, or fit for purpose; and they may make the customer feel good about themselves or confer social status (Kumar & Reinartz, 2016). Customer-based pricing factors this value into the price – for example, brands like IKEA (saves space), Uber (saves effort and money), TripAdvisor (saves time), PayPal (convenient), The Body Shop (sustainable), Jeep (durable), Apple (usability/fitness for purpose), and Mercedes (confers social status). However, it is difficult to equate customer benefits to a price equivalent.

Value-Added Pricing

Perhaps the simplest value-based pricing approach, it assumes that the supplier adds customer value to create a USP rather than discounting the product. This helps to build prestige, avoids a price war, potentially encourages customers to buy products more suited to their needs, and garners satisfaction, creating improved profit opportunities for sellers. As such, sellers can differentiate themselves from competitors, building distinctive market positions. An example is the British shoe manufacturer Clarks, which is pricey but renowned for comfort and durability.

Everyday Low Pricing

Everyday low pricing (EDLP) keeps prices consistently low rather than using sales promotions or discount campaigns. Customers can depend on the seller for repeat purchases rather than shopping around, thereby deriving value from cost savings and convenience. In return, the seller enjoys customer loyalty, a settled customer base and, consequently, predictable cash flow and reduced borrowing (Olbrich et al., 2017). The Irish clothing chain Primark use this approach.

Good-Value Pricing

Good-value pricing balances quality, service levels, and fairness. It is used by budget suppliers like the UK short-haul airline easyJet and motel chains such as Travelodge or Motel 6. It may increase customer loyalty in categories where purchases are habitual or frequent. Some organisations establish endorsed good-value sub-brands which leverage the parent company's brand equity, such as Courtyard by Marriott.

Demand Pricing

Demand pricing is synchronised with the vagaries of the market. By capturing data on customers' value perceptions and upper price limits, organisations use meticulous market research and knowledge of price elasticity at multiple possible pricing points. Pricing maximises the profitability of each sale and considers the declining costs per unit which volume manufacturing brings. However, sellers must not be exploitative: if a shop triples the price of bottled water during a heatwave, it may fuel a customer backlash and lose goodwill.

Price Skimming

Price skimming is a specialised form of demand pricing used by companies holding a significant advantage (Du & Chen, 2017) over previously sold products. Typically, this strategy is used in the consumer electronics industry, and it links to Rogers' (2010) diffusion of innovations model (Figure 8.2).

Innovators constitute 2.5% of the population. They pay high prices for technologically advanced products at the beginning of the product life cycle, take risks associated with these products (e.g. unreliability or design flaws), and provide feedback to manufacturers. An innovator in one product category, such as hi-fi equipment, may be an innovator in similar categories, such as personal computers, but not in unrelated categories, like mountaineering equipment. They are highly motivated specialists in product categories which interest them. In price skimming, firms charge very high prices at launch – leveraging innovators' motivation – to recoup R&D costs and maximise profit. However, this market segment is quickly exhausted, so the seller drops the price to sell to the next segment: early adopters.

Early adopters constitute around 13.5% of the market. More demanding of reliability than innovators and more price conscious, they are still willing to take a risk on a relatively unknown product. Early adopters are materialistic, enjoying modern gadgets and the trappings of success, and are influential and well respected amongst peers.

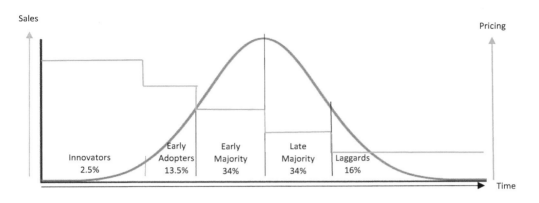

Sales

Pricing

Innovators
2.5%

Early
Adopters
13.5%

Early
Majority
34%

Late
Majority
34%

Laggards
16%

Time

FIGURE 8.2
Adaptation of Rogers' (2010) diffusion of innovations model to demonstrate price skimming, showing sales volumes in blue and pricing in red.

Therefore, their recommendations resonate with the mass consumers on whom the product depends. Once early adopters have bought, the manufacturer drops the price again to sell to the next segment – the early and late majority.

The **early majority** and **late majority**, each constituting around 34% of the market, are psychographically and behaviourally similar. They are both 'average consumers', but the early majority are slightly less risk averse, less price conscious, and more motivated by recent technology. The firm drops its price first to sell to the early majority and then to the late majority. When the late majority segment becomes saturated, the product is late in its life cycle, has usually lost the competitive advantage once derived from its technology, has long since recouped the R&D costs plus plenty of profit, and no longer has the volume potential or profitability to merit significant marketing spend (Jahanmir & Lages, 2016). Continuing to sell such a dated product may damage brand credibility. The only remaining consumers are laggards.

Laggards are extremely risk averse, wary of innovation, may have low levels of disposable income, and are only prepared to spend small amounts once products are tried and tested. They have little brand loyalty and exhaustively evaluate alternative products within elongated decision-making processes. Laggards make up only around 16% of the population and necessitate a price drop from the late majority. Some organisations may consider laggards so unprofitable, unresponsive, and difficult to service that they avoid them by **demarketing** their products and services to them (i.e. trying to reduce rather than increase demand) or by withdrawing the product during the early or late majority stage.

ETHICS QUESTION

Do you consider that price skimming raises any ethical concerns? For example, does it exploit the people who are willing to pay most at the start of the product life cycle? Make a few bullet points on the nature of each of these concerns, and for each one, explain how you might mitigate the negative effects.

Psychological Pricing

The most widespread psychological pricing tactic is to price products ending in 99 pence or cents rather than rounding up to the next pound, dollar, or euro, because the initial, unconscious customer perception is of a savings several times larger than in reality. Likewise, retailers understand price points representing typical customers' budget limits within product categories (Hanna & Dodge, 2017).

Customary Pricing

This involves charging customers what they are used to paying. Sellers may do this for price elastic products which customers buy habitually over many years (e.g. a brand of chocolate bar). This is problematic, because inflation devalues currency, so that a dollar in 2030 is worth less than in 2020, and therefore a manufacturer charging the same price year after year will erode their profit margin. Therefore, sellers may sometimes reduce the quantity sold instead of increasing the price. In 2016, Food giant Mondelez attracted criticism for reducing the 'peaks' and increasing the 'gaps' in its Toblerone bars to cut costs and keep its price around £1 or $1.40. It eventually reverted to the original proportions – around 33% bigger – but also increased the price by around 200% to compensate (Guardian, 2018).

Second Market Discounting

This enables firms to profit from less lucrative secondary markets, utilising their resources more fully and filling in troughs in demand. A restaurant may supplement its peak trade and cover overhead by attracting less profitable customers during weekdays, generating incremental profit without undermining the price expectations of core customers. Larger companies often use second market pricing to sell inexpensively in less economically advanced countries. In this case, they must safeguard against grey imports, or sellers shipping back discounted product to undercut local sellers in higher-priced markets.

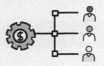
Types of Competitor-Based Pricing

If a rival cuts prices, an organisation must react by (i) reducing their own price, (ii) improving customer perceptions of their own product to differentiate, (iii) increasing both the product quality and price to move upmarket, or (iv) fighting the rival with a budget sub-brand.

By matching the rival's price reduction ('meet-the-competition' pricing) or beating it ('undercutting the competition'), the organisation may trigger a price war, distressing its brand, lowering customers' price expectations, and undermining its profits (Sotgiu & Gielens, 2015), but it may prevent the rival poaching its customers and gaining market share.

Improving customer perceptions is more economically sustainable, but if the product is not actually being improved, changing perceptions may be unachievable and require significant marketing spend.

Increasing product quality and price is challenging. Although counterintuitive, raising prices as rivals cut theirs could increase customer perceptions of brand prestige and worth, making them less price sensitive and more profitable.

Launching a budget sub-brand entails significant marketing spend but enables an organisation to compete in a lower priced but profitable market segment without jeopardising brand equity. Renault achieved this with their Dacia brand (Steenkamp, 2017).

The two most prominent competitor-based pricing options are penetration pricing and predatory pricing, which have these characteristics:

PENETRATION PRICING

▶ Prices dropped discernibly but not deeply discounted

▶ Leverages on price elasticity and customers' perceptions of value

▶ Low price increases market share

▶ Necessitates comprehensive intelligence on competitors' pricing

▶ Therefore, difficult in marketplaces where prices fluctuate frequently

▶ Difficult where competitor salespeople routinely sell below published prices

▶ Can be difficult to restore prices to a higher level

▶ Risks triggering a prolonged price war which damages brand equity and profitability

PREDATORY PRICING

▶ Firm drastically reduces prices to damage a competitor by taking their customers

▶ Only feasible for financially stronger organisations that can absorb low or no profit margins

▶ A commercial war of attrition in which the firm 'starves' competitors into submission

▶ If the rival collapses, the aggressor often hikes prices to recover lost income

▶ It then often raises prices to maximise the profit opportunity presented by less competition

▶ Illegal in many countries, as it is considered anti-competitive and bad for consumers

Types of Cost-Based Pricing

By starting with the costs and working forwards to a selling price, cost-based pricing focuses on the product and the organisation's financial needs. The main financial considerations are (i) research, development, and design; (ii) overhead like business premises, machinery, and wages; (iii) manufacturing costs, like materials used in the production; (iv) the distribution and selling of goods; (v) margin required by channel partners; and (vi) a fixed profit margin for the organisation. Adding these factors should give a total price, but certain elements of customer-based or competitor-based pricing may be used to 'round off' the price.

The costs underpinning prices are fixed, variable, and total costs. **Fixed costs** are incurred regardless of how many units are produced (e.g. factory rental, heating and lighting, wages, and interest payments). Unless the firm can sell enough units to cover these, it will be economically unsustainable. **Variable costs** change with the number of units manufactured (e.g. a factory manufacturing 1 million bottles weekly has a lower per-bottle cost than a factory producing 250k bottles weekly). **Total costs** are the sum of all fixed and variable costs. An organisation which has reduced costs (e.g. Ryanair, which does not offer complimentary food) may undercut the competition. Therefore, cost-based and competitor-based pricing often exist in tandem.

Cost-Plus Pricing

This is simply adding predetermined profit margins (e.g. 20% or $10) to costs, and prevails in service industries.

Break-Even Volume

This is critical, particularly in cost-plus pricing. It is the number of unit sales required to cover all costs before a profit is possible, and is calculated using this equation:

Fixed Cost/(Price − Variable Cost) = Break-Even Volume

For example, a picture framer has fixed costs of £800 per month (e.g. rent, utilities), the price for framing each picture is £48, and the variable cost for each picture is £16. In this case, £800/(48 − 16) = 25. She must frame 25 pictures per month before generating profit at a rate of £32 per frame (i.e. the £48 selling price minus the £16 variable cost). Therefore, if she wished to make a £1,600 profit per month, she must generate £32 profit from each of 50 frames – a grand total of 75 pictures per month.

Break-Even Price

A closely related approach is to calculate the break-even price by using this equation:

Variable Cost + (Fixed Cost/Number of Units sold) = Break-Even Price

If the variable cost of framing a picture is £16, the fixed monthly costs are £800, and the desired number of pictures framed is 100, then the calculation would be £16 + (£800/100) = a break-even price of £24 per picture. So, if she wishes to frame 100 pictures monthly, the first £24 of each sale covers costs and break even, whilst every additional £1 charged will generate an additional £100 profit each month.

Target Profit Pricing

Target profit pricing uses break-even price as a base value and then adds profit per unit (and therefore overall profit) by setting a higher sales volume objective, reducing costs, charging a higher price, or a combination of these tactics.

Mark-Up Pricing and Profit Margins

Mark-up pricing and profit margin targets are common approaches. Mark-up pricing takes the bought-in price and adds a predetermined percentage profit. For example, if a store buys a jacket for £100 and applies an 80% mark-up, it must sell the jacket for £180. Mark-up is therefore expressed as a percentage of the bought-in price. Alternatively, a firm may desire a predetermined margin. Using the above example, if the store targeted a 50% profit margin, it must price the jacket at £200, because 50% of that £200 would be profit margin and the other 50% the bought-in price. Margins are expressed as a percentage of the selling price rather than the bought-in price. A 100% margin equates to a 50% mark-up.

MARKETING MANAGER TASK

As a marketing manager for Zomotor, Dylan must ascertain how much value Chinese customers might attach to different features of a forthcoming car, and to warranties and breakdown coverage.
Make a list of the types of people Dylan should speak to and explain your rationale. Compile some key questions which you may need to ask them and decide what methods you will use to collect this data. Finally, explain how you might analyse and present the findings to your directors.

In addition to customer-based, competitor-based, and cost-based pricing, firms may also use product-mix, adjustable, promotional, or discount pricing. These are shown in Table 8.2 and are discussed in detail next.

TABLE 8.2

Types of product-mix, adjustable, promotional, and discount pricing.

Product-Mix Pricing	Adjustable Pricing	Promotional Pricing	Discount Pricing
Product line pricing	Segmented pricing	Cash-back deals and	Volume discounts
Optional-product pricing	Location and time pricing	rebates	Seasonal discounts
Product bundle pricing	Demand and dynamic pricing	Warranties, servicing, and finance	Promotional discounts
Captive-product pricing	Geographical pricing	Special-event pricing	Trade-in allowances
By-product pricing	Uniform delivered pricing	Loss leaders	
	Freight absorption pricing		
	Zone pricing		

Product-Mix Pricing

When a product is priced in the context of a range of product, this is product-mix pricing. It involves the seller 'looking at the big picture', and using one of several approaches.

Product Line Pricing

In the product line pricing approach, sellers encourage customers to trade up and accessorise by placing different product versions within a stepped pricing hierarchy. It is intended that customers intending to purchase a basic version will be enticed to a more expensive one with higher profit margin. Car manufacturers rely greatly on this technique.

Optional-Product Pricing

Motor manufacturers also use optional-product pricing to encourage customers into more profitable purchases. By offering accessories and optional extras, such as heated leather seats, roof bars, and iridescent paintwork, some customers will upgrade to more profitable cars.

Product Bundle Pricing

Product bundle pricing is much loved by fast-food outlets. Perhaps a customer intends to buy a small burger and soft drink. However, by offering a package of medium-sized burger, small fries, and large drink, and pricing the package lower than if all items were bought individually, the restaurant entices customers into increasing their spend. The drink and fries would be sold cheaper than if ordered separately, but the profit is still healthy (financially, at least) and incremental, and the customer probably feels satisfied by the deal and more likely to return.

Captive-Product Pricing

Captive-product pricing entails a relatively expensive and profitable subsidiary product being sold to operate a less expensive core product. For example, technology firms sell printers cheaply, knowing that customers will later need to purchase profit-laden ink cartridges. The seller can use the strategy if the customer cannot switch to a rival's consumable product – usually guaranteed through product design – but may jeopardise customer goodwill and repeat purchases unless they also demonstrate customer value.

By-Product Pricing

Finally, by-product pricing is the cheap sale of commodities which are superfluous to the manufacturing process, presenting an incremental profit and relieving a stock burden. The brewing industry produces yeast-based by-products which it sells to makers of spreads such as Marmite, whilst sherry and bourbon distillers sell used oak casks to whisky distilleries.

Adjustable Pricing

Many circumstances necessitate pricing strategy adjustments: entering a new market, selling to several segments, responding to changes in customer demand, and attacking or defending against a competitor. These can require nuanced, segmented pricing approaches to maximise profit and serve diverse audiences.

Segmented Pricing

This involves pricing the same product or service differently depending to specific customer segments. For example, an art gallery may price admission lower for pensioners, children, and the unemployed – 'customer-segmented pricing' – to be inclusive and socially just.

Location and Time Pricing

A football club may charge different prices to watch the same match depending on the seat position, view, and experience. This is location pricing. Time pricing uses the same principle but charges more when a product or service is provided during a time rather than a place, which is more desirable, like an airline charging more for midday flights than midnight flights.

Demand and Dynamic Pricing

Demand pricing and dynamic pricing develop this idea by linking price to the circumstances of the sale. For example, taxis often cost more after public transport has finished for the night (demand pricing), and television auction sites often drop prices as more customers buy (dynamic pricing). Many global companies use international pricing, reducing prices in poorer regions where consumers have less to spend, to gain their customers and make a reduced profit rather than no profit. By charging more in wealthier markets, they reinforce brand prestige, imply added value, and increase their profit per unit.

Geographical Pricing

Several forms of geographical pricing can also be used in international trade. Many sellers adopt **uniform delivered pricing**, applying the same prices globally. Usually, the seller would use the average anticipated freight charge, meaning that nearer accounts slightly subsidise farther ones. This prevents distant customers from feeling alienated but can allow aggressive competitors to undercut a nearby company. A similar strategy is

freight-absorption pricing, where sellers absorb all or most of the shipping costs. This contrasts with **zone pricing**, which charges according to customer location, ensuring competitiveness when supplying nearer customers and covering costs when supplying distant ones. However, this can alienate overseas customers and encourage them to seek a local supplier.

NEW MEDIA QUESTION

Imagine you are the marketing director of a company which produces apps. Having designed an app to help students learn common marketing definitions, you wish to implement a 'freemium' pricing strategy, in which users can access some content interspersed with adverts for free or can pay a monthly subscription to access premium content without adverts. Write down which content and features you would make available to each type of user and why.

Promotional Pricing

Promotional pricing constitutes offering temporary price inducements to entice customers to buy, and is summarised as follows.

CASH-BACK DEALS AND CASH REBATES

► Often offered through retail partners

► Encourage customers to buy within a pre-defined promotional period

► Even when the customer has bought using finance, they can receive the money as a lump sum

► Builds upon consumers' short-term cash-flow issues

WARRANTIES, SERVICING, AND FINANCE

► Free or subsidised extended warranty periods, servicing packages, or interest-free finance

► Benefits the customer, but its cost is not apparent

► Avoids distressing the brand through overt discounts

SPECIAL-EVENT PRICING

▶ Used to maximise sales volumes in a given period (e.g. during the FIFA World Cup)

▶ Used to counter lulls in market demand (e.g. when an old product is being withdrawn)

▶ Alternatively, used during busy periods to generate footfall, build market share and awareness, damage the opposition, or increase units sold and therefore overall profit

LOSS LEADERS

▶ Products priced eye-catchingly low

▶ Especially popular in supermarkets and retail stores

▶ Attract customers' attention and generate footfall so the store can profit from these incremental customers' additional, non-discounted items

METRICS QUESTION

Having used extremely discounted hand sanitiser gel and face masks as loss leaders to entice shoppers, your local supermarket wishes to ascertain what effect this has had on other, more profitable sales. List three ways in which they could find this out, and three key performance indicators (KPIs) against which they might measure the success of the strategy.

PHOTO 8.3
Tesco offers price discounts to its Clubcard members.

Discounts

Discounts can be problematic. They use price elasticity to encourage customers to buy sooner or more, but may undermine brand equity and value perceptions, sensitising customers to price. However, offering early payment discounts – around 3% to key accounts – may help maintain a healthier cash flow.

Volume Discounts

The most common discount in B2B sales is a volume discount offered to supply a product at a reduced price per unit if the buyer increases the order quantity. Such an offer needs careful handling, as customers sometimes exaggerate their requirement to flush out the salesperson's best price.

Seasonal Discounts

These encourage customers to buy during periods of low demand. For example, a horticultural wholesaler may offer 30% to 40% discounts to garden centres on hosepipes, wheelbarrows, and spades during autumn and winter. The garden centre can therefore achieve better profit upon resale, whilst the wholesaler can alleviate stock pressure, generate income, and operate year-round instead of seasonally.

Promotional Discounts

Promotional discounts may be granted to retailers to encourage them to help coordinate a sales campaign or product launch. To avoid distressing the product or alienating smaller channel partners, these discounts may be bundled with promotional support for advertising and local below-the-line marketing activities which benefit both parties.

Trade-In Allowances

Very popular with car dealerships, these guarantee customers a minimum trade-in price for their current item when buying a new item. Naturally, people's existing cars have a predetermined value judged by independent industry valuers, and dealerships only offer more attractive trade-in values by increasing the new vehicle price commensurately.

Sustainability and Pricing

Some pricing may not be intended to be financially sustainable (e.g. deep discounts) but to achieve short-term objectives. Firms must be clear on desired time frames or self-harm. Pricing can also address environmental sustainability. By placing a small levy on single-use plastic bags, governments have encouraged recycling, drastically reducing waste and addressing an environmental concern through pricing. Through similar demarketing approaches, in which demand is deliberately reduced, governments have encouraged smoking cessation (Shiu et al., 2009), responsible alcohol consumption, and reductions in non-essential city driving (Wright & Egan, 2000). As such outcomes impact positively on other parties, such as the families of previously heavy drinkers, these approaches are stakeholder-focused and embrace both economic sustainability and social sustainability, addressing the 'triple bottom line' of profit, planet, and people (Elkington, 2013).

SUSTAINABILITY QUESTION

Manufacturers are under increasing pressure to ease the burden which consumption of their products places upon the environment – in particular, by reducing the use of single-use plastics and unnecessary or unrecyclable packaging. If you were a politician charged with reducing environmental impact, what policies would you introduce, and how would you help manufacturers to adopt more sustainable practices? List three or four alternatives, and explain your rationale.

PHOTO 8.4
Wetherspoons is a pub chain famous for its range of competitively priced drinks and food.

The Price Setting Process

Organisations must follow a structured process when setting prices. As constant price re-evaluation should take place, it is a cyclical process. Although firms may vary the process depending upon whether they are pricing a new or existing product, operating amongst new or existing clients, and in a competitive environment or a monopoly, the process should include the following (Figure 8.3).

1. Situation analysis

   ▶ Where the organisation is at that point in time

   ▶ Macro environmental, micro environmental and internal factors – especially customers and competitors

   ▶ Comprehensive market research

2. Pricing objectives

   ▶ To serve organisational and commercial objectives

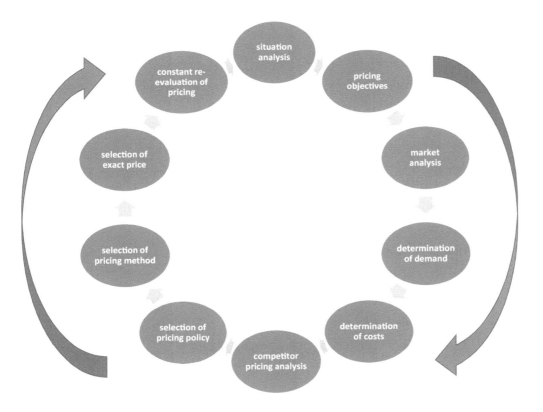

FIGURE 8.3
The price-setting process.

3. Market analysis
   - ▶ Consumer confidence
   - ▶ Elasticity of demand (customer tolerance of specific price rises and responsiveness to specific price cuts)
   - ▶ Ability to pay within its target market (including availability of finance if selling 'big ticket' products)
   - ▶ Customers' price sensitivity

4. Determination of demand
   - ▶ Expected customer numbers at specific pricing levels

5. Determination of costs
   - ▶ Fixed costs
   - ▶ Variable costs
   - ▶ Total costs
   - ▶ Break-even profits
   - ▶ Break-even volumes

6. Competitor pricing analysis
   - ▶ Explore rivals' prices
   - ▶ Examine rivals' product specifications and the perceived value and actual costs attached to each individual specification
   - ▶ Make direct comparisons with competitor product and benchmark wherever possible
   - ▶ Perhaps undertake perceptual mapping, comparing competitor products by three variables as per the example below, to visualise the differentiatedness of a product and avoid commoditisation

7. Selection of a pricing policy
   - ▶ Must be customer, competitor, or cost based

8. Selection of a pricing method
   - ▶ Refine to an exact, nuanced, and individual stance on pricing
   - ▶ Fulfil all stakeholder needs
   - ▶ Blend elements of the three major pricing strategies

9. An exact price

10. Constant reassessment of pricing
    - ▶ The pricing decision is never complete
    - ▶ Constantly monitor customers

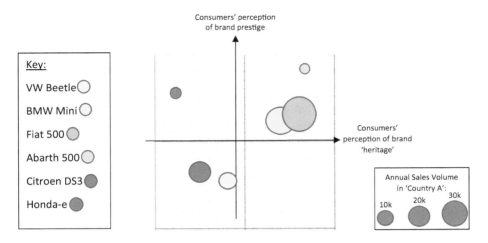

FIGURE 8.4
Perceptual map of consumers' perceptions of 'heritage' motor car brands.

▶ Constantly monitor competitors

▶ Constantly monitor external and internal environments

▶ Anticipate changes early enough to mitigate against threats and capitalise upon opportunities

MARKETING DIRECTOR TASK

As Zomotor's marketing director, Lee will be launching a new car in Europe in six months' time. The competition is fierce, with several rivals selling well-established, high-quality products to a discerning audience. The new car must grow market share, build brand equity, recover R&D costs, and generate a healthy profit. It will be sold to retail customers through franchised dealerships, leased through finance companies, and sold to industrial clients (car fleet operators) by Zomotor's B2B salespeople. Help Lee by devising a comprehensive pricing approach which caters for these segments whilst delivering your commercial objectives. Which pricing strategies will you use? What advantages and disadvantages could each bring for Zomotor and its customers?

Chapter Summary

Pricing influences profits profoundly. Simply selling large volumes or quantities may not generate a healthy profit – and may even generate an unsustainable loss – unless the price is correctly pitched. However, price setting is a tightrope: pricing too high, whilst providing seemingly healthy profit per unit, may discourage customers from buying and drive them towards competitors, undermining the firm's overall profits and damaging market share. Conversely, pricing too low may attract more customers and increase sales volumes but erode profit per unit until the break-even volume is unattainably high and the product sustains unacceptable losses. Customers rarely choose the cheapest product – house, car, holiday, ring, laptop, college course, or T-shirt. Instead, they seek a balance of factors, including price.

Key Learning Outcomes

► Many pricing strategies are employed, sometimes in combination.

► Pricing strategies should fit the commercial context in which an organisation operates.

► Each strategy has advantages and limitations to different stakeholders.

► Pricing, commercial performance, and stakeholder needs are interconnected and interdependent.

Recommended Further Reading

Du, P., & Chen, Q. (2017). Skimming or penetration: Optimal pricing of new fashion products in the presence of strategic consumers. *Annals of Operations Research, 257*(1–2), 275–295.
Fisher, M., Gallino, S., & Li, J. (2017). Competition-based dynamic pricing in online retailing: A methodology validated with field experiments. *Management Science, 64*(6), 2496–2514.
Nagle, T. T., & Müller, G. (2017). *The strategy and tactics of pricing: A guide to growing more profitably*. Routledge.

References

Albanese, P. (2015). Inside economic man: Behavioral economics and consumer behavior. In *Handbook of contemporary behavioral economics* (pp. 25–45). Routledge.
Bös, D. (2015). *Pricing and price regulation: An economic theory for public enterprises and public utilities* (Vol. 34). Elsevier.
Coglianese, J., Davis, L. W., Kilian, L., & Stock, J. H. (2017). Anticipation, tax avoidance, and the price elasticity of gasoline demand. *Journal of Applied Econometrics, 32*(1), 1–15.
Diallo, M. F., Coutelle-Brillet, P., Riviere, A., & Zielke, S. (2015). How do price perceptions of different brand types affect shopping value and store loyalty? *Psychology & Marketing, 32*(12), 1133–1147.
Elkington, J. (2013). Enter the triple bottom line. In *The triple bottom line* (pp. 23–38). Routledge.
The Guardian. (2018). https://www.theguardian.com/business/2018/jul/20/toblerone-to-revert-to-original-shape-but-with-bigger-size-and-price
Hanna, N., & Dodge, H. R. (2017). *Pricing: Policies and procedures*. Macmillan International Higher Education.

Jahanmir, S. F., & Lages, L. F. (2016). The late-adopter scale: A measure of late adopters of techno-logical innovations. *Journal of Business Research*, *69*(5), 1701–1706.

Kumar, V., & Reinartz, W. (2016). Creating enduring customer value. *Journal of Marketing*, *80*(6), 36–68.

Lee, K. Y., Jin, Y., Rhee, C., & Yang, S. B. (2016). Online consumers' reactions to price decreases: Amazon's Kindle 2 case. *Internet Research*, *26*(4), 1001–1026.

Olbrich, R., Jansen, H. C., & Hundt, M. (2017). Effects of pricing strategies and product quality on private label and national brand performance. Journal of Retailing and Consumer Services, 34, 294–301.

Payne, A., Frow, P., & Eggert, A. (2017). The customer value proposition: Evolution, development, and application in marketing. *Journal of the Academy of Marketing Science*, *45*(4), 467–489.

Rogers, E. M. (2010). *Diffusion of innovations*. Simon and Schuster.

Shiu, E., Hassan, L. M., & Walsh, G. (2009). Demarketing tobacco through governmental poli-cies – the 4Ps revisited. *Journal of Business Research*, *62*(2), 269–278.

Sotgiu, F., & Gielens, K. (2015). Suppliers caught in supermarket price wars: Victims or victors? Insights from a Dutch price war. *Journal of Marketing Research*, *52*(6), 784–800.

Steenkamp, J. B. (2017). Global brand equity. In *Global brand strategy* (pp. 243–273). Palgrave Macmillan.

Wright, C., & Egan, J. (2000). De-marketing the car. *Transport Policy*, *7*(4), 287–294.

Glossary

Break-even price: the selling price at which the seller covers costs but makes no profit

Break-even volume: the sales volume at which the seller covers costs but makes no profit

By-product pricing: the pricing of a commodity which is wastage from another indus-trial activity

Captive product pricing: the pricing of a product which must be used as a component of a larger product

Cash-back deals/cash rebates: offering money back as an incentive to buy or lease something

Competitor-based pricing: basing one's prices upon competitors' pricing

Cost-based pricing: basing prices upon one's costs

Cost-plus pricing: adding a predetermined profit to the break-even price before selling

Customary pricing: selling at a price to which customers are accustomed

Customer-based pricing: basing prices on customer-focused factors

Demand pricing: changing pricing as customer demand fluctuates

Demarketing: intentionally reducing demand for one's product or service

Distress a brand: damage perceptions of a brand, often through discounting

Dynamic pricing: see *demand pricing*

Early adopters: consumers who buy products early in the product life cycle

Early majority: the 'mass market' consumers who buy products earlier in the life cycle

Everyday low pricing (EDLP): offering constant low pricing rather than sporadic discounts

Fixed costs: remain constant regardless of how many units are made and sold

Freight-absorption pricing: absorbing the cost of all transportation into prices

Geographical pricing: the pricing of something differently according to customer location

Globalisation: trading globally, often with some uniformity of approach

Good-value pricing: conveys value for money

Innovators: the motivated consumers who buy products at the start of the product life cycle

Laggards: the risk-averse consumers who buy products at the end of the product life cycle

Late majority: the 'mass market' consumers who buy products later in the life cycle

Location and time pricing: tailoring prices to the time and place in which the sale will occur

Loss leaders: underpriced items, which attract customers to more profitable items

Margin: the percentage or amount of money in the price which constitutes profit

Mark-up pricing: adding a predetermined percentage or amount of profit to the buy-in cost

Monopolistic competition: many producers selling different products which resist direct comparison

Oligopoly: a market dominated by a small group of large sellers

Optional-product pricing: selling a base product cheaply and its accessories more profitably

Penetration pricing: dropping the price slightly to gain market share

Perceptual map: a graph expressing three variables against which brands/products can be compared

Predatory pricing: trying to damage or eliminate a competitor with unsustainably low prices

Price elastic: the demand for something fluctuates considerably when pricing changes a little

Price inelastic: the demand for something remains constant when pricing changes a lot

Price skimming: stepping down prices as a product ages and attracts different customer segments

Product bundle pricing: offering a package deal to incentivise customers to buy additional items

Product-line pricing: using pricing to position products within a firm's product portfolio

Product-mix pricing: a type of pricing which incentivises purchases across the firm's product range

Promotional discounts: short-term discounts to accompany a promotional event

Promotional pricing: temporary price inducements to entice customers to buy

Psychological pricing: a type of pricing which considers customers' unconscious perceptions of price and value

Pure competition: many suppliers and customers prevent one seller from dictating price trends

Pure monopoly: there are no competitors, and firms can price as high as customers will tolerate

Return on capital employed (ROCE): a measure of company profitability

Return on sales (ROS): net profit generated by each monetary unit (e.g. dollar, euro, pound) of sales

Seasonal discounts: applied at certain times of the year

Second market discounting: applying discounts to trade with a secondary market segment

Segmented pricing: dividing the market into segments and pricing for each

Special-event pricing: offering temporary pricing to support a special event

Stock turn: the number of times annually that the entire stock is sold and replaced

Total costs: fixed costs plus variable costs

Trade-in allowances: applying a 'part exchange' discount to a new sale for the item it is replacing

Uniform delivered pricing: a type of pricing which includes the same delivery charge, regardless of location

Value-based pricing: see *customer-based pricing*

Variable costs: production and trading costs which decrease (per unit) and volumes increase

Volume discounts: offering discounts which increase if a customer buys a greater volume

Zone pricing: applying different prices to different geographical regions

Pricing Case Study: Zambia's Trade Kings Group

In 1995, a Zambian businessperson named Mr Patel developed Blue Boom Detergent Paste – described on the company website as a "high quality, locally produced but affordable washing and cleaning solution" – and the Blue Boom brand from his garage in the country's capital, Lusaka. Despite enduring difficult economic and political conditions, he was able to build his business by purchasing a textile trading outfit and then a bakery, and by sourcing local products from Zambian suppliers. Today, his Trade Kings Group is the most popular brand in Zambia and the dominant manufacturer of fast-moving consumer goods (FMCG) in sub-Saharan Africa. Zambia itself is a rugged, landlocked country in southern Africa. Lusaka lies 4,500 miles (a 130-hour drive) south of the Mediterranean

continued

Coast and 1,000 miles (a 24-hour drive) west of the Indian Ocean. As a quickly growing city of over 3 million people, its airport is being redeveloped, and it is also on the south-north Cape to Cairo Railway and the east-west Transafrican Highway 9.

Trade Kings Group has a number of subsidiary companies: Bigtree Beverages sell soft drinks, colas, bottled water, fruit juices, and energy drinks; Bigtree Brands and Royal Oak make baby cereal, infant nutrition products, teas, coffees, and baking products; Dairy Gold produce juices, creams, milk, and the Maheu drink traditionally consumed by sub-Saharan African families in the evening; Swiss Bake sell biscuits and cookies through their Chelsea and Amazon brands; and Yoyo Fun Snacks is a youthful company producing savoury snack foods such as potato chips.

Despite lacking the financial power of longer established European and North American counterparts such as Unilever, Procter & Gamble, and Reckitt Benckiser, the company appears well-poised to grow domestically by acquiring brands to enter new product categories, and internationally by growing its market share in Northern Africa and perhaps expanding into the Middle East, south Asia, and southern Europe. Many of its prominent products, such as the Mr Boom bathroom and kitchen cleaners, appear very similar to established European and North American products like Mr Muscle, Cillit Bang, and Dettol, which are sold in Western supermarkets at much higher prices than own-label products.

Imagine that you work for a major international marketing agency and have just been awarded a contract to help Trade Kings to grow their small presence in Egypt and to plan a stepped approach to entering southern Europe. For each of these target territories, identify three core products or subsidiary companies which you believe would help to establish Trade Kings. For each product or company in both regions, suggest two pricing strategies which you believe would be most successful. Give a balanced, critical rationale for your strategic recommendations.

Sources

African Business Magazine website. Retrieved December 24, 2020, from https://africanbusinessmagazine.com/top-african-brands/africas-top-100-brands-2020/

Statista website. Retrieved December 24, 2020, from https://www.statista.com/topics/2870/zambia/

Trade Kings website. Retrieved December 24, 2020, from www.tradekings.co.zm

9 | Consumer and Buyer Behaviour

LEARNING OBJECTIVES

▶ To assess the role of consumer behaviour in marketing

▶ To evaluate how the characteristics of the buying situation influence consumer behaviour

▶ To understand how social, psychological, and personal drivers affect an individual's buying behaviour

▶ To explain the process by which consumers make buying decisions

▶ To highlight the basic differences between consumer behaviour and organisational behaviour

Introduction

We think of marketing as the activity and process for creating, communicating, delivering, and exchanging offerings that have value for customers and satisfy their needs. It goes to say that customer behaviour consists of customers' actions taken while searching for, purchasing, using, evaluating, and disposing of products and services that they expect will satisfy these needs (Blythe, 2013; Stankevich, 2017).

Why do individuals or organisations buy the products and services they do? What criterion do they use when they buy? Where do they like to shop, or what vendors do they choose and when? Marketers want to know the answers to these questions as, once they have these answers, they have a better chance of communicating about products and services that consumers will want to buy. As both consumer and business markets are in a state of continuous change, marketers also need to understand any new and emerging contexts to conduct marketing activities successfully. It is therefore essential to recognise that buyer behaviour influences, at all times, how marketers communicate

PHOTO 9.1
Consumers make buying decisions every day.

and deliver products that offer value to customers. Indeed, marketing and consumer behaviour stem from the marketing concept, which maintains that the essence of marketing consists of satisfying customers' needs, creating value, and retaining customers. Therefore, studying consumer and organisational behaviour results in an understanding of *why* and *how* customers make purchase decisions. That is what the study of buyer behaviour is all about.

Buyer behaviour is the behaviour of consumers in different buying situations as they go through a decision-making process when making consumption decisions. For example, the widespread adoption of digital technologies has connected individuals and organisations in a way not imagined as possible only a few years ago. As the environment around us changes, so does our purchasing behaviour. Buyers buy things every day, exchanging money for products and services. However, our decisions to buy have implications for ourselves and our friends, family, stakeholders, and the environments surrounding us. For example, in markets we see people eating more convenience food, more family members are working to pay household bills, and more single-person households means that many consumers prioritise convenience in their buying decisions. This chapter will highlight the underlying tenets to consumer behaviour and follow this discussion with some insights on the differences between consumer and organisational behaviour.

Consumption and Consumer Behaviour

Consumer behaviour is recognised as a highly complex set of processes. Our understanding of this subject is formed by consumer psychology and theories of human behaviour, which are, in themselves, extensive subject areas. To understand consumer behaviour, we need to look at it in the context of the rest of the marketing elements, as the way a consumer behaves influences segmentation, marketing planning within an organisation, and the marketing mix. Indeed, for marketers, a detailed understanding of each aspect of behaviour will help modify the marketing mix elements to suit each situation better. This understanding of customers can be gained by answering the following questions, as they help define the key dimensions of behaviour.

Who Buys?

Most of the time, consumer purchases are *individual*. For example, when purchasing a chocolate bar, a person may make an impulse purchase upon seeing an assortment of confectionery at a supermarket checkout. However, decision-making can also be made by a *group*, such as a household. In such a situation, any number of individuals may interact to influence the purchase decision. Even more, each person may assume a role in the decision-making process. These specific roles have been classified by Blackwell et al. (2005) in five distinct categories:

1. The *initiator* is the person who starts (i.e. initiates) the process of considering a purchase. In some cases, information about the considered product or service may be gathered by this person to help the decision.

2. The *influencer* is the person who tries to persuade others in the group about the outcome of the decision. Typically, influencers gather more detailed information about the product or service they consider and often attempt to impose their choice criteria on the final decision.

3. The *decider* is the individual with the power and/or financial authority to make the ultimate choice regarding which product or service to buy.

4. The *buyer* is the person who conducts the transaction. The buyer calls the supplier, visits the store, makes the payment, and ensures delivery of the product or service.

5. The *user* is the actual consumer/user of the product or service that has been purchased.

How Do They Buy?

How consumers buy has been traditionally regarded as a decision-making process beginning with the recognition that a problem or a need exists. Many researchers have developed theories and models depending on various factors and findings. The common consensus is that the consumer purchasing theory (i.e. how consumers buy) involves several stages, which generally involve the recognition of need or problem, information search, comparing the alternatives, purchase, and post-purchase evaluation. These stages are detailed later on in this chapter.

Where and When Do They Buy?

Consumers make purchases for different reasons that involve underlying motivations and the importance of the purchase for the individual or the group. The time and place of purchase used to be at a physical point of sale, such as a supermarket. However, we notice that this is no longer the case, as the scope and opportunity of when and where to buy have been significantly extended by e-commerce systems and the growth of digital markets.

Buying Situation

Consumer buying situations and consumers' involvement are often influenced by different factors, such as self-image, perceived risk, social factors, and hedonistic drivers (Laurent & Kapferer, 1985). In particular, three types of buying situations have been identified: extensive problem-solving, limited problem-solving, and habitual problem-solving:

PHOTO 9.2
Buying online represents a significant shift in consumer behaviour that has changed the way businesses interact with consumers.

▶ *Extensive problem-solving* involves buying decisions, often associated with specialty products, where consumers take a significant period of time to decide. This is often due to the risk associated with the buying decision. For example, choosing what university to attend is an example of extensive problem-solving. There is risk associated with the decision, and it can be difficult to compare alternatives. Careful consideration and research is needed in order to solve extensive problem-solving buying situations.

▶ *Limited problem-solving* involves buying decisions, often associated with shopping products, where a consumer takes a limited amount of time to decide. The consumer has some experience with the product in question, so that an information search may be limited or internal through memory. However, a certain amount of external search and evaluation may occur before a purchase is made (e.g. checking prices). This situation allows marketers to affect purchase by stimulating the need to search (e.g. advertising) and reducing the risk of brand switching (e.g. warranties).

▶ In *habitual problem-solving*, a consumer repeat-buys the same product with little or no evaluation of alternatives (e.g. buying the same breakfast cereal on a weekly shopping trip). The consumer may recall the satisfaction gained by purchasing a brand and automatically repurchase it. Advertising may effectively keep the brand name in the consumer's mind and reinforce already favourable attitudes.

PHOTO 9.3
Purchasing bed linens is an example of a limited problem-solving purchase.

Factors Influencing the Buying Decision

Like marketing itself, the study of consumer behaviour is a combination of other disciplines, such as economics, psychology (the study of the human mind and mental factors that affect behaviour), sociology (the study of the development, structure, functioning, and problems of human society), and anthropology (which compares human societies cultures and development). As a result, many factors can influence the outcomes of consumer purchasing decisions. Some of these factors are specific to the buying situation: what exactly is the consumer buying and for what occasion? Other factors are specific to each individual, such as an individual's background and preferences, personality, and motivations. For marketers, an understanding of these factors provides a better understanding of the buying situation. Here, we group these influencing factors into social, cultural, psychological, and personal determinants of consumer behaviour.

MARKETING ASSISTANT TASK

Tannya is undertaking an audit of all branded materials in the franchised dealerships in Mexico to check which ones are damaged or display out-of-date logos, fonts, colour schemes, and slogans. Tannya was alarmed to find that nearly half of all dealer demonstrator vehicles used for customer test drives either had decals (i.e. temporary vehicle livery) which were obsolete or had no decals at all. In a number of cases, this seemed to be because dealer staff were using demonstrator cars for their own private use or because they were being used as courtesy cars for customers whose cars were being serviced. Whilst this was undoubtedly helping dealerships by reducing their vehicle running costs, it was also undermining their attempts to build brand recognition in their local sales territories, simultaneously hurting Zomotor's performance.

Tannya also found that some dealerships had signage which was up to 12 years old and two rebrands which were out of date. The dealers had not ordered replacement signage to reduce their overhead, and Zomotor's regional managers had either not noticed or not believed that they could persuade or force the dealer to replace the materials. Tannya realises that a comprehensive understanding of all elements of Zomotor branded materials within dealer premises is needed. Please help Tannya by producing a list of all such materials (e.g. brochures, flags) and, for each one, explain the potential impact on the dealer's B2C sales performance if the materials are obsolete.

Social Factors

Social factors are external environmental variables that can influence buying decisions. These sociological drivers for consumer behaviour recognise that sociology has contributed to understanding consumer behaviour by looking at peers and reference groups, family, and self-image.

Reference Groups

Reference groups, which often include an opinion leader, serve as information sources that can influence an individual's attitude or behaviour. Religious groups, political groups, and subcultures are all examples of groups that exert influence. Although their impact varies across products and brands, reference groups are recognised as having a great potential of influencing consumer behaviour. For example, the brand or model chosen in the case of conspicuous products (e.g. clothing or cars) is often strongly influenced by what consumers perceive as being acceptable to their reference group. In this case, the reference group may consist of family members, a group of friends, or work colleagues.

Socialisation is the gradual moulding of a person's behaviour by comparison with a group. This process is a vital issue not only in sociology but also in marketing. So, marketers frequently use reference groups and opinion leaders to model the use of the products in group situations, showing how the person who uses the product can become popular within a desirable group of people.

Reference groups influence their members by the roles and norms expected of them. There are three main types of reference groups: associative (groups to which an individual already belongs), dissociative (groups to which an individual wishes to dissociate from or discriminate against), and aspirational groups (groups to which the individual would like to belong). For example, ASOS, the online fashion retailer, bases its marketing strategy on the aspirant group theory: the company copies the style of clothing worn by film stars and models and sells its clothes to aspirant consumers who wish to dress like them.

▶ *Associative* reference groups often include a person's nuclear family (extended family, friends, colleagues, neighbours), consumer action groups (either ongoing, such as government action groups, or ad hoc, such as action protest or support groups), online consumer blogging, and branded websites (e.g. corporate websites or brand communities).

▶ *Dissociative* reference groups are those from whom the individual may wish to dissociate themselves. There are often cultural reasons for this dissociation, as there are certain groups that people universally dissociate from, such as paedophiles, arsonists, murderers, drug dealers, corrupt officials, and terrorists. There are also

PHOTO 9.4
Religious affiliation is an example of a reference group that can influence consumer behaviour.

celebrities that some consumers may dissociate with based on negative publicity or personal likes and dislikes. Some individuals dissociate themselves from certain companies because of a mismatch in values, commercial practices, or targeting children.

▶ *Aspirational* reference groups are those that the consumers themselves against or perhaps aspire to their achievements and lifestyles. The most referenced are opinion leaders and celebrities. Opinion leaders are those whose knowledgeable and insightful views we value as the basis for our thinking and decisions. The estimation is that opinion leaders make up about 10% of the population, influencing consumers about what to buy and where to eat (Keller & Berry, 2013). There are opinion leaders in politics, business, technology, education, and many other areas. Celebrities are individuals that we admire, follow, and look at in an aspirational way. They are always in the news through media coverage, positive or negative influence listings. However, the influence can be lost as quickly as it is gained. Very often, marketers use celebrities as brand ambassadors in advertising or to launch new products.

Family

The family is the first reference group for many individual attitudes and behaviours. At the most basic form, a family consists of two or more persons related by blood, marriage, or adoption, who live together.

The family is also the prime target consumer segment for marketers. Marketers recognise that although families operate as units when it comes to consumer behaviour, there are important dynamics in family decision-making. Therefore, marketers focus on each family member's relative influence regarding consumption, such as the children's role in family decision-making. Many consumer studies classify family consumption decisions as husband-dominated, wife-dominated, joint, or autonomic decisions (Meier et al., 1999; Ganesh, 1997). However, the consensus is that the relative influence of one partner depends mainly on the product or service category (Chandrasekar & Vinay Raj, 2013; Moss, 2017). Over the past several decades, marketers have also noticed a trend toward children playing a more active role in what the family buys and the family decision-making process (Taneja, 2019).

The family life cycle represents the life stages of a typical family. It is a composite variable that combines marital status, size of family, age of family members (focusing on the age of the oldest or youngest child), and employment status of the head of household. It then classifies the family into a 'typical' stage. The parents' ages and the relative amount of disposable income are inferred from the family's stage in the cycle. Generally, the family life cycle starts with bachelorhood/bachelorette stage and moves on to marriage to create the family unit. Marriage usually leads to a growing family (with the birth of children) and later to family reduction (as the children grow and leave the household). The cycle ends with the end of the family unit due to the death of one spouse.

PHOTO 9.5
Family is a significant influence on consumer behaviour.

Geo-demographics

Geo-demographics is another method of socially classifying households. This classification is based on geographic location, and the analysis uses population census data. Marketers group households into geographic clusters based on information such as age, occupation, accommodation type, car ownership, number and age of children, and ethnicity. These clusters can be identified by postcodes, which makes targeting by mail easier. For example, in the UK, several systems are used, such as MOSAIC (developed by Experian) and ACORN (A Classification of Residential Neighbourhoods).

ETHICS QUESTION

Health and fitness have been a significant part of Western culture. Even more, American media, in particular, has driven healthcare to become a point of cultural reference in contexts and countries that have adopted the American way of life. With a rise in the number of health clubs, fitness-related services, and wearable technologies that monitor heart rate, body fat, and calories, many consumers have increasingly become more conscious of their lifestyles. Businesses decide the type of products to offer based on these trends, with food companies modifying their products to cater to these health-conscious consumers. Indeed, many food companies have introduced variants of their products that are 'light', 'fat-free', or 'no preservatives', even though these new offers are not always the healthier option (e.g. some of these products might have a higher level of sugar compared to their 'not-as-healthy' options). Examine how consumers, buying behaviour might be influenced by the 'healthy' messages conveyed by such companies.

Cultural Factors

Marketing communication at a global scale is assumed to have created a global, homogeneous consumer culture. However, in practice, in many areas of consumers' lives (e.g. music, sports), it's been noted that globalisation has been the reason for the revival of local cultural identities in different parts of the world (Giddens, 2003; de Mooij, 2011).

Culture

Culture is a very complex belief in human behaviour. It includes human society and refers to the traditions, norms, taboos, values, and basic attitudes of the entire society to which an individual belongs. Culture also provides the framework within which individuals and their lifestyles develop. Therefore, cultural norms are the rules that govern behaviour and are based upon values (i.e. beliefs about what attitudes and behaviour are desirable).

Cultural values express the collective principles, standards, and priorities of a society. However, cultures constantly evolve, so marketers must monitor the sociocultural environment to market existing products more effectively and develop new products congruent with changing cultural trends. However, understanding these cultural changes is not easy given the diversity of factors that affect cultural changes within a given society, such as new technologies, population shifts, resource shortages, and customs from other cultures.

We learn cultural norms and customs mostly from family and peers and begin to understand at a very young age that some behaviours are appropriate and others are not. Individuals also form their ethical values during childhood, learning them from parents, friends, teachers, and other significant adults. The contents of media, advertising, and other marketing communications reflect these cultural values and convey them effectively to all members of society. As a result, culture is acknowledged to be one of the key drivers of consumer behaviour. Some of the main elements of culture are discussed here:

▶ *Language* affects purchasing behaviour in many ways, given that recognising and consequently acting on marketing communication relies on understanding the language and specific words and sentence constructions within the language. For example, slang terms may not be fully understood by all non-native speakers of the language.

▶ *Rituals* are symbolic activities consisting of multiple behaviours, are repeated periodically, and occur in a fixed sequence. For example, weddings generally follow a well-defined path.

▶ *Customs* are norms of behaviour that originated at some point in the past. Some of these can stem from religious beliefs or shared beliefs. For example, many traditions associated with Christmas emerged from a combination of pagan, pre-Christian, and Christian beliefs.

▶ *Religion* influences consumers' behaviour in many ways, from rules about what to wear and when to consume certain foods. An example is the symbolic meal taken by Christians during communion.

▶ *Rites of passage* are events that move an individual from one state to another. For example, turning 21 years old in some cultures is considered becoming an adult.

SUSTAINABILITY QUESTION

Consciousness and interest toward the environment have become essential features in Western societies, and now many companies use these concepts in their marketing to enhance the appeal of their products. However, this is an aspect that considerably varies across cultures, as not all of them are equally receptive to it in the same way. For example, China has been traditionally less concerned by environmental issues than others, although this may be changing. Indeed, China has started paying more attention to environmental concerns, which represents a massive opportunity for many companies in the country. The companies are also responding to increased consumer awareness of global warming and the desire to be more eco-conscious, which results in greater demand for green products. The question for you to consider is 'Do consumers react differently to green products depending on their country of origin?', and if so, why?

Subculture

A subculture is a group of individuals who share the same values, customs, and traditions. These can be defined as a nation, a religion, racial groups, or groups of people sharing the same geographic location. In other words, they are groups of individuals within a society who share common behaviours and cultural meanings. It is important to note that although a subculture shares most of the mainstream culture within which it is embedded, its members have a distinct and identifiable set of behavioural norms and customs, which distinguishes that from the rest of the culture.

Subcultures may be based on gender type, age, special interests, or ethnic background, or even how members interpret communication messages. For example, a subculture of conspiracy theorists will interpret all official statements as evidence of a cover-up. Some of the key subcultures are:

▶ *Age subcultures*, also known as the 'generation gap', exist because members have different attitudes and behaviours. Some of the age subcultures are teenagers, Generation Z, millennials, baby boomers, the over-50s, and many others. Marketers need to be aware that, in some cases, individuals retain attitudes that were current in their youth (e.g. music likes and dislikes), and in other cases, individuals' behaviours change as they age.

▶ *Geographic subcultures*. For example, in the UK, Wales and Scotland regard themselves as separate from England, and they have different languages and cultures. These differences can be significant for marketers. They need to recognise

PHOTO 9.6
Subcultural affiliation can influence a consumer's beliefs, values, and norms.

differences between subcultures and, importantly, address them accordingly, perhaps by using local dialects in any promotional communication.

▶ *Ethnic subcultures* are a growing group of consumers. There are two groups here:
those individuals who emigrate from their country of origin and therefore are considered members of their home country culture, and those whose were born in a
host country of parents who came from another country.

▶ *Gender subcultures* are also significant for marketers, although there are relatively
few products or services that are gender specific.

▶ *Brand-based subcultures* also exist (e.g. Harley-Davidson owners).

Social Class

Social class is an essential determinant of consumer behaviour. It has remained a predictive measure of consumption, although consumption patterns are likely to vary within
each identified social class (Wacquant, 2019). Social stratification, as social class is
sometimes referred to, is the separation of members of a society into a hierarchy of
distinct status classes. Members of each class have a comparatively similar status, and
members of all other classes have either more or less status.

Some form of class structure (or social stratification) has existed in all societies
throughout history (Meyer, 2018). In contemporary societies, better-educated people
or those who have prestigious occupations have more status relative to other members

of the same society. Belonging to a given social class is also reflected in differences in the values, attitudes, and behaviours (including consumer behaviour) among members of different social classes. Social class is a continuum along which society's members, usually as households, are placed into one stratum; they are 'assigned' to a social class according to their relative prestige within that society.

When measuring social class, marketers are concerned with classifying individuals into social class groupings. These are effective ways to identify and segment target markets. There are two basic methods for measuring social class: subjective measurement and objective measurement. Subjective measures rely on an individual's self-perception. In contrast, objective measures use specific socioeconomic measures, either alone (as a single-variable index) or in combination with others (as a composite-variable index). Composite variable indexes, such as the Index of Status Characteristics (Warner et al., 1977) and the Socioeconomic Status Score, combine several socioeconomic factors to form one overall measure of social-class standing.

METRICS QUESTION

Choose a company that sells its products and/or services through its own shops or other retailers. Now consider how metrics might help this company monitor its current and potential consumers' behaviour. In particular, look at (i) traffic patterns (i.e. how customers move through the store, (ii) dwell time (i.e. how long consumers spend inside specific sections of the store, and (iii) traffic patterns (i.e. how your consumers move throughout the store). How do you think store design impacts customer experience? What specific attributes do stores incorporate that might enhance (or detract) from the customer experience?

Psychological Factors

Psychological drivers for consumer behaviour are varied and relate to the consumer's motivation, learning, socialisation, attitudes, and beliefs. Marketers recognise the importance of contributions from psychology (e.g. drive and motivation), research on goals and incentives, learning studies, studies about attitude formation and change, and studies of personality and self-concept.

Motivation

Motivation is the driving force that compels all consumers to act. It represents an individual's reasons for behaving in a particular way and drives consumers to take action by producing a psychological tension caused by unfulfilled needs. Individuals strive to reduce this tension by selecting goals and subsequent behaviour that they anticipate will fulfil their needs and relieve them of the tension they feel. For motivation to be useful in marketing practice, it is helpful for marketers to understand its role in a specific purchasing situation. In other words, marketers need to understand what triggers consumers to set goals, take action, and solve their need-based problems.

It is worth noting that these needs can be psychological needs, social needs, esteem needs, and needs of security and self-actualisation, as identified by Maslow's widely accepted theory of human motivation, known as the hierarchy of needs (Maslow, 1943). The theory identifies five basic levels of human needs, which rank in order of importance from low-level needs (biogenic) to higher-level needs (psychogenic). It suggests that individuals will seek to satisfy lower-level needs before higher-level needs emerge.

▶ *Physiological* needs are the first and most basic level of human needs and are dominant when chronically unsatisfied. They are those things that are required to sustain biological life: food, water, air, shelter, clothing, and sex (biogenic needs).

▶ *Safety and security* needs become the driving force behind consumer behaviour after physiological needs have been satisfied. They include order, stability, routine, familiarity, and control over one's life and environment. Health and the availability of healthcare are important safety concerns.

▶ *Social* needs relate to such things as love, affection, belonging, and acceptance.

▶ *Egoistic* needs can take an inward or outward orientation or both. Inwardly directed ego needs reflect an individual's need for self-acceptance, self-esteem, success, independence, and personal satisfaction with a job well done. Outwardly directed ego needs include the needs for prestige, reputation, status, and recognition from others.

▶ *Self-actualisation* refers to an individual's desire to fulfil their potential to become everything they are capable of becoming.

An individual's motivation levels also vary depending on the individual, the type of purchase, and the purchase occasion. For example, research conducted by Nwankwo et al. (2014) suggests that the motivations for buying luxury goods focus on the desire to portray a specific social class, to communicate a desired self-image, and to provide self-concept reinforcement, a visible proof that the consumer can afford higher-priced products.

Attitudes

Attitudes are an orientation that a person holds that are rooted in the thoughts and values that a person believes. In the marketing context, it is a conviction about a product or service on one or more choice criteria (e.g. beliefs about a Volvo car might be that it is safe, reliable, and of high status). It is also an overall favourable or unfavourable evaluation of a product or service. Attitudes are consistent views encompassing individuals' beliefs and emotions about products, services, brands, and organisations.

An attitude is recognised as being a learned predisposition to behave in a consistently favourable or unfavourable way towards a given object. It is important to note here that, in the context of consumer behaviour, an object broadly includes the product, brand, service, price, package, and many other aspects. We all form our attitudes from direct experiences with the product or service or from word of mouth, exposure to media, and other information sources. They reflect either favourable or unfavourable evaluations of the attitude object, and they motivate consumers either to buy or not to buy particular products or brands. Given that consumers generally buy products towards which they have favourable feelings, marketers must ensure that consumers maintain positive attitudes following each purchase and remain loyal customers.

Attitude structure can be defined in terms of three components, also known as the tri-component attitude model, which proposes cognitive, affective, and conative components of an attitude (Cavell, 1990; Agyeiwaah et al., 2021; Asiegbu et al., 2012).

▶ The *cognitive* component represents the knowledge and perceptions acquired by combining direct experiences with the attitude object (i.e. beliefs) and related information gathered by an individual from different sources.

▶ The *affective* component reflects emotions and feelings, considered evaluations because they capture the person's overall assessment of the attitude object. Affect-laden experiences manifest themselves as emotionally charged conditions (e.g. happiness or sadness), which may enhance the consumer's positive or negative experiences and recollections of those experiences.

▶ The *conative* component is the likelihood or tendency an individual will undertake a specific action or behave in a particular way about the attitude object. In many cases, the conative component includes the actual behaviour itself. Marketers often regard the conative component as an expression of the consumer's intention to buy.

In most cases, attitudes precede and guide behaviour. Sometimes, consumers act first and only afterwards do they develop attitudes about actions already undertaken, creating conflicting thoughts about the attitude object, known as cognitive dissonance. Because important purchase decisions (i.e. buying a new home) require compromise and choices among similar alternatives, post-purchase conflicts are common. Marketers must ensure that customers resolve cognitive conflicts by changing their attitudes to conform to their behaviour. The broad view is that attitudes are consistent with the behaviour they reflect. In other words, a positive attitude towards a product will result in the consumer purchasing that product. Research, however, does indicate that, despite their consistency, attitudes are not necessarily permanent. They do change, and sometimes even frequently, as they are affected by situations, events, or circumstances that influence the relationship between attitudes and behaviour.

Perception, Learning, and Experience

Information processing refers to the method by which a stimulus is received, interpreted, stored in memory, and later retrieved (Blackwell et al., 2005). Therefore, it is viewed as the link between external influences, including marketing activities, and consumers' decision-making process. Two critical aspects of information processing are perception and learning.

Perception is sensing the world and the situations around and then taking a decision accordingly. It is all about how individuals develop an understanding of the world around them by processing information gleaned through the senses. It is also about creating a view of the world through both synthesis and analysis. Consumers constantly reject most of the stimuli they receive and only take in information that is of direct interest to them at that particular point, leaving gaps in individuals' knowledge that need to be filled in. As a result, each of us has a somewhat different understanding of how the world is made up and what the rules are.

One of the problems with perception is that it is difficult to change. Changing people's perceptions of the world is not easy. Everything we take in is interpreted in the light of what we already know (known in psychology as the 'law of primacy'), and generally, we are relatively comfortable with our worldview. Furthermore, there is always a natural suspicion about being manipulated – individuals tend to resist being influenced by other people unless they have specifically requested some information.

On the other hand, learning is a relatively permanent change in behaviour that is linked to experience. However, behaviour is not the only type of learning, as individuals also learn by physical behaviour or by interpreting symbols and their meanings. Effective learning is learning to value some aspects of our environment and to dislike others. This type of learning also influences consumers' development of favourable or unfavourable attitudes towards a company or a brand.

In consumer behaviour, learning is an ongoing process that is dynamic, adaptive, and subject to change. Here, learning does not include behaviour associated with instinctive responses or temporary states of an individual, such as hunger, fatigue, or sleep. Instead, it is the research of products and services before the consumer decides to buy a product. Therefore, learning is the process by which consumers change their behaviour after they gain information or experience a product. Experience is recollecting a lesson from the past experiences of a product, service, or brand. Learning and experience both again play an essential role in influencing consumers' behaviour, as it influences their purchase decision. Marketers use the learning to focus on consumer satisfaction to reinforce behaviour, such as after-sales services, personalised relationships such as special offers, birthday discounts and gifts, and customer rewards for their purchases with loyalty schemes.

MARKETING MANAGER TASK

Dylan has found that, despite a fresh and comprehensive model range and strong national marketing, footfall at Zomotor's Chinese dealerships is disappointing. In other words, the number of retail customers who are visiting the dealerships is below the number anticipated. In a few instances, Zomotor has recognised localised issues, such as the dealership building being a long way back from the roadside behind a line of trees, a temporary lack of easy access to the dealership caused by roadworks, or a major advertising campaign by a rival dealership on the opposite side of town. However, in most cases, those rival dealerships located on the same roads as Zomotor dealerships – clustered together on a street lined with motor franchises – have not been affected to the same extent.

Dylan is trying to establish what Zomotor and its dealerships are doing incorrectly or less effectively than their competitors and why they are failing to attract as many retail customers as expected. Help Dylan by making a list of potential explanations. In particular, focus on internal factors, such as the dealership not cleaning its display vehicles and placing them at the boundary of their site. For each potential reason you provide, analyse the effect this would have on the retail customer and their perception of Zomotor.

Personal Factors

A large portion of what motivates us to purchase products and services is our desire for pleasure. Since basic survival needs have generally been taken care of (in most wealthier parts of the world, in any case), we look to satisfy our emotional needs. Personal drivers, therefore, become important factors that influence consumers' buying decisions.

Lifestyle

Lifestyle represents the beliefs, activities, values, and ways of living of individuals. It consists of a combination of demographic characteristics, such as education and income, as well as psychographic characteristics around personality and motives. Lifestyle analysis has implications for marketing, since lifestyles have been found to correlate with purchasing behaviour (O'Brien & Ford, 1988).

People originating from different cultures, subcultures, occupations, and even social class have different living styles. Lifestyle can confirm the interest, opinions, and

TABLE 9.1

Taylor Nelson's lifestyle typologies based on consumer lifestyle category.

Lifestyle Category	Characterised by	Percentage of the Population
Belonger	Places value in home, family, country, and establishment.	19
Survivor	Disposed towards identification with groups and accepting of authority. Self-expression and creativity are irrelevant.	16
Experimentalist	Attracted to all that is new and different. Always looking for new ideas, items, and experiences.	12
Conspicuous consumer	Energies directed towards the consumer dream via material possessions. Take their cues from reference groups; noncritical of advertisers; followers of fashion.	18
Social resistance	Seek to maintain the status quo, controlling self, family, society, suppressing self in favour of duty and moral obligation.	15
Self-explorer	Self-aware and self-concerned people consider self-expression important.	14
Aimless	Uninvolved and alienated, aggressive towards the system, resentful of its failure to provide employment.	6

activities of people. Different lifestyles affect the purchase pattern of consumers. Therefore, marketers can develop more profound insights into consumer behaviour by understanding how consumers spend their time and what they think of various elements of their environment and getting a clearer idea of consumers' motives.

Taylor Nelson's Social Value Group typologies show that consumers' values and lifestyles influence consumer perceptions. It has been recognised as a useful conceptual tool for understanding consumer behaviour in many areas such as leisure (Gratton & Taylor, 1991) and tourism (Dalen, 1989), product innovation, purchasing, branding, advertising and food consumption (Nelson, 1986; Skelly & Nelson, 1966; Caulkin, 1987), new product development (Nelson, 1986), retailing (Powderly & MacNulty, 1990), and organisational structures and dynamics (MacNulty, 1985).

Personality

Personality is the internal trait characteristics within an individual. The word 'personality' is frequently used to refer to an individual's capacity for popularity, friendliness, or charisma. Nonetheless, these might be specific personality dimensions that an individual might possess – after all, we all have a personality, which provides the essential differences between one individual and another. That is why *personality* is also defined as 'the relative stable organisation of a person's motivational dispositions arising from an interaction between biological drives and the social and physical environment' (Eysenck, 1975).

Similar to lifestyle, marketers can use any personality trait to segment the consumer target market. Traits are individuals' distinct ways of responding to the social and physical environment, such as sociability, honesty, anxiety, independence, and aggression. The significant factors related to personality indicate that consumers may be high or low, or in between, along the continuum of traits. Most consumers, however, are scoring in the middle – this is sometimes referred to as the multi-trait approach because several dimensions measure holistic personality. Single-trait approaches, on the other hand, focus on one dimension.

The big five personality factors, as developed by John and Srivastava (1999), are:

- ▶ *Emotional stability*: calm/anxious, secure/insecure, self-satisfied/self-pitying
- ▶ *Extraversion*: sociable/retiring, fun-loving/sober, affectionate/reserved
- ▶ *Openness to experience*: imaginative/practical, independent/conforming, variety seeker/OK with routine
- ▶ *Agreeableness*: soft-hearted/ruthless, trusting/suspicious, helpful/uncooperative
- ▶ *Conscientiousness*: organised/disorganised, careful/careless, disciplined/impulsive

METRICS QUESTION

Opinions are formed from attitudes and beliefs. Part of the opinion process is the comparison of things. Trustpilot.com is a digital platform that aims to bring businesses and consumers together to encourage trust and stimulate collaboration. The website hosts reviews to help consumers shop with confidence. In groups, go to Trustpilot.com and explore how comparisons are made in a variety of product fields. Next, examine the rankings for a preferred product or services found on the Trustpilot website and discuss how attitudes influence such ranking and comparison processes. Examine how attitudes (opinions) might change once a viewer (i.e. consumer) has examined the rankings and comparisons.

The Consumer Decision-Making Process

As consumers, how much do we really make choices? At the superficial level, we have a vast number of options when deciding to purchase any products or services, from groceries to cars and from computers to mobile phones. However, how much *real* choice do we have about buying particular products or services at a more fundamental level?

Consumer decision-making is a complex process. The consensus amongst marketing researchers (Turley & LeBlanc, 1993; Stankevich, 2017; Karimi et al., 2018) is that it primarily consists of three distinct but interrelating stages: input, process, and output.

▶ The *input stage* includes two influencing factors. First, we have external social and cultural influences, such as culture, family and friends, reference groups, and social class. Second, we have the marketing mix elements in the product or service itself, its price, promotion, and distribution channels. It is worth noting that this stage also includes the methods by which information from organisations is transmitted to customers.

▶ The *process stage* is all about how consumers make decisions regarding the purchase. At this stage, the psychological factors (e.g. motivation, personality, attitudes, and perception) affect how the external inputs influence consumers' recognition of a need for a product or service, pre-purchase search for information, and evaluation of available alternatives. Noticeable here is that the experience gained by customers through the evaluation of alternatives in turn affects their existing psychological attributes.

▶ The *output stage* involves two post-decision activities: the actual purchase behaviour and post-purchase evaluation.

PHOTO 9.7
Sales promotion is a key tool in promoting need recognition during the input stage of the consumer decision-making process.

The specific elements of the three stages (i.e. input, process, and output) are discussed in more detail below.

NEED RECOGNITION/AWARENESS

Need recognition or awareness is the point where a consumer realises that they have a need to fulfil. This need recognition state can be the result of either internal stimuli (e.g. feeling hungry or thirsty) or external stimuli (e.g. interactions with friends, reference groups, or advertising messages). Need recognition can be seen also be seen as the perceived discrepancy between a *desired state* and what we perceive as our *actual state*. For example, nobody wants to feel thirsty (desired state), but I am thirsty (actual state). A perceived discrepancy is simply the difference between our desired and actual state: if there is a difference, then we become aware of a problem. It should be mentioned here that past experiences and individual motivations often moderate the perception of the desired state and the perception of an actual state.

There are various levels of needs and problems, such as:

▶ Routine problems, which require little search and evaluation because the decision has been made before and it is simply repeated.

▶ Planning problems, which can be seen ahead of time and there is time to make a decision. For example, if you expect to buy a new car sometime in the future, you may start taking note of different brands and designs and noticing any kind of related advertising. Similarly, if you expect that your mobile phone will be due for a replacement in the next few months, you may ask friends and family members about their experiences with brands, features, and retailers more than you would otherwise.

▶ Evolving problems come up expectedly, but they do not require an immediate decision, and so the consumer gathers information in a leisurely way. For example, adoption of new fashion may take a while for some consumers; a consumer may be aware of a fashion but choose to wait for a period to see the extent to which it meets social approval.

▶ Emergency problems, on the other hand, are unexpected problems that cannot be postponed and must be dealt with immediately. If your laptop computer suddenly fails and you have assignments to do this week, then what might have been an evolving problem that could have been postponed suddenly becomes an emergency. In such a situation, the amount of time expected to be spent on research and evaluation is substantially reduced; you will find suppliers that you have already known and perhaps seek a brand that you already trust, with relatively little consideration of features and value.

Problem-Solving

Information Search

The information search stage shows consumers what options are available. Generally, search behaviour is of two types: *internal search*, which involves scanning an individual's memory to recall previous experiences with products or brands, and *external search*, which involves looking elsewhere for information about the product or service, such as personal sources (i.e. friends and family) or public sources (i.e. online reviews by experts and other customers).

Nevertheless, not all decision-making situations require the same intensity of information research. When the individual has no established criteria for evaluating a product or service, more extensive problem-solving happens. If, however, consumers have already established the essential criteria for evaluating a product or service, a more limited problem-solving occurs, as the individual might only need more information to simply decide amongst the different models and brands available on the marketplace. When consumers have previous experience with the product, service, or brand, they will buy items often and almost instinctively – this is referred to as routinised response behaviour.

Consumer decision-making is different for high-involvement as compared to low-involvement situations. Consumer involvement (i.e. the degree of personal relevance that a product or service holds for the consumer) is another aspect of the information search stage. Based on the level of involvement, we talk about:

► *High-involvement purchases*, or those purchases that are very important in terms of the perceived risk. As a result, they generally cause extensive problem-solving and information processing on the consumer's part. For example, both cars and fashion represent high-involvement purchases: cars because of the perceived high financial risk and fashion because of the perceived high social risk.

► On the other hand, *low-involvement purchases* have little perceived risk, are mostly not very important, and cause limited information processing on the consumer's part.

PHOTO 9.8
University choice is an example of a high-involvement purchase.

Identification and Evaluation of Alternatives

Once the consumer has searched for available options to solve their problem and satisfy their need, they must decide which option to choose. This decision is a function of the criteria used to make an evaluation and how vital those criteria are. As already mentioned, people have limited capabilities for processing information. It is impossible to know everything about every possible alternative available, and an individual's criteria and motivations are often contradictory. We can, however, evaluate criteria as one of three types:

1. *Affective* evaluations are usually based on an impulse, as they involve an immediate emotional response to the product or service considered.

2. *Attitude-driven* evaluations are based on instant impressions, intuitions of feelings; in this situation, alternatives are not compared according to their features.

3. *Attribute-based* evaluations are based on a judgement on the attributes, or product features, of an alternative.

Classic consumer decision-making models assume that attribute-based evaluations are generally used by consumers looking to purchase a product or service. Indeed, a significant part of the earliest stage of information gathering and search for alternatives is gathering information about what criteria should be used for making comparisons and finding out what the alternatives are. So, by the time the consumer has finished their information gathering, they will have a list of available alternatives and a list of criteria to compare them against. Attribute-based evaluation rules can be classed into two groups:

▶ *Non-compensatory rules* are non-negotiable, specific criteria that must be met, otherwise the product or service alternatives are eliminated, regardless of how attractive other criteria might be. These rules are shortcuts that are only used to quickly select one or a brief list of acceptable options. For example, consider a personal budget as the specific criteria: if an individual cannot afford the alternative, they have to select something else, regardless of how much they like other features.

▶ *Compensatory rules* are attractive features on some criteria that compensate for unattractive features of other criteria. These rules allow consumers to trade one or more criteria for others when evaluating alternatives, and an attractive feature can compensate for an unattractive one. It also allows consumers to trade one or more criteria for others (i.e. an attractive feature can compensate for an unattractive feature). For example, consider what is meant when somebody says, 'It is a long walk across campus to the school café, but the quality of the coffee is so much better there'. The attractive feature (in this case, the better quality of the coffee) compensates for the unattractive feature (long walking distance).

In practice, when faced with a complicated or new decision task, most consumers tend to use non-compensatory and compensatory rules in sequence. Therefore, the first task for the marketer is to ensure the brand is known. Following this, the marketer must ensure it is acceptable to the customer (i.e. the brand should be in the consumers evoked set, or the set of brands from among all possible brands in a category that are known to the consumer).

MARKETING DIRECTOR TASK

Lee has realised that, if Zomotor is to attract a higher proportion of millennial customers to the brand, it must allow them a greater level of control over their choice of product. Currently customers can choose from a limited number of cost and non-cost options to add to their new cars, but a large proportion of those are 'linked options'. That means that if, for example, a customer chooses Option A, they must also buy Option B but are unable to choose Option C. Until recently, consumers seldom questioned manufacturers using such practices – indeed, there are times when two options are simply incompatible with each other, such as a sunroof and a soft-top – but increasingly customers are demanding a more democratic approach when speccing their new purchase.

continued

> As marketing director, Lee is working with product managers in Zomotor's largest markets, to analyse which car specifications they are able to make independent orderable options and which they must keep as standard specification or linked options. Whilst giving consumers more choice is likely to attract them and endear the Zomotor brand to them, it may also cause logistical complications, such as increased shipping costs for the manufacturer and significant delays in delivery, especially if two ordered options are produced by suppliers who are geographically distant from each other or where options must be added in different locations or in a specific order. Help Lee by making a list of the ten options which are likely to be the most emotive to millennial consumers; decide which you believe should be offered as independent orderable options, linked options, and standard specifications; and explain your rationale for each, taking into account both the customer's and the manufacturer's needs.

Purchase Decision

Having decided on evaluation criteria and evaluated all available options, the consumer decides to buy one preferred brand or to buy none. Purchases can be classified into three types: planned purchase, partially purchase, and impulse purchase (Kacen & Lee, 2002). Hoyer et al. (2012) also state that a number of factors can affect the purchasing process. For example, the desired product may not be available in the stock, in which case the purchase process is delayed, and the consumer may consider buying the product through online stores rather than visiting traditional physical stores.

The model or the brand to be purchased is usually seen as the decision process that has already happened, but there are also further tasks, such as deciding which model to buy and which retailer to purchase from. This may require a new information-gathering and decision-making process in itself. For example, should the consumer buy from a high street store or via an online retailer? Some retailers will allow repayments over time, and others insist on paying upfront. Some retailers may have to order in a product, or there may be a time delay if purchased online.

Post-Purchase

For most consumers, it is not the purchase itself that solves the problem that was recognised at the beginning of the process but the act of consuming the product or service purchased. The actual consumption allows an individual the opportunity to decide if the purchase process, as a problem-solving activity, has been successful. That is, does the alternative that has been chosen solve the problem first recognised? To settle this question, the consumer needs to consider whether the decision made was the best one and decide whether or not they are satisfied with the decision.

Many companies tend to ignore this final stage in the decision-making process, as it takes place after the transaction has been completed. However, marketers recognise that this stage can be the most important one, as it directly influences future decision-making processes by the consumer for the same product or service. Indeed, as the consumer decision-making process is a repetitive action (Ofir & Simonson, 2007), a good experience is essential in decreasing the uncertainty when the decision to purchase the same product or service is considered in the future.

This process includes cognitive dissonance, satisfaction and dissatisfaction, attribution, and equity. Dissonance means disagreement. How the customer feels about the purchase will significantly influence whether they will purchase the product again or consider other products in the category or other brands. Customers are more likely to feel dissonance when they consider that they do not have all the information required or do not know how to judge the information they have. Because dissonance is an uncomfortable state, the consumer may use one or more of the following tactics to reduce their dissonance:

▶ Try to persuade friends and family of the positive features of the brand, as the opinion of peers, friends, and family regarding the purchases made is recognised as one of the most critical factors affecting the outcome of post-purchase evaluation (Perrey & Spillecke, 2011)

▶ Look to known satisfied owners for reassurance

▶ Seek out advertisements that support the original reason for choosing the product

Marketers can help reduce post-purchase uncertainty by aiming specific messages at reinforcing consumer decisions by complimenting their astuteness, offering stronger guarantees or warranties, increasing the number and effectiveness of their services, or providing detailed leaflets on how to use their products correctly. The need to remove customer doubts is a strong reason why follow-up calls are a standard part of the sales and service process for many industries, such as car sellers, insurance companies, and banks.

STAKEHOLDER QUESTION

We generally consider individual attitudes to be relatively consistent with behaviour. Nevertheless, we also know that they are influenced by many other personal, social, and cultural factors. 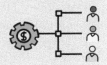 In many purchasing situations, consumers will also experience post-purchase dissonance (e.g. when a person may strongly prefer one brand but purchase a discounted brand because of budgetary requirements). Consider the

continued

following situation: a university student has just purchased a new laptop. In small groups, reflect on the factors that might cause the student to experience post-purchase dissonance and consider how they might try to overcome it. Further, discuss what the laptop retailer can do to help reduce the student's dissonance. And finally, consider how the laptop manufacturer can help.

Organisational Buying Behaviour

There is a different set of behaviour considerations when we look at organisational behaviour. Organisational behaviour, which is referred to as business-to-business (B2B) marketing, is the decision-making process associated with the purchase, production, and transformation of products and services for the purposes of adding value, and selling these outputs at a profit. B2B marketing represents a substantial component of the global economy. While this textbook outlines a number of characteristics associated with B2B markets, such as business segmentation (see Chapter 5), organisational decision-making units, the organisational decision-making process, and business buyer behaviour (see Chapter 14), the focus here is on the unique characteristics associated with organisational buying behaviour and the types of business products associated with B2B markets.

Buyer Behaviour

The main differences between organisational behaviour and consumer behaviour are the market size; demand characteristics; purchase volume; use of reciprocity and negotiation type; and buying nature, complexity, and size.

Market Size

Business markets deal with far fewer customers than consumer markets, but the transactions are far larger. Business markets often operate on what is known as the Pareto principle, which posits that 80% of the wealth (in business markets, this translates to revenue) is concentrated amongst 20% of the population (on business markets, this translates to buyers; Sanders, 1987). The relevance of this to business markets is that business markets are concentrated and are dominated by few players. In business markets such as breweries, 43% of all beer sales are concentrated amongst three dominant manufacturers (InBev, Heineken, and Carlsberg) (Conway, 2021). This leads to the stability of markets and long-term investments in businesses as ongoing entities.

Demand Characteristics

Demand characteristics are the business equivalent of consumer needs. In business markets, demand characteristics are influenced by derived demand, inelasticity, and joint demand.

Derived demand is the principle that demand is dependent upon the need for goods or services further down the supply chain. For example, the demand for timber is dependent upon a number of factors which include the demand for furniture, housing, consumer packaging, and other paper-based products. Business demand is interlinked and determined by the needs of buyers further downstream.

Business markets can also be characterised as inelastic, which means that demand for goods and services are often not impacted by price. This is often due to the complexity of business products being made from a number of different component parts. For example, if the price of a computer CPU increases dramatically, the demand for that component part is unlikely to change, nor would consumer demand for computers be greatly impacted. However, if there is a shortage of CPU chips, this will greatly impact the demand for other computer component parts such as motherboards or graphics cards, as the demand for these component parts are jointly connected.

Use of Reciprocity and Negotiation Type

One of the benefits to suppliers and buyers is the use of reciprocity in business markets. Reciprocity is a mutually beneficial exchange where both buyer and supplier receive equivalent value. Buyers are often able to extract concessions, in the form of discounts, when negotiating with suppliers. This is due to the nature of the business buy, where buyers purchase in large volumes and commit to long-term relationships. In these types of negotiations, a supplier might require a buyer to purchase their products as part of this negotiation. For example, an automobile manufacturer might require a supplier to buy a fleet of cars in exchange for doing business with a supplier. This is an example of business reciprocity, where each business is buying from the other.

Buying Nature, Complexity, and Size

Buying decisions within organisations often involve many different decision makers within the organisation. It can also involve buying complex technical goods and services that cost large sums of money and are bought in large quantities. Business organisations can enter into complex contracts that can legally guarantee buying commitments, lead times, and technical specifications. As a result, many organisations hire trained, professional purchasing agents to help manage the complexity of the buying decision.

Types of Business Products

Buyer behaviour and the decision-making process that organisations go through when making purchases are influenced by the types of products organisations buy. There are seven types of business products that organisations purchase, and these influence the level of buyer involvement in the buying process:

Raw materials: Raw materials are often unprocessed, commodity goods that manufacturers transform in the production of goods. Agricultural products, metals, ore, timber, and oil are all examples of raw materials.

Major equipment: Major equipment is the large capital investments organisations buy to add value to goods. In the cloud computing industries, these are industrial-sized mainframe computers and coolant systems that keep them from overheating.

Accessory equipment: Accessory equipment is similar to major equipment but on a much smaller scale. These are secondary components that aid in the transformation of goods and services. Using the cloud computing example, an organisation might need to buy hardware such as desktop or laptop computers to efficiently manage the system and run the business.

Component parts: Component parts are completed (or nearly completed) materials that are used in the production of another product. For example, televisions comprise a number of component parts made by different manufacturers that are then assembled. The completed television is then shipped to retailers to be sold or directly to consumers.

Process materials: Process materials are raw materials that have been processed and then integrated into another product. Corn syrup is an example of a processed material. It is made from the starch of corn, glucose, maltose, and other ingredients. Corn syrup is then used in the manufacture of other food products, such as soft drinks, breakfast cereals, confectionery, and other everyday household food items.

Business services: Organisations use external business services to help them maintain high levels of business performance. Business organisations might use external consultants to provide strategic recommendations that can be incorporated into strategy.

Supplies: Supplies are the everyday materials business need to function. These materials might include janitorial supplies or stationery.

Chapter Summary

Buyer behaviour refers to both customer and organisational behaviour. Marketers need to understand why customers make purchases and recognise the need to research behaviour to understand how and why individuals and organisations perceive and accept products and services. Social, psychological, and personal factors influence buying behaviour, and these determinants need to be considered when creating effective marketing mix strategies. Even more, the decision-making process needs to be understood, given that the actual purchasing is only one stage of this process and not all decision processes lead to a purchase.

Key Learning Outcomes

Consumer behaviour is a fundamental part of marketing activities within organisations. It is also a highly complex set of processes that enable marketers to understand how, why, when, and where individuals buy products and services.

Diverse factors influence consumer behaviour, such as social, psychological, and personal drivers. Culture and sub-culture, family and friends, individual lifestyle and personality, motivations, and attitudes all converge to influence the products and services an individual consumes.

The decision-making process includes several stages pre- and post-purchase. At each stage, individuals go through different degrees of involvement, and marketers have to understand how to 'move' the potential consumers through pre-purchase events to have a better chance of conversion to purchase and repeat purchase.

Recommended Further Reading

Boardman, R., & McCormick, H. (2019). The impact of product presentation on decision-making and purchasing. *Qualitative Market Research: An International Journal, 22*(3), 365–380.

Boulet, M., Hoek, A. C., & Raven, R. (2021). Towards a multi-level framework of household food waste and consumer behaviour: Untangling spaghetti soup. *Appetite, 156*, 104856.

Gu, S., Ślusarczyk, B., Hajizada, S., Kovalyova, I., & Sakhbieva, A. (2021). Impact of the COVID-19 pandemic on online consumer purchasing behavior. *Journal of Theoretical and Applied Electronic Commerce Research, 16*(6), 2263–2281.

Loxton, M., Truskett, R., Scarf, B., Sindone, L., Baldry, G., & Zhao, Y. (2020). Consumer behaviour during crises: Preliminary research on how coronavirus has manifested consumer panic buying, herd mentality, changing discretionary spending and the role of the media in influencing behaviour. *Journal of Risk and Financial Management, 13*(8), 166.

Voramontri, D., & Klieb, L. (2019). Impact of social media on consumer behaviour. *International Journal of Information and Decision Sciences, 11*(3), 209–233.

References

Agyeiwaah, E., Dayour, F., Otoo, F. E., & Goh, B. (2021). Understanding backpacker sustainable behavior using the tri-component attitude model. *Journal of Sustainable Tourism, 29*(7), 1193–1214.

Asiegbu, I. F., Powei, D. M., & Iruka, C. H. (2012). Consumer attitude: Some reflections on its concept, trilogy, relationship with consumer behavior, and marketing implications. *European Journal of Business and Management, 4*(13), 38–50.

Blackwell, R. D., Miniard, P. W., & Engel, J. F. (2005). *Comportamento do consumidor* (9th ed.). Pioneira Thomson.

Blythe, J. (2013). *Consumer behaviour* (2nd ed.). Sage.

Caulkin, S. (1987, July). The fall and rise of brands. *Management Today*, 45–49.

Cavell, T. A. (1990). Social adjustment, social performance, and social skills: A tri-component model of social competence. *Journal of Clinical Child Psychology, 19*(2), 111–122.

Chandrasekar, K. S., & Vinay Raj, R. (2013). Family and consumer behaviour. *International Journal of Management and Social Sciences Research, 2*(7), 17–20.

Conway, J. (2021). Global market share of the leading beer companies in 2020, based on volume sales. *Statista.* https://www.statista.com/statistics/257677/global-market-share-of-the-leading-beer-companies-based-on-sales/

Dalen, E. (1989). Research into values and consumer trends in Norway. *Tourism Management, 10*(3), 183–186.

de Mooij, M. (2011). *Consumer behaviour and culture: Consequences for global marketing and advertising* (2nd ed.). Sage.

Eysenck, H. J. (1975). The measurement of emotions: Psychological parameters and methods. In L. Levi (Ed.), *Emotions: Their parameters and measurement* (pp. 439–467). Raven Press.

Ganesh, G. (1997). Spousal influence in consumer decisions: A study of cultural assimilation. *Journal of Consumer Marketing, 14*(2), 132–155.

Giddens, A. (2003). *Runaway world: How globalization is reshaping our lives.* Taylor & Francis.

Gratton, C., & Taylor, P. (1991). *Government and the economics of sport* (1st ed.). Longman.

Hoyer, W. D., MacInnis, D. J., & Pieters, R. (2012). *Consumer behavior.* Cengage Learning.

John, O. P., & Srivastava, S. (1999). *The big-five trait taxonomy: History, measurement, and theoretical perspectives* (Vol. 2). University of California.

Kacen, J. J., & Lee, J. A. (2002). The influence of culture on consumer impulsive buying behavior. *Journal of Consumer Psychology, 12*(2), 163–176.

Karimi, S., Holland, C. P., & Papamichail, K. N. (2018). The impact of consumer archetypes on online purchase decision-making processes and outcomes: A behavioural process perspective. *Journal of Business Research, 91,* 71–82.

Keller, E., & Berry, J. (2013). *The influentials: One American in ten tells the other nine how to vote, where to eat, and what to buy.* Simon and Schuster.

Laurent, G., & Kapferer, J. N. (1985). Measuring consumer involvement profiles. *Journal of Marketing Research, 22*(1), 41–53.

MacNulty, W. (1985). UK social change through a wide-angle lens. *Futures, 17*(4), 331–347.

Maslow, A. H. (1943). A theory of human motivation. *Psychological Review, 50*(4), 370–396.

Meier, K., Kirchler, E., & Hubert, A. C. (1999). Savings and investment decisions within private households: Spouses' dominance in decisions on various forms of investment. *Journal of Economic Psychology, 20*(5), 499–519.

Meyer, J. W. (2018). The evolution of modern stratification systems. In D. B. Grusky & K. R. Weisshaar (Eds.), *Social stratification: Class, race, and gender in sociological perspective* (4th ed., pp. 1116–1125). Routledge.

Moss, G. (2017). *Gender, design and marketing: How gender drives our perception of design and marketing.* Routledge.

Nelson, R. (1986). Institutions supporting technical advance in industry. *American Economic Review, 76,* 186–189.

Nwankwo, S., Hamelin, N., & Khaled, M. (2014). Consumer values, motivation and purchase intention for luxury goods. *Journal of Retailing and Consumer Services, 21*(5), 735–744.

O'Brien, S., & Ford, R. (1988). Can we at last say goodbye to social class? An examination of the usefulness and stability of some alternative methods of measurement. *Journal of the Market Research Society, 30*(3), 289–332.

Ofir, C., & Simonson, I. (2007). The effect of stating expectations on customer satisfaction and shopping experience. *Journal of Marketing Research*, *44*(1), 164–174.

Perrey, J., & Spillecke, D. (2011). *Retail marketing and branding: A definitive guide to maximizing ROI*. John Wiley & Sons.

Powderly, J., & MacNulty, C. (1990). Consumer trends: A turbulent time ahead. *Marketing*, *11*, 33–34.

Sanders, R. (1987). The Pareto principle: Its use and abuse. *Journal of Services Marketing, 1*(2), 37–40.

Skelly, F., & Nelson, E. (1966, Summer). Market segmentation and new product development. *Scientific Business*, 13–22.

Stankevich, A. (2017). Explaining the consumer decision-making process: Critical literature review. *Journal of International Business Research and Marketing*, *2*(6), 7–14.

Taneja, C. (2019). Categorising products strategically basis children's influence in urban Indian household. *International Refereed Social Sciences Journal*, *10*(2), 1–13.

Turley, L. W., & LeBlanc, R. P. (1993). An exploratory investigation of consumer decision making in the service sector. *Journal of Services Marketing, 7*(4), 11–18.

Wacquant, L. J. (2019). Making class: The middle class (es) in social theory and social structure. In *Bringing class back in* (pp. 39–64). Routledge.

Warner, W. L., Meeker, M., & Fell, K. (1977). Index of status characteristics. In D. C. Miller & N. J. Salkind (Eds.), *Handbook of research design and social measurement* (3rd ed.). Sage.

Glossary

Attitudes: an orientation that a person holds that are rooted in the thoughts and values that person believes

Buyer: the person who conducts the transaction

Consumer behaviour: the behaviour of consumers in different buying situations as they go through a decision-making process when making consumption decisions

Culture: the traditions, taboos, values, and basic attitudes of the entire society to which an individual belongs

Decider: the individual with the power and/or financial authority to make the ultimate choice regarding which product or service to buy

Evaluation of alternatives: a consumer's choice of options

Extensive problem-solving: buying decisions often associated with specialty products, where decisions take a significant period of time to decide

Family: two or more persons related by blood, marriage, or adoption who live together

Habitual problem-solving: when a consumer repeat-buys the same product with little or no evaluation of alternatives

Influencer: the person who tries to persuade others in the group about the outcome of the decision

Initiator: the person who starts (i.e. initiates) the process of considering a purchase

Information search: shows consumers what options are available

Learning: the process by which consumers change their behaviour after they gain information or experience a product

Lifestyle: an individual's beliefs, activities, values, and ways of living

Limited problem-solving: buying decisions, often associated with shopping products, where consumers take a limited amount of time to decide

Motivation: the driving force that compels all consumers to act

Need recognition: the awareness of the need is the point where a consumer realises that they have a need to fulfil

Organisational behaviour: the decision-making process associated with the purchase, production, and transformation of products and services for the purposes of adding value, and selling these outputs at a profit

Perception: sensing the world and the situations around and then taking a decision accordingly

Personality: the internal trait characteristics within individuals

Reference groups: serve as information sources that can influence an individual's attitude or behaviour

Social class: the separation of members of a society into a hierarchy of distinct status classes

Subculture: the group of individuals who share the same values, customs, and traditions

User: the actual consumer/user of the product or service that has been purchased

---

Marketing's Quest for Cool

This exercise is dedicated to marketing's quest to find cool in consumer culture. What do marketers mean by 'cool'? Well, it is not easy to define.

From a consumer perspective, cool means different things to different people. For some people, cool means being unique or different. It means standing out from the crowd and not following the mass popular trends. It is being true to yourself and authentic. For other people, cool means what is fashionable or trendy. It means fitting in with your social group, not standing out and conforming to what your friends do.

For marketers, cool takes on a whole new meaning. When marketers try to reach youth markets, cool is a key driver in creating a distinctive brand identity that resonates with youth culture. Marketers try to manufacture cool in order to reach teen and young adult markets (ages 11–20).

The challenge for marketing is appearing to sell something to someone (which is what marketers do) is not cool. While a very small number of marketers can defy trends and manufacture cool, most marketers try to become cool by mirroring/replicating what is already cool in culture. The ability to find cool and study cool can be an important form of marketplace competitive advantages. One way that marketers try to be cool is to find what is cool in youth cultures. In

continued

some case, marketers seek out trendsetters in culture. Marketers then study these trendsetters by watching their habits and behaviours. They conduct ethnographic research, netnography, and focus group studies. Marketers observe what youth cultures do, what they listen to, where they go, what they wear, what they like and dislike, and what meanings and practices resonate with this group. They then try to package that information into product and service offerings. Marketers embed trendsetting language, clothing, imagery, music, and imagery into their marketing communications. The try to mimic the cool trends within culture. By studying cool, marketers try to become cool themselves.

continued

Pre-class Assignment

Please post in the discussion forum and/or be ready to discuss in your seminar group.
What is cool?

Cool can take different forms in culture. Choose a cultural category (you do not have to choose them all) and express "what is cool?" When thinking about cool, think about the following categories:

Brands

Music

Clothing/fashion

Film

Social media platforms

Experiences (experiences might be shared activities/things you do, either physically together or digitally)

You can use your opinions, pictures, or hyperlinks. What do you think is cool? Do you agree with your classmates? (Note: It is OK to agree/disagree, but be respectful of other people's opinions.)

In-Class or Post-Reflective Assignment

Consider the role marketing plays in the production and dissemination of cool. Do you think that marketers can be trendsetters in the manufacture of cool? Alternatively, do marketers represent the mass market that forces cool trends and cool people to move on? Reflecting on your own experiences of cool, consider the relationship between cool and marketing. In reflecting on these experiences, here are additional questions to consider:

1. What do you think about the marketer's ability to manufacture cool?
2. Are there differences between what cool people think is cool and what the mass market thinks is cool? If there is a difference, what is it?
3. How do you know when something is cool?
4. Reflect back on what was cool ten years ago. What was cool then? What does the marketing of cool look like today? Has it changed?
5. Drawing from examples of cool products, films, TV, fashion, and so forth, how do you think marketers find what is cool today? Where would they find cool?

Bibliography

Frontline. (2001). The merchants of cool. Public Broadcast System. https://www.pbs.org/video/frontline-merchants-cool/

Gladwell, M. (1997). The coolhunt. The New Yorker, pp. 17, 78–88.

LEARNING OBJECTIVES

► To identify major ethical issues facing marketers

► To explore how sustainability considerations can shape marketing strategies

► To analyse the role of corporate social responsibility

► To evaluate the impacts of organisations' ethical stances upon stakeholders

PHOTO 10.1
The betting industry has introduced measures to discourage gambling addicts from overspending.

DOI: 10.4324/9781003170891-11

Introduction

In this chapter, we will explore how the expectations placed upon organisations have changed over time, and how these changes in consumer attitudes have encouraged, and even compelled, organisations to present themselves to their markets in more ethically aware and stakeholder-focused ways. We will trace the evolution of ethical marketing practice and discuss the major underlying philosophical beliefs which shape them. We will then go on to explore how sustainability concerns have come to occupy a central position within firms, breaking them down into categories and noting how they are often mutually supporting rather than existing in isolation. Finally, we analyse the ethos and objectives of corporate social responsibility, the types of initiative which it comprises, and the outcomes which these initiatives engender for firms, customers, other stakeholders, and society more generally.

Marketing Ethics

Marketing in the Dock

The confrontational comedian Bill Hicks once asked if anyone in his audience worked in advertising or marketing, and then he infamously suggested that they kill themselves – to warm applause. This may seem shocking when we consider the positive value which marketing delivers to many stakeholders, but marketing has not always been as inclusive, interactive, and ethical as it is today, and many people still hold negative perceptions of it. Some of the accusations levelled at marketing include the following:

▶ It encourages a culture of **unnecessary consumption** which **depletes the earth's resources** and skews people's priorities away from what is really important.

▶ It encourages **conspicuous consumption** and ownership as an indicator of social acceptance, which excludes or **marginalises the less wealthy**.

▶ It reduces complex needs to **oversimplifications** and makes sweeping, stereotypical generalisations about people, thereby essentialising them and **perpetuating social inequalities**.

▶ It **exploits anxieties** in its audience, picking away at emotions such as embarrassment, disappointment, loneliness, desperation, pride, jealousy, and fear.

▶ It presents a **misrepresentation of reality** by accentuating the positives and minimising the negatives of a brand, product, or service – the **selective inclusion and omission of information**.

▶ It is **manipulative**, and much of its **influence is covert**.

ETHICS QUESTION

Imagine that you are a defence lawyer given the task of defending marketing against charges of being unethical. Whilst it would be unrealistic to say that marketing is never applied unethically by unprofessional practitioners, you need to outline the most important ways in which marketing makes a positive, ethical contribution to business, consumers, and society. With the help of bullet point prompts and PowerPoint slides if necessary, prepare a five-minute speech in which you explain the ethical value of marketing.

The above list – by no means exhaustive – grows yet further when we consider some of the dubious practices which have been carried out by unethical marketers:

▶ The use of political donations and **lobbying** to influence lawmakers into favouring one's organisation

▶ The **demarketing** of certain products, services, and companies to parts of the population deemed undesirable or unprofitable (e.g. credit card companies cherry-picking affluent customers but rejecting poorer ones)

▶ Political **spin** (i.e. presenting information to the public in an unrepresentatively positive light)

▶ **Cultural appropriation** (e.g. corporations coldly using hip hop culture to sell more products)

▶ **Anti-competitive practices** and predatory pricing (i.e. when an established seller 'starves' a new rival company out of the market with aggressive short-term price cuts, thereby reducing competition and being able to increase prices unopposed)

MARKETING ASSISTANT TASK

In Mexico, Zomotor is organising a 'ride and drive' event in which public sector vehicle fleet managers can test drive Zomotor's new van (light commercial vehicle) and obtain details from representatives. To make the event more enjoyable and to attract more guests, Zomotor would like to create a memorable experience which is fun for guests and allows them to socialise with Zomotor staff in an informal, relaxed manner. Possible experiences are (i) a sumptuous banquet in a castle, (ii) a jungle safari, and (iii) coral reef diving. Marketing assistant Tannya has been asked to make a list of ethical considerations which should underpin the choice of experience (e.g. how to choose who to invite, how much to spend, and how to communicate the invitation). Help Tannya by setting out ethical guidelines for Zomotor to follow, explaining why each one is important.

PHOTO 10.2
Darlington Building Society has an ethical code of practice built upon its Quaker roots. It has never offered high loan-to-value mortgages, which risk overstretching borrowers.

Four Common Approaches to Marketing Ethics

Many firms adopt one of four ethical stances in their marketing (Table 10.1).

In UK law, all advertisements must be 'legal, decent, honest and truthful', and ethical organisations try to adhere to these criteria across their marketing activities. In other words, they stay within local and international regulations, avoid offending the audience's sensibilities, present accurate and representative information, and refrain from misleading people.

Two Moral Dilemmas and Several Ethical Positions

Deep down, we are all moral philosophers. We may not categorise our moral beliefs or associate them with terminologies or schools of thought, but most of us are unconsciously competent in knowing what we believe to be right or wrong, even if our beliefs are not universal. Take, for example, the famous Trolley Problem (Thompson, 1976; Foot, 1978).

In the first scenario, a runaway trolleybus is hurtling towards five people tied to the track. An innocent bystander, you find yourself next to a lever which, if pulled, will divert the trolleybus away from the five people who are currently facing death, but towards one person tied to another track. By pulling the lever, you can save five lives but, in doing so, condemn one person to death who would have otherwise survived.

TABLE 10.1

Ethical marketing stances.

Stance	Meaning	Favourability
Caveat emptor	In Latin, 'buyer beware'; this means that it is the customer's responsibility to look after themselves, not the seller's job	Low
The ethics code	Do not simply meet one's obligations, but aim for higher ethical standards	Mid to High
Consumer sovereignty	"The customer is king/queen" – gives them the information and freedom to make appropriate choices	High
Caveat venditor	In Latin, 'seller beware'; this means that it is the seller's responsibility to ensure that the customer makes a suitable purchase decision which is in their own best interests	High

PHOTO 10.3

Timpsons, whose business centres around locksmith and dry cleaning services, is a highly ethical business which trains and recruits ex-offenders, provides employees with a final salary pension, and provides other major benefits.

What would you do? Most students, although harbouring reservations, say that they would pull the lever, because the net result would be four fewer fatalities.

Now imagine a second scenario. Once more, a runaway trolleybus is hurtling down-hill towards five people tied to the track, but this time, you are an innocent bystander on a railway bridge, standing immediately behind a very large man. Again, if you do not intervene, five people will die. However, you now have the opportunity to push the large man off of the bridge onto the track, where he would – at the expense of his life – derail the trolleybus and save the five currently condemned victims. What would you do now? Faced with this scenario, many of the students who would have intervened before become reluctant to do so. But why, if the basic effects are the same? The answer seems to be that, by being in direct contact with the person whose death will result from your actions, and by having a less passive role in their death, we are confronted by our choices and unable to detach reason from emotion.

If you would refuse to intervene in either scenario because you are not prepared to kill someone – even if in doing so you save five other lives – then you are taking a **deontological** approach. This means that you are adopting an **idealistic** standpoint which focuses on your duties as a responsible member of society, and you will not compromise your principles. In short, you believe in **ordinary decency**, that some things are just wrong and cannot be done under any circumstances. If you would intervene in both scenarios, then you are taking a **teleological** approach. This means that you are adopting a **consequentialist** and **relativist** standpoint which gauges how to attain the maximum benefit for the largest number of people. You are focused on the outcomes of your actions and embrace **situationalism**, the ability to view moral decisions through the lens of the situation or context in which it is posed.

The above standpoints occur not only in hypothetical dilemmas but also in business decision-making. Marketers may be guided in their actions by **contractualism** – the

PHOTO 10.4
IKEA reduces unnecessary wastage by selling slightly damaged goods for heavy discounts and encouraging recycling.

rules, obligations, and duties implicit within their roles. However, this should be the lowest acceptable standard against which they operate, and they should seek **moral equity** (inherent justice and fairness) in everything they do.

Useful Questions to Ask Oneself When Facing Ethical Dilemmas

In the face of ethical dilemmas, it is useful for marketers to ask themselves the following questions about their actions:

1. Am I adhering to the desired ethical standards of my profession?
2. Have I considered the consequences of my actions on all stakeholders?
3. Would I feel comfortable explaining my actions to a live television audience?
4. Am I treating others as I would wish others to treat me?

METRICS QUESTION

Think of famous brands which may have failed one of the previous four 'litmus test' questions on ethical practice. What did those brands do, how did their failings impact on others, and how has it made you feel about those brands? Draw a graph or chart which attempts to quantify how ethical or unethical each brand has been, comparing them with more ethical brands.

Ethical Transgressions in Marketing Communications

Although all aspects of marketing should conform to the highest ethical standards, ethical transgressions in marketing communications attract widespread criticism for their negative impact upon society. The International Chamber of Commerce has set out codes of practice for advertising (1997), direct marketing (2001), sales promotion (2002), sponsorship (2003), selling to children and young adults (2003), and digital marketing (2004). The codes state that marketers should *not* do any of the following:

▶ Offend audience members purposely

▶ Denigrate sections of society

▶ Mislead

▶ Abuse the trust placed in them by audiences

▶ Imitate competitors

▶ Design marketing communications to look like they are not marketing communications

▶ Fabricate testimonials

▶ Obscure the conditions of customer promotions or make participation difficult

▶ Charge payment for unsolicited goods (i.e. products or services not requested by the customer)

▶ Use data for purposes other than that stated, or for inappropriate purposes

▶ Share someone's data to third parties without that person's consent

▶ Disguise offers as invoices or bills

▶ Take advantage of young audience members' lack of maturity and experience, or undermine their familial loyalty

Additional laws and guidelines apply to harmful products such as alcohol and tobacco, limiting or banning their promotion in certain circumstances.

NEW MEDIA QUESTION

Imagine that you are a marketer for a major brand of single malt scotch whisky. You would like drinkers of other single malts, of blended whisky, and of other spirits to try your product. You would also like your existing customers to choose your brand more consistently when making their single malt purchases. However, you wish for consumers to drink responsibly and not to drink drive, and you wish to avoid glamourising your product to minors. In the context of your social media activities, how would you achieve this?

Offensiveness in Advertising

When advertisers offend audience members, it is big news and can damage the brand. Naturally, the incremental publicity may help to build awareness. For example, the Italian fashion brand, Benetton, has featured challenging images of human hearts, new-born babies, and breastfeeding mothers to convey their 'United Colours of Benetton' message. Whilst none of these images *should* be found offensive, many people were shocked by them or felt them inappropriate to the context and deliberatively provocative. However, it is worth noting that Benetton adverts were perhaps slightly ahead of society's sensibilities, whereas truly offensive advertising content usually conveys meanings which modern society has rejected. For example:

▶ PlayStation's 'White Is Coming' and Nivea's 'Re-civilize Yourself' campaigns were considered **racist**, as they alluded to the **power and cultural dominance** of white people over People of Colour.

▶ Irish betting company Paddy Power's posters seemed to trivialise and joke about the possibility of pensioners being knocked down on a pedestrian crossing. Whilst many enjoyed this irreverent humour, some charities and spokespeople complained that it **perpetuated negative attitudes towards a vulnerable minority group**.

▶ A significant proportion of men, and even more women, in adverts are **portrayed in a sexualised context**. Moreover, many television adverts are filmed with a **male gaze**, in which the camera lingers disproportionately long on the physical attributes of females deemed attractive.

▶ Some adverts reinforce unhelpful gender roles or draw upon negative stereotypes, such as the mother who feels neglectful of her children whilst at work, or the father who lacks his wife's childcare ability. Home gym equipment manufacturer Peloton attracted criticism in 2019 for an advert storyline in which a man gave his wife or girlfriend an exercise bike for Christmas, ostensibly with the intention of enabling her to preserve her physical attractiveness to him. Audiences found it **paternalistic, sexist, patronising**, and against the prevailing zeitgeist.

▶ Elsewhere, adverts have attracted criticism for being **vulgar** or displaying **poor taste**, taking an unsympathetic attitude towards **suffering**, including **nudity** or sexual **innuendo**, using **indecent language**, portraying **antisocial behaviour**, or broaching topics which are deemed **too personal** or sensitive.

Sometimes, advertisers may be a force for good but still attract criticism. When feminine hygiene products were first advertised on UK television, many viewers did not wish to be confronted by a supposedly taboo subject whilst watching programmes with their families. However, in helping to break down the taboo and encourage open, healthy discussion about sanitary care, marketing adopted a progressive role, moving society's attitudes forwards.

STAKEHOLDER QUESTION

As a marketer for a fashion company, you wish to portray your range of dresses and suits positively in television, print, and billboard adverts, encouraging women to perceive them as sophisticated, sexy, and empowering. However, you must be very careful 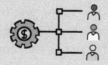 not to objectify women through the 'male gaze' or to alienate women of differing body shapes and sizes. What process would you put into place to ensure that you are acting ethically towards stakeholders? Make a list and prepare to discuss your rationale for each proposed action.

Untruthfulness in Advertising

There are numerous ways in which marketers may manipulate audiences to give a false impression of their brands. As consumers are becoming more aware of marketing 'tricks' and empowered to demand high standards of organisations, untruthfulness thankfully appears to have retreated, but the main forms of untruthfulness in advertising are as follows (Table 10.2).

TABLE 10.2

Main forms of untruthfulness in advertising.

Untruthfulness	Meaning
Lying/false advertising	Asserting verbally that a falsehood is true, or that a truth is false, to the benefit of the organisation and detriment of the customer
Subliminal ('hidden') branding	Branding which targets audiences' unconscious minds rather than attempting conscious interaction. One example is the use of advertising images within other televised content for such a minute time that it is imperceptible to audiences but is internalised by them unconsciously. This is now widely banned. Another example would be the use of specific colour schemes, graphics, and fonts to allude to a product which is banned from being advertised, such as cigarette brands on Formula 1 cars.
Misrepresentation	Making claims about a product, service, or company which are partially true but presented in an unbalanced and misleading manner to trick consumers
Exaggeration	Over-emphasising the benefits of a particular product or service
Misuse of statistics	Omitting statistical information, obscuring the context of statistics, or skewing statistics to present them in a way which is disproportionately favourable to the brand being advertised (Di Domenico & Visentin, 2020)
Use of pressure	Applying unfair coercion on consumers to force them to buy something; for example, deliberately encouraging children to pester their parents for goods, or communicating an imminent expiry date for an oversubscribed customer offer
Poor taste	Resorting to vulgar, embarrassing, or offensive images and messages, such as gratuitous sexual innuendo, which may be deemed more offensive in some cultures than in others (Javalgi & La Toya, 2018)
Use of dubious brand/ product comparisons	Making comparisons to products, brands, or services which are not direct competitors; for example, a motor manufacturer comparing the benefits of its mid-range car to a competitor's budget spec version

---

GLOBAL MARKETING QUESTION

Although taste is largely subjective, varying from one person to another, there are commonly accepted and expected standards within each culture or country. Imagine that you are a marketer for a fun, rebellious brand such as Cheetos, Peperami, or Tango, and you have been asked to prepare a marketing plan to take the brand into another country which is much more socially conservative than the UK or US. Go to your brand's website and identify what changes you might need to make to the imagery, tone, messages, and other aspects of the marketing to be acceptable in your host market.

Sustainability in Marketing

If a practice is sustainable, it can be continued for a long time into the future. The recent focus by consumers, businesses, and governments on **sustainability** stems from a recognition that many current practices cannot be continued for much longer. For example, burning fossil fuels for energy at current levels cannot be continued much longer, as it is depleting non-renewable resources, polluting the atmosphere, and contributing to other environmental and ecological damage. Using current levels of **single-use plastics** in product packaging cannot be continued much longer, as this nonbiodegradable material accumulates in landfill sites or is carried into oceans, where it kills marine creatures. It is unlikely that developed economies' current meat consumption levels can be continued much longer without preventing the production of the pulses, cereals, and vegetables which can feed more members of the earth's rising population per hectare of land.

SUSTAINABILITY QUESTION

What do you think are the top ten changes which your university or workplace could make to improve sustainability, and how would it make those changes? Try to look beyond 'green' initiatives.

Sustainability is the focus of multiple stakeholders (e.g. producers, marketers, consumers, governments) on the adoption and expansion of business and consumption practices which are benign enough to have long-term viability. The four main categories of sustainability are human, social, economic, and environmental, and their main concerns are summarised in Table 10.3.

TABLE 10.3
The four main categories of sustainability.

Sustainability Categories	Key Concerns
Human capital	Education
	Knowledge
	Training
	Skills
	Health
	Nutrition
	Resource access
Social capital	Social cohesion
	Societal wellbeing
	Rights and laws
	Equality
Economic capital	Profitability
	Standards of living
Environmental capital	Land
	Air
	Natural resources
	Seas, rivers, and lakes
	Flora and fauna

MARKETING MANAGER TASK

In China, Zomotor has a renewed focus on environmental capital, not only in its production plants and assembly lines, but in all aspects of its business. As marketing manager, Dylan has been asked to suggest how the company might differentiate itself from the competition in its marketing messages by communicating its sustainability credentials and commitment to the environment. In particular, Zomotor would like to target consumers who are heavily motivated by conservation and preservation of natural landscapes. Help Dylan by suggesting ways in which Zomotor might do this, and explain the rationale behind your suggestions.

Sustainable marketing has two main characteristics: (i) it considers the needs of business and the needs of consumers; and (ii) it considers future needs, rather than simply current needs. This differentiates it from basic marketing, societal marketing, and strategic marketing, as we see in Figure 10.1.

FIGURE 10.1
Sustainable marketing and its focus on business and
consumer needs of the future.

Why Sustainability Is Important,
and What Marketers Can Do

Land Usage

The global population in 2021 is 7.8 billion. This is expected to rise to 8.5 billion by
2030, 9.7 billion by 2050, and 10.9 billion by 2100 (UK Government, 2021). With
an ever-larger number of people to feed, clothe, and satisfy as consumers, weightier
demands are placed upon the planet. To produce a kilogram of fruit, potatoes, brassica,
or root vegetables requires less than one square metre of land. However, one kilogram
of mutton or beef takes 370 or 326 square metres, respectively, and cheese production
requires 88 square metres per kilogram (Statista, 2021). If an expanding global population continues to favour foodstuffs which require large amounts of land (and water
and chemicals) to produce, it will exhaust land capacity, leading to the malnutrition
of the poorest, or it will need to create more agricultural land by deforestation and the
destruction of other important environments. Therefore, there is an ethical obligation for
governments, businesses, and marketers to avoid encouraging audiences to consume
unnecessarily high amounts of resource-intensive foods. Naturally, it is unlikely that a
butcher would demarket meat as a commodity; to do so would be to undermine its core
product and potentially make itself redundant. However, it is possible for butchers to
engage in product innovation and sell items within their product range which are more
sustainable. For example, they can create pies or sausages which use meat but also have
a high content of cereals, nuts, vegetables, fruits, spices, and pulses. In doing so, they
are able to differentiate themselves from competitors, and maintain or increase pricing
and profit levels, whilst simultaneously reducing their ecological footprint.

Water Usage

Globally, one in three people have no access to clean, safe drinking water, and half cannot access safe sanitation services (WHO, 2019). A single cotton shirt requires around

PHOTO 10.5
IKEA displays recycling information on its products.

2,500 litres of water to produce, and the Aral Sea has shrunk by 90% due to irrigation for cotton production (Common Objective, 2021). This casts the phenomenon of 'fast fashion' and the throwaway clothing culture as very problematic. Marketers can help in a number of ways: (i) by raising awareness of their companies' water-saving initiatives and buy raw materials from suppliers who actively seek to reduce water usage, thereby driving consumer awareness of the issue and placing ethics amongst their buying criteria; (ii) by involving their brands in projects such as Fairtrade or the Better Cotton Initiative until industry norms become more ethical; (iii) by advising consumers how to preserve water elsewhere (e.g. in their selection of a machine wash cycle); and (iv) by marketing more durable, timeless products which can be worn for many years, rather than 'trendy' or flimsily made clothes with built-in obsolescence which will be thrown away and replaced after few uses. Adventure clothing company Patagonia went one step further on Black Friday 2011 with its 'Don't Buy This Jacket' campaign, in which it communicated the environmental cost of its top-selling jacket, and asked customers to reflect carefully on whether they actually needed a product before buying it (Patagonia, 2011).

Poverty

Over 700 million people worldwide exist in extreme poverty, living on less than $1.90 per day, and nearly 100 million of these have been plunged into that situation by the effects of the COVID-19 pandemic, particularly in sub-Saharan Africa, Latin America, the Caribbean, the Middle East, and North Africa (World Bank, 2021). Increasing numbers of marketing academics are focusing on the needs of bottom-of-pyramid (BoP) populations – the 2.7 billion global consumers who survive on less than $2.50 per day

(Prahalad, 2004). For many years, businesses had overlooked this segment of society, despite it being the largest globally, as they did not consider it to be profitable enough to merit significant attention. However, Prahalad (2004) and others have contested that not only do these consumers deserve to have their needs served, but they also constitute a very viable, profitable audience due to their large number. The proportion of China's population who are BoP has decreased from around 20% in 2015 to around 5% in 2021, as the effects of China's 'economic miracle' continues to lift people from poorly paid, precarious employment into more stable, better-paid jobs. India's BoP market – currently the world's largest – is set to halve over the next decade as the Indian economy develops in a manner similar to what has been seen in China over the last 25 years. Whilst the proportion of people in Nigeria classed as BoP is expected to decline gradually until it is below 50%, this is outstripped by a larger population growth, which means the overall BoP population will climb. In South Africa, BoP consumers spend more on alcohol and tobacco than on housing, which presents marketers with the opportunity to switch consumers into alternative, healthy products and services (Euromonitor, 2017). The organisation with perhaps the greatest focus on BoP-specific product development is Unilever, which operates the Pureit brand of household water purifiers for the Indian market. Other product and service categories which are particularly important to BoP consumers are public transport, healthcare, education, and leisure.

Food Poverty and Malnutrition

Around 9% of the world population, or 690 million people, live in food poverty and suffer malnutrition (United Nations, 2021). Many of these are BoP consumers, but others live in developed economies, such as those of Western Europe, where millions of people have relied on charitable food banks for basic sustenance since government cuts to public expenditure since the 2007–2009 financial crisis. As around 17% of global food production is wasted, and this results in 8%–10% of global greenhouse gas emissions (UNEP, 2021), it makes good sense to divert surplus food to poorer consumers before it spoils. In doing so, not only is there a strong environmental and social benefit, but food producers and retailers also have a chance to receive at least some income for the goods and to save time and money on disposal. Smartphone apps similar to those such as Too Good to Go are able to facilitate this (Apostolidis et al., 2021).

Pollution and Global Warming

As economies strive to free themselves from fossil fuel usage and transition towards consumption of 'cleaner' energy from solar and wind power and other sources, marketers have an important role to play, not just in making harmful products such as high-polluting cars socially unattractive (Wright & Egan, 2000) but also in encouraging adoption of newer technologies and alternative solutions. For example, choosing and owning an electric car is a daunting task for most people, whose experience is usually of petrol or diesel vehicles. They may struggle to balance their needs for convenience, ease of use, cost, and functionality in the purchase decision-making process, and marketers can help present the information clearly. Additionally, they can communicate customer objections and needs to their companies to ensure that products are designed which meet those needs and are adoptable.

MARKETING DIRECTOR TASK

Zomotor's global marketing director, Lee, is due to attend a senior executive meeting to decide how to market the company's new 'Charge' vehicles. These are the electric variants of existing car models which can be recharged at an external charging point or through a domestic electric socket and which deliver a range of up to 200 miles from a 90% charge. Rather than waiting for consumer society to get used to the idea of electric vehicles, Zomotor wish to be more active in converting new and existing customers to electric. Initially, they must convince innovators and early adopters, but then they will need to encourage the mass market to make the switch. Using the Western Europe market as an example, suggest strategies which Lee might adopt, explaining why they are likely to be successful.

Corporate Social Responsibility

Corporate social responsibility (CSR) is the collective term for business strategies which embrace the doing of charitable, philanthropic, or activist activities and the support of ethically oriented initiatives. It is divided into four major categories:

1. Environmental responsibility: looking after the planet and its flora and fauna

2. Ethical responsibility: behaving in a fair manner to all stakeholders

3. Philanthropic responsibility: nurturing communities and helping people

4. Economic responsibility: being profitable and using investment wisely

The Friedman Doctrine (Friedman, 1970) asserted that "the social responsibility of business is to increase its profits" and to serve shareholders rather than stakeholders. His idea was partially derived from that of the economic philosopher Adam Smith, who imagined an 'invisible hand' unintentionally bestowing societal benefits as it pursued self-interest but not intentionally as an end in itself. He also seemed to favour the adage 'let the market decide', which essentially means that customers will decide which companies they like or dislike and make it clear through their purchase decisions, so

PHOTO 10.6
The National Trust must generate money to maintain its tourist attractions, even when they are closed, and direct debit memberships help to achieve this.

that organisations can interpret their healthy profits as a sign that they do not need to change into more benevolent operations. However, many more recent commentators (e.g. Klein, 2007) have dismissed this as a morally, ethically, socially, and economically incorrect approach which impoverishes the many to enrich the few. Instead, they have encouraged the concept of CSR. Moreover, millennials and Generation Z consumers – those born since around 1980 – are much more likely than previous generations to expect and demand that businesses seek solutions to society's ills (Digital Marketing Institute, 2021).

Many organisations have recognised CSR not just as an ethically sound way to conduct themselves, but one which can add a great deal of value to their businesses (He & Harris, 2020). By acting responsibly and seeking to use their power and resources to produce stakeholder benefits – and especially by visibly supporting good causes – they can generate positive public relations, reduce overall marketing costs, differentiate themselves from their competitors, engender customer loyalty (Nassar & Battour, 2020), attract new customers, make customers less price sensitive, reduce their tax liabilities, and build strategic alliances with other organisations.

PHOTO 10.7
Fast fashion takes a huge toll of the earth's resources, but Primark has launched recycling initiatives to counteract this.

Some examples of CSR initiatives include the following:

▶ Adopting progressive approaches to employment contracts, such as by offering flexible working, career breaks, and extended maternity/paternity leave

▶ Ensuring that a robust **Equality, Diversity, and Inclusion** framework is adopted

▶ 'Greening' the organisation's operations to reduce its carbon footprint or environmental impact

▶ Introducing favourable terms for suppliers and channel intermediaries

▶ Participating in broader initiatives by bodies such as Fairtrade

▶ Facilitating employees' volunteering activities and matching funds which they raise (up to a stipulated level)

▶ Donating money or products to good causes

Chapter Summary

In this chapter, we have explored some of the underlying assumptions about businesses' responsibilities to customers and other stakeholders and ascertained how these assumptions have changed over the years. In particular, millennial and Generation Z consumers are much more likely than previous consumers to demand that organisations contribute to solving society's ills (Hassan et al., 2021). We have identified a number of common

PHOTO 10.8
Drivers choose Volvo for many reasons, but often for the safety and comfort of their families.

ethical dilemmas which are faced by marketers, and by organisations more broadly, and discussed the implications of these dilemmas to concerned parties. As we have seen, sustainability is a concept which has established itself as fundamental to business. However, it relates not only to environmental or 'green' issues, as is sometimes supposed, but also to social, societal, and financial factors. The key to achieving a sustainable approach is to adopt a long-term perspective which considers all stakeholders, rather than a short-term focus on purely business needs. In doing so, companies can add value to the customer proposition, differentiating themselves from their competitors, and giving themselves a competitive advantage. Firms which embrace CSR are best placed to act ethically and reap the rewards.

Key Learning Outcomes

▶ Marketers are faced with many ethical considerations, and their responses are scrutinised by their various audiences.

▶ Sustainability in marketing instils a perspective which focuses not simply on the organisation's short-term needs but on stakeholders' long-term needs.

▶ CSR encompasses a variety of charitable and social initiatives undertaken by organisations.

▶ Organisations' ethical stances may empower stakeholders, satisfy them, and bond them more closely to the brand.

Recommended Reading

Agudelo, M. A. L., Jóhannsdóttir, L., & Davídsdóttir, B. (2019). A literature review of the history and evolution of corporate social responsibility. *International Journal of Corporate Social Responsibility*, *4*(1), 1–23.

Ferrell, O. C., & Ferrell, L. (2021). New directions for marketing ethics and social responsibility research. *Journal of Marketing Theory and Practice*, *29*(1), 13–22.

Kemper, J. A., & Ballantine, P. W. (2019). What do we mean by sustainability marketing? *Journal of Marketing Management*, *35*(3–4), 277–309.

References

Apostolidis, C., Brown, D., Wijetunga, D., & Kathriarachchi, E. (2021). Sustainable value co-creation at the Bottom of the Pyramid: Using mobile applications to reduce food waste and improve food security. *Journal of Marketing Management*, *37*(9–10), 856–886.

Common Objective. (2021). *Report on water usage in the fashion industry*. Retrieved December 5, 2021, from https://www.commonobjective.co/article/the-issues-water

Di Domenico, G., & Visentin, M. (2020). Fake news or true lies? Reflections about problematic contents in marketing. *International Journal of Market Research*, *62*(4), 409–417.

Digital Marketing Institute Article. (2021). *16 brands doing corporate social responsibility successfully*. Retrieved December 6, 2021, from https://digitalmarketinginstitute.com/blog/corporate-16-brands-doing-corporate-social-responsibility-successfully

Euromonitor. (2017). *Top 5 bottom of the pyramid markets: Diverse spending patterns and future potential*. Retrieved December 6, 2021, from https://www.euromonitor.com/article/top-5-bottom-pyramid-markets-diverse-spending-patterns-future-potential

Foot, P. (1978). The problem of abortion and the doctrine of double effect. In P. Foot (Ed.) *Virtues and vices, and other essays in moral philosophy*. Basil Blackwell.

Friedman, M. (1970). A Friedman doctrine: The social responsibility of business is to increase its profits. *The New York Times Magazine*.

Hassan, S. M., Rahman, Z., & Paul, J. (2021). Consumer ethics: A review and research agenda. *Psychology & Marketing*, *39*(1), 111–130.

He, H., & Harris, L. (2020). The impact of Covid-19 pandemic on corporate social responsibility and marketing philosophy. *Journal of Business Research*, *116*, 176–182.

Javalgi, R. G., & La Toya, M. R. (2018). International marketing ethics: A literature review and research agenda. *Journal of Business Ethics*, *148*(4), 703–720.

Klein, N. (2007). *The shock doctrine*. Knopf.

Nassar, R. M., & Battour, M. (2020). The impact of marketing ethics on customer loyalty: A conceptual framework. *International Journal of Business Ethics and Governance*, *3*(2), 1–11.

Patagonia. (2021). *'Don't buy this jacket' 2011 campaign analysis*. Retrieved December 5, 2021, from https://eu.patagonia.com/gb/en/stories/dont-buy-this-jacket-black-friday-and-the-new-york-times/story-18615.html

Prahalad, C. K. (2004). *Fortune at the bottom of the pyramid: Eradicating poverty through profits*. Prentice Hall.

Statista Data. (2021). *Land used to produce one kilogram of food product as of 2018, by type (in square meters per kilogram)*. Retrieved December 5, 2021, from https://www.statista.com/statistics/1179708/land-use-per-kilogram-of-food-product/

Thompson, J. J. (1976). Killing, letting die, and the trolley problem. *The Monist, 59*(2), 204–217.

UK Government. (2021). *'Trend Deck 2021: Demographics' report*. Retrieved December 5, 2021, from https://www.gov.uk/government/publications/trend-deck-2021-demographics/trend-deck-2021-demographics#:~:text=The%20global%20population%2C%20the%20total,and%2010.9%20billion%20by%202100

United Nations. (2021). *Food data*. Retrieved December 5, 2021, from https://www.un.org/en/global-issues/food

United Nations Environment Programme. (2021). *UNEP food waste index report 2021*. Retrieved December 6, 2021, from https://www.unep.org/resources/report/unep-food-waste-index-report-2021

World Bank. (2021). *Extreme poverty, 2015–2021 data*. Retrieved December 5, 2021, from https://www.worldbank.org/en/topic/poverty

World Health Organization. (2019). *1 in 3 people globally do not have access to safe drinking water report*. Retrieved December 5, 2021, from https://www.who.int/news/item/18-06-2019-1-in-3-people-globally-do-not-have-access-to-safe-drinking-water-unicef-who

Wright, C., & Egan, J. (2000). De-marketing the car. *Transport Policy, 7*(4), 287–294.

Glossary

Anti-competitive practices: marketing practices (usually unrealistically low pricing) designed to eradicate the competition and create a monopoly

Cherry-picking: choosing the easiest, most profitable business whilst neglecting the rest

Consequentialism: considering the consequences of a strategy to decide whether it is ethical

Conspicuous consumption: consuming a product or service as a public display of wealth or style

Consumption: the use of a product or service by a consumer

Contractualism: being ethically guided by the obligations and duties of one's role

Cultural appropriation: taking and adopting aspects of a different (usually weaker) culture for profit or self-interest

Demarketing: using marketing approaches to reduce demand for a product, service or brand

Deontology: the belief that some actions are ethically indefensible, regardless of the outcomes

Idealism: instead of being pragmatic, sticking rigidly to one's own vision of what is right

Lobbying: building relationships with politicians to influence decisions in one's own favour

Male gaze: the way in which cameras often film women as a man might look at them (i.e. lingering on aspects of appearance deemed sensual or attractive)

Moral equity: an inherent sense of justice and fairness

Ordinary decency: adhering to the sensibilities and values of normal people

Relativism: weighing up the possible benefits of an action against its costs, especially ethically

Situationalism: judging ethical decisions based upon the context or situation in which they occur

Spin: presenting facts in a way which is designed to convey certain meanings but ignore others

Sustainability: a mindset which focuses on the long-term needs of multiple stakeholders

Teleology: approaching ethical decisions by considering how to bring the greatest benefit to the most people

Ethics Case Study: Dove's #ShowUs Initiative

Dove is an instantly recognisable American personal care brand which specialises in moisturising soaps and beauty bars, lotions and body washes, facial and hair care products, and deodorants and antiperspirants. Conforming closely to the 'caregiver' brand archetype (Mark & Pearson, 2001), its brand values embrace nourishment, soothing, and gentleness. Operated by the UK fast-moving consumer goods (FMCG) giant, Unilever, Dove launched its Campaign for Real Beauty in 2004, which sought to instil confidence in women and children. Research undertaken by three partner universities and Dove's marketing agency, Ogilvy & Mather, found that only 2% of women considered themselves 'beautiful'. Therefore, Dove set out to broaden its audiences' understanding of beauty, changing its 'brand essence' marketing approach to a point-of-view approach which adopts women consumers' perspectives and reflects their self-concepts. Beauty, argued Dove, should be a source of confidence rather than anxiety, and it is something not restricted to models and 'classically' glamorous women but available to people of all ages, sexual orientations, body shapes, abilities, ethnicities, and skin tones. By featuring 'regular women' with 'real curves' on billboard advertisements, and by asking viewers to vote whether they found the subjects beautiful, Dove generated huge amounts of word of mouth and PR – worth around 30 times the value of the paid-for media space – and doubled its sales to $4 billion within three years.

In 2019, Dove decided to build upon its reputation for redefining beauty by adopting an even more inclusive approach called Project #ShowUs. This initiative aimed to dismantle gender stereotypes by inviting female photographers to photograph a diverse range of women, depicted in real-life situations without any

continued

digital distortion or photo enhancement techniques. Once more, the women represented all ages, body shapes, skin tones, and ethnicities, and a significant number of them are LGBTQ+ or gender non-binary, have visible disabilities, or have skin conditions such as alopecia. Additionally, rather than creating visual content solely for its own marketing purposes, Dove, along with partners Getty Images and Girlgaze, is compiling the world's largest library of royalty-free stock photos of women by women. In doing so, it helps women to feel represented in the portrayals of women which they see in everyday situations, broadening society's view of women, dismantling stereotypes, and having a positive impact upon their self-esteem, health, relationships, and opportunities. Each of the women photographed has, for the first time on Getty Images, been able to apply their own photo tags and search descriptions. The male gaze, it seems, is finally being challenged in a meaningful way.

Imagine that you have been hired to work alongside Dove and its creative marketing agency to extend the ethos of Dove's #ShowUs initiative to its range of products for males, which are branded as Dove Men+Care. Dove has already started to challenge toxic masculinity and to redefine what it means to be a man, asserting that strength is derived from caring for others and oneself. What other messages would you wish to embed within the initiative? What approaches would you take to ensure audience engagement and to blur the boundaries between consumers and the brand, driving the co-creation of value? Explain your rationale and the intended outcomes.

Sources

Digital Agency Network website. (2021). 'Dove is proud not to #ShowUs unrealistic images of women in media, with the help of Getty Images' report. Retrieved December 8, 2021, from https://digitalagencynetwork.com/dove-is-proud-not-to-showus-unrealistic-images-of-women-in-media-with-the-help-of-getty-images/

Dove website. (2021). Report on #ShowUs campaign. Retrieved December 8, 2021, from https://www.dove.com/uk/stories/campaigns/showus.html

Mark, M., & Pearson, C. S. (2001). *The hero and the outlaw: Building extraordinary brands through the power of archetypes.* McGraw Hill.

Shorty Awards website. (2021). Report on Dove's #ShowUs campaign. Retrieved December 8, 2021, from https://shortyawards.com/4th-socialgood/project-showus

continued

Unilever website. (2021). Project #ShowUs: Dove's disruptive new partnership to shatter stereotypes. Retrieved December 8, 2021, from https://www.unilever.com/news/news-search/2019/project-showus-doves-disruptive-new-partnership-to-shatter-stereotypes/

11 | Services, Relationship, and Internal Marketing

LEARNING OBJECTIVES

▶ To explore the benefits of relationship marketing to organisations and customers

▶ To identify the types and dimensions of relationships important to marketers

▶ To analyse the characteristics of services and their influence

▶ To critique the importance of marketing to the organisation's internal stakeholders

Introduction

In this chapter, we will explore the concept of relationship marketing to understand the mutual benefits which it brings to organisations and their stakeholders, and the marketing of services. To do this, we examine the constituents and characteristics of relationships and services and consider how customers derive value from each. Internal marketing – the marketing of an organisation to its workforce – may be considered relationship marketing to internal stakeholders. As we shall see, the world has largely moved on from the days of transactional marketing, in which organisations only interacted with customers at the point of purchase or when reacting to incoming enquiries.

Defining Relationship Marketing

Relationship marketing seeks to "identify and establish, maintain and enhance and, when necessary, terminate relationships with customers and other stakeholders, at a profit so that the objectives of all parties are met, and this is done by mutual exchange and fulfilment of promises" (Grönroos, 1997, p. 322). It entails an organisation regularly providing value to its stakeholders. It builds networks, manages services, establishes strategic alliances, builds customer intelligence, and creates market-oriented communications.

DOI: 10.4324/9781003170891-12

The Chartered Institute of Marketing defines relationship marketing as "the *management process* of *identifying*, *anticipating* and *satisfying* customer requirements *profitably*" (CIM, 2017), while Berry's (1993, p. 25) seminal paper describes it as "*attracting, maintaining* and *enhancing* customer relationships", and Gordon (1998, p. 9) saw it as

PHOTO 11.1
Some services are hedonic, especially when they provide an 'experience', such as go-karting.

PHOTO 11.2
Restaurants sell products but rely very heavily on delivering good service.

"creating *new value* with *individual customers* and then *sharing the value benefits* with them *over the lifetime of association*". By focusing on the phrases and words which we have emphasised, we can see what relationship marketing entails (Table 11.1).

TABLE 11.1

Elements of relationship marketing.

Term	Meaning
Management process	Not a product or outcome, but the route to success
	Longitudinal, ongoing, iterative, circular, unending
Identifying	Looking, listening, asking and researching
	A focus on customers
Anticipating	Scanning the horizon for evolving opportunities and threats
	Proactive, not reactive
Satisfying	Fulfilling and exceeding expectations
	Achieving 'customer delight'
Profitably	Generating a benefit not only for stakeholders, but for the organisation
	Benefits may be in cash flow, market share, brand equity, or planning
	Many benefits derive from customer lifetime value (CLTV)
Attracting	Generating awareness, interest, desire and action (AIDA)
	Instilling brand awareness and engagement
Maintaining	Retaining customers rather than losing and replacing them
	Incentivising the relationship, erecting barriers to exit
Enhancing	Adding customer value, aligning customer and organisational objectives
	Constantly re-evaluating customer needs and wants
New value	Saving customers time, space, money, effort, or risk
	Helping them feel good about themselves, or enabling them to shine
Individual customers	Using interactive technology to individualise contact
	Avoiding generic, meaningless segmentation definitions
Sharing the value benefits	Ensuring that customers, stakeholders, and the organisation all benefit
Over the lifetime of association	Seeking multiple customer contact points
	Adding value at each point rather than simply at point of purchase

The Evolution of Relationship Marketing

From the 1950s and 1960s, marketing slowly evolved through the following phases, from a 'transactional marketing' to a 'relationship marketing' paradigm:

▶ Basic marketing (focus on 'selling', no dialogue, high customer churn rates)

▶ Reactive marketing (responding to customers, little dialogue)

▶ Accountable marketing (using customer feedback to fulfil duty of care)

▶ Proactive marketing (frequent contact between supplier and customer)

▶ Partnership marketing (continuous contact between supplier and customer)

From the 1970s to the 1990s, service-oriented industries became more dominant in economically developed regions, focusing on the provision of intangible goods (services). Relationship marketing became dominant, providing the interaction between customers and firms vital to service industries, and differing from transactional marketing in the following ways:

▶ Taking a long-term perspective

▶ Deferring some of the organisational benefits, such as profits

▶ Retaining customers for future sales opportunities

▶ Prioritising good customer service

▶ Contacting customers frequently

▶ Targeting high customer commitment

▶ Basing supplier-customer interactions on cooperation, trust, collaboration, and interdependence rather than manipulation

▶ Producing customer value across the entire company rather than solely in the production of superior goods

---

ETHICS QUESTION

Relational marketing is generally considered more ethical than taking a transactional approach to customers. However, some commentators have suggested that some organisations are becoming too intrusive, instigating inappropriately frequent and trivial contact through new media and other channels. From your own experiences, what is your opinion? List examples of times when you have welcomed unsolicited contact from brands who sell to you, and times when this uninvited contact has been an annoyance. Analyse why you felt the way you did – what was it that engaged or annoyed you?

The term 'relationship marketing' was introduced by Berry (1983) and developed by Christopher et al. (1991) eight years later. They focused on firms pushing customers up the ladder of loyalty, increasing their potential profitability during the relationship – **customer**

PHOTO 11.3
Retail banks are no longer foreboding institutions with high counters and thick screens but casual spaces which are customer centric.

lifetime value (CLTV) – through carefully designed interventions. Grönroos (1997) conceptualised relationship marketing as a 'new marketing paradigm' – a new belief system at the very heart of marketing. If done well, organisations can inhabit customers' 'social landscapes' rather than being a one-dimensional business entity. Its ethos extends to all stakeholder groups (Gummesson, 1999) including employees, suppliers, channel intermediaries, and shareholders (Sheth & Parvatiyar, 1995), who are each engaged through value exchange. These stakeholder partnerships have been categorised (Morgan & Hunt, 1994) as follows:

Internal partnerships encompass employees, other departments and business units.

Supplier partnerships encapsulate suppliers of goods and services to the firm.

Lateral partnerships are formed with competitors, local and national governments, and not-for-profit organisations.

Buyer partnerships are forged with end-user customers and intermediate customers, such as downstream channel partners.

Relationships within these partnerships are ordered as follows:

First order relationships entail marketplace-based direct contact with the organisation's stakeholders (e.g. firm-customer) which provide focal firm experiences

Second order relationships are networks of relationships between participants (e.g. competitor-customer)

Third order relationships occur within participants' organisations or larger social units (e.g. employee-employee or customer-customer)

As we have seen, relationship marketing acknowledges consumers' roles in the buying process and attempts to define and communicate the value which they expect from brands (Sheth, 2017). It demands that organisations design processes which create and support customer value. Customer-focused organisations have rejected the **transactional perspective** of the mid- to late 20th century, which drew on classical economic theory to conceptualise customers as passive entities in a product-oriented marketplace exchange. Instead, they have adopted a **relational perspective,** understanding customers as engaged consumers who co-produce value with suppliers and each other through sociality, goodwill, and altruism driven more by social and psychological fulfilment than economic considerations.

New Media and Relationship Marketing

The internet and interactive technology have shaped the demands and expectations of consumers, and social media is now key to relationship marketing. It provides a bountiful source of **volunteered data** – self-disclosed information which can be used for segmentation and to target individual consumers. Social media hosts identify **consumer tribes** (Cova et al., 2007), where members cluster around shared interests and values, facilitating the interactivity and responsiveness which many of today's B2B and B2C customers expect. Finally, social media communications, when compared with other marketing communications media, cost relatively little, have a wide reach across large and diverse customer populations, and enjoy high levels of credibility amongst many audiences.

Stakeholders in Relationship Marketing

Whilst much of the literature explores the benefits of relationship marketing to 'customers' and the organisation, it is more accurate to consider a broader range of beneficiary stakeholders who belong to different types of market. Payne et al. (2005) suggested that there are 'six markets':

Supplier markets comprise upstream channel partners who supply goods or services to the firm (e.g. gearboxes, stationery, or shipping).

Referral markets include people or organisations who recommend the firm to potential customers through word of mouth or testimonials (e.g. industry journalists).

Influence markets contain anyone who can positively influence the marketing environment in which the firm operates (e.g. agencies).

Recruitment markets are potential employees and the organisations from which they may be recruited (e.g. universities, employment agencies).

Internal markets are the firm's current employees – internal marketing being the marketing of an organisation to the people who work there.

Customer markets are those customers who buy from a firm. These are perhaps the stakeholders afforded the greatest consideration by theorists and practitioners. However, the model suggests that to service their needs, the firm needs to look after the other five markets or risk inefficiency, inconsistency, and poor credibility.

To service those markets, an organisation would follow a variation of these stages (Table 11.2).

The final three stages are core responsibilities of internal marketing, discussed later in the chapter.

TABLE 11.2

Steps to servicing markets.

Stage	Outline	Entails
1	Map the service delivery system	Being explicit about how and when the firm will provide a service to the customer
2	Identify critical service issues	Ascertaining what could go wrong, when, why, and to what effect
3	Set service standards and monitor	Setting key performance indicators (KPIs) against which service is appraised, and implementing them
4	Develop customer communications	Enabling dialogue with customers and communicating relevant messages
5	Train staff to be customer oriented	Embedding knowledge, skills, and practices to deliver excellent service
6	Incentivise employees for good service	Rewarding staff for providing staff – and each other – with excellent service
7	Instil a relationship marketing ethos	Ensuring staff are service minded and market focused

Dimensions of Relationships

Expectation and Satisfaction

Customers judge the performance of a product or service after purchase by comparing it with the expectations and beliefs which they had of it prior to purchase (Sachdev & Verma, 2002) – an informal 'gap analysis'. If post-purchase reality falls below pre-purchase expectations, dissatisfaction ensues, and the customer is unlikely to make repeat purchases. If the reality exceeds expectations, customer delight may be generated, resulting in loyalty and customer adoption of the brand. To achieve customer satisfaction, organisations must understand customer expectations (Ho & Zheng, 2004), and how they are formed. Factors in the formation of expectations include:

1. The customer's previous experience of the organisation

2. Their experience of its competitors, external factors (e.g. culture, class, and generation)

3. Individual factors (e.g. personal attitudes, prejudices, and values)

4. The marketing communications of the organisation and its competitors

PHOTO 11.4
Hospitals are towards the 'service' end of the product-service continuum.

But what do customers actually expect? Often, expectations increase as the price increases. Customers usually have dual level expectations of processes (e.g. friendliness and speed of service), determining what is sufficient and what is desirable. Customers often also expect relationships with their suppliers. Recently, customers have started seeking personalisation of the product and service, a high level of product and service choice, more contact along the length of their relationship, and a high degree of responsiveness – for firms to invite their input, listen to them, and adapt their processes and behaviours accordingly without a significant delay. These recent expectations appear to stem from Generation Y and Z consumers accustomed to the speed and interaction provided by the internet.

Trust

Trust is a state of mind, attitude, or feeling which a person develops if they believe that they can rely with confidence on another party (Moorman et al., 1992). By sensing the trustworthiness, reliability, and integrity of another (Morgan & Hunt, 1994), people are willing to surrender an element of control in an exchange relationship (Schurr & Ozanne, 1985), believing that the resulting vulnerability will not be exploited or abused. Building and nurturing trust is central to relationship marketing and is essential if customers are to become committed and stay loyal to a brand (Bejou & Palmer, 1998), and it is derived from several areas:

Branding: consistently expressing and according with the customer's worldview or sense of tradition (e.g. Hovis bread, Jaguar cars).

Product quality: making well-constructed, durable, and reassuring goods (e.g. Worcester-Bosch boilers, Bosch power tools).

Integrity: safeguarding customers' privacy and security (e.g. dealing with customers in a transparent and honest manner) and attracting recommendations.

Demonstrating the necessity of one's offering: evidencing that the purchase has substantial outcomes rather than being frivolous.

Familiarity and repeated exposure: instilling a sense of the brand's omnipresence and continuity by being visible to the customer for a long time (e.g. Hershey's chocolates).

Provision of high-quality information: enabling customers to make informed choices based upon clear, comprehensible, and relevant information.

Fulfilment of promises: preferably on time, in full, and with no errors (OTIFNE). However, the service recovery paradox suggests that consumers may have more trust in an organisation which has quickly and satisfactorily fixed a problem, such as broadband service interruption, than a firm which has never had to fix such a problem. This is because the customer has observed proof of the firm's competence and willingness, should the need for further assistance arise.

After-sales support and guarantees: reducing risks associated with a poor purchase decision and offering peace of mind.

Consumer communities and third party recognition: boosting customer enjoyment by linking them with like-minded others and conferring social status.

SUSTAINABILITY QUESTION

As relationship marketing can instil trust between stakeholders and organisations, it seems logical that local and national governments could use relationship marketing to increase the trust and commitment which people have towards their environmental policies. For example, by building a stronger relationship with its local population, a city council could perhaps encourage more people to recycle waste paper and plastic or to share car journeys. If you were in charge of stakeholder communications for the Singaporean government, what initiatives would you implement to build trust with citizens and encourage them to be 'greener'? Explain the rationale for your strategic suggestions.

Categories of Trust

Trust may be categorised as benevolent, credibility, overall, contractual, competence, or goodwill trust (Godson, 2009), as defined by the following prerequisites or antecedents (Table 11.3).

Commitment

Commitment is the belief that a relationship with a partner is so beneficial or important that it merits a significant amount of effort or resources being dedicated to its nourishment to ensure its longevity (Morgan & Hunt, 1994). It is "an implicit or explicit pledge of relational continuity between exchange partners" (Dwyer et al., 1987). This psychological attachment may be defined as affective, normative, or continuance commitment (Table 11.4).

Trust and commitment are interrelated. Trust produces commitment, which in turn drives loyalty. However, commitment fluctuates during the life of a relationship.

TABLE 11.3

Prerequisites of trust.

Type of Trust	Prerequisites
Benevolent	The customer believes that the seller is ethical and will act in the best interests of the customer
Credibility	The reputation of the seller reassures the customer that it has the ability to deliver upon its promises
Overall	The general feeling of trust when benevolent and credibility trust are both strong
Contractual	Legal, contractual mechanisms instil peace of mind where trust might otherwise be low
Competence	From the reputation or observed performance of a seller
Goodwill	The customer feeling that the seller intends to do what is right and honourable rather than the bare minimum; ongoing dialogue encourages collaboration

TABLE 11.4

Prerequisites of commitment.

Types of commitment	Prerequisites
Affective commitment	A 'feeling' commitment arising from a desire to commit, or a liking of the brand
Normative commitment	Commitment arising through an obligation (usually social or contractual)
Continuance commitment	Commitment existing through necessity or lack of choice

Commitment, Power, and Dependence

Commitment is linked to the phenomena of power and dependence. A balance of power – power symmetry – between both parties is ideal, but rarely achievable. If one party has too much power, there is a risk that the other party can be overwhelmed or yield too little influence, unless the larger party is careful to be ethical. There are five forms of power (French et al., 1959):

Legitimate power derives from formal authority (e.g. the power of an insurance loss adjuster).

Referent power derives from one party's ability to build a strong relationship.

Expert power derives from expertise or access the party has to valuable information.

Reward power derives from incentivisation of one partner by another (e.g. through commission payments).

Coercive power uses force to place sanctions on a partner's undesired behaviours (e.g. enforcing penalties for late deliveries).

In many supplier-customer relationships, all five types of power can coexist (Godson, 2009). The mix of their presences and the extent of **power asymmetry** partially determines how relationship marketing is undertaken. A degree of **dependence** between partners encourages relationship-building through actions such as **idiosyncratic investments** (i.e. investments made by each partner for shared benefits within that specific relationship). **Interdependence**, where both parties depend on each other, produces barriers to relationship dissolution. However, too much dependence can lead a partner to be vulnerable to the other and deter them from seeking fruitful, alternative opportunities.

STAKEHOLDER QUESTION

Imagine you are the key account manager for a cosmetics manufacturer, charged with nurturing relationships with the biggest stores so they sell your products enthusiastically and represent your brand well. You may be competing for shelf space against many other manufacturers.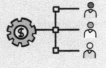

▶ With whom in the stores do you try to build trust and commitment?

▶ How do you do this?

▶ What factors might make you feel more trusting of, and committed towards, your major stores?

Loyalty

Loyalty is cognitive and behavioural; in other words, it relates to how people think and how they behave. It represents a tendency for someone to favour one entity, such as a brand (Storbacka et al., 1994; Javalgi & Moberg, 1997), above others. Loyal customers respond with biased behaviours towards one or more sellers. For instance, a consumer who has developed loyalty towards Apple over several years would favour an Apple product over that of competitors when choosing a replacement smartphone or tablet, even if alternative suppliers could offer comparative benefits, and Apple would carry an advantage into the process which would be difficult for challengers to overcome. Loyalty is also interpreted as the likelihood that a customer will buy a particular brand in any one purchase occasion (Keiningham et al., 2005). Some customers are loyal to two or more suppliers in the same industry (**polygamous loyalty**), for instance, by undertaking their weekly grocery shop from two supermarkets. Others are loyal to just one (**monogamous loyalty**). Today's consumers are more likely than ever to display polygamous brand loyalty rather than switching from one monogamous relationship to another (Uncles et al., 2003).

The **long-term value** of customers usually increases as their relationship with a brand lengthens. This is partially because the high costs of customer acquisition are absorbed in year 1, but also because long-term customers are more likely to

▶ trade up to a more expensive product when they replace their old one

▶ purchase accessories

▶ buy from their current supplier without first checking the competition

▶ attach a value to the supplier-customer relationship, making them less price conscious

▶ recommend the brand to their peers

The Ladder of Loyalty

The **relationship ladder**, or **ladder of loyalty** (Christopher et al., 2002), expresses the development of loyalty throughout the customer journey. Relationship marketing helps to bring about these changes. Each 'customer' type on the ladder of loyalty has different characteristics, and a firm's relationship marketing strategy should tailor its tasks to their potential. They term their 'customers' as follows (Table 11.5).

TABLE 11.5

Customer types by stages of the relationship.

Customer Type	Characteristics	Relationship Marketing Tasks
Prospect	Possible future customer Need products/services which the firm sells	Firm must encourage trial behaviour (e.g. dine at a restaurant for the first time)

Customer Type	Characteristics	Relationship Marketing Tasks
Customer	Current customer – already bought from firm Relatively uncommitted to firm	Encourage repeat purchases (e.g. through loyalty cards)
Client	Repeatedly buys from firm More likely to buy from firm again, more frequently, or with a higher order value	Encourage client to be more monogamously loyal
Supporter	Client who is so loyal that they wish to see the firm prosper Often follows the firm on social media and interacts with it	Engage the supporter to harness their potential for word of mouth (WOM) communications
Advocate	Passionate, 'brand-insistent' customers Monogamously loyal Spread positive WOM	Harness their goodwill to build a partnership
Partner	Extremely committed customers (often B2B and in specialised industries) Have blurred boundaries between themselves and their supplier firm	Work together for mutually beneficial outcomes and efficiencies Perhaps plan 'idiosyncratic investments' specific to that partnership

Source: Adapted from Christopher et al. (2002).

At the beginning of the relationship, **offensive marketing** attempts to win the customer, whilst later on, **defensive marketing** attempts to keep them.

MARKETING MANAGER TASK

Zomotor China's marketing manager Dylan has been tasked with designing a relationship marketing processes for drivers of the firm's vans (i.e. commercial vehicles and small trucks). For each customer type listed above, and using a table to present the information, list at least one specific action which Dylan might adopt to push his customers further up the ladder of loyalty. (For example, you might wish to invite 'clients' to a vehicle launch event in a dealership in which a respected home improvement vlogger is meeting the audience.) For each suggestion, explain your rationale, saying why it is likely to be effective, and what you wish to achieve.

Stages of the Relationship

There are often considered to be eight phases of relationships within marketing:

1. **Awareness**: partners note each other's potential to service their needs
2. **Exploration**: they search for solutions and undertake a trial period
3. **Expansion**: initial benefits enjoyed are scaled up
4. **Commitment**: either implicit or explicit – intent to preserve the relationship
5. **Termination**: if one or both partners withdraw from the arrangement
6. **Dissolution**: an agreed separation
7. **Customer exit**: dissatisfied customers may voice their frustrations
8. **Supplier withdrawal**: firms 'sack' unprofitable or troublesome customers

Many relationship marketing theories draw upon research into marriage and interpersonal relationships. Duck (1991) reduced relationship formation into four elements – (i) awareness of partnership opportunities, (ii) the ability to attract partners, (iii) relationship-building skills, and (iv) relationship maintenance and repair skills. Cross (1992) expanded this to five elements: (i) awareness, (ii) identity, (iii) relationship, (iv) community, and (v) advocacy. Waddock (1989) reduced it to three: (i) recognition of potential partnership benefits, (ii) initiation of partnership, and (iii) partnership establishment and maturity. Scanzoni (1979) was yet more reductive, boiling relationships down to (i) exploration, (ii) expansion, and (iii) commitment.

Internal Marketing

The internal environment of an organisation can be understood as the '5 Ms':

▶ Men/women: staff, skills, training, knowledge, personal attributes, goodwill, and relationships

▶ Money: money, financial streams, and income

▶ Machinery: the things used by the firm to undertake its core business (e.g. printers, ovens)

▶ Materials: the things used by the machinery to produce the thing to be sold (e.g. paper, pastries)

▶ Minutes: available time to plan and undertake initiatives

Internal marketing is a form of relationship marketing targeted at the first of these Ms: the organisation's staff. It aims to win over 'hearts and minds', and strives for openness and interaction rather than a top-down, hierarchical, unilateral imposition of strategy. Although most of the literature on internal marketing discusses the interaction between the 'organisation' and 'its employees' (Ahmed & Rafiq, 2003), many of the actions actually occur between individuals, such as a line manager and one staff member (Hume & Hume, 2014).

The Core Aims of Internal Marketing

The theoretical literature on internal marketing offers little practical advice to marketing managers on how internal marketing should be operationalised, but closer analysis reveals 13 key desired outcomes (Table 11.6).

METRICS QUESTION

If you were a company director who had recently implemented a range of internal marketing initiatives, what metrics would you use to ascertain its effectiveness? Provide a list of six key performance indicators (KPIs), explaining why each one is relevant and describing how you would collect the information.

TABLE 11.6

Aims of internal marketing.

No.	Desired Internal Marketing Outcome
1	To bring the advantages of traditional external marketing approaches to a firm's dealings with its employees (Christopher et al., 1991)
2	To improve staff performance levels (Sanchez-Hernandez & Miranda, 2011)
3	To facilitate better relational networks and interactivity (Lings, 2004)
4	To recruit, satisfy, and retain staff (Quester & Kelly, 1999; Gounaris, 2006)
5	To orient staff towards their external customers (Awwad & Agti, 2011; Day, 2012)
6	To accommodate and facilitate resource management strategy (Collins & Payne, 1991)
7	To encourage colleagues to treat each other as 'internal customers' and to consider their jobs as 'internal products' (Greene et al., 1994)
8	To motivate staff towards the achievement of organisational goals (Conduit & Mavondo, 2001)
9	To stimulate internal market research and exchange, easing the transmission of organisational knowledge and the propagation of organisational competences (Lindner & Wald, 2011)
10	To instigate effective internal communications (Kale, 2012)
11	To streamline internal processes, integrate previously separate functions, and discourage a silo mentality (Kelemen, 2000; Hume & Hume, 2014)
12	To stimulate organisational change (Winston & Cahill, 2012)
13	To manage the organisational culture (Kelemen & Papasolomou-Doukakis, 2004)

Implementation of Internal Marketing

The tools used for internal marketing are, on the whole, well worn:

▶ Notice boards

▶ Internal emails and intranet pages

▶ Town hall meetings (in which the boss informally updates a department or workforce with the latest developments and invites questions)

▶ Staff competitions and incentives

▶ Brown bag lunches (in which nominated staff members informally explain their roles to colleagues over sandwiches)

▶ 'Away days' (where staff bond away from the work environment)

▶ Training sessions

▶ Job shadowing

▶ Staff representation at board level

Limitations of Internal Marketing

Internal marketing theory suffers from a lack of practitioner-focused advice, insufficient scrutiny of ways in which it might be enabled by digital technology and new media, and little research on how the spark of internal marketing passes from one individual to another (i.e. a lack of dyadic perspectives). In practice, it often suffers from being prioritised by organisations much lower than external marketing activities, through uncertainty around who is responsible for it, and by it being implemented incorrectly (either intentionally or otherwise; Brown, 2021; Brown et al., 2019), resulting in internal demarketing (Vasconcelos, 2008), in which the organisation becomes less attractive to some or all of its staff.

MARKETING DIRECTOR TASK

Zomotor's global marketing director, Lee, must decide which values to promote prominently within the internal marketing strategy. These should bring a positive impact to staff and consequently to external customers. They must also decide which 13 core aims listed above are most important to deliver. Help Lee by prioritising the 13 aims in descending order of importance, explaining your rationale, and suggesting ways to achieve the top three aims. Use a table to do this.

Services Marketing

Services marketing emerged in the early 1980s as academics recognised how the significant differences between products and services demand different approaches. Numerous industries primarily sell services, with notable examples being tourism, hospitality, professional services, healthcare, financial services, telecommunications, entertainment, insurance and banking, and education. Services fall into five main categories:

1. Goods rental (e.g. of cars, cement mixers, or graduation gowns)
2. Place rentals (e.g. of a hotel room, theatre seat, or restaurant table)
3. Shared space access (e.g. to parks, tennis courts, or VIP areas)
4. Expertise hiring (e.g. of lawyers, builders, or dentists)
5. Systems access (e.g. to broadband, car insurance, or banking facilities)

Service Characteristics

Services have been considered as experiences, interactions, processes, value exchanges, performances and deeds, but what links all services is a set of characteristics which sets them apart from products (Table 11.7).

Service Marketing Characteristics

These service characteristics dictate that services marketing also has particular characteristics:

▶ The firm must sell an intangible concept (e.g. holiday, insurance).

▶ It must use tangible products to deliver the service (e.g. cruise ship, dentist's drill).

TABLE 11.7

Characteristics of services.

Characteristic	Meaning
Intangibility	They are not objects which can be touched
Inseparability/simultaneity	Their production and consumption occur together
Perishability	They cannot be stored
Variability/heterogeneity	They cannot be replicated exactly
Lack of ownership	The purchasers cannot take them away
User participation/customer contact	They require interaction between producer and consumer

▶ Storage and stock maintenance are not required.

▶ Customers are usually less price sensitive than when buying products.

▶ It is a value creation process.

Clearly, these factors can make services attractive to sell. Suppliers do not have to account for expensive warehouse space, time-consuming haulage and logistical issues, the financial burden of holding stock, or the repair of faulty goods. This often reduces overhead significantly.

Categories of Services

Services are sometimes classified as high contact or low contact, according to how much personal interaction there is between the customer and service provider. For instance, a massage would be high contact and broadband provision low contact. Services are also often classed as 'search goods', which may be evaluated by customers in advance, 'experience goods', which may be evaluated by customers after purchase or consumption, or 'credence claims', which are difficult or impossible for customers to evaluate at any point. Other theorists have categorised services according to what is processed:

People processing services entail the application of expertise directly onto the customer (e.g. hairdressing, aromatherapy)

Information processing services require the use of data (e.g. finance and insurance)

Mental stimulus processing services help refine the customer's knowledge or cognition (e.g. education, coaching, or psychotherapy)

Possession processing services maintain things owned by the customer (e.g. upholsterers or gardeners)

Services and the Extended Marketing Mix

The original Marketing Mix '4 Ps' from the 1960s became the Extended Marketing Mix '7 Ps' in the 1980s, partially to accommodate the needs of services marketing. 'Processes' encapsulates the way in which the firm serves its customers – for example, how it undertakes the sales transaction or deals with faulty goods. 'People' emphasises how human factors influence this service and add customer value – such as through friendliness and expertise. 'Physical evidence' (sometimes 'physical environment') plays a particularly important role in reinforcing customers' positive brand perceptions when purchasing services, as it provides sensual evidence which is otherwise difficult for an intangible service to convey. For example, wall photographs of exotic locations, the branding of professional industry associations, and comfortable waiting areas help convey professionalism and reassure customers of travel agents, despite their core service

PHOTO 11.5
Although Superdry sells products, store atmospherics and an enjoyable servicescape encourage customers to engage with the brand and to reject inferior competitors.

being inscrutable. Even the original '4 Ps' of the Marketing Mix have been reinterpreted to take into account services marketing: 'product' now includes the services which form part of the customer offer, such as wake-up calls in hotels; 'price' extends beyond the amount charged, also describing the timing and method of payment; 'place' includes the number, locations, functions, and characteristics of intermediaries who provide a service; and 'promotion' is sometimes now interpreted to consider how elements of the marketing communications mix can come into play during the provision of service.

SERVICESCAPES

Servicescapes (Bitner, 1992), which relate to 'physical evidence', are analyses of the environments in which services occur, and of the roles which those environments play in service delivery. They cover factors such as the design and 'personality' of retail areas. For instance, over the last 25 years, the customer areas of most retail banks have become gradually less formal, replacing queues with furnished waiting areas, and replacing high counters and glass screens with low desks and open spaces, soft lighting, ambient background music, customer-facing display screens, and customer information written in a friendly, conversational tone. As

continued

such, servicescapes are designed around three major considerations – the **ambience, functionality**, and **symbolism** which they convey to customers – and may be categorised as **lean servicescapes** if they are simple, functional spaces such as vending machines or drive-through kiosks, or **elaborate servicescapes** if they comprise a more complicated architecture and increased customer interaction, such as gyms and hotels.

NEW MEDIA QUESTION

If you study at a university, it should be an environment with a distinct servicescape which underpins the institution's brand and enables the organisation to convey how it wishes to serve its stakeholders (particularly its students) and transfer value to them. However, as many students compile a shortlist of possible universities online before application, they will not experience the ambience 'in the flesh'. If you were a marketing manager for a university business/management school, how would you communicate your servicescape to prospective applicants? In a table, list four or five actions which you would undertake, explain how you would do them, and why you think they might be effective.

Measuring Service Quality

Measuring the performance of an organisation's service provision is increasingly important to marketers, who must demonstrate a return on investment and enhance customer engagement. The Nordic School sought to measure service quality across two dimensions: the 'technical quality' of what is delivered and the 'functional quality' of how it is delivered. Whilst technical quality lends itself readily to numerical analyses, functional quality is far more subjective and therefore requires a qualitative approach of observation, interviews, and focus groups.

SERVQUAL

The dominant model in measuring service quality is 'SERVQUAL' (Parasuraman et al., 1988). It encourages a gap analysis, ascertaining the customer's perceptions and expectations of service delivery before attempting to understand why there may be a gap between them. Using five dimensions of service quality – reliability, assurance, tangibles, empathy, and responsiveness – it also provides a questionnaire which is readily adoptable by practitioners. There are numerous opportunities for gaps to open between customer expectations and perceptions of quality, and organisations should monitor and manage these. SERVQUAL was subsequently adapted by Cronin and Taylor (1992) to form SERVPERF, another prominent model which dispenses with expectations to focus purely on customer-perceived performance. Having eliminated one measurable variable, it is considered by many academics to be of less diagnostic value and importance than SERVQUAL.

Service-Dominant Logic

Along with the 'customer co-creation of value' and the increased focus on sustainability, perhaps the most significant development in marketing theory in the 21st century has been the conceptualisation by service-dominant logic (S-D logic) by Vargo and Lusch (2004). It is a framework which challenges the traditional notion of 'goods and services' and therefore represents a paradigm shift in marketing – a whole new way of understanding the function of marketing. After its subsequent development, it offers 11 'foundational propositions', as follows:

1. All exchanges (i.e. interactions between people) come from service.
2. Indirect exchange obscures the fundamental basis of exchange.
3. Goods distribute services (e.g. a bicycle is a distributor of travel).
4. Strategic benefits come from operant resources (i.e. invisible, intangible resources stemming from knowledge or capabilities drive long-term, overall benefits).
5. All economies are ultimately service economies.
6. Multiple actors co-create value, including the beneficiary.
7. Actors are unable to deliver value, simply to participate in the creation and offer of value propositions (i.e. as it requires cooperation between more than one person).
8. A service-centred view is customer oriented and relational (i.e. focuses on relationships).
9. Social and economic actors are always resource integrators (i.e. they use things to achieve a purpose).
10. Value is always determined by the beneficiary.
11. Value co-creation is coordinated through actor-generated institutions and through institutional arrangements.

GLOBAL MARKETING QUESTION

We know from Hofstede (1984) that consumers in different countries and cultures have different characteristics; their expectations of influencing power, their acceptance of gendered roles and macho references, and their avoidance of uncertainty, all differ broadly between cultures. How do you think this might affect the applicability of the S-D logic? Choose two dissimilar countries and a product or brand, then go through the list of S-D logic's 11 'foundational propositions', briefly stating how each one might be affected.

In the 16 years after its initial publication, the original article on S-D logic has attracted over 17,000 academic citations, and Vargo and Lusch's later articles developing it have produced an even greater combined number, demonstrating the extent to which the concept undermines so many areas of modern marketing theory.

Chapter Summary

As we have seen, many organisations sell services rather than products. In fact, firms which sell products almost invariably supply a service, without which the product would not be viable. However, services have several characteristics which differentiate them from products and demand special consideration from marketers. This is especially true as countries develop away from heavy industry and become 'service economies' built upon industries like finance, insurance, education, research, and business services.

We have also explored how organisations have moved away from a transactional paradigm, in which they were simply reacting passively to incoming customer queries, to a relationship marketing paradigm in which they build multiple meaningful interactions with customers, with the aim of stepping them up the ladder of loyalty by retaining, maintaining, and enhancing the long-term relationship. One part of relationship marketing which is often overlooked by marketers and under-resourced by firms is internal marketing, which is the marketing of the employer to the workforce. Internal marketing is especially effective at managing the culture by encouraging interdepartmental collaboration, customer-centricity, and adoption of brand behaviours.

Key Learning Outcomes

▶ Relationship marketing benefits organisations and customers reciprocally and mutually.

▶ Relationship dimensions include commitment, trust, loyalty, expectation, satisfaction, power, and dependence.

▶ Services are influenced by characteristics such as intangibility, inseparability, variability, perishability, user participation, and lack of ownership.

▶ Internal marketing is important is aligning the organisational culture towards external stakeholders.

Recommended Reading

Brown, D. M. (2021). *Internal marketing: Theories, perspectives and stakeholders*. Routledge.
Grönroos, C. (2020). Service marketing research priorities. *Journal of Services Marketing, 34*(3), 291–298.
Sheth, J. (2017). Revitalizing relationship marketing. *Journal of Services Marketing, 31*(1), 6–10.
Steinhoff, L., Arli, D., Weaven, S., & Kozlenkova, I. V. (2019). Online relationship marketing. *Journal of the Academy of Marketing Science, 47*(3), 369–393.

References

Ahmed, P. K., & Rafiq, M. (2003). Internal marketing issues and challenges. *European Journal of Marketing, 37*(9), 1177–1186.
Awwad, M. S., & Agti, D. A. M. (2011). The impact of internal marketing on commercial banks' market orientation. *International Journal of Bank Marketing, 29*(4), 308–332.
Bejou, D., & Palmer, A. (1998). Service failure and loyalty: An exploratory empirical study of airline customers. *Journal of Services Marketing, 12*(1), 7–22.
Berry, L. L. (1983). Relationship marketing. In L. L. Berry, G. L. Shostack, & G. D. Upah (Eds.), *Emerging perspectives on services marketing* (pp. 25–28). American Marketing Association.
Bitner, M. J. (1992). Servicescapes: The impact of physical surroundings on customers and employees. *Journal of Marketing, 56*(2), 57–71.
Brown, D. M., Dey, B., Wappling, A., & Woodruffe-Burton, H. (2019). Internal demarketing in the UK civil service since the 2007–9 financial crisis. *Strategic Change, 28*(5), 355–368.
Chartered Institute of Marketing. (2017). https://www.cim.co.uk/media/4772/7ps.pdf
Christopher, M., Payne, A., & Ballantyne, D. (1991). *Relationship marketing: Bringing quality customer service and marketing together*. Butterworth-Heinemann.
Christopher, M., Payne, A., & Ballantyne, D. (2002). *Relationship marketing: Creating stakeholder value*. Elsevier.
Collins, B., & Payne, A. (1991). Internal marketing: A new perspective for HRM. *European Management Journal, 9*(3), 261–270.
Conduit, J., & Mavondo, F. T. (2001). How critical is internal customer orientation to market orientation? *Journal of Business Research, 51*(1), 11–24.
Cova, B., Kozinets, R. V., & Shankar, A. (Eds.). (2007). *Consumer tribes*. Routledge.
Cronin Jr, J. J., & Taylor, S. A. (1992). Measuring service quality: A reexamination and extension. *Journal of Marketing, 56*(3), 55–68.
Cross, R. H. (1992, October). The five degrees of customer bonding. *Direct Marketing*, 33–58.
Day, G. S. (2012, Fall). Aligning the organization with the market: Reflections on the futures of marketing. *MIT Sloan Management Review*, 67–93.

Duck, S. (1991). *Understanding relationships*. Guildford Press.

Dwyer, F. R., Schurr, P. H., & Oh, S. (1987). Developing buyer-seller relationships. *The Journal of Marketing, 51*(2), 11–27.

French, J. R., Raven, B., & Cartwright, D. (1959). The bases of social power. *Classics of Organization Theory, 7*, 311–320.

Godson, M. (2009). *Relationship marketing*. Oxford University Press.

Gordon, I. (1998). *Relationship marketing: New strategies, techniques, and technologies to win the customers you want and keep them forever*. John Wiley & Sons.

Gounaris, S. P. (2006). Internal-market orientation and its measurement. *Journal of Business Research, 59*(4), 432–448.

Greene, W. E., Walls, G. D., & Schrest, L. J. (1994). Internal marketing: The key to external marketing success. *Journal of Services Marketing, 8*(4), 5–13.

Grönroos, C. (1997). Keynote paper: From marketing mix to relationship marketing-towards a paradigm shift in marketing. *Management Decision, 35*(4), 322–339.

Gummesson, E. (1999). Total relationship marketing: Experimenting with a synthesis of research frontiers. *Australasian Marketing Journal (AMJ), 7*(1), 72–85.

Ho, T. H., & Zheng, Y. S. (2004). Setting customer expectation in service delivery: An integrated marketing-operations perspective. *Management Science, 50*(4), 479–488.

Hofstede, G. (1984). *Culture's consequences: International differences in work-related values* (Vol. 5). Sage.

Hume, C., & Hume, M. (2014). Augmenting transcultural diffusion through knowledge management: The critical role of internal marketing. *Handbook of Research on Effective Marketing in Contemporary Globalism, 104*.

Javalgi, R., & Moberg, C. R. (1997). Service loyalty: Implications for service providers. *Journal of Services Marketing, 11*(3), 165–179.

Kale, S. H. (2012). Internal marketing: An antidote for Macau's labor shortage. *UNLV Gaming Research and Review Journal, 11*(1), 1.

Keiningham, T. L., Perkins-Munn, T., Aksoy, L., & Estrin, D. (2005). Does customer satisfaction lead to profitability? The mediating role of share-of-wallet. *Managing Service Quality: An International Journal, 15*(2), 172–181.

Kelemen, M. (2000). Too much or too little ambiguity: The language of total quality management. *Journal of Management Studies, 37*(4), 483–498.

Kelemen, M., & Papasolomou-Doukakis, I. (2004). Can culture be changed? A study of internal marketing. *The Service Industries Journal, 24*(5), 121–135.

Lindner, F., & Wald, A. (2011). Success factors of knowledge management in temporary organizations. *International Journal of Project Management, 29*(7), 877–888.

Lings, I. N. (2004). Internal market orientation: Construct and consequences. *Journal of Business Research, 57*(4), 405–413.

Moorman, C., Zaltman, G., & Deshpande, R. (1992). Relationships between providers and users of market research: The dynamics of trust within and between organizations. *Journal of Marketing Research, 29*(3), 314–328.

Morgan, R. M., & Hunt, S. D. (1994). The commitment-trust theory of relationship marketing. *Journal of Marketing, 58*(3), 20–38.

Parasuraman, A., Zeithaml, V. A., & Berry, L. L. (1988). Servqual: A multiple-item scale for measuring consumer perceptions of service quality. *Journal of Retailing*, *64*(1), 12.

Payne, A., Ballantyne, D., & Christopher, M. (2005). A stakeholder approach to relationship marketing strategy: The development and use of the 'six markets' model. *European Journal of Marketing*, *39*(7–8), 855–871.

Quester, P. G., & Kelly, A. (1999). Internal marketing practices in the Australian financial sector: An exploratory study. *Journal of Applied Management Studies*, *8*(2), 217–229.

Sachdev, S. B., & Verma, H. V. (2002). Customer expectations and service quality dimensions consistency: A study of select industries. *Journal of Management Research*, *2*(1), 43.

Sanchez-Hernandez, M. I., & Miranda, F. J. (2011). Linking internal market orientation and new service performance. *European Journal of Innovation Management*, *14*(2), 207–226.

Scanzoni, J. (1979). Social exchange and behavioral interdependence. In *Social exchange in developing relationships* (pp. 61–98). Academic Press.

Schurr, P. H., & Ozanne, J. L. (1985). Influences on exchange processes: Buyers' preconceptions of a seller's trustworthiness and bargaining toughness. *Journal of Consumer Research*, *11*(4), 939–953.

Sheth, J. N., & Parvatiyar, A. (1995). The evolution of relationship marketing. *International Business Review*, *4*(4), 397–418.

Storbacka, K., Strandvik, T., & Grönroos, C. (1994). Managing customer relationships for profit: The dynamics of relationship quality. *International Journal of Service Industry Management*, *5*(5), 21–38.

Uncles, M. D., Dowling, G. R., & Hammond, K. (2003). Customer loyalty and customer loyalty programs. *Journal of Consumer Marketing*, *20*(4), 294–316.

Vargo, S. L., & Lusch, R. F. (2004). Evolving to a new dominant logic for marketing. *Journal of Marketing*, *68*(1), 1–17.

Vasconcelos, A. F. (2008). Broadening even more the internal marketing concept. *European Journal of Marketing*, *42*(11–12), 1246–1264.

Waddock, S. A. (1989). Understanding social partnerships: An evolutionary model of partnership organizations. *Administration & Society*, *21*(1), 78–100.

Winston, W., & Cahill, D. J. (2012). *Internal marketing: Your company's next stage of growth*. Routledge.

Glossary

Advocate: a customer who actively promotes a brand to others
Affective commitment: a type of commitment due to 'liking' a brand
Coercive power: obtained through force
Consumer tribes: social clusters of people interested in the same product type or brand
Customer lifetime value (CLTV): the amount of value (chiefly profit) which a firm may expect to derive from a customer of the entire course of their relationship
Defensive marketing: aimed at customer retention
Expert power: derived from one's expertise
First-order relationships: direct contact with the organisation's stakeholders

Idiosyncratic investments: made by a partner in a project or opportunity specific to that partnership
Influence markets: anyone who can positively influence the marketing environment in which the firm operates
Information processing: services requiring the use of data
Internal demarketing: reducing the attractiveness of an organisation to its employees
Internal marketing: marketing to one's employees
Lateral partnerships: partnerships with competitors, local and national government, and not-for-profit organisations
Legitimate power: derived from authority or rank
Mental stimulus processing: services which help refine the customer's knowledge or cognition
Monogamous loyalty: loyalty to one brand in a product or service category
Normative commitment: arises from an obligation
Offensive marketing: aimed at attracting new customers
Polygamous loyalty: loyalty to two or more brands in a product or service category
Possession processing: services which maintain things owned by the customer
Prospect: a potential new customer
Referent power: derived from one party's ability to build a strong relationship
Relationship marketing: managing commercial relationships through marketing approaches
Reward power: derived from incentives
Second-order relationships: networks of relationships between participants
Servicescapes: the environments in which services occur, and the roles those environments play in service delivery
Services marketing: the marketing of services rather than products
Third-order relationships: occur within participants' organisations or larger social units
Volunteered data: personal data given freely by prospects and customers, usually online

Relationship Marketing Case Study: Handelsbanken's Local Relationship Banking

Handelsbanken ('the trade bank') is one of the largest Scandinavian brands. Based in Stockholm, Sweden, it offers banking and insurance services to corporations and private individuals. With nearly 400 branches in its home country, the firm considers its 'home markets' as the Nordic countries (i.e. Finland, Norway, and Denmark) along with the Netherlands and the UK, whilst maintaining a presence in China, the US, Spain, France, Poland, Germany, Luxembourg, and Singapore. In

continued

the UK, its organic growth has resulted in over 200 branches, although the brand is not widely known there amongst retail consumers, as many of its branches are away from areas of high pedestrian footfall and it relies on word-of-mouth recommendations from satisfied customers who perceive high levels of friendliness from an organisation competing in an industry which can often feel impersonal, computer-driven, and quick to punish customers' minor mistakes. In 2020, Handelsbanken announced the closure of many of its Swedish branches to accelerate investment in internet services, responding to changes in customer behaviour which are driven by technological advances. Typically, Handelsbanken customers are financially prudent, have a healthy (though not necessarily high) income, and are likely to represent a low credit risk – although a customer's ability to take on credit is assessed through conversations between the client and account manager rather than through the digital credit checks which are standard within the industry.

Outside Sweden, Handelsbanken is noticeably differentiated from other major banks through its adoption of a self-professed 'relationship banking' approach, in which generally even modest savers are allocated a specified contact, or dedicated account manager, within their local branch, rather than simply being served by whoever is available at the time, as would be the case in other retail banks. Likewise, the financial products themselves are highly individualised. For example, rather than advertising specific mortgage lending rates to a mass market, they are decided (within certain parameters) by local branch staff, who have the autonomy to tailor offerings to their clients' needs and circumstances. When agreeing overdrafts with customers, they ascertain their individual requirements and arrange a loan which is manageable, in the best interests of the customer, and "reflects our mutual relationship". Moreover, the bank is unusual in offering rates which are calculated against its costs, rather than pinning them against government rates and what the market will tolerate, although some online reviewers have found scrutiny of their transactions intrusive, suggesting that Handelsbanken achieves good results by cherry-picking low-risk customers and monitoring them very closely.

Imagine you are a Handelsbanken branch manager in one of its non-Swedish markets – perhaps Denmark, Finland, or Norway. Your branch has been operational for five years, and in the past two years it has acquired a healthy number of new customers who are young (21–25), well educated (75% to degree level), and developing well-paid careers (80% are in managerial or technical positions earning at least 140% of the national average salary). Handelsbanken's corporate goal of attracting more profitable business than competitor consumer banks is

continued

achieved by focusing continually on customer satisfaction and costs. It aims to attract customers for life, who then recommend the bank to their family, friends, and associates. Handelsbanken has adopted a business model which is not reliant upon short-term customer transactions but which aims to broaden and deepen relationships with their customers over time. In a table, explain what actions you would take at each stage of the relationship to encourage them up the ladder of loyalty and what customer responses you anticipate each action would elicit. How would you increase their customer lifetime value and reinforce the strong relationships?

Sources

Customer reviews of Handelsbanken, Money Saving Expert website discussion, August 22, 2012. Retrieved December 24, 2020, from https://forums.moneysavingexpert.com/discussion/4138881/handelsbanken

Financial Times article. *Handelsbanken to close almost half of Swedish branches*, September 16, 2020. Retrieved December 24, 2020, from https://www.ft.com/content/7b1dccc7-2e7d-4d8e-9ac3-0c666b14d998

Handelsbanken global website. Retrieved December 24, 2020, from www.handelsbanken.com

Handelsbanken UK website. Retrieved December 24, 2020, from www.handelsbanken.co.uk

12 | # Principles of Integrated Marketing Communications

LEARNING OBJECTIVES

▶ To locate the marketing communications mix within the broader land-scape of marketing

▶ To compare mass and personal communications

▶ To evaluate planning and budgetary approaches for marketing communications

▶ To analyse how to create an integrated marketing communications strategy which helps deliver organisational objectives

Introduction to Principles of Integrated Marketing Communications

In this chapter, we will focus on the major principles of the marketing communications mix. Sometimes termed the promotions mix or promotional mix, it combines a number of elements and tools to convey messages from an organisation to its audiences. The number of available media for transmitting these messages is growing, largely due to the proliferation of digital technologies and the liberalisation of broadcasting in recent years (Kitchen, 2017). This looks likely to continue, as consumers become increasingly internet savvy, demand immediacy and interaction, and move away from the traditional retail model of shopping in centralised, physical stores. However, marketers should not assume that older means of communicating such as print media will die out; rather, they are likely to support new media in different ways. One of the most difficult tasks for practitioners is to convey meanings about their organisation so that their intended audiences understand them correctly (Ots & Nyilasy, 2017). Another challenge is to anticipate how the communication may also find its way to unintended or secondary audiences, and the commercial impact which this may have. We will contextualise

DOI: 10.4324/9781003170891-13

321

marketing communications by locating them within the broader marketing mix, assess the differences between personal and mass communications, ascertain appropriate ways to plan a communications strategy, and analyse how and why communications should be integrated rather than acting in isolation.

MARKETING ASSISTANT TASK

In her role as marketing assistant for Zomotor Mexico, Tannya must evaluate the relative strengths of different advertising media. She needs to consider billboards, newspapers, magazines, television, radio, social media, and cinema. For each of these, she must judge their effectiveness in the following areas: the number of people who can be reached, overall cost, cost per prospect, memorability, Zomotor's control over the message, how quickly the adverts can be released, and the ability to target specific segments. Help Tannya by producing a table with the different media along the x-axis and their characteristics along the y-axis, and in each cell write 'strong', 'weak', or 'neutral' to indicate their potential effectiveness for Zomotor in advertising the new model to their target audiences.

PHOTO 12.1
IKEA uses outdoor, print, and broadcast advertising to lure customers into its stores.

The Communication Process

Whenever one person or entity wishes to communicate something to another, they must encode into a message the meaning which they wish to convey and transmit it via a medium to the recipient. Then the recipient must decode the message which they have received to extract its meaning.

Consider an example of an interpersonal communication: the love letter. First, Romeo wishes to communicate his thoughts and feelings to Juliet, so he decides what words to use to convey them as accurately as possible (i.e. message encoding). He realises that, even if Juliet reads his words, she still may not appreciate the strength of Romeo's emotions, so he tries to anticipate how his words will be interpreted by Juliet when she reads them. Next, Romeo decides which channel to use to send his message. Living in 21st-century Verona, he can choose from a letter, an email, or even an announcement in the local newspaper. A traditionalist, he writes a letter and posts it (i.e. chooses a media). When Juliet receives it, she reads it, interprets the words and phrases, and derives meaning from it (i.e. message decoding). The complexity of language, and of individuals' experiences and knowledge, means that Juliet will derive slightly different meanings from the letter than those intended by Romeo, but hopefully she understands very well the main content.

Communications between an organisation and its audiences work in the same way, and may be summarised as shown in Figure 12.1.

As we see, when a marketer communicates with an audience, they have much in common with Romeo. Their messages are influenced by their knowledge and experience of the world and language, their ability to communicate well, and the culture in which they exist. Additionally, they must reflect their organisation's wishes. After encoding meanings into a message, they transmit it by their choice of media. However,

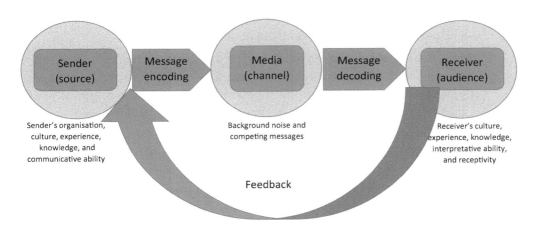

FIGURE 12.1
The communication process.

they must try to make the message heard above the background noise of compet-ing communications, which may come from other marketers or from society more broadly. This may be achievable by making the communication fun or unusual or by conveying a particularly impactful benefit. The receiver decodes the message, but this is influenced by the culture in which they exist, their experience and knowledge of the world and language, their ability to interpret messages, and the receptiveness to the communication. The sender will enjoy some sort of feedback from the receiver – this may be an enthusiastic/interested response, an unenthusiastic/uninterested response, or silence – and be able to refine future messages accordingly. The marketer's task is more complicated than Romeo's in one crucial aspect: they must often communicate with several audiences of differing importance and influence. This is discussed more in Chapter 5.

Differentiate, Reinforce, Inform, Persuade

'Differentiate, reinforce, inform, persuade' (DRIP) is a common marketing mantra to remind us of what marketing communications should do.

> **Differentiate**: say how your brand, product, or service is different from – and better than – the competition. Failure to do this results in commoditisation, meaning that customers have little reason to choose one competitor instead of another, apart from price. This can lead to an unprofitable price war and extreme cus-tomer price sensitivity, which undermines the organisation's brand and its commercial objectives. Therefore, marketers should convey customer benefits (Bruhn & Schnebelen, 2017).

> **Reinforce**: where a brand is established and popular, marketers reinforce the rea-sons for this. It is easy for customers gradually to forget a supplier which they buy from infrequently, and the reasons why they ever bought from them, so marketers must remind them of these reasons.

> **Inform**: a marketing communication should provide the audience with some sort of information. This does not necessarily require words. For instance, a television advert for a car could deliver much information by how, where, and by whom the car is driven, the production techniques, photography, and music.

> **Persuade**: unless the communication has influenced audience members to think or behave differently in relation to the brand, it has failed to market effectively (Duralia, 2018). For example, a billboard advert for a washing machine may persuade an audience member to associate that particular brand with washing machines, to visit a retailer or the company's website for more information, or to include that manufacturer within their 'evoked set' of preferred suppliers when they next purchase a washing machine.

ETHICS QUESTION

As a marketer for a holiday park, you need to market holidays in your lodges. You realise that, after the COVID-19 pandemic, self-contained holiday accommodation will be very sought after, as it reduces the risk of infection or of the holiday being cancelled. To what extent would you target potential holidaymakers who are in the 'vulnerable' categories (e.g. ageing or disabled), and what types of message would you try to convey to them? Identify and discuss any ethical dilemmas.

From the Extended Marketing Mix to the Marketing Communications Mix

As we have seen, the extended marketing mix comprises the 7 Ps of product, price, place, promotion, people, process, and physical evidence. Of these, promotion has sometimes been referred to as the promotional mix, but it is now more commonly known as the marketing communications mix. Promotion entails communicating messages and meanings to audiences by marketing to them (or with them). The marketing communications mix, often shortened to 'marcomms', comprises several instruments. The first five instruments are well established: advertising, personal selling and sales management, public relations (PR), direct marketing, and sales promotion. Three recent additions to the list have been sponsorship, packaging or point of sales, and digital or online, although some commentators believe that digital/online should not be treated as a separate instrument but as running through all the others, as it is accepted practice for digital marketing to occur in tandem with other forms of marketing rather than in isolation. If we could place advertising and sales promotion within a marketing 'family tree', it would resemble Figure 12.2.

In recent years, an increasing number of theorists have questioned the marketing mix, believing it to be too 'inside-out' in its perspective (i.e. presenting customers with something ready-made and focused on the organisation's interpretations of customers rather than involving customers and other external stakeholders earlier to impose their ideas upon the design of the marketing strategy). In particular, relationship marketing theorists, and those interested in the customer co-creation of value, have made this criticism. Therefore, it is unsurprising that the integrated marketing communications (IMC) mix has more recently attracted similar criticisms for the same reasons (e.g. Finne & Grönroos, 2017). Therefore, we need to remember these ideas when we analyse the use of marcomms and consider how we might integrate customers more within marcomms strategies.

FIGURE 12.2
The marketing communications mix and the extended marketing mix.

Instruments of the Integrated Marketing Communications Mix

Each element of the marketing mix (product, price, place, and promotion) has numerous instruments: areas of marketing with which they are concerned, or things which they do for the organisation. For example, products address customer needs through their specifications, features, benefits, quality, options, branding, and services. Prices convey cost to customers through published prices, discount structures, incentives, payment periods, and credit terms. Place conveniently gets products to customers via transport and logistics, inventory control, channel intermediaries, and the locations in which the organisation or product is present.

Promotion also has a job to do, and this is to communicate the value or suitability of the product or service to existing and potential customers. To do this, an organisation reaches them via advertising, sales promotion, and the other instruments of the marketing communications mix in Figure 12.2. Some theorists list exhibitions and trade fairs as an additional instrument, but we have included them in personal selling and sales management.

Taking into consideration recent theoretical and practical developments, we can describe the main instruments of the IMC mix as follows:

Advertising: the use of overtly sponsored messages and spaces by an organisation for the purposes of promoting or selling their product, service or brand. Adverts may be hosted by intermediaries in several different formats, such as print or broadcast media.

Sales promotion: the use of short-term incentives for customers to trial or buy items which they would otherwise be less likely to purchase during that time period. These inducements to buy have an expiry date to stimulate demand and may include coupons or discounts.

Public relations: the building and maintaining of a favourable reputation by an organisation by disseminating information which influences public perceptions, increasing their awareness and acceptance of the organisation.

Direct marketing: communicating directly with preselected audience members, rather than face-to-face or through media, to sell to them or elicit another response which will lead towards purchase. Mailshots and telephone calls are common examples.

Sponsorship: supporting a person, team, organisation, activity, or event for exploitable commercial potential. Typically, the sponsor expects to gain favourable brand exposure to a target audience, and to gain credibility by association with the sponsored entity.

Personal selling: face-to-face selling in which the organisation's representative may attempt to encourage the prospect to purchase through persuasion, presentation of relevant information, and objection handling.

Sales management: the strategic use of a salesforce to sell to potential or existing customers, and to encourage customers to become more loyal and committed to the organisation.

Packaging: the wrapping which protects and preserves a product but which may also use graphics to reinforce the brand, informing customers and encouraging them to purchase the item.

Point-of-purchase or point-of-sale material: branded product cabinets, totems, furniture, flags, livery, and other equipment visible to customers at the point of purchase, which reinforces their positive brand perceptions.

Digital and online marketing: marketing communications which are mediated by technology (e.g. websites, smartphone apps, SMS texts).

SUSTAINABILITY QUESTION

As a marketer for a confectionery company, you know that packaging plays a major role in increasing sales of your Easter eggs. However, the volume of packaging used is disproportionate to the quantity of chocolate sold or the level of protection which it needs. You realise that your packaging is unnecessarily contributing to landfill waste but do not wish to risk losing sales to competitors. Make a list of possible initiatives which you might try, their commercial risks (if applicable), and how you might try to implement them.

PHOTO 12.2
Universities like Northumbria University make use of television and radio adverts, targeted emails, and heavy online presences to recruit students.

Tools of the Integrated Marketing Communications Mix

Marketers contact, engage, and communicate with members of their intended audiences by using the tools of the IMC mix (Manser Payne et al., 2017). Almost all organisations use more than one such tool, often simultaneously but perhaps varying the intensity with which they use each. They are a little like ingredients which are added at various times and in different quantities. The work with each other and should be mutually complementary. The main tools use for contacting audiences and their members are listed in Table 12.1.

Certain tools and media belong in more than one category. For example, product placement – where a brand pays to have its product made visible – does not only occur in broadcast media contexts such as television shows but also in interactive video games. It is also tempting to consider some of these listed contact tools simply as advertising media, but that would be to underestimate the extent to which other instruments of the marketing communications mix make use of them. One example might be a petrochemicals company which influences its audience's perceptions of its brand by

TABLE 12.1

Marketing communications tools and media.

Tool	Examples
Broadcast media	Television, radio
Print media	Newspapers, magazines
Outdoor media	Billboards, vehicle ads, transport hub ads
Digital media	Social media adverts, apps, internet, advergames, paid search (Valos et al., 2017)
Point-of-purchase media	Packaging, point-of-sale display, in-store media
Viral and WOM media	WOM, electronic word of mouth (EWOM), guerrilla and ambush marketing
Product placement/brand entertainment	Product placement, flash mobs
Events and sponsorship	Trade shows, sponsorship (e.g. people, teams, events; Turner, 2017)
Public relations and publicity	Providing favourable stories about the organisation to journalists, publishing editorials
Direct marketing	Leaflets, fliers, mass emails
Sales promotion	In-store discount weekends, 'Black Friday'
Personal selling	B2B field sales, in-store sales assistance

reaching them through television, not by using paid advertisements but by providing television journalists with 'good news' stories to air – public relations.

The media used by marketers may be paid, owned or earned:

Paid media belong to other organisations (e.g. television broadcasters, billboard owners, and newspaper companies). Marketers pay to have their messages displayed by those organisations. Therefore, it may be expensive to the brand and less credible to audiences, but it allows the marketer a high degree of control over the message and how it is conveyed.

Owned media are those channels which are controlled by the marketer's organisation (e.g. their own blogs and vlogs, brochures and leaflets, smartphone apps, and websites). These allow the marketer total control over the message and may be very cost-effective but are unlikely to benefit from as much passing footfall as with paid media.

Earned media are social, viral, or customer led. Perhaps the most prominent example is WOM and EWOM, in which audience members are sufficiently motivated to transmit messages about the brand to their peers. Online reviews (such as those on TripAdvisor), the views of trusted online community members, and social media 'shares' or 'reposts' also constitute earned media. Communications

329

transmitted through earned media are usually considered highly credible by audience members; they are often very inexpensive, long-lasting, and are able to cross national and cultural boundaries. However, the marketer has very little control over the message. In fact, much recent research has focused upon negative WOM and EWOM, and the prevalence of 'shilling', in which an interested party such as a rival hotelier posts biased content such as an unfairly critical hotel review to gain a competitive advantage.

We compare different forms of media in more detail in the next chapter.

NEW MEDIA QUESTION

As a marketer for a motorcycle manufacturer, you wish to lower the brand's average customer age by using new media to target Generation Y (millennials) and Generation Z. You realise that much of your current online content – YouTube videos and a Facebook discussion group – are likely to be less attractive to your target audience than the Generation X and Baby Boomer consumers who dominate your customer base. Which websites and online spaces will you use to engage younger audiences, how, and why?

Personal and Mass Market Communications

Marketers have several key decisions to make when designing a communications strategy. Perhaps the key decision is whether to use personal communications or mass market communications (Percy, 2018). Most organisations use both, but the proportions used of each can be critical.

Personal Communications

These are marketing communications in which a representative of the selling organisation interacts with an individual within the target audience. For instance, if a salesperson instigates a telephone conversation with a customer to talk about product benefits, that is a personal communication, as it is tailored specifically to that customer and takes their individual needs into account.

Personal communications are strong in the following areas:

▶ Capturing and keeping the prospect's attention

▶ Guiding the prospect through complicated information, such as technical specifications

▶ Facilitating instant, two-way feedback

▶ Allowing their success to be measured

However, personal communications also suffer the following limitations:

▶ They are labour intensive, and therefore the cost per prospect reached is high.

▶ They are slow, which makes it time-consuming or impossible to reach a large audience.

Mass Communications

In contrast to personal communications, mass communications do not rely on personal contact and interaction between the organisation's representative and an individual prospect or customer. Instead, they reach multiple members of the target audience remotely – sometimes even millions simultaneously – by taking a less individualised, more generic approach. An example of a mass communication would be a television advert.

Mass communications are strong in the following areas:

▶ They reach a large audience quickly.

▶ By reaching so many prospects, the cost per person reached is low (although the overall cost may be high).

However, mass communications also suffer the following limitations:

▶ They may struggle to be impactful or grab the prospect's attention.

▶ They provide little assistance to prospects' comprehension of complicated information.

▶ Communication is unidirectional (one-way) from the organisation to the audience, rather than dialogical (a two-way conversation), which deprives the organisation of useful feedback and the audience of a voice.

▶ Measuring their effectiveness is difficult, as feedback is delayed and it is difficult to filter out other factors which may have influenced prospects.

GLOBAL MARKETING QUESTION

As a marketer for a lawnmower manufacturer, you are using mass communications to transcend national boundaries and expand sales internationally. However, you have noticed that your online content and broadcast communications – which were originally designed for the

continued

European and Australian markets – are having little effect in South Asia and Latin America. Why might this be? How would you find out the possible causes? What changes could you make to rectify the problem?

As we see, both personal and mass communications have their pros and cons, so many organisations use a mix. For example, if a construction company was building a new housing development, they might advertise on local radio and in newspapers and magazines, harnessing mass communications to build awareness of their products, and including a call to action (CTA), such as encouraging prospects to visit a show home. If they are successful in this, a sales representative at the show home would use personal communications, ascertaining the prospect's requirements and expectation and gently persuading them to place an order.

Integrated Marketing Communications

'Integrated' is a word often used to describe how marketing communications should be managed. This is because any form of communication is more effective and efficient if it works alongside other communication forms. In effect, each communication is like a soldier which needs to synchronise its actions with the other soldiers in its unit rather than acting alone.

The most common aims of IMC are summarised in Table 12.2.

Aims of marketing communications.

TABLE 12.2

Aims of marketing communications.

Dialogue	Stimulating two-way conversations between the organisation and its customers
Selective communication	Communicating only relevant content to targeted groups, rather than generic content to one untargeted group
Customer empowerment	Enabling customers to access relevant content when they need it
Information provision	Providing information which customers need to make informed purchase decisions or to get the most out of the product
Defence	Safeguarding the organisation's reputation and its position against competitors
Selling (softly)	Encouraging prospects to buy product for the first time (i.e. customer acquisition) or an existing customer to make repeat or additional purchases
Brand awareness	Building awareness of the organisation's brand amongst prospects

Brand confidence	Building affinity between prospects/customers and the brand through confidence and trust
Relationships	Constructing long-term relationships, rather than one-time transactions
Satisfaction	Stimulating customer satisfaction by meeting and exceeding their expectations, and by adding customer value
Retention	Instilling customer loyalty through satisfaction and brand affinity to discourage them from seeking products from alternative suppliers
Globalisation	Some organisations may use marketing communications to expand their presence internationally

STAKEHOLDER QUESTION

As a marketer for a photocopier manufacturer, you have used the aims in the above table when designing an IMC strategy targeting major companies who might buy over 50 photocopiers in a single order. However, to be successful in that market segment, your 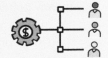 firm will need the support and presence of its local dealerships and service agents. Explain which IMC actions you would undertake, and how, to communicate effectively with your dealers and agents to gain their loyalty and assistance.

Forms of Integration and Barriers to Integration

Brands may strengthen their marketing communications by integrating on a number of levels (Anabila, 2020). Broadly speaking, these are based around six considerations:

1. *Images*: pictures, symbols, typefaces, designs, and language (e.g. phrases, tone)

2. *Functions*: the objectives of individual communications should align to serve an overarching purpose

3. *Timings*: the release of communications should be synchronised carefully so that they reinforce each other

4. *Consumers*: segmenting consumer markets and targeting them with communications which are segment specific but unified by certain brand-related elements

5. *Stakeholders*: as with the consumer approach above, but targeted at stakeholders such as channel intermediaries, governments, and charities

6. *Relationships*: considering the evolving requirements of customers throughout their relationships with the brand, and shaping communications which fit those longitudinal journeys (Šerić et al., 2020)

However, organisations are often hindered by the following factors in their attempts to integrate their communications:

Functional specialisation and structures within organisations can encourage a 'silo mentality' in which colleagues in sales, marketing, and other functions consider their areas so specialised that they are unable to adopt a more holistic, 'one organisation' mindset.

Functional specialisation within communications agencies has a similar effect. If an organisation, for instance, appoints a creative marketing agency to handle its national television adverts, but the agency has little experience of press or outdoor advertising, it is less likely to adopt a 'joined-up' approach with another agency which the organisation has hired for that purpose (Key & Czaplewski, 2017; Laurie & Mortimer, 2019).

Company politics, and particularly distrust or jockeying for position between senior managers, may prevent them from collaborating sufficiently to produce coherent and cohesive communications.

Inadequate internal communications can prevent managers and staff from uniting around a common vision or understanding of the organisation's ethos, leading to disjointed external communications.

Management misperceptions of the ease or importance of integration can discourage its adoption (De Pelsmacker et al., 2018).

MARKETING MANAGER TASK

In China, Dylan is managing an IMC strategy to support a new car model, the Zappy. He has commissioned a creative marketing agency to design the artwork, a field marketing agency to supply temporary B2B salespeople, and a communications agency who will book media space and liaise with broadcasters and publishers. However, he is concerned that they are working as three separate entities rather than in a consistent, 'joined-up' manner. Make a list of five initiatives which Dylan might introduce to overcome this problem and bring the agencies together, including your rationale.

Planning an Integrated Marketing Communications Strategy

Successful organisations never fully take a break from their marketing communications. They appraise, adjust, and redesign but never entirely cease communicating. We may

FIGURE 12.3
Integrated marketing communications planning process.

therefore understand the process of planning marketing communications as a cycle (Figure 12.3).

In this process, the marketer first undertakes a **situation analysis,** which not only identifies general opportunities and threats in the organisation's macro and micro environments, and strengths and weaknesses in its internal environment, but also analyses factors which are specific to communications. This knowledge suggests how the marketer can shape and target their communications both defensively and offensively, enabling them to set appropriate **communications objectives**. When the marketer is clear about what they want to achieve, and in what timescale, they can undertake **budgeting**. Ideally, they would use an objective and task approach to allocate the correct amount of money to achieve the objectives. However, it is common for organisations to allocate insufficient funds, which can result in the objective not being met. By having a clear **segmentation strategy**, the marketer identifies the most suitable audience to target. This is done with a **creative strategy**, combining the content, tone, and style to be conveyed through identified **customer touchpoints** – times and places at which the customer comes into contact with the organisation and can be influenced by its communications. **Evaluation** of the effectiveness of communications should occur constantly to ensure that budget is spent on actions which will address the objectives and create return on investment (ROI). However, a more formal evaluation is likely to occur at predetermined points against specific key performance indicator (KPI) metrics. These measures, and the actions taken in response to them, may be considered **control mechanisms**, keeping the communications strategy on course (Porcu et al., 2017; Porcu et al., 2019).

Communications Objectives

After undertaking the situation analysis to ascertain 'where we are now', marketers must define communications objectives (i.e. 'where do we want to be at a specific point in the future?') which are consistent with the broader commercial objectives of the organisation (Patti et al., 2017). These broader objectives are influenced by factors such as the economy and the strength of the firm's product line, and may be to increase market share, to improve profit margins, to move upmarket, or to reduce overhead. When writing specifically about advertising, Colley (1961) suggested the following as suitable, measurable goals in his DAGMAR model, which stands for 'defining advertising goals for measured advertising result' (Table 12.3).

These goals are more applicable to business-to-consumer (B2C) than business-to-business (B2B) markets, and they reflect the stages in the customer journey.

TABLE 12.3

Goals for advertising and for integrated marketing communications.

Goals	Description
Category need	Persuading a prospect that they need to buy something from a product or service category where the firm is active, to fulfil their requirement (e.g. a travel agency may, before promoting its own brand, persuade prospects that they need a vacation and should buy a package holiday)
Raising brand awareness	Making more prospects aware of the firm's brand and making it more memorable to them
Raising brand knowledge/ understanding	Enabling audiences to understand the brand, its products, services, meanings, and (most crucially) its customer benefits
Improving brand attitude	Encouraging audiences to like the brand, identify with it, or think of it favourably
Brand purchase intention	Converting uncommitted prospects into ones who intend to buy the firm's products or services; to do this, the firm may try to place the brand in prospects' evoked set (i.e. their shortlist of preferred brands from which they will buy certain goods)
Purchase facilitation	Making it easier for prospects to buy from the organisation, perhaps by offering interest-free finance packages for expensive purchases such as cars, house extensions, or cruise holidays
Purchase	Taking prospects to sale by gaining commitment and facilitating the transaction in which they place a purchase order

Goals	Description
Satisfaction	Ensuring that customers' expectations are met and exceeded, and that they recognise and appreciate the good product and service quality which the firm has provided
Brand loyalty	Bonding customers to the brand psychologically by breaking down barriers, personalising the contact, and making the firm less replaceable to the customer

Source: Adapted from Colley (1961).

Therefore, as the firm works its way from the goals listed near the top of the table to those listed further down, the proportion of audience members in each stage will decrease. For example, if a construction company wishes to attract customers to order house extensions and targets all 1,000 homeowners in a village, it will attempt to raise 'category need' awareness (i.e. of the availability of house extensions) in all 1,000 audience members. However, 50 householders may have absolutely no need for an extension (e.g. if they live alone and/or have no available land) and will effectively 'switch off', becoming unreceptive or unresponsive to the firm's communications. Therefore, when the firm then progresses to raising brand awareness, there will only be 950 audience members remaining. This thinning-out process continues at each stage until perhaps only 10% of prospects purchase, and only 3% repurchase.

MARKETING DIRECTOR TASK

Lee, Zomotor's marketing director, is coordinating a television advertising campaign for Europe. Its key aim is to increase recognition of the Zomotor brand amongst millennials and to raise awareness of its youthful brand attributes, especially in connection with its new small and sporty city car. Several competitors have been criticised and fined for breaching ethical guidelines by misrepresenting product details and offending viewers. Lee and their team wish to safeguard the reputation of Zomotor and respect their diverse audiences and stakeholders. To help Lee, list ways in which the television advertising campaign risks falling short of Zomotor's high ethical standards, and explain what actions Lee could take to mitigate those threats.

Communications Budgeting

Effective IMC depends upon an appropriate budget. Advertising practitioners often say that share of voice (i.e. the percentage of their industry's advertising communications

PHOTO 12.3
Helping customers to become familiarised with products and to decipher specialist jargon is one element of integrated marketing communications.

attributable to their firm) results in the same market share (i.e. the percentage of their industry's sales achieved by their firm). For instance, if Nokia is responsible for 10% of marketing communications in Europe by smartphone manufacturers (by spending 10% of the European smartphone industry marcomms budget), it could expect to sell 10% of the smartphones sold in Europe. Naturally, this is a generalisation which does not account for the strength of each company's strategies and the relative position of market strength from which they start the year. However, budgeting is certainly extremely important and, as with marketing more generally, marketing communications are often allocated budgets by one of the following methods:

Marginal analysis is the process of predicting the increase in sales, income, or profit which is likely to result from a specified increase in spend. For example, spending $5 million on marketing communications might be expected to generate $10 million of profit within a year, whereas spending an additional $5 million might only generate a further $7 million of profit. In this instance, the firm may decide not to spend the second $5 million but instead to invest it in developing its product range or network of retailers.

Inertia is much less complicated: it is simply taking the same approach which has always been taken, rather than analysing and making a new decision. It often leads to strategic drift and deteriorating sales because it ignores changes in the marketplace.

Arbitrary allocation is similarly unsatisfactory, and is the allocation of funds to marketing communications with little consideration of the objectives or needs. It often results in insufficient funds, which usually erode share of voice and market share, or in excess funds, which are often spent unnecessarily and wastefully.

Affordability means allocating what senior managers believe the firm can afford to spend. However, if a firm has small cash reserves, it may benefit financially from the stimulus of marketing communications.

Percentage of sales is a similar approach, allocating a proportion of the previous year's income. Often firms use the same percentage each year. This means that if they have had a poor year, they risk perpetuating this poor performance by underinvesting in the marketing the following year. It can therefore lead into a cycle of decline.

Competitive parity is a budgetary method which pitches the firm's marketing communications spend against that of its competitors. For example, the second most popular smartphone manufacturer in a country may decide to spend 80% of what the market leader spends. These percentages are often unchanged from previous years and, whilst they stabilise the firm's market position, they may prevent it from gaining market share by capitalising upon its new product development or competitors' temporary weaknesses.

Objective and task is the final and most satisfactory budgetary method. It entails analysing the communications objectives which the firm has, the tasks necessary to fulfil those objectives, and the costs of undertaking those tasks. By extrapolating backwards from the result to the spend, this approach is far more likely to deliver upon the company's ambitions.

Budgetary Influences

Organisations' marketing budgets may be influenced by several factors. Commercial considerations include the size and potential of the market and the strength of the competition, whilst factors internal to organisations include the market share objectives which they harbour, and whether they wish to reduce their variable and total costs by manufacturing in great quantities to achieve economies of scale (Belch & Belch, 1998). The characteristics of the organisation and its senior managers is also very influential. In a 'sales organisation' which focuses heavily on its market presence, larger budgets are likely to be allocated for marketing purposes, and this is especially true of companies fronted by bold, ambitious leaders.

Even when budgets have been passed, unanticipated factors may lead to budgetary changes part way through an accounting period. These include unforeseen opportunities or threats, perhaps caused by the actions of competitors – crises such as the collapse of channel partners, macroenvironmental factors like recessions or emerging trade wars, or even internal factors such as errors and omissions within the planning process. Although many of these reduce budgets, some, such as company takeovers or rising share prices, may increase them.

Chapter Summary

The IMC mix is an essential area of marketing, in which organisations communicate messages to their target audiences. In doing so, they intend to provide to customers the information needed to make a purchase decision, to convey their products and brand in a positive light, to differentiate themselves against the competition by demonstrating customer benefits, and to persuade prospects and customers to purchase or to become more committed to the brand. Often, several different instruments of the IMC mix will be used in the same campaign to complement each other or to target more than one market segment. Much communication is non-verbal and non-textual, relying on symbols, imagery, and other audio-visual cues to reinforce or replace the printed and spoken word. An organisation may employ several specialist agencies on one campaign. Communicating with audiences is a skilled function because, when they decode messages, they are almost certain to extract a slightly different understanding to the meaning which was intended and encoded by the sender. Moreover, marketing messages are increasingly likely to reach secondary or unintended audiences due to the growing proliferation of media and the interconnectedness of consumers.

Key Learning Outcomes

▶ The IMC mix is the 'promotion' P of the extended marketing mix, and it is an important part of an organisation's broader marketing landscape.

▶ Mass and personal communications have different characteristics and may have different immediate objectives, but they should complement each other and work toward the same overall marketing objectives.

▶ Organisations must plan their marketing communications carefully to ensure consistency, integration, and alignment with customer needs; this may need a pragmatic approach to budgeting.

▶ To create an IMC strategy which helps deliver organisational objectives, marketers must overcome organisational silos and adopt a holistic mindset.

Recommended Further Reading

Anabila, P. (2020). Integrated marketing communications, brand equity, and business performance in micro-finance institutions: An emerging market perspective. *Journal of Marketing Communications*, 26(3), 229–242.

Bruhn, M., & Schnebelen, S. (2017). Integrated marketing communication – from an instrumental to a customer-centric perspective. *European Journal of Marketing*, 51(3), 464–489.

Duralia, O. (2018). Integrated marketing communication and its impact on consumer behavior. *Studies in Business and Economics*, 13(2), 92–102.

References

Belch, G. E., & Belch, M. A. (1998). *Advertising and promotion: An integrated marketing communications approach* (4th ed.). McGraw Hill.

Colley, H. R. (1961). *Dagmar*. Association of National Advertisers.

De Pelsmacker, P., Geuens, M., & Van Den Bergh, J. (2018). *Marketing communications: A European perspective* (6th ed.). Pearson.

Finne, Å., & Grönroos, C. (2017). Communication-in-use: Customer-integrated marketing communication. *European Journal of Marketing, 51*(3), 445–463.

Key, T. M., & Czaplewski, A. J. (2017). Upstream social marketing strategy: An integrated marketing communications approach. *Business Horizons, 60*(3), 325–333.

Kitchen, P. J. (2017). Integrated marketing communications: Evolution, current status, future developments. *European Journal of Marketing, 51*(3), 394–405.

Laurie, S., & Mortimer, K. (2019). How to achieve true integration: The impact of integrated marketing communication on the client/agency relationship. *Journal of Marketing Management, 35*(3–4), 231–252.

Manser Payne, E., Peltier, J. W., & Barger, V. A. (2017). Omni-channel marketing, integrated marketing communications and consumer engagement: A research agenda. *Journal of Research in Interactive Marketing, 11*(2), 185–197.

Ots, M., & Nyilasy, G. (2017). Just doing it: Theorising integrated marketing communications (IMC) practices. *European Journal of Marketing, 51*(3), 490–510.

Patti, C. H., Hartley, S. W., van Dessel, M. M., & Baack, D. W. (2017). Improving integrated marketing communications practices: A comparison of objectives and results. *Journal of Marketing Communications, 23*(4), 351–370.

Percy, L. (2018). *Strategic integrated marketing communications*. Routledge.

Porcu, L., Del Barrio-Garcia, S., Alcántara-Pilar, J. M., & Crespo-Almendros, E. (2019). Analyzing the influence of firm-wide integrated marketing communication on market performance in the hospitality industry. *International Journal of Hospitality Management, 80*, 13–24.

Porcu, L., Del Barrio-García, S., & Kitchen, P. J. (2017). Measuring integrated marketing communication by taking a broad organisational approach: The firm-wide IMC scale. *European Journal of Marketing, 51*(3), 692–718.

Šerić, M., Ozretić-Došen, Đ., & Škare, V. (2020). How can perceived consistency in marketing communications influence customer – brand relationship outcomes? *European Management Journal, 38*(2), 335–343.

Turner, P. (2017). Implementing integrated marketing communications (IMC) through major event ambassadors. *European Journal of Marketing, 51*(3), 605–626.

Valos, M. J., Maplestone, V. L., Polonsky, M. J., & Ewing, M. (2017). Integrating social media within an integrated marketing communication decision-making framework. *Journal of Marketing Management, 33*(17–18), 1522–1558.

Glossary

Affordability: allocating a budget based upon what the organisation can afford

Arbitrary allocation: allocating a budget without carefully considering how much is appropriate

Audience(s): the target(s) of marketing communications, comprising potential customers

Category need: the customer realisation that they need a particular category of product or service

Communication: the act of sending or receiving information to another person or people

Competitive parity: allocating a budget based on how much competitors allocate

Decoding: deciphering and interpretating the meaning from a message received

Differentiate: to explain why your brand, organisation, product, or service is different to those of your competitors

Earned media: communication channels which must be achieved through the marketer's efforts

Encoding: placing meaning into a message before sending it

Functional specialisation: when different departments or agencies specialise in one communication type

Inertia: making no budgetary decision, instead simply repeating previously allocated amounts

Inform: to convey information to an audience

Marginal analysis: allocating a budget to achieve the organisation's desired product margin

Marketing communications mix: the collected instruments through which organisations communicate with customers and stakeholders

Mass communications: those communications targeted at large groups of unidentified individuals

Message: the information being conveyed through a marketing communication

Noise: the background effect of other communications, above which the marketer must make their communication heard by the target audience

Objective and task: allocating a budget by identifying targeted outcomes, then ascertaining the resourcing levels needed by processes to achieve those outcomes, and funding accordingly

Owned media: communication channels owned by the marketer's organisation

Paid media: communications channels which the marketer's organisation pays to use

Percentage of sales: allocating a budget which is a proportion of the previous year's sales revenue

Personal communications: those communications targeted at identified individuals

Persuade: to influence an audience member to think, feel, or act differently

Reinforce: to strengthen a previously communicated message

Integrated Marketing Communications Case Study:
The Town of Salla, Climate Change, and the 2032 Summer Games

Salla is a town of 3,500 people in Lapland, the northern half of Finland. Located a two-hour drive east of Rovaniemi, the regional capital, a little more than 20 minutes to the Russian border and nearly 50 miles to the nearest train station, its website describes it as being "in the middle of nowhere" (www.lapland.fi). However, it has a rich skiing heritage dating back 5,000 years, a skiing school catering to all abilities, 15 slopes, and 6 lifts, all situated in a sparsely populated wilderness which is snow covered for much of the year. Besides skiing, tourists can visit a reindeer farm, see the aurora borealis (northern lights), kayak, trek, snowshoe, cycle, ice-fish, snowboard and snowmobile, dog sled, ride sleighs, climb mountains, discover the local Second World War history, spot wolves, stay in wooden cabins, and sample the local Sami culture. In short, Salla is a beautiful, pristine environment associated with winter sports – an entirely unlikely venue for the Summer Olympic Games. But in February 2021, it launched its 'Salla 2032 Summer Games Candidate City' campaign – not a formal application to host an event, but a marketing communications campaign to raise awareness of climate change and global warming. It studiously avoids any mention of the 'O' word (which is legally protected) but alludes to that organisation throughout.

Salla's spoof campaign mascot is a cartoon reindeer named Kesa (Finnish for 'summer'), which is visibly sweating and wilting in the heat, and the campaign logo is a simple line drawing of a mountain melting into a puddle whilst what resemble some famous sporting rings are reimagined as an approaching, increasingly warm sun.

Another promotional photograph shows an ageing local couple wearing summer attire, sitting on picnic chairs on a ski run. The wife is casually fanning herself whilst her husband holds a reflective mat beneath his chin to get an even suntan. The slogan reads, 'Warm heart, we have it. Warm place, coming soon'. Adhering to all other protocol connected with making an official games bid, Salla also created uniforms, a bid book, a range of promotional activities, and a campaign film which depicts locals struggling to prepare for the 2032 Summer Games by adapting traditional winter pursuits for a snow-free environment. The town's mayor, Erkki Parkkinen, explains that as inhabitants of Lapland's coldest town, they experience the effects of global warming before almost everyone else globally, and therefore they feel responsible for transmitting environmental messages early and attempting to preserve their inherited environment. The municipality

continued

343

of Salla (www.savesalla.com) and the House of Lapland body for promoting the region (www.lapland.fi) worked with the Brazilian marketing agency Agencia Africa, which has formerly represented brands such as Budweiser and KraftHeinz, and with Fridays for Future (www.fridaysforfuture.org), the environmental campaign group started by young activists including Greta Thunberg.

Imagine you are a senior partner in a marketing communications agency which has been recruited by House of Lapland to build upon the work already done, creating additional campaign communications which are consistent and integrated, to increase the impact of the campaign globally. Using the following table as a guide, choose three media or channels which you would use from each media type (paid, owned, and earned media) and give the rationale for your choices (about 100 words in bullet points for each choice). Try to consider the strengths and weaknesses of any potential choice within the context of the campaign and its audiences.

Media Type	Choice of Media/Channel	Rationale
Paid media	1.	1.
	2.	2.
	3.	3.
Owned media	1.	1.
	2.	2.
	3.	3.
Earned media	1.	1.
	2.	2.
	3.	3.

Sources

Agencia Africa. Retrieved February 28, 2021, from www.africa.com.br

Fridays for Future. Retrieved February 28, 2021, from www.fridaysforfuture.org

House of Lapland. Retrieved February 28, 2021, from www.lapland.fi

Marcomm News article. #SaveSalla – Finnish Arctic town gains the world's attention with a bid for 2032 Summer Games. Retrieved February 28, 2021, from https://marcommnews.com/savesalla-finnish-arctic-town-gains-the-worlds-attention-with-a-bid-for-2032-summer-games/

Municipality of Salla. Retrieved February 28, 2021, from www.savesalla.com

13 | Advertising, Sales Promotion, Public Relations, and Sponsorship

LEARNING OBJECTIVES

▶ To compare the effectiveness of different advertising media for an advertising campaign

▶ To assess the suitability of different forms of sales promotion to stimulate sales volumes

▶ To critique the role of public relations in establishing and maintaining a healthy corporate reputation

▶ To analyse credible approaches to sponsorship

Introduction

In this chapter, we build upon the principles of integrated marketing communications explored in the previous chapter to analyse several of its instruments in more depth. These are advertising, sales promotion, public relations, and sponsorship. They are closely related to each other, as they all seek to influence a mass audience from a distance. Furthermore, they should operate in conjunction with each other rather than in isolation. To help our understanding of them, we will consider some of the psychological factors which dictate audience expectations and responses. These may be influenced by cultural considerations such as the recipient's nationality, social class, and membership of subcultures.

Advertising

Advertising is a paid form of marketing communication which uses media owned by a third party to reach its target audience remotely. For example, a consumer electronics manufacturer such as Samsung may pay billboard owners, television and radio

DOI: 10.4324/9781003170891-14

channels, and website owners to show adverts which will reach its desired audience segment. Whilst much advertising is concerned with reaching consumers and end users, B2B advertising is also important (Cortez et al., 2020), as is the effect of adverts being received by secondary or non-targeted audiences which may also play a significant role in the brand's success.

Setting Advertising Objectives

An organisation's advertising objectives are shaped by various important factors. Just a few of these would be the **strength of the organisation**, the **strength and aggression of its competitors**, the **desirability of its products or services**, the type of **information needed by its customers**, its **position within the marketplace**, the **loyalty of its customer base**, and the **aspirations of its leaders**. The advertising objectives for a product or service sit within the broader advertising objectives for the brand, which in turn sit within the broader marketing and commercial objectives of the brand. If we were to visualise the position of the product/service advertising objectives within the broader landscape of organisational objectives, it would look like Figure 13.1.

When defining a marketing communications objective, marketers must make five decisions:

1. What they wish to improve or increase

2. By how much

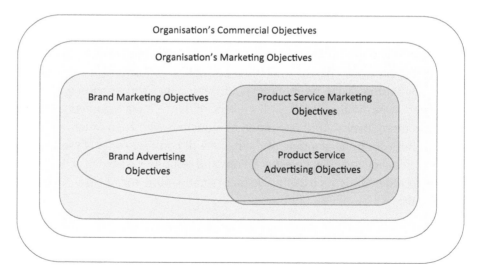

FIGURE 13.1
Advertising objectives within a broader landscape of organisational objectives.

3. For which product, service, or brand

4. In which market or segment

5. Within what timescale

For example, when launching a new version of its iPhone, Apple might set the following objective (with numbers added to demonstrate its constituent parts):

We aim (1) to increase our share of the smartphone market (2) by 15% (3) through sales of our new iPhone (4) to 18–30-year-old inhabitants of Cuba (5) between March 2025 and September 2026.
In another example, Harley-Davidson might set the following objective:

We intend (1) to reduce the average customer age (2) by five years (3) of our entire range of motorcycles (4) in the US and Japan (5) by the end of the 2020s.

ETHICS QUESTION

A betting firm, or bookmaker, would like to attract new customers during a FIFA World Cup football tournament. It would also like to encourage lapsed customers to return and for current customers to bet on a wider range of outcomes, such as the time of the first goal or the number of free kicks. In small groups, discuss what ethical issues these aspirations might raise, the potentially damaging effects which some stakeholders might experience, and the ways in which the firm might mitigate these negative outcomes.

Building a Customer Profile

To be successful, the marketer must segment the market using one or more criteria. The only possible exception would be if they sold a very undifferentiated product of near-universal appeal, such as salt. As we have seen previously, marketers can use profile, behavioural, or psychographic segmentation.

Profile segmentation splits the market based upon the audience members' easily identifiable characteristics, such as age, location, gender, nationality, income level, occupation, and educational attainment level. Some marketers and theorists treat sociographic and demographic (or socio-demographic) considerations separately and others within profile segmentation.

Behavioural segmentation focuses on what audience members do, such as where they shop, how often, what they buy, how much they spend, and who else they include in the purchase decision.

Psychographic segmentation groups audience members by their common beliefs, perspectives, aspirations, identities, and other psychological factors.

By using these three types of segmentation, marketers can then choose media and messages which are most likely to impact their target market. However, it is useful to ask these additional questions:

▶ How, and for what purpose, will the prospect use the product? (e.g. if they are buying a dress, will they wear it for dinner parties, holidays, clubbing, or work?)

▶ What benefit does the prospect wish to derive from the product? (e.g. if buying a table from IKEA, are they motivated by saving money, saving space, easy assembly, modern styling, breadth of choice, ease of transaction, copying their friends and neighbours, or enjoyment of the IKEA brand and customer experience?)

▶ How will the prospect pass through the adoption process of awareness, interest, evaluation, trial, and adoption? (e.g. are they likely to be impulsive, spending little time and effort evaluating the product's suitability and the available alternatives, or will they instead be very cautious and deliberate at length?)

▶ How ready is the customer to buy? (e.g. do they need more information or to arrange finance?)

▶ How loyal is the customer? (e.g. monogamously loyal to one brand, polygamously loyal to several brands, or willing to switch brands repeatedly?)

STAKEHOLDER QUESTION

We normally think about advertising in terms of its relevance to, and impact on, the people who might buy the organisation's products or services: customers and consumers. However, as 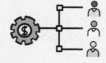 with any form of marketing communication, the messages and content do not simply transmit to the target audience without any leakage. Instead, stakeholders who are outside that target audience also receive these communications. This may be because they watch a television programme or read a magazine which is not typical of people in their age group or location, or because they may be considered non-normative in some other way. Likewise, people who have a relationship with the firm which is not primarily as a customer – perhaps as part of

continued

their jobs – will also receive certain advertising content and messages which may not have been intended for them. Examples are employees of the firm, employees of the firm's business partners, financiers, government officers, and members of the local community around the firm's premises. Choose any three stakeholders of a frozen food manufacturer, make bullet points to say what different meanings they might derive from its television adverts, and suggest the commercial or relational implications for each point.

Involvement, Attitude, and Values

To design a successful advertising campaign, marketers must consider their audience members' likely levels of involvement, the attitudes which they hold towards the brand and its products, and the values which guide them in their decision-making.

Involvement

Involvement is the level of time, effort, and thought invested by a customer on a purchase decision. Involvement is usually very low for inexpensive and frequent purchases, where the repercussions of making a poor decision are not serious (e.g. washing powder or kitchen cleaner). Involvement is usually much higher if the purchase is high value, infrequent, highly differentiated from the competition, a complicated item, and carries high repercussions for a poor decision (e.g. a house, car, or university degree programme).

When buying **high-involvement products**, customers usually consider several alternatives in a lengthy decision-making process, rank them (at least informally), and buy the top-ranking product. If they are satisfied with the product, they are likely to be loyal to that brand in the future. When buying **low-involvement products**, customers usually purchase their favourite product which they usually buy and, unless they feel particularly dissatisfied during its consumption, they will default to that choice next time within a very short decision-making process, but through inertia rather than brand loyalty.

Attitude

Attitude is an audience member's stance towards a product or brand. It heavily influences their behaviour, engagement, and purchased intention, and is split into three components:

Affective attitude is emotional and concerns gut feelings, prejudices, and deep-seated beliefs.

Cognitive attitude is rational and encapsulates knowledge, understanding, and interpretation of information appertaining to a thing or person.

Conative attitude is concerned with translating these thoughts and feelings into actions, behaviours, and intentions.

These customer attitudes can be influenced by marketing communications and may occur in different sequences. For example, when choosing a crib for their baby, a parent may begin with an affective attitude influenced by parental love and ingrained cultural representations of cribs, such as in the Nativity. They may then progress to a period of cognitive attitude, in which they seek and process technical information on the safety and stability of competing products. Finally, they may pass into a conative attitude stage, when they decide what to buy, when to buy it, and where they will place it within their newly decorated nursery. Some products or services (e.g. car insurance policies) may begin with cognitive rather than affective attitude. Others will begin with conative attitude. Marketers must understand which attitudes will prevail at which junctures in the customers' journey towards purchase.

Values

Values are intrinsic, deeply ingrained beliefs which individuals derive from membership of cultural groups. Our values may be influenced by our parents and upbringing, our teachers and education, the country where we were raised, the media to which we have been exposed, the friendships we have made, the music we listen to, the books we read, and many more factors which make us who we are. These values frame our attitudes and guide our personal actions. For example, someone whose parents encouraged the values of self-sufficiency and a spirit of adventure is likely to harbour strong attitudes relating to freedom, fearing unnecessary commitments or becoming trapped, whilst seeking products which enable sustainability, exploration, and independence. They are more likely to respond favourably to adverts which convey freedom and exploration and less well to ones which convey routine or obligation. This means that advertisers need to transmit appropriate messages through suitable media or risk alienating their target audience.

Persuasion in Advertising

Advertising must inform its audience members, but this alone may not change their behaviour. To do this, it must persuade them to buy or use something, or at least to respond favourably to a new stimulus. Usually this can be achieved only if the following three conditions are in place:

1. The sender of the message is trusted, trustworthy, skilled, empathetic, and benevolent

2. The message evokes in audience members an appropriate range of emotions

3. It supports its call to action (CTA) with reasonable, logical facts and information

The Persuasion Process

There are six sequential stages in the persuasion process which audience members must pass through for the advert to be a success. To achieve these stages, marketers need to be skilled and careful:

▶ To ensure the advert comes into contact with the intended audience member, they must select the right medium and use it in an appropriate place at a suitable time. For example, to advertise business attire to office workers, a poster on a train station platform might reach plenty of office-bound passengers, but only during commuting hours.

▶ To attract people's attention, adverts must carry a relevant message presented accessibly and attractively.

▶ To ensure comprehension, adverts should be uncluttered, written in simple language, and convey meaning visually.

▶ To instil belief and trust, the medium and message should both be perceived as credible.

▶ To remain memorable, an advert should be simple, infectious, and employ a 'hook' which comes readily to audience members' minds – perhaps a catchphrase, jingle, or character.

▶ To inspire an outcome, the CTA must be clear, simple, and explicit.

NEW MEDIA QUESTION

A university wishes to increase applications for undergraduate study from 17- and 18-year-olds and aims to do so by taking them through the six sequential stages of the persuasion process identified above. It realises that to engage with a young audience and to maximise its impact within a reasonable budget, it must use a blend of online and offline approaches. For each of the six stages, make bullet point notes of two or three actions which the university could take to attract new applicants, being careful to maintain a blend of online and offline actions.

FIGURE 13.2
The sequential stages of the persuasion process in advertising.

Using Rationality and Emotion

Consumers are driven by a mixture of rationality and emotion. If they see a television advert in which a car sweeps gracefully through an exotic mountain pass, they may unconsciously imagine themselves in that situation and indulge in the fantasy presented to them. This may well raise their awareness of the car brand and the product shown, enhance their perceptions of both, and instil feelings of aspiration. This is particularly the case during the early stages of the decision-making process, when the consumer has recognised a need for a new car or is trying to reduce the large number of choices down to an evoked set (i.e. a shortlist of manufacturers and models from which they will choose). However, as they near their decision, they are more likely to drill down into the technical specifications and detail of the products – the fuel efficiency, tax efficiency, luggage capacity, and service intervals – as these less 'sexy' considerations impact the viability of the purchase choice.

To reflect this phenomenon, firms often use production-heavy adverts containing impactful elements, such as lively music when trying to build brand awareness, but more staid communications as the final purchase decision is approached. However, not all purchases require the same amount of deliberation as a car. For instance, choosing which confectionery or chocolates to buy does not pose a financial risk to the consumer, as it is a low-cost, routine, often impulsive purchase. Therefore, a brand such as Hershey's, the American chocolate manufacturer, or Chupa Chups, the Spanish confectioner, would not need a stepped approach to build upon its hedonic (i.e. focused on fun) advertising content.

Selecting Advertising Media

As we saw in the previous chapter, media are the means by which marketing messages are communicated from the sender to the receiver. The sender is almost always an organisation. The intended receivers in B2C markets are usually consumers, but as almost all products pass through intermediaries, organisations will also have to communicate with their business partners (e.g. manufacturers communicating with retailers and wholesalers). In B2B markets, the sender may wish to communicate with different members of decision-making units (DMUs), such as directors, purchasers, accountants, and users. Marketers must select media which are appropriate for the message, will help the organisation to fulfil its communications objectives, and are suitable for the target audience.

Advertising media fall into the following main categories, with some examples provided:

Print: newspapers, magazines, brochures
Broadcast: television, radio

Outdoor: billboards, vehicles, transport hubs

Digital: own website, third-party websites, apps, SMS, social media, blogs/vlogs, user-generated content (UGC), electronic word of mouth (EWOM)

Social: word of mouth (WOM)

When selecting advertising media, practitioners consider the following criteria:

Organisational and marketing objectives: what the organisation needs to be delivered by the advert, and by the marketing campaign more broadly. It is influenced by the organisation's situation. For example, if it has a strong new product, it may require its advertising to leverage the product to gain market share or to justify the relatively high purchase price which will recoup R&D costs and boost short-term profit margins.

Audience characteristics and needs: what potential customers, both individually and collectively, require from the adverts. For instance, if confronted by a complicated technological innovation, they may need to see product demonstrations or receive guidance.

Product/service characteristics: the specifics of the product or service which must be considered when deciding how to communicate to audiences. For example, a product such as a sports car may benefit from an advert expressing concepts like freedom, power, or control, whereas a home computer may need more data-focused communication.

Reach: the number of people who may be reached through a specific type of advert or media.

Targetability: the extent to which specific market segments may be targeted by the advert type.

Total cost: how much the advert will cost when all resources are accounted for (e.g. production costs, media space, and agency fees).

Cost per contact: the total cost divided by the number of potential customers reached.

Credibility: the extent to which audiences find the advert believable and trustworthy.

Brand fit: the closeness of the advert to the brand's image.

Media control and availability: how quickly the organisation can make their advert public, and the level of control which they can exert over the message and its presentation.

Audience interaction: the extent to which audience members can respond to the advert and interact with the organisation and/or each other.

MARKETING ASSISTANT TASK

Zomotor Mexico is launching a new small car, which it will also sell in the other countries of Central America. Tannya, the marketing assistant, has been asked to undertake some preparatory work, analysing the suitability of different media for Zomotor's pre-launch product advertising. Using the table below, help Tannya by allocating each media type a score of 1 (poor) to 10 (excellent) for their performance against the given criteria.

	Org objectives	Audience needs	Product characteristics	Reach	Targetability	Total cost	Cost/contact	Credibility	Brand fit	Media control	Interaction
Newspapers											
Magazines											
Brochures											
Television											
Radio											
Billboards											
Vehicles											
Transport hubs											
Own website											
Third party website											
Apps											
SMS											
Social media											
UGC											
EWOM											
WOM											

It is tempting to see digital advertising as wholly efficient and the perfect way to reduce wastage of marketing spend. However, for the vast majority of firms, it must work in tandem with other media, such as print, outdoor, and broadcast. Furthermore, the effectiveness of digital advertising is hindered by four market inefficiencies:

1. Difficulties in measuring the effectiveness of adverts

2. Frictions between advertising channel members (e.g. between the needs of creative agencies and media booking agencies)

3. Ad blocking (e.g. the ability of website users to pay a premium to block adverts, such as on the language tuition site, Duolingo)

4. Ad fraud (e.g. when the firm's efforts are undermined by spurious online copycat brands; Gordon et al., 2021)

Sales Promotion

Sales promotion is another element in the marketing communications mix which uses both media and non-media marketing. If you have seen a television advert offering attractive deals for a limited period on cars, sofas, or kitchens, you have witnessed a sales promotion which uses media marketing. If you have been lured into a coffee shop by a poster in the window promising half-price drinks for students during university freshers' week, then you have been influenced by a sales promotion which uses non-media marketing. Sales promotions may be consumer sales promotions, or trade promotions which aim to stimulate sales to business customers and channel intermediaries. For example, a timber producer may offer a sales promotion to construction companies or DIY stores.

A sales promotion is a temporary, time-bound offer made by a seller to its customers and prospects. It is intended to stimulate incremental sales to boost total profit, market share, sales volumes, or stock rotation times (i.e. the length of time needed to sell stock). Perhaps the organisation has too much stock, which it needs to turn into cash. Perhaps it feels as though it is losing its position in the marketplace due to its competitors' actions or dwindling brand awareness. Or maybe it simply wants to ensure that it attracts lots of customers during the most opportune season for selling – such as a travel agent needing to sell most of its package holidays during the winter. For such organisations, sales promotions are often the answer.

The main characteristics of sales promotions are as follows:

▶ They are **temporary and short term**, both in their communication and in their effect.

▶ They mainly seek to influence the **latter stages of customers' decision-making process**, helping to push a sale 'over the finish line'.

▶ They are **subservient to other elements** of the marketing communications mix (e.g. supporting the firm's advertising or PR).

▶ They encapsulate a **range of techniques**.

SUSTAINABILITY QUESTION

Sustainability is the extent to which a course of action is viable in the long term – environmentally, economically, and socially. Find an example of a sales promotion which is happening near you. It might

continued

be a special meal deal at your university's restaurant, a discounted weekend tuition offer from your driving instructor, or a summer clearance sale by a local car dealership or furniture retailer. Analyse the impact which the promotion might have on environmental, economic, and social sustainability – on the living world, on the finances of the firm and its stakeholders, and on social groups and society.

Business-to-Business and Business-to-Consumer Sales Promotions

When offering sales promotions to corporate customers or channel intermediaries such as dealers, wholesalers, or retailers, firms usually offer one of, or a combination of, the following B2B incentives (Table 13.1).

Naturally, these are designed to focus both the downstream intermediary firms and their staff to sell the manufacturer's products keenly, rather than being passive or favouring competitor products. However, firms have a much wider and more sophisticated choice of sales promotion types when approaching consumers (Table 13.2).

TABLE 13.1

B2B sales incentives.

Promotion	Description
Training	Training of intermediaries employees to help them sell on products, pushing them down the supply chain to consumers
Contests	Competitions to reward top-selling salespeople and channel partners
Point-of-purchase support	Help and financial support to provide point-of-purchase materials (e.g. flags, signage, or display cabinets) to reinforce the brand and stimulate impulse purchases
Trade allowances	Time-bound discounts encouraging a dealer, wholesaler, or retailer to increase stock levels of a product
Dealer loaders	Financial rewards to dealers for displaying and pushing a product to customers
Push money	Commission paid to dealer or retailer employees to push certain products

TABLE 13.2

Types of sales promotion.

Promotion	Description
Money off/price deal	A price reduction (e.g. '50% off' or 'half price')
Free extra	More product for the usual price (e.g. '25% extra', '2 for the price of 1', 'free kid's meal with every adult meal', or 'free gift with purchase')

continued

TABLE 13.2 (CONTINUED)

Promotion	Description
Loss leader	Luring customers into a store by promoting one heavily discounted product, then benefitting from the additional footfall by selling other, more profitable items
Loyalty rewards	Issuing customers with points which can be redeemed against the cost of future purchases
Coupons (printed or mobile)	Giving away coupons which customers can redeem to claim a discount
Contests	Entering purchasers of a specific product into a competition (e.g. a prize draw to win a holiday in the Caribbean)
Rebates	Refunds given to customers if they commit to the sale quickly (e.g. construction companies offering '5% rebate when you move in' to prospects who pay their deposit before month-end)
Point-of-sale displays	Offers of discounted fast-moving consumer goods (FMCG) or similar low-price items, often in supermarkets, which are promoted by in-store products displays and branded signage. Often used to encourage consumers to trial a newly launched product, such as a new flavour of nachos.
Samples	Free trial samples to encourage consumers to purchase something for the first time

METRICS QUESTION

If Coca-Cola decided to launch Coca-Cola chewing gum by promoting it initially through supermarkets, which promotional methods would you use, and how might you measure their success? Choose three alternatives, list your rationale for each choice, discuss the limitations of each, and explain what sort of measure or target you would use to establish if the promotion technique had been successful.

From the customer's perspective, a sales promotion may enable them to buy something which they could not previously afford or to buy it sooner than they could ordinarily afford it. It may enable them to buy a better version of their planned purchase – perhaps a larger television or faster laptop. It may even encourage them to buy in greater quantity than they anticipated; for example, if a supermarket sells a case of 32 premium beers for only slightly more money than 24 premium beers during a FIFA Football World Cup competition. Customers may be incentivised to purchase by discounts, free upgrades or increased product size, coupons or vouchers, free samples, and competitions (Ofo-su-Boateng, 2020). 'Buy-one-get-one-free' (BOGOF) is a particularly simple and effective message often used as an incentive (Ben Said et al., 2019).

The Need for Caution in Sales Promotions

Sales promotions can damage companies if used carelessly. If a furniture store, for instance, runs countless promotions in which sofas and tables are heavily discounted, consumers eventually refuse to shop at the store when it is not running a promotion, as they believe that they will get a better deal by waiting for another promotion to come along. This means that the store can only sell at a discount, slicing into its profit margins and undermining the prestige and aspirational nature of its brand. In effect, it cannibalises its own sales and undercuts its own pricing structure (McColl et al., 2020). Naturally, this effect can also occur in the B2B arena and between manufacturers and retailers, as we explore in the next exercise.

MARKETING MANAGER TASK

Zomotor China's Marketing Manager, Dylan, has been seconded to Zomotor UK for six months as part of his professional development. In the UK, around 22% of annual new car sales take place in each of March and September, making it crucial for motor manufacturers to hit their sales volume targets in those months. It is nearing the end of March, and Zomotor UK risks missing its monthly sales target by around 5%. Dylan would like to offer a special deal to some of Zomotor UK's largest dealers to buy and register additional cars before the month-end, but is worried that (i) those dealers will then expect a special deal every month; (ii) the dealers will be too busy selling the March-registered cars in April to do their April targets; and (iii) that they might pass on any discounts to customers, which would distress the market by producing localised price fluctuations. Help Dylan by suggesting three possible approaches which he might consider adopting, and stating the advantages and disadvantages of each approach to Zomotor and its dealer network.

Public Relations

The Chartered Institute of Public Relations (2019) defines PR as "the discipline which looks after reputation, with the aim of earning understanding and support and influencing opinion and behaviour. It is the planned and sustained effort to establish and maintain good will and mutual understanding between an organisation and its publics". A communication tool, it is used by organisations to generate goodwill from their publics – their customers and prospects, employees, investors, governments, channel intermediaries, and anyone else with an interest in the organisation (Johnston & Sheehan, 2020).

PR helps to project the 'personality' of the organisation. It is not simply there to resurrect public goodwill when things have gone wrong, like Volkswagen's emissions scandal or BP's oil spillage. Instead, organisations should be undertaking PR constantly, feeding positive stories about themselves to media partners (e.g. newspaper journalists, bloggers and vloggers, or television programme editors). This helps to reduce the gap between how the organisation sees itself (or wishes others to see it) and how others actually perceive it.

PR must be integrated with the other elements of the marketing communications mix to convey the brand and its values, the corporate identity, and its connection to communities. For example, a sportswear manufacturer might make press releases about its charitable work with a disabled sports foundation, the success of an elite athlete who wears the company's products, or the results of a 'customise a sneaker/trainer' competition for its social media followers. Figure 13.3 shows the different audiences targeted by PR.

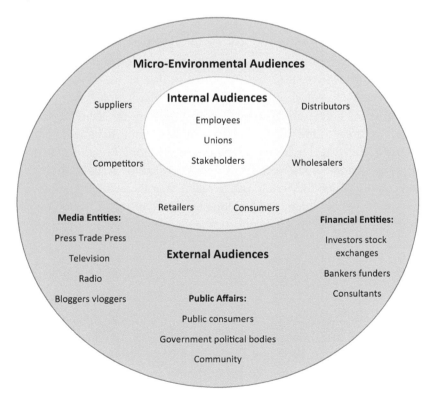

FIGURE 13.3
Audiences targeted by public relations.

Characteristics of Effective Public Relations

To achieve its corporate objectives, PR must be sufficiently attractive to be transmitted by the firm's media partners and to be received favourably by the targeted audiences. The major criteria which PR must fulfil are as follows:

1. Buzz: PR must be current, relevant, and newsworthy if it is to be adopted by media partners and capture the attention of audiences.

2. Accuracy: It must be accurate, honest and transparent.

3. Authority: It should generate respect and credibility by adopting a trustworthy tone of approachable authority – usually assisted by provision of an expert opinion.

4. Interest: There should be an element of human interest.

5. Contact: It should include contact details, usually of the press department or PR director.

MARKETING DIRECTOR TASK

Zomotor's marketing director, Lee, wishes to address the brand's underperformance in Hong Kong, where it has a much lower market share than elsewhere in China. They realise that Hong Kong is culturally distinctive from other provinces and that its inhabitants perhaps derive different messages and values from the Zomotor brand. They wish to demonstrate to the local population that Zomotor recognises Hong Kong's uniqueness and that it is a 'friend' to the people of Hong Kong, but they must be careful not to alienate audiences elsewhere. Help Lee by suggesting three stories and three media which they could use to reach their target audiences, giving your rationale. Think about which specific Hong Kong audiences they should target and how they can adhere to the characteristics of effective PR.

Sponsorship

Sponsorship is a form of marketing communication in which an organisation supports a person, event, or another organisation. A person could be, for example, a sportsperson or someone undertaking a challenge. An event might be a sporting event, or perhaps a cultural gathering such as a music concert. Another organisation may be a governing body such as FIFA (which manages global football) or the owner of a venue. But **sponsorees** (the people or entities being sponsored) are not limited to these examples. The **sponsor** (the supporting organisation) could be any business entity which intends to gain brand equity from being associated with its sponsoree. For example, a smartphone or a nutrition or automotive brand may feel that, through sponsorship of the Olympic Games or FIFA World Cup, it can reach a new audience or enhance its existing relationships for commercial purposes. **Sponsorship** constitutes some form of payment in return for these commercial benefits.

Sponsorship, unlike most other elements of the marketing communications mix, cannot convey the features and benefits of individual products or service, and it is unable to be used without the support of other elements. However, it is strong in these aspects:

▶ Increasing consumer/customer awareness of the brand and products

▶ Building the prestige and acceptability of the brand

▶ Increasing the likelihood that audience members will purchase from the brand

Whilst sponsorship tends to be most effective when there is a close match between the sponsor organisation and the entity being sponsored (e.g. a pizza brand or wine company sponsoring a food and drink festival), this is not necessary for the partnership

PHOTO 13.1
If a firm sponsors a shopping mall, all the stores within the mall can benefit from the association.

PHOTO 13.2
Sponsorship is so prevalent that we tend to notice it more by its absence than its presence, such as when we see a football top without an advert across it.

PHOTO 13.3
Many Newcastle United Football Club fans disliked the Sports Direct-sponsored signage which used to adorn their stadium, St James Park.

to be a success. For example, football leagues and football clubs have often received high-worth sponsorships from airlines, insurance companies, banks, telecommunications providers, consumer electronics manufacturers, betting firms, and brewers.

Habitzreuter and Koenigstorfer (2021) noted that sports sponsorship linked to corporate social responsibility (CSR, or policies adopted by organisations to ensure they act ethically) manipulates consumers' perceptions of the sponsor brand. However, sponsors should consider the context in which their brand is linked to that of their sporting partner, as this too will affect audience perceptions. Likewise, if entering a partnership is beneficial to a sponsor, it must also consider what effect relationship dissolution will have on its brand. A small minority of sponsorships end due to a sponsored sportsperson or public figure becoming the focus of negative news – as we have seen with Lance Armstrong, Tiger Woods, and Oscar Pistorius. However, most sponsorship deals end for commercial reasons, such as a need for the sponsor to target a new audience or to capitalise on a new event or emerging public figure. The likelihood of a sponsorship being dissolved is also influenced by factors internal to the brand. For example, if the sponsor has a primarily B2B focus, the likelihood is reduced, but if sophisticated technology is central to the relationship or brand, the likelihood is increased (Jensen & Cornwell, 2021).

GLOBAL MARKETING QUESTION

An airline has decided to be the official sponsor of a highly successful English Premier League football club. Many of its matches will be broadcast around the world. Not only will it play league and cup games, but during the summer break, it will also play in a friendly tournament in the airline's home country as part of the deal. The airline's name will be displayed across the players' shirts during home games, their adverts will be displayed on digital hoardings by the pitch, and for five years the stadium will officially adopt the airline's name. As the audience will be global, the airline's brand will be beamed to viewers in Europe, Africa, the Americas, Asia, and Australasia – from luxury penthouse to shanty town, from bustling metropolis to remote farmstead. Considering the cultural differences between viewers across the world and the volatile nature of competitive elite sport, what are the major threats or challenges which the airline could face over the course of its sponsorship deal, and how should it deal with them?

Chapter Summary

Advertising, sales promotion, public relations, and sponsorship are elements of the marketing communications mix which help to convey meanings about the brand and its products and services to its customers and prospects. They must work in conjunction with all other elements of the marketing communications mix to deliver consistent messages and ensure consistency. Whilst PR should be ever-present, as the organisation strives to generate and spread positive stories about itself through third-party media, the other elements may be used intermittently whenever they are most needed. For example, a major advertising campaign may be used if the firm is due to launch a new product – the initial adverts on television, billboards, and online may be intended to build customer awareness of the product, then later adverts on radio and in newspapers and magazines may provide those prospects with more detailed information to assist their decision-making. The use of these communications elements is influenced simply by customer needs, competitor actions, and the organisation's commercial and marketing objectives.

Key Learning Outcomes

A range of advertising media are available to marketers, with each media representing a different balance of strengths and limitations which demand careful scheduling and blending together within a marketing communications strategy.

Sales volumes may be stimulated by the use of sales promotions, in which customers and prospects are incentivised to purchase something which they may otherwise not, to purchase in greater quantity, or to bring forward a purchase in time.

Public relations helps to establish and maintain a healthy corporate reputation when an organisation channels positive messages to audiences through a range of unpaid media. PR constitutes far more than simply restoring public goodwill after a crisis.

Sponsorship approaches should be credible to target audiences and encourage them to perceive the brand more positively due to the association with a respected person or entity.

Recommended Further Reading

Cortez, R. M., Gilliland, D. I., & Johnston, W. J. (2020). Revisiting the theory of business-to-business advertising. *Industrial Marketing Management, 89,* 642–656.

Gordon, B. R., Jerath, K., Katona, Z., Narayanan, S., Shin, J., & Wilbur, K. C. (2021). Inefficiencies in digital advertising markets. *Journal of Marketing, 85*(1), 7–25.

Habitzreuter, A. M., & Koenigstorfer, J. (2021). The impact of environmental CSR-linked sport sponsorship on attitude toward the sponsor depending on regulatory fit. *Journal of Business Research, 124,* 720–730.

Jensen, J. A., & Cornwell, T. B. (2021). Assessing the dissolution of horizontal marketing relationships: The case of corporate sponsorship of sport. *Journal of Business Research, 124,* 790–799.

Johnston, J., & Sheehan, M. (Eds.). (2020). *Public relations: Theory and practice.* Routledge.

McColl, R., Macgilchrist, R., & Rafiq, S. (2020). Estimating cannibalizing effects of sales promotions: The impact of price cuts and store type. *Journal of Retailing and Consumer Services, 53,* 101982.

References

Ben Said, Y., Bragazzi, N. L., & Pyatigorskaya, N. V. (2019). Influence of sales promotion techniques on consumers' purchasing decisions at community pharmacies. *Pharmacy*, *7*(4), 150.

Chartered Institute of Public Relations. (2019). Website content. Retrieved May 18, 2022, from https://www.cipr.co.uk/CIPR/About_Us/About_PR.aspx

Ofosu-Boateng, I. (2020). Influence of consumer sales promotion on consumers' purchasing behaviour of the retailing of consumer goods in Tema, Ghana. *Journal of Marketing Management*, *8*(1), 24–36.

Glossary

Advertising: a paid form of promoting a brand, product or service through a third party's media

Affective attitude: an audience member's stance towards a brand, product, or service based upon their gut feelings, prejudices, and deep-seated beliefs

Attitude: an audience member's stance towards a brand, product, or service

Audience: the people (targeted or otherwise) who receive a marketing communication

Behavioural segmentation: splitting a large population into smaller groups based upon the things they do

Broadcast media: television and radio – media which broadcast communications to receivers

Buzz: the 'interest factor' which encourages individuals to talk about a brand or its promotional activities

Cognitive attitude: an audience member's stance towards a brand, product, or service based upon their knowledge, understanding, and interpretation of information

Conative attitude: an audience member's stance towards a brand, product, or service based upon how their thoughts and beliefs shape their actions (the behavioural response)

Dealer loaders: financial rewards to dealers for displaying and 'pushing' a product to customers

Digital media: media owned by the promoting organisation or a third party which use digital technology to reach an audience. The main forms are websites, apps, SMS, social media, blogs/vlogs, user-generated content (UGC), WOM, and EWOM

Involvement: the level of time, effort, and thought invested by a customer on a purchase decision

Loss leader: an offer which drives footfall by promoting one heavily discounted product, increasing the number of potential purchasers of other, more profitable items

Outdoor media: promotional media which are located outdoors (e.g. billboards, vehicles, transport hubs)

Point of purchase/point of sale: the location where customers purchase a product, such as a checkout desk

Print media: places where printed marketing communication may be found (e.g. newspapers, magazines, brochures)

Profile segmentation: splitting a large population into smaller ones based upon their identifiable characteristics, such as age, gender, or location

Psychographic segmentation: splitting a large population into smaller ones based upon what people think and believe, their values and mindsets (e.g. 'environmentally conscious', 'anti-authority')

Public relations (PR): the element of the marketing communication mix tasked with managing reputation, understanding, and support of the organisation

Push money: offered to retailers and dealers and/or their staff to incentivise them to focus on selling a particular product or a particular manufacturer's products

Reach: the breadth of audience or number of prospects which a marking communication will enjoy

Rebates: refunding a percentage of the transaction price to the customer to encourage purchase

Sales promotion: a temporary, time-bound offer made by a seller to its customers and prospects which is intended to stimulate incremental sales

Samples: small amounts of a promoted product (typically food and drink) which allow customer trial behaviour and the adoption of a product by first-time buyers

Sponsorship: a form of marketing communication in which an organisation supports a person, event, or another organisation for commercial gain

Targetability: the extent to which a marketing communication can be aimed successfully at a particular market segment

Trade allowances: time-bound discounts encouraging a dealer, wholesaler, or retailer to increase stock levels of a product

Values: intrinsic, deeply ingrained beliefs which individuals derive from membership of cultural groups

Advertising Case Study: Walkers Crisps Dividing Opinions With Bread

In the UK, crisps are a ubiquitous snack food. Comprising a large handful of deep fried, flavoured, salted, and cooled potato slices, a bag of crisps is a favourite snack of workers, students, and people travelling on public transport. They are inexpensive, tasty, convenient, and sold at every corner shop, newsagent, and supermarket. Amongst people eating their lunch outside the home, crisps are second only to sandwiches in popularity. Crisps often accompany sandwiches too, served beside them on the plate or eaten

continued

immediately before or after them from the lunchbox. In fact, many stores offer shoppers a bundled lunchtime deal of sandwich, soft drink, fruit or vegetable slices, and packet of crisps. Over the years, many children, taking their first baby steps into cookery, have placed crisps between two slices of bread to make a 'crisp sandwich', often attracting criticism from their parents or teacher, who may tell them to eat properly and not to play with their food. However, it becomes apparent that this habit often sticks, with many adults surreptitiously still undertaking this unsophisticated culinary improvisation as a guilty pleasure. Around 30% of crisp sandwich-eaters only do so at home, and around 20% do so entirely in secret; it appears to be a slightly stigmatised practice. The UK's leading crisp brand, the PepsiCo-owned Walkers Crisps, seized upon the opportunity to generate buzz and consumer word of mouth from observational humour linked to this phenomenon in a 2021 television advertising campaign.

Many of Walkers' recent television adverts have used the phrase 'Too Good to Share' to express its crisps' role in constructing indulgent 'me time'. Many more adverts have used English football legend and popular television presenter, Gary Lineker, in the role of a 'nice guy' turned selfish through his determination not to share his crisps. In its '#CrispIN or #CrispOUT' advertising campaign, launched with 60-second television advertising spots, they leverage a trivial but polarising debate ('is it OK to put crisps in sandwiches?) by amusingly depicting the shocked, dismayed, and disgusted reactions displayed towards crisp sandwich–eating friends, spouses, and co-workers. As with dunking biscuits in tea or spreading Marmite on toast, people either love crisp sandwiches or find the idea abhorrent. However, even amongst the '#CrispOUTers', who would never use their crisps as filling, the concept is deeply nostalgic and British, evoking memories of schooldays which are comforting and grounding at a time when COVID-19 and political turbulence is placing British consumers in flux. This is at the heart of the advert's success. Let's check out the figures provided by Kantar, a market research company working with Walkers:

▶ it was in the top 3% of UK adverts for expressiveness (i.e. its propensity to provoke a facial expression from someone viewing it)

▶ it was in the top 2% for making viewers smile

▶ it was in the top 21% for stimulating enjoyment amongst viewers (presumably, some viewers were too repulsed by this carb-in-carb, hard-in-soft food portrayal to enjoy watching)

continued

367

- ► it was in the top 25% for creating 'brand love'
- ► it was in the top 6% for salience (i.e. its ability to grab attention and be memorable)
- ► despite being in the bottom 10% of ads for persuasiveness, it was in the top 10% for driving brand awareness – much more important for a low-cost, low-risk, routine, or impulse purchase

Imagine that you are Walkers Crisps' UK brand manager, in charge of developing the brand through its marketing communications. You have the opportunity to build upon the crisp sandwich theme in subsequent advertisements and within your public relations and sales promotions. First, list reasons why it is important or beneficial to Walkers for the audience to find the advertising campaign humorous, nostalgic, expressive, and salient. Then make bullet points on how you would try to replicate these results through your PR and sales promotions, engaging customers and refreshing their awareness of the brand through humour and nostalgia. Briefly say if any of the characteristics or outcomes of this advertising campaign give any cause for concern or pose any threats, and offer ways in which you might mitigate those threats.

Sources

Marketing Week article. *April's most effective ad revealed: Walkers 'CrispIn or CrispOUT'*. Retrieved June 17, 2021, from https://www.marketingweek.com/april-effective-walkers/

Walkers Crisps website. Retrieved June 17, 2021, from https://walkers.co.uk

YouTube video of Walkers Crisps' television advert. *#crispIN or #crispOUT*. Retrieved June 17, 2021, from https://www.youtube.com/watch?v=XLCEvDaNy7Y

14 | Personal Selling and Sales Management

Introduction

If you have bought a smartphone or perfume from a store, or a package holiday from a travel agent, you have probably experienced a salesperson at work. However, much sales activity is not consumer focused, but between businesses. For instance, smartphone manufacturers, perfumiers, and tour operators first sell products and services to retailers, negotiate pricing, and arrange promotional duties. Of the seven elements of the extended marketing mix, 'promotion' divides into the marketing communications mix, containing personal selling and sales management, although sales and marketing often feel like separate entities (Johnson & Matthes, 2018). Understanding how to design and manage the sales function is critical to commercial success.

Sales and the Organisation

Sales management is a strategic function. Organisations target prospects for their potential profitability and compatibility, nurturing mutually rewarding relationships and an exchange of value. Personal selling involves a representative presenting, negotiating, and persuading. It demands research, market awareness, and relationship management skills. To sell cars, a motor manufacturer will need dealership salespeople to sell to retail customers (B2C selling). The firm would also need to sell to dealerships, leasing companies, and fleet operators (B2B selling).

FIGURE 14.1
The relationship of personal selling and sales management to the marketing mix and the marketing communications mix.

B2B and B2C sales differ because, compared with individuals, businesses tend to

▶ Be fewer in number

▶ Be easier to identify and target

▶ Have formalised decision-making processes

▶ Buy less frequently

▶ Buy in greater quantity

▶ Have larger order values

▶ Be sold to on their own premises

Antczak and Sypniewska (2017) asserted that personal selling should help create a suitable customer base and underpin the firm's market stance by capitalising upon the firm's promotional strategy and marketing information to influence clients, consumers, and other audiences, then feeding intelligence back to the marketing strategists.

Categories of Sales

Sales types are often categorised as follows:

TRADE SALES

▶ To organisations in an industry in which the selling firm specialises (e.g. a wheelchair manufacturer to healthcare providers)

▶ Few buyers and sellers

▶ Selling new or existing products to new or existing customers

▶ Repeat customers, where nurturing relationships is crucial; this is achieved through information, expertise, logistical solutions, good service, and trust

MISSIONARY SELLING

▶ Raises awareness of the brand amongst non-customers

▶ Focuses on influencers and key prospects

▶ Tries to place the brand within the prospect's evoked set (the mental shortlist from which they choose suppliers)

▶ Puts in place the conditions for future, rather than immediate, sales

TECHNICAL SELLING

▶ Used where purchase decisions require high levels of expertise and where bad purchases have serious consequences

▶ Less reliant on persuasion than other sales

▶ Salespeople usually have engineering or technological backgrounds

▶ They are well remunerated through a higher basic wage

NEW BUSINESS SALES

▶ Selling to prospects rather than existing customers

▶ Common amongst new organisations and those entering new markets or segments

▶ Reliant on persuasion

▶ Salespeople usually have lower basic salaries and higher commissions

KEY ACCOUNT MANAGEMENT

▶ Selling to major clients

▶ Retention and development of profitable client relationships rather than winning new customers

▶ Dedicated salespeople

▶ Close cooperation between supplier and buyer organisations

PHOTO 14.1
When consumers are persuaded to buy products which they cannot afford, especially on credit, the effects can be very negative.

Categories of Salespeople

Roles within sales vary widely depending on the product or service sold and the customer relationship (Table 14.1).

Managing Salespeople

Good salespeople do not necessarily make good sales managers, as the skills in each role differ. Salespeople usually influence sales individually below management level by developing customer accounts, but sales managers influence sales by planning strategically and directing junior colleagues.

The sales manager's seven key roles are as follows:

Recruitment: finding staff with the required skills, attributes, and experience, liaising with recruitment agencies, shortlisting candidates and interviewing them.

Training: ensuring team members develop relevant skills, such as negotiating skills, prospecting techniques, and product knowledge.

TABLE 14.1

Types of sales roles.

Role	Duties	Example Products
Inside order-takers	Process orders from customers who are already committed to buy	Wholesaler stock for supply to retailers
Outside order-takers	Order replacement stock for retailers	Chocolate bars
Delivery salespeople	Replenish customers' inventories from a van	Automotive spares
Political or indirect salespeople	Win significant contracts to supply major clients such as governments	Submarines
Creative salespeople	Aggressively seek clients using problem-solving pitches	Printer/photocopiers

Motivation: maximising salespeople's potential, partially through commission, competitions, and other incentives, and partially through team spirit and professional pride.

Planning: suggesting sales force tactics and setting collective and individual targets (for sales volumes, model mixes, market penetration, profitability, and order size) to meet the firm's commercial objectives.

Organisation: resourcing individuals to perform their duties, implementing procedures and practices which streamline activities.

Monitoring: checking salespeople's progress against agreed targets.

Controlling: taking early, corrective actions if salespeople are not on course to fulfil these objectives.

Sales and the Consumer Decision-Making Process

The salesperson's tasks are partially dictated by consumer psychology and the steps which customers take when buying. Consumers and business purchasers follow slightly different decision-making processes.

Consumers usually spend their own money on things they will use themselves, and follow the logical progression as shown in Figure 14.2.

| Need recognition | Information seeking | Evaluation of alternatives | Purchase decision | Post-purchase evaluation |

FIGURE 14.2
The consumer decision-making process.

PHOTO 14.2
Clarks shoe shops rely on good service and gentle sales skills to match customers to appropriate products. Their ticketed service ensures that all customers benefit from this.

Need recognition: identifying a problem or requirement. Two examples are *assortment depletion* (items have become worn out or used up and need replenishing) and *assortment extension* (when they wish to add additional items to their existing stock). Their perceived needs may be **utilitarian** (e.g. necessities like soap or train tickets) or **hedonic** (e.g. 'feel-good' items like bracelets or paintings).

Information seeking: finding out possible ways to fulfil their need.

Evaluation of alternatives: comparing relevant products, services, and suppliers against purchasing criteria.

Purchase decision: choosing one specific product, service, or supplier, and buying.

Post-purchase evaluation: after buying, judging if the purchase fulfilled their needs successfully.

The decision-making process lengthens if the purchase is made very infrequently, is of high value, or if a poor choice carries serious consequences (e.g. a house or car).

Sales and the Organisational Decision-Making Process

In organisations, where one or more people purchase on behalf of their employer, the process is more complex and formalised (Figure 14.3).

Need recognition: like consumers, organisational decision makers start by identifying a problem, lack, or requirement.

Development of product or service specifications: carefully drawing up criteria (often weighted) which must be fulfilled to address the need.

FIGURE 14.3
The organisational decision-making process.

PHOTO 14.3
During and since COVID-19–related lockdowns, more consumers order online and collect in store.

Search for alternative products and suppliers: where the order value is high, prospective suppliers need to tender by completing a comprehensive questionnaire about the proposed products, services, parts, support, deliveries, pricing, and other aspects of supply.

Product and service evaluation: judging the suitability of the product/service against the identified purchasing criteria.

Select and order: purchasing the most appropriate goods from the most suitable supplier.

Evaluate the supplier's services and goods: ensuring the order is fulfilled and organisational needs satisfied properly.

Factors Influencing the Decision-Making Process

Salespeople must ascertain customers' purchasing criteria and tailor their approach accordingly. For example, if a customer highly values ease of product usage, the salesperson may use a product demonstration to gain their confidence. However, the decision-making process may be complicated by **environmental stimuli** such as work distractions, the buyer's **affective state** (or emotions), introduction of **unexpected information** from rival suppliers or the buyer's colleagues, and **conflicts** (e.g. the need to conform to the finance directors' economic parameters whilst meeting the expectations of end users). These are compounded by personal factors like the customer's **demographic** (i.e. age, class, nationality), the **context or situation** surrounding their decision (e.g. hurriedly due to an emergency), and the **level of authority or involvement** which they enjoy. Salespeople must therefore gauge these factors as early as possible. Customers often buy if their **affiliation** or connection to the product or brand conveys success, if they enjoy perceived **power** within the buyer-seller relationship, and when they feel the negotiated deal represents an **achievement**. Salespeople can play to these factors.

Psychology in Personal Selling

The salesperson's task is further complicated by decision-making psychology in both B2B and B2C. Just as in pricing, the notion of 'economic man' (Albanese, 2015) or 'economic woman' is idealistic and overlooks customers' individual and often irrational idiosyncrasies.

▶ Customers' **perceptions** of goods and suppliers may be shaped by external influences such as their previous experiences of a product and word-of-mouth communications.

▶ People may draw upon **internal search** or **external search** – remembering internalised experiences and accounts or gathering of new knowledge.

▶ Preferences may be influenced by **personality traits** – analytical people may prefer detail and fresh information and avoid **heuristics** (decision-making shortcuts or rules of thumb).

▶ Customer **motives** for choices vary in type and strength, and their **knowledge and capabilities** (e.g. their experience) affect their decision.

▶ Their **attitudes** – and their affective (emotional), cognitive (reasoning) and conative (behavioural) differences – make the sales process highly individual.

ETHICS QUESTION

If you had the chance to sell an unsuitable photocopier to a prospect at month-end, and this would trigger a significant monthly commission, would you do it? What factors influence your decision?

Types of Demand

The decision-making process is influenced by the type of customer demand. Salespeople should identify these and modify their approach.

Derived demand: demand for products or services which service another demand (e.g. a T-shirt printer which enables the customer to sell more T-shirts).

Elastic demand: stimulated by favourable economic circumstances or price drops (e.g. cruises).

Inelastic demand: largely unaffected by economic circumstances or price fluctuations (e.g. essential commodities such as petrol).

Joint demand: when demand for one product is linked to demand for another (e.g. the demand for gin influencing the demand for tonic water).

Fluctuating demand: when factors like pricing, seasonality, taxation levels, and availability make goods significantly more desirable at certain times (e.g. bikinis, fireworks).

Types of Purchase

Different purchase characteristics also call for different sales approaches.

New-task buying: when customers purchase items or categories of product for the first time, so spend more time collecting information and researching alternative products and suppliers.

A straight rebuy:

PHOTO 14.4
Routine, low-cost purchases rely less on sales techniques and more on visibility to convert prospects into customers.

when they replace a used item or replenish diminishing stock of something, so seek less new information and make no supplier comparisons.

A modified rebuy:

a hybrid situation where customers know from experience the purchase parameters but seek a slightly different replacement product (e.g. a smartphone user wishing to upgrade).

Specific Requirements Within Business-to-Business Sales

B2B salespeople must consider the roles and methods within customers' decision-making units (DMUs), their supplier selection criteria, factors influencing their decision. The DMU typically constitutes a combination of the following people (Table 14.2).

TABLE 14.2

Members of the organisational decision making unit.

Member	Common roles
Initiators	Recognise initial business need, begin purchase process, invite salespeople
Gatekeepers	Present a barrier between the decision maker and salespeople (e.g. receptionists)
Users	Operate the product within an organisation (e.g. van drivers, hospital porters)
Influencers	Inhabit many levels of seniority, are often not readily identifiable. May even be external (e.g. Managing Director's golf partner), but have trusted opinion
Deciders	The most powerful decision-making unit members make the final decision; normally senior, supported by colleagues
Buyers	Procurement specialists, issue required specifications, handle quotations, negotiate deals, co-ordinate purchase administration

STAKEHOLDER QUESTION

If you were trying to sell office furniture to a firm, what approaches would you take to each of the DMU members described above? What specialist information might different stakeholders need?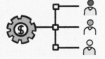

Supplier Selection Criteria

Salespeople try to ascertain the organisation's criteria for selecting a supplier. If it needs high **technical ability**, it may wish to inspect the supplier's factory or speak with engineers to ensure that procedures meet their standards. Where **managerial ability** is critical, the DMU may request to meet senior managers to coordinate supply schedules and support mechanisms. If the suppliers' **financial strength** is paramount, the DMU may check its creditworthiness very carefully. If **ability to deliver** was either in doubt or the main criteria, it might check production capacities, stock inventories, and customer testimonials. **Price** is seldom the key consideration. Many industrial customers rate the **fitness for purpose** of the product and its **reliability** much higher. For example, a construction company would rather avoid penalties and wasted wages by buying a reliable digger than save a comparatively smaller sum by purchasing a cheaper, less reliable alternative.

Organisational Decision-Making Unit External Influences

Organisational DMUs are influenced by external factors, which Reid et al. (2017) categorise as physical, technological, economic, political, legal and ethical, and cultural.

▶ **Physical** factors include the geographical proximity of supplier and customer, which is important if the product is perishable, stock is needed at short notice, or local suppliers are more attractive to end users (e.g. local farmers supplying restaurants).

▶ **Technological** considerations include the compatibility of the customer's processes with the supplier's technology and the relative technological sophistication of the supplier's product. Suppliers of accountancy software may attract scrutiny in this area.

▶ **Economic** influences include confidence in the economy, taxation, and the firm's competitive and financial position.

▶ **Political** factors include potential trade tariffs, sanctions, and government grants and interventions.

▶ **Legal and ethical** factors dictate the standards to which products should conform and the procedures governing buyers and sellers.

▶ **Cultural** factors encapsulate the values, norms, accepted traditions, beliefs, and practices which dictate business behaviour between customers and suppliers, varying between countries, regions, and even industries.

Buyers' Risk Reduction Strategies

Poor purchase choices may harm an organisational decision maker's career and reputation and their firm's finances, so they reduce risk through several means:

▶ Issuing specific specifications required from suppliers

▶ Inspecting goods prior to order and delivery

▶ Visiting supplier premises

▶ Quality control of samples before ordering larger amounts

▶ Inserting penalty clauses for late delivery or faulty goods

▶ Requesting customer testimonials

▶ Negotiating lower prices which thereby restrict potential losses

SUSTAINABILITY QUESTION

If you managed procurement for Marks & Spencer and had been approached by a supplier of seafood, what sustainability considerations might you have, and how would you manage them?

In some cases, buyers may purchase from incumbent (current) suppliers as they are a known quantity and a lower risk. New suppliers may struggle to gain a foothold and, even then, gain only small orders before attempting to increase **share of customer**. Some customers multisource all orders; for example, a firm operating 1,000 cars may buy a fifth from each of Ford, General Motors, Toyota, Volkswagen-Audi, and Fiat-Chrysler in case one of them experiences parts supply shortfalls or a collapse in their used vehicle resale values.

MARKETING ASSISTANT TASK

Zomotor has recently been very successful in its conquest sales by targeting Mexican fleet operators with demonstration vehicles, competitive vehicle finance packages, and bespoke after-sales support. However, after winning many corporate accounts, Tannya wishes to penetrate these fleets and supply at least 20% of the vehicles sold to those corporate customers within three years. Design a strategy to achieve this, explaining necessary salesperson actions and the supporting activities of other departments.

After the Sale

Salespeople should follow up customers after a sale. Post-purchase evaluation informs whether a customer considers the product or service satisfactory and would buy again. If so, the salesperson may move a customer up the ladder of loyalty to the 'client' stage, then to 'advocate' and 'partner'. This helps to increase

- ▶ Repeat purchase value and frequency
- ▶ Share of customer
- ▶ Positive WOM recommendations
- ▶ Operating cost savings
- ▶ Salesperson productivity

During post-purchase evaluation, the customer compares prior expectations with actual performance. If expectations exceed reality, the customer may experience **buyer's remorse**. This regret in their purchase decision is a form of **cognitive dissonance** (Festinger, 1957) – the uncomfortable psychological state felt through unfulfilled expectations of an item or event – and usually damages repeat business. Apart from judging purchases against their **expected performance**, customers also compare them with their **ideal performance**, which is above expectations and a best-case scenario.

The Business-to-Business Sales Process

As we have seen, the salesperson's job continues after the sale, but it also starts before the first appointment. The main stages are shown in Table 14.3.

Objection Handling

The power of personal selling is in its personalisation: the way each prospect's concerns can be treated instantly and specifically. If any customer objections remain

TABLE 14.3

Stages in a sales appointment.

Stage	What the salesperson does
Prospecting	Defines the target market, generates sales leads, contacts those leads
Qualification	Questions the prospect to find vital information and ascertain the possibility of selling to them
Appointment making	Arranges a meeting with the correct decision-making unit members
Preparation	Researches the organisation, plans their day's activities (maybe targeting several companies in the same area), collates necessary information, checks demonstration product reliability
Ice-breakers	Humanises the experience and relaxes both parties, instigates casual conversation, but also extracts useful business information. In some countries (e.g. Sweden), less informal talk is expected, whereas in others (e.g. UK), preamble is normal
Need identification	Asks questions about the prospect's requirements, focuses the appointment on a potential sale, reminds the customer of their need
Presentation	Explains how the salesperson's proposed solution would service the customer's need
Objection handling	Overcomes obstacles to sale, diffuses concerns, finds alternative solutions
Negotiation	Agrees on supply price and terms
Closing the sale	Asks customer to commit to an order

unaddressed, the sale is unlikely to proceed, so the salesperson must isolate and nullify them. By repeating and rephrasing the customer's explanation, the salesperson demonstrates understanding of the concerns. If the objection is unjustified, the salesperson may tactfully explain why, perhaps by apologising for not clarifying this earlier. However, if the objection is justified, the salesperson may persuade them that the benefits outweigh the disadvantage, confirming that the objection has been overcome rather than making assumptions. Occasionally, objections remain and the sale falters due to underlying factors outside the salesperson's control: perhaps the prospect is not the authorised decision maker, in which case the salesperson should ascertain who is and include them; perhaps the product is superfluous to customer needs, in which case the salesperson should seek a prospect with more potential; or perhaps the customer has insufficient budget, in which case finance options or deferred payments may solve the issue. Sometimes sales fail due to a lack of empathy, understanding, trust, or 'personal chemistry' between buyer and seller. If a salesperson suspects this, they may request a colleague take over the account.

Negotiation

Negotiation demands patience and skill. Both parties must have slightly unaligned interests (e.g. one wishes to charge more and the other to pay less) but believe that an agreement is beneficial and attainable. Astute negotiation manages social and psychological factors, like the need for each party not to feel 'beaten', and tangibles like products and resources. Blythe (2004) proposed eight stages of sales negotiation:

- ▶ **Preparation** of parameters and objectives for the discussion (e.g. prices)
- ▶ **Discussion** to ascertain each other's requirements and bargaining position
- ▶ **Signals** that progress is being made through negotiation
- ▶ **Proposition** of a suggested win-win solution, fulfilling both parties' needs
- ▶ **Presentation** of the benefits of this proposal
- ▶ **Bargaining** to secure a reciprocal benefit for what they are offering
- ▶ **Closing** the negotiation by summarising the terms and committing to buy/sell
- ▶ **Agreement** through a signed contract

Closing

Many salespeople struggle to close a sale. Some lack confidence, talk after the customer has decided to buy, and risk inadvertently dissuading them. There are several established closing techniques, all leveraging psychology.

Assumptive closes entail asking which of two options the customer would like (e.g. 'would a Tuesday or Thursday delivery be better for you?'). By not asking a question which can be answered with 'yes' or 'no', and by establishing an assumption that only the details of the order need confirming, the salesperson makes it awkward for the customer to say no.

The **order-book close** is an assumptive close in which salespeople write product specifications on an order form, making it socially awkward for the customer to halt the sale. Salespeople must beware, however, that assumptive closing can alienate prospects, and customers pressured into a sale may block the process later (e.g. by cancelling a direct debit) or become resentful, troublesome, loss-making customers.

The **puppy-dog close** is often used when the product being sold will bring convenience or pleasure to the prospect but they are baulking at the commitment. It involves leaving it with them so they become reluctant to return it after a trial period. For example, a B2B salesperson selling a coffee vending machine may leave a demonstrator in the customer's reception area for a month so that removing it afterwards would disappoint and inconvenience the decision maker and influencers.

An **immediate-gain close** is appropriate if a product bestows clear customer benefits, and allows the salesperson to push for commitment by saying 'if we process the order now, you get the benefits immediately'.

The **sales manager close**, common in car dealerships, entails the salesperson declaring that they have no more discount but that, if the customer can order immediately, they can ask their sales manager for exceptional discount or free extra specification. Usually the tactic is spurious: the private conversation with the sales manager is an irrelevance, as the salesperson already has the additional negotiating leeway but is using it as leverage.

Processing the order ensures smooth order fulfilment and delivery.

Follow-up, in person or by telephone or email, checks that the customer is satisfied with the purchase.

Efficient Salespeople

Efficient salespeople use time efficiently. They **minimise travel time**, maximising customer contact, perhaps by travelling outside office hours, avoiding rush-hour traffic, and clustering appointments geographically or linearly along a motorway. Some organisations use **telesales** – office-based staff who contact customers remotely, especially for order-taker duties and missionary sales which require uncomplicated, low-risk decisions. The **telemarketing** function may undertake less specialised elements of customer contact, generating and qualifying leads, taking after-sales queries and routine orders, and following up promotional offers. This frees salespeople to use their specialist skills more efficiently and broadens the relationship between customer and firm.

MARKETING MANAGER TASK

Dylan is assisting his boss in designing a training programme for Zomotor salespeople, who are undertaking insufficient appointments and spending too long travelling. Their sales conversion rate (i.e. the percentage of appointments resulting in a sale) is also low. Help Dylan to write a report explaining how to address this within the training programme. Which messages will you embed, which learning strategies will you use, and how will you ensure the training has been effective?

Key Accounts

Why Are Key Accounts Important?

A **key account** or **major account** is a customer which contributes a significant percentage of the selling organisation's sales or profits. The seller may be vulnerable if the customer changes supplier. To retain them may require bespoke after-sales support, larger discounts, and widespread collaboration from within the seller firm and its channel partners (e.g. dealers and agents). Major accounts often have long selling cycles involving multiple decision makers. As the account is strategically important, it represents a risk, so mistakes should be eradicated, value conveyed, and relationships nurtured.

Key Account Management

Salespeople attempt to **penetrate the account** by increasing their **share of customer** (i.e. gaining a greater percentage of their purchases) and trying to achieve **preferred supplier status**, where they are invited to pitch before any competitors. An established supplier may attempt to gain a **solus agreement**, in which they give extra support in return for being the only supplier, or perhaps a **dual-badge agreement**, where preferential terms guarantee a position as one of two suppliers. Securing either addresses sellers' sales volume aspirations and leverages economies of scale. It also develops the supplier-customer relationship, fostering a common culture and **spirit of partnership**, where both parties share resources and the interfirm boundaries are blurred through synergistically integrating shared functions.

Successful Salespeople

Successful salespeople believe in the product and firm they are representing, draw upon recognised sales techniques and product knowledge, understand and identify with their customer base, and remain motivated even when working alone and faced with setbacks. They must fit the firm's ethos, their supervisor's management style, the sales type, and the working environment. Some people say that good salespeople are born, not made. Whilst certain personalities (e.g. extraversion) may enjoy sales more, training, knowledge, and experience are equally important. Good salespeople may not be talkative; listening is vital. Ideally, sales teams should be diverse to encompass broad skill sets.

Training Salespeople

Effective training is motivational and empowering, reducing staff churn rates (i.e. employees who leave). Well-trained salespeople require less supervision but make more and higher-value sales. Customers also benefit from fewer mistakes and greater empathy. Whilst salespeople need structured training, both during induction and throughout their careers, it is vital where staff are inexperienced or expensive to recruit, if order values are high, and if the products or customers are complicated and technically oriented. Training programmes cover **sales skills and administration, customer and market intelligence, company information**, and **product knowledge**, although areas like legislation may be included. They are planned around stated objectives relating to salesperson and company needs, the key points are signposted through repetition and reinforcement, and these are often revisited in follow-up sessions. As trainees may be at different career stages, training should be differentiated, learner oriented, and contextualised. The tutor, perhaps using role-plays, can provide individualised feedback on behaviours and translate these into plans for achieving specific goals. A blend of training methods like this is more engaging:

Lectures to reach a wide audience, imparting facts quickly but lacking interaction, engagement, and learner differentiation

Hands-on experience to help kinaesthetic learners (who learn by doing rather than seeing or hearing) and enable salespeople to recall first-hand experiences when talking to clients

Instructional videos to demonstrate sales skills

Role plays to provide safe spaces for honing those skills

Field visits and joint appointments where experienced colleagues can provide post-appointment feedback

Discussion groups where best practice can be shared

Training films, which embed consistency across a large trainee cohort in multiple locations, but lack differentiation

Motivating Salespeople

An effective salesperson has **intrinsic motivation** (i.e. inner drive and purpose) but also needs **extrinsic motivation** (by external factors). The best salespeople have expectancy, instrumentality, and valence: **expectancy** is a belief that, by sacrifice, their performances will improve; **instrumentality** is the belief that improved performances will be rewarded; and **valence** is the valuing of those rewards.

Financial Motivation

Salespeople may be motivated through remuneration. Most earn a basic salary, plus a commission (bonus payment) determined by their performance. Additional to the **salary-plus-commission** approach, some salespeople have **salary-only** packages, whilst others are paid **commission only**. Typically, salespeople earn commission for meeting or exceeding monthly **sales volume, profit**, and **model-mix targets**. Targets should stretch salespeople but be attainable (Herweg & Rosato, 2020). Sales jobs commonly offer 70%–90% as a basic salary, allowing enough security to take a mortgage or plan a family, with the remainder as commission. Salary-only sales positions are rarer and often key account management (KAM) roles, those requiring technical expertise, or those producing high-value but infrequent sales. Commission-only positions are often for part-time salespeople who cold-call (i.e. visit without appointment) householders to sell double glazing or conservatories. Some salespeople strive for every available penny or seek the spotlight, some desperately avoid the social stigma of being in the bottom-performing group of colleagues, whilst others try to develop themselves (Good et al., 2020).

Non-financial Motivation

Salespeople also respond to non-monetary incentives. Hitting targets may matter as much as commission. **Sales meetings, competitions**, and **league tables** offer recognition, positive or otherwise. Successful salespeople may earn **holidays**, upgraded **company cars**, membership of the company's **millionaires' club**, or **lunch of the month** with their boss. Competitions constitute **gamification of the sales role. Branded gifts and factory visits** may engender affinity to the brand. Esteem, recognition, social acceptance, and fulfilment of objectives drive many salespeople. Individuals also respond to **hygiene factors** (Herzberg, 1987), such as appropriate resources, friendly feedback, administrative support, empowerment, team spirit, job security, and prompt payment of expenses and commission.

Managing Sales Performance

Managing sales entails **managing individuals, teams**, and **processes** (Kim & Jung, 2018) but also **forecasting**, overseeing **complementary sales activities**, and ensuring compliance with **ethical standards**. The sales function is costly, requiring salaries, commission, company cars, fuel, tax, pensions, travel, insurance, conferences, and administrative support. Performance management is critical. Splitting regions into sales territories allows comparison of performances between salespeople, clarifies their remit, provides customers with a specified contact, and reduces travel. Territories may be allocated by customer type, sector, or product.

Sales Forecasting

Accurately predicting individual salespeople's performance for the week, month, or quarter is vital for planning manufacturing production slots, finance, personnel coverage, purchasing, invoicing, goods logistics, and other resources. Therefore, sales managers use sales meetings and conference calls to gather detail from the sales team and identify any assumptions or inaccurate variables rendering their forecasts inaccurate. At the national or regional level, sales forecasts should account for economic and commercial conditions in the industry and country.

METRICS QUESTION

What metrics might you use when setting salespeople objectives or when measuring their performance, and why?

Complementary Sales Activities

Complementary sales activities, designed to maximise salesforce effectiveness, include the following:

- *Telesales calls* to qualify customers, follow up demand, arrange sales appointments, and perhaps sell remotely.
- Corporate hospitality, such as golf days, humanises the relationship between the firm or salesperson and the customer and their firm in an informal, relaxing environment which can uncover additional sales opportunities and leverage feelings of reciprocity.
- *Trade fairs and conferences* drive prospects and customers to the salesperson, reducing their travel and prospecting. They also help launch products, take orders, enhance the brand image, undertake competitor intelligence and product knowledge, outflank non-exhibitors, and bring sales staff together for morale-boosting social events like restaurant meals.

To be ethical, salespeople and managers should distinguish between corporate hospitality and bribery, between a fair profit margin and exploitation, and understand the importance of confidentiality (Rousselet et al., 2020). Most importantly, they should work within the principles of **caveat venditor** ('the seller must beware that it fulfils it ethical obligations to buyers') rather than **caveat emptor** ('the buyer must beware that it is vigilant towards the possibility of sellers acting unethically').

MARKETING DIRECTOR TASK

Zomotor recently launched several new models popular within the retail sector (i.e. individual owner-drivers). Lee wishes to increase Zomotor's presence within major fleets (i.e. firms running 500 cars or more) from 6% market share to 10% within five years. They have $5 million per year to spend on additional salespeople and sales support to achieve this objective. Write a report showing how they might spend this money, organise their resources, and target major fleet operators.

Chapter Summary

Sales management ensures a sustainable customer base is nurtured profitably. Salesforces are expensive but enable direct interpersonal contact between firms and consumers (in B2C markets) or the customer's decision maker(s) (in B2B markets). A well-trained,

PHOTO 14.5
The customisation inherent within LEGO is maximised by offering a choice of products reminiscent of those found in pick 'n' mix sweet shops.

motivated, and able salesperson can enhance the firm's brand image, maximise profits, encourage customers to consider less popular products, and harvest considerable market intelligence (a resource lamentably underutilised by many organisations). Firms should carefully recruit, train, motivate, remunerate, and manage salespeople, adequately resourcing and supporting them to maximise their effectiveness.

Key Learning Outcomes

▶ Sales databases underpin all effective prospecting and sales activities.

▶ The B2B sales process is usually more formalised and objective than B2C sales.

▶ Personal selling is a costly but effective way to make sales.

▶ Sales management strategies should fit organisational objectives and customer requirements.

Recommended Reading

Good, V., Hughes, D. E., & LaBrecque, A. C. (2020). Understanding and motivating salesperson resilience. *Marketing Letters*, 1–13.
Herweg, F., & Rosato, A. (2020). Bait and ditch: Consumer naïveté and salesforce incentives. *Journal of Economics & Management Strategy*, 29(1), 97–121.

Rousselet, E., Brial, B., Cadario, R., & Béji-Bécheur, A. (2020). Moral intensity, issue characteristics, and ethical issue recognition in sales situations. *Journal of Business Ethics*, *163*(2), 347–363.

References

Albanese, P. (2015). Inside economic man: Behavioral economics and consumer behavior. In *Handbook of contemporary behavioral economics* (pp. 25–45). Routledge.

Antczak, A., & Sypniewska, B. A. (2017). Personal selling in the service sector as one marketing promotional tool. In A. Antczak & B. A. Sypniewska (Eds.), *Cross-cultural personal selling* (pp. 35–56). Palgrave Macmillan.

Blythe, J. (2004). *Sales and key account management*. Cengage Learning EMEA.

Festinger, L. (1957). *A theory of cognitive dissonance*. Stanford University Press.

Herzberg, F. (1987, September–October). One more time: How do you motivate employees? *Harvard Business Review*, *65*(5), 109–120.

Johnson, J. S., & Matthes, J. M. (2018). Sales-to-marketing job transitions. *Journal of Marketing*, *82*(4), 32–48.

Kim, S. K., & Jung, Y. S. (2018). Regaining control of salesforce. *Industrial Marketing Management*, *73*, 84–98.

Reid, D. A., Plank, R. E., Peterson, R. M., & Rich, G. A. (2017). Examining the use of sales force management practices. *Journal of Business & Industrial Marketing*, *32*(7), 974–986.

Glossary

Closing: gaining commitment to buy towards the end of the sales conversation

Cognitive dissonance: the uncomfortable psychological state when realities fall short of expectations

Creative salespeople: salespeople using problem-solving pitches

Delivery salespeople: salespeople who replenish customers' stock from a van

Derived demand: demand for something which services another demand

Elastic demand: demand which fluctuates significantly as prices change

Heuristics: decision-making shortcuts/rules of thumb

Inelastic demand: demand which fluctuates little as prices change

Inside order-takers: order processing staff

Joint demand: demand for one product which is linked to demand for another

Key account management (KAM): nurturing the organisation's most valuable customer relationships

Missionary selling: using sales-like approaches to raise brand awareness and affinity

Modified rebuy: buying from experience, but choosing something slightly different to last time

New business sales: sales to prospects who are not already the seller's customer

New-task buying: buying something for the first time

Outside order-takers: salespeople who replenish retailers' stock

Political/indirect salespeople: salespeople supplying major client contracts (e.g. governments)

Prospecting: identifying and contacting potential new customers

Qualification: questioning prospects or customers to extract useful information

Straight rebuy: replacing old or used items with identical new ones

Telesales: sales activity in which the seller and prospect are remote from each other

Trade sales: sales to an organisation in the seller's specialist industry

Technical selling: selling complicated goods or services

Personal Selling and Sales Management Case Study: Caudalie

Caudalie is a Parisian family firm which makes skincare and haircare products from extracts of grapes and grape vines – 'vinotherapie'. Launched in 1995, Caudalie's products offer anti-ageing properties which have been celebrating by industry publications such as *Marie Claire*, which awarded the firm its 2018 Prix d'Excellence de la Beauté. The brand is eco-friendly, an attribute which helped the founder win the French Legion of Honour award in 2018, and belongs to the '1% for the Planet' initiative, donating 1% of its global turnover to organisations which protect the environment. It embraces a number of good causes (e.g. a campaign to plant 8 million trees by 2021) and has a 'cosm-ethics' charter banning ingredients such as parabens, mineral oils, synthetic colouring agents, and animal-derived products.

The product is sold through a very small number of Vinotherapie spas and a slightly larger number of boutique spas around the world. Outside France, its products are available in Europe through pharmacies; in the US through the luxury American beauty retailer, Bluemercury, and the French beauty retailer, Sephora; and in Asia via Sephora and other department stores. By 2018, it was present in over 40 countries, where its products could be purchased at around 20,000 locations. Despite being a wealthy country which is easily accessible from Paris, the Netherlands has relatively few outlets stocking Caudalie products (e.g. only four retailers in Amsterdam), and these are mainly chemists and perfumiers rather than spas. Consequently, Caudalie is missing an opportunity to penetrate a lucrative market.

Imagine you are the European marketing director for Caudalie, and you have decided that you wish to penetrate the Netherlands market, both by increasing

continued

sales volumes through your current outlets and by selling through department stores, hotels, and leisure spas. Visit the company's website to familiarise yourself fully with the product range, and formulate a plan for a sales team of two executives to use when approaching potential retailers, by explaining the following: (i) How would you ascertain which retailers are suitable? (ii) How would you make initial contact with them, ensuring you get to the decision maker? (iii) What activities would you undertake before the appointment? (iv) In an appointment, what unique selling propositions (USPs) would you emphasise to differentiate your brand positively from the competition? (v) If the decision maker wishes to place an order but is hesitating anxiously instead of signing the contract, what actions would you take? Make bullet points for each question.

Sources

Caudalie UK website. Retrieved December 30, 2020, from https://www.uk.caudalie.com

Cult Beauty website. Retrieved December 30, 2020, from https://www.cultbeauty.co.uk/caudalie

Look Fantastic website. Retrieved December 30, 2020, from https://lookfantastic.com

15 Channel Management

LEARNING OBJECTIVES

▶ To explore the importance of designing and managing an effective route to market

▶ To compare the roles and duties of different channel intermediaries

▶ To analyse how power and conflict can undermine channel efficiency

▶ To evaluate different approaches to balancing intermediary and customer requirements

PHOTO 15.1
Amazon sell their own and other companies' products direct to customers.

DOI: 10.4324/9781003170891-16

Introduction

Most manufacturers use partner organisations to reach customers through a 'channel'. Without these partners, they would have to sell and deliver direct to customers, which would be logistically and commercially unviable. Clearly, a Nike truck will not deliver sports shoes from the factory to our homes. Some exceptions exist (e.g. service providers like solicitors or dentists usually interact directly with customers). However, most firms have **downstream channel partners**, who help to market, move and sell goods; and **upstream channel partners**, who supply the resources needed by the firm. Each type adds value within the supply chain. When you buy a bottle of hand sanitiser, think of the organisations involved and how they have contributed (see Table 15.1).

'Channel length' refers to the number of intermediary levels in the channel, and 'channel width' is the number of individual partners at each intermediary level. For instance, a manufacturer selling through 200 different retail companies, but without any brokers, agents, or wholesalers, would have a short but wide channel.

Push and Pull Strategies

Some manufacturers use **push strategies**, in which they persuade or incentivise their downstream channel partners to take lots of stock, which therefore puts pressure on them to sell product to end users. In this approach, the manufacturer is 'pushing' product down through the channel. Some manufacturers use **pull strategies**, in which they appeal directly to end users via branding, marketing communications, and other elements of the marketing mix. By making the brand and its products desirable in this way, customers are persuaded into the firm's retail partners to order or buy products, which then forces retailers to order stock for wholesalers and wholesalers from

TABLE 15.1

Core functions of channel partners.

Organisation	Core functions
Supplier to the manufacturer	Provides the ingredient commodities and packaging
Manufacturer	Makes the core product, bottles it and packages it
Logistics company	Transports the product from manufacturer to wholesaler
Wholesaler	Stores product, breaks into smaller quantities, sells with other products, delivers to retail premises
Retailer	Displays product where consumers can access it, sells with other products, serves consumer

PHOTO 15.2
UK stationery retailer WHSmith is an authorised reseller of Apple products.

the manufacturer (for example). In this approach, the manufacturer 'pulls' demand up through the channel. In practice, most organisations use a combination of both approaches.

Upstream Channel Partners

Upstream partners may supply raw materials (Srivastava Dabas et al., 2012). A car manufacturer like Zomotor would need sheet metal for vehicle bodywork, and also materials which are not in the end product but used during manufacture. For example, the company BOC supplies industrial gases to the healthcare, welding, and automotive sectors. Other organisations supply machinery rather than materials. For instance, Thyssenkrupp supplies machinery to the mining, cement, steel, chemical, and fertiliser industries. Some upstream partners supply components found in the firm's end products. For example, Bosch supplies central heating units found in construction companies' buildings. Certain upstream partners supply services (information, finance, or expertise) rather than goods (Palmatier et al., 2016). A manufacturer might need information from engineering companies on the properties of plastics to ensure it designs a viable product, finance from banks to help with product development and launch costs, and lawyers' expertise to ensure conformity to legal standards. These partners are 'upstream' because they are further away from the consumer than the originating firm in the supply chain (Rosenbloom et al., 2004).

PHOTO 15.3
Car dealerships often have franchise agreements to sell the products of one or more motor manufacturers.

Downstream Channel Partners: Retailers and Wholesalers

Downstream channel partners, or 'channel intermediaries', are located between originator firms (usually manufacturers) and end users (Claro & Claro, 2010) in the marketing channel. The two major ones are retailers and wholesalers, which perform the following functions:

RETAILERS

▶ Provide product knowledge, expertise, and sales advice (Dukes & Geylani, 2016)

▶ Attract footfall

▶ Prepare and order stock and display products

▶ Serve customers and answer queries

▶ Arrange deliveries

▶ Provide information and demonstrations

▶ Offer variety

▶ Undertake local promotional activities

▶ Maintain a customer database

▶ Complete the sales paperwork

▶ Provide after-sales support and service, and maintain sold products

WHOLESALERS

▶ Accommodate large incoming deliveries

▶ Accumulate and store products (also called warehousing)

▶ Break bulk (also called allocation)

▶ Offer variety, enabling retailers to order flexibly in small quantities in response to their quickly evolving local market demands (Rosenbloom & Andras, 2008)

▶ Make fast, last-mile deliveries to retailers

▶ Share stock burden (i.e. the money tied up in products before they are sold), reducing the effects of seasonality

▶ Negotiate terms with their suppliers

PHOTO 15.4
Department stores usually sell a large range of higher-quality brands, such as perfume and cosmetics.

- ▶ Drive downstream promotional activities through retailers

- ▶ Stock inventory

- ▶ Check credit of retailers

- ▶ Are aware of pricing and competitors' activities

- ▶ Gather and disseminate information down to retailers and up to the manufacturer, helping them to make informed competitive decisions (Boyaci & Gallego, 2004)

ETHICS QUESTION

A local convenience store (a neighbourhood store or, in the UK, a corner shop) might sell canned and frozen food, fruit and vegetables, bread, confectionery, newspapers and magazines, flowers, soft drinks, alcoholic drinks, tobacco products, and lottery tickets. What should it take into consideration to ensure it is trading ethically and legally?

Other Downstream Channel Partners

Franchisees

These independent companies represent a brand within an agreed sales territory. A Zomotor car dealership owned by a family firm or bank would be an example. The franchisee receives resources such as sales, display and demo stock, corporate branding, manufacturer warranty and after-sales work, sales leads, the knowledge that no other competitor will be given that manufacturer's franchise locally, and the prestige and peace-of-mind associated with the manufacturer's brand. In return, they take bulk deliveries, hold stock in their compound, display and sell goods, contribute to local promotional campaigns, share stocking and marketing costs, provide local market knowledge, attract footfall, serve customers, negotiate sales, order appropriate stock, drive sales volumes, and manage the customer relationship.

Brokers and Agents

These may be middlemen which eat into profit margins, but they also find customers, whether in B2B or B2C. In Central London, the agency TKTS sells last-minute, discounted tickets for West End musicals. It is highly visible to tourists and Londoners alike and captures significant footfall, freeing theatres for their theatrical productions. In this way, TKTS (a not-for-profit service) adds value to its upstream partners (the theatres) and to customers by offering advice and accessibility (Cui & Shin, 2017). Brokers and agents may be invaluable where a manufacturer wishes to enter a new market and lacks experience of customers there.

Finance and Insurance Partners

These may be crucial, especially in the sale of big-ticket items to consumers: high-value products purchased infrequently, such as cars or furniture. Customers often cannot afford to pay cash for expensive items, so use finance packages instead, perhaps paying 25% of the cash price as a deposit, then 3% monthly for three years, until the purchase price and interest are repaid. This gives sellers a larger potential market, disguises a large and off-putting sale price, and allows them the opportunity to sell customers replacement products toward the end of the agreement before they shop around (Chen & Popovich, 2003).

Marketing Agencies

Although marketing agencies constitute service providers rather than supply chain intermediaries, they sit between the firm and its customers, facilitating trade. Field marketing agencies deploy temporary salesforces on behalf of client organisations (Mullin, 2018); for example, salespeople in B2B contexts for motor manufacturers wishing to penetrate the fleet market, and in B2C contexts for lottery operators wishing to gain more customers. This 'outsourcing' allows the originator firm to keep its headcount low, devolving to the agency responsibility for wages, redundancy packages, and holiday and sickness entitlement.

Logistics Companies, Importers, Exporters, Haulage, and Shipping Companies

These downstream channel partners handle deliveries and transportation and are related to wholesalers (Aykol & Leonidou, 2018). However, title (i.e. ownership) of the products being moved rarely passes to them, so they are considered service providers. Selling platforms such as eBay and Amazon offer another interface between firms and customers.

Specialist Channel Intermediaries

These operate in sectors which modify original products before selling on to the end user. For example, a motor manufacturer may provide chassis to conversion companies which then turn them into ambulances, motorhomes, vehicle transporters, hearses, mobile libraries, mobile decontamination units, mobile surgical clinics, or other applications and then sell the end products.

STAKEHOLDER QUESTION

Make a list of as many stakeholders as you can who are involved in bringing a sports drink to your table. What function does each perform?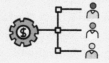

How Channel Partners Add Value

Channel partners have been conceptualised as comprising either a supply chain or a demand chain. Theorists imagining a supply chain believe that organisations make and sell things, and that these sales organisations require assistance to push product down the supply chain, applying stock pressure to intermediaries who subsequently market and sell them to their customers. Contrastingly, theorists imagining a demand chain believe organisations should research, sense, and respond to customer needs, listening first and acting second, adding value through collaboration (Emmett & Crocker, 2016). In his 'value chain' theory, Porter (1980) famously illustrated how an organisation should add value through its functions and processes. By streamlining all areas, firms could gain competitive advantage by operating more cost-efficiently than the competition, pricing their products higher, differentiating themselves, reducing waste, producing better quality goods, and selling in greater volume.

MARKETING ASSISTANT TASK

In Mexico, Tannya must help to recruit a new dealership in Chetumal, a coastal city of 150,000 people near the border with Belize. As a state capital, its economy benefits from the presence of government officers, and it is a major regional hub, attracting visitors to its shopping mall, beachside bars, and restaurants. The nearest major dealerships are five hours away in Cancun and Campeche. Tannya wishes to develop a checklist of customer-focused aspirations which any new dealership should fulfil. She knows that customers need ample free parking, complimentary Wi-Fi, and separate sales and servicing waiting areas with sofas and televisions. Help Tannya by adding ten items to her list, explaining the importance of each to customers.

Intensive, Exclusive, and Selective Channels and Networks

It is crucial that manufacturers choose their channel partners carefully, considering their commercial objectives, customer requirements, and market characteristics. One of the most fundamental decisions, especially in B2C trading, is whether to have an intensive, selective, or exclusive network of partners (Frazier & Lassar, 1996), the characteristics of which are shown in Table 15.2.

Channel Levels and Considerations

A channel level is one layer of intermediaries between the firm and its customers. If there are no intermediaries because the firm sells direct to end users, this is a direct

PHOTO 15.5
Some shops sell goods bearing their own name rather than those of other brands.

TABLE 15.2
Characteristics of intensive, selective, and exclusive network types.

Intensive network	Selective network	Exclusive network
Very many partner organisations in a territory	Intermediate number of partner organisations in territory	Very few partner organisations in a territory
Includes retailers and maybe wholesalers, brokers, agents, and dealers	Includes retailers and maybe wholesalers, brokers, agents, and dealers	Focused on retailers and agents or dealers
High anticipated sales volume	Medium anticipated sales volume	Low anticipated sales volume
Products are usually small, low cost, simple, low risk, routine, or compulsive purchases, requiring little decision-making	Products are medium cost, size, risk, and complexity, purchased only semi-frequently, requiring some decision-making	Adopted where consequences of a poor consumer decision are high (Trivedi, 1998), product is expensive, bought very infrequently, is complicated, or requires detailed decision-making

Intensive network	Selective network	Exclusive network
Customers prepared to travel very short distances to buy	Customers prepared to travel intermediate distances to buy	Customers prepared to travel great distances to buy
Very loose contractual agreement and little manufacturer control over intermediary and brand standards	Standard contractual agreement and moderate manufacturer control over intermediary and brand standards	Very stringent contractual agreement and significant manufacturer control over intermediary and brand standards
Provides blanket coverage of sales territory	Provides selective coverage in heavily populated areas (Frazier, 1999)	Provides sales representation in a few, strategic centres
Example: Cadbury's, confectionery manufacturer selling through neighbourhood stores	Example: Sony, consumer electronics manufacturer selling through electrical stores	Example: Ferrari, supercar manufacturer selling through exclusive dealerships

PHOTO 15.6
Municipal market halls such as this provide space for specific small traders to sell their goods; for example, butchers and greengrocers.

marketing channel. However, most channels contain one or more levels of inter-mediary, so are indirect marketing channels. Some firms have different numbers of channel levels depending on the customer type. For example, a motor manufacturer selling chassis cabs to a corporate customer may have no intermediaries, relying on

PHOTO 15.7
Large shopping centres often cluster competitors, such as chain restaurants, together so that they all benefit from an increased footfall of customers prepared to purchase.

its own salespeople to deal with customers, whereas it may sell cars to retail customers via a network of franchised dealerships. Likewise, a firm's number of channel levels may vary from one market to another – in its largest market, it might be 'firm > wholesaler > retailer > customer', whereas in a smaller market, it might be 'firm > agent > customer'. Channel members are linked to each other by the following 'flows':

> *Flow of products*: for example, downstream from the manufacturer to a wholesaler via large truck deliveries into large depots and then downstream to retailers based in smaller premises via transportation.

> *Flow of payments*: for example, upstream from retailers paying wholesalers, and from wholesalers paying manufacturers, for products which they have ordered or received.

> *Flow of ownership*: for example, from a manufacturer to a wholesaler at discounted terms accounting for storage, transportation, marketing, and interest costs, and their need to profit when selling the products on to retailers.

> *Flow of promotional activities*: for example, typically downstream from the manufacturer, which uses the marketing communications mix to make their product as attractive as possible before tasking their channel intermediaries with

promoting product to consumers or partners further downstream through more localised activities like regional trade fairs (Mehta et al., 2002).

Flow of information: constant and in both directions; for example, providing downstream partners with product, technical, and general market information, and upstream partners with detailed customer feedback and local market intelligence.

Choosing a Channel Structure

When deciding what sort of channel to operate, a firm must consider market requirements (i.e. the channel needs or their targeted customer segments) and the objectives to be delivered. Each segment may value different channel competences. For example, millennials and Generation Z consumers may demand greater interactivity with the channel than baby boomers or Generation X consumers, as they are 'digital natives' rather than 'digital immigrants' in an electronically enabled world. In this instance, the firm's channel objective may be to deliver products to customers within specified time frames, influencing its choice of channel (Goering, 2012). Firms must also increase profits by minimising costs wherever possible without damaging customer satisfaction. The major considerations when choosing a channel structure and design are as follows:

▶ **Channel intensity and exclusivity** dictates how many channel partners are appointed, where, and the level of control which the firm has over them. It is influenced by customer purchase frequency, the consequences of a poor purchase choice, market potential compared to overall population size, and customer service demands. For these reasons, Coca-Cola is available at many more outlets than Rolex watches.

▶ **Market conditions and product characteristics** impact channel decisions. If a firm has growth aspirations in a buoyant market, more intermediaries are often needed to provide more contact with prospects and customers.

▶ **Product characteristics** have storage and transport implications. Large products are usually more expensive and difficult to manage and must be moved in smaller quantities. Products which are less frequently purchased by customers may require long-term storage, and perishable goods may need refrigerated transport and warehouses. Customers buying technologically advanced or legally stringent products need more guidance, placing demands upon downstream partners.

▶ **The firm's characteristics, demands, and ambitions** influence channel structure and partner choice. Manufacturers of prestigious, high-priced products require partners with equally aspirational brands. Likewise, if the manufacturer demands impeccable customer service or has ambitions of reaching a specific customer segment, its partners must help deliver these objectives.

▶ **The competitive landscape** dictates that, if a firm is operating in a monopolistic market (i.e. without significant competitors), it has more freedom to decide how to trade with customers. However, if constantly attacked by competitors on product specification, price, customer service, or other differentiating factors, it must appoint channel partners which help it mitigate those threats and build its own competitive advantage – perhaps through allowing flexible customer ordering.

▶ **The location of customers** directly affects channel design. If a car manufacturer has open points (i.e. areas without dealer representation) in major towns and cities, it will neglect market potential there and either struggle elsewhere to compensate or suffer a disappointing market share.

▶ **The territory to be covered** is a closely related consideration. Any channel intermediary must have not sufficiently large and equipped premises, and enough staff members such as salespeople, to service the sales territory and penetrate the market sufficiently.

▶ **Storage, distribution factors**, **tariffs, and costs** influence the speed with which goods must be transported (e.g. if they are perishable or are supplied to customers under emergency conditions). This dictates the number of intermediaries and their location relative to target customers. The firm and its partners must consider the product characteristics, relative costs, and reliability levels of alternative methods of transportation (e.g. between road haulage and train), the traceability and security of products during transit, the speed of transportation, competitors' methods, and customer service demands (Zimmerman & Blythe, 2017).

▶ **The number of channels required** is the final consideration. Organisations may consider it advantageous to sell direct to major B2B customers, building closer relationships and controlling the account, whilst selling to B2C customers through channel intermediaries which will absorb transaction costs and time.

SUSTAINABILITY QUESTION

Manufacturing a product and moving it down through the supply chain, via wholesalers and retailers, to end consumers may take a significant toll on the environment. Make a list of resources which might be used up, or environmental damage which might be incurred, in the process. For each listed item, also suggest how the negative impact might be reduced.

Areas Requiring Agreement Between the Firm and Its Channel Partners

As the English adage goes, 'marry in haste, repent at leisure' (i.e. rushing into inappropriate commitments brings long-term suffering). Firms can appoint channel intermediaries quickly and easily, perhaps to fill an open point, but unsuitable partners can hinder each other for years. Therefore, it is important for both to ensure that their aspirations, objectives, motives, and capabilities are aligned (Carson & Ghosh, 2019). There are two key areas where the partners should agree: price expectations and sales and service territories.

Agreement on Price Expectations

Price plays a huge role in positioning a brand and generating profit, so is highly emotive to commercial organisations. Some firms prefer large profit margins and high prices to differentiate themselves from the competition, communicate prestige, and produce commercial sustainability. However, if a channel intermediary (maybe a retailer) would rather 'pile them high and sell them cheap', prioritising sales volumes over profit margins, then the partnership will be unviable.

Agreement on Sales and Service Territories

This is another emotive issue. Firms need retailers to drive sales volumes within their respective territories to fulfil their wider objectives, including profit and market share. Many downstream intermediaries want the biggest possible territory because it provides more prospects and prevents (or discourages) competitors from selling the same products within that area. However, territories which are oversized or overpopulated with prospects cannot be covered properly by a retailer's salespeople, and if it is under-resourced, this will undermine the firm's efforts. In many countries, and also in the European Union, a manufacturer cannot prevent retailers from selling outside their territories, as this constitutes anti-competitive practice (Iacobucci & Winter, 2017).

Managing the Channel

After carefully selecting channel partners, firms must manage them to ensure they deliver the required objectives. On the one hand, the firm needs to keep its partners focused, incentivised, and stretched if it is to grow, but if it pushes its partners too hard, it risks alienating them, driving them away, and potentially encouraging them to form alliances with rivals. Therefore, astute channel management is vital.

Motivation

Motivation of channel partners entails setting testing yet achievable targets and linking these to bonus or commission payments, which may be payable to the partner organisation and perhaps also staff within it (Gilliland & Kim, 2019). Monthly, quarterly, and annual targets frequently cover sales volumes, percentage of customers purchasing finance and insurance products, market share, profit per unit, customer satisfaction score, and adherence to agreed channel standards. Money, recognition (e.g. through competitions), awards, and career progression can motivate individuals.

Training

Training maximises the staff resource and helps safeguard the firm's reputation through knowledgeable service. Frequent product knowledge training ensures that customer-facing staff offer accurate advice but also allows salespeople to understand their products' competitive advantages, enabling them to explain to customers how they add value. This should make the customer less cost sensitive and more profitable, impacting positively on volumes and profit margins.

Targeting

Having targeted its channel intermediaries against key performance indicators (KPIs) important to the overall objectives, the firm must then undertake frequent evaluation of its partners' performance across multiple metrics. Where it appears that a partner is beginning to underachieve, the firm can make timely remedial interventions to help them get back on course.

Channel Conflict

An unwanted phenomenon between channel partners is channel conflict, which occurs due to misalignment of their objectives, which is almost inevitable to some extent. It may also occur due to interpersonal clashes, so managers tasked with maintaining the relationship should be personable, trained, and skilled in conflict avoidance and resolution. Having precise contracts stipulating which partner is responsible for each task reduces the risk of domain dissensus – the uncertainty where each partner simultaneously believes the other should be undertaking a specific function.

METRICS QUESTION

If you were a regional sales manager for Nike, and you had 100 retailers selling Nike product in your region, what targets would you set them to stretch and measure their performance? Make a table listing your three preferred types of target in the left-hand column and your commercial rationale in the right-hand column.

PHOTO 15.8
Some shops specialise in the retail of second-hand or reconditioned goods.

Channel Integration

Channel conflict can be largely avoided and control gained through **vertical integration**, where the manufacturer buys each channel intermediary (e.g. wholesaler, dealer) positioned between themselves and the market. This contrasts with **horizontal integration**, where one wholesaler company, for example, might buy other competing wholesalers (Takata, 2016), and with **co-marketing**, where two organisations pool their marketing resources to provide each other representation alongside their own brand – an approach not limited to channel partners.

Power in Channel Relationships

To mitigate channel conflict, firms may consider the effects of different power types within the channel. Based on French et al.'s (1959) seminal sociological theory of power types, these are as follows:

Referent power occurs when partners tries to emulate their leader. For example, if dealer- or retailer-employed staff enjoy representing a well-established, respected manufacturer with a strong brand, they may try to emulate some of its competences.

Legitimate power derives from legal, contractual, or hierarchical dominance over a partner. Hopefully, a cordial working relationship can be maintained without making 'legalistic pleas' (i.e. resorting to pointing out contractual obligations), but sometimes the 'power of power' (i.e. knowing which partner holds power without necessarily exercising it) influences partners' behaviours.

Coercive power goes one step further, constituting the use of direct force to achieve one's wishes at the partner's expense. It is usually overt but may also be used covertly; for example, by a manufacturer deliberately punishing an uncooperative partner by making late or incorrect deliveries or late payment of volume discounts.

Reward power uses incentives to positively reinforce desired behaviours and may be achievable through commission, competitions, or even praise.

Expert power is achieved by people or organisations which have earned respect due to their expertise, knowledge, or professionalism. Often an astute salesperson can acquire this by demonstrating sales prowess and the positive benefits which it can bestow on partners.

MARKETING MANAGER TASK

In China, Dylan is visiting a dealership to finalise the details of a new franchise agreement in the major north-eastern city of Dalian. With a population of nearly 7 million, the Dalian metropolitan area is a major open point, damaging Zomotor's market share in China and depriving it of sales, parts, and servicing revenue. However, the dealer's owner is known to negotiate hard for preferential treatment from business partners (e.g. flexibility over stock levels and interest charges). To help Dylan prepare, list areas which the owner may seek to negotiate, and for each, briefly explain how Dylan may achieve reasonable compromises or the original conditions. You may do this by explaining why the conditions are fair, or by granting a concession to the dealer in return for one of equal value.

Exclusivity and Selling an Entire Product Range

The firm decides how intermediaries should represent its brand and manage its products. As discussed, it may pursue an intensive, exclusive, or selective network, depending on the nature of the product, number of customers, their purchase frequency, and the difficulty of their decision-making. **Exclusive distribution** through very few partners enables them to sell their products against limited competition, making them more likely to invest heavily in the brand (e.g. by purchasing expensive branded signage). However, there are two more contractual mechanisms which grant 'exclusivity': exclusive dealing and tying agreements.

Exclusive Dealing

An exclusive dealing agreement stipulates that the partner may not represent competitor brands. This prevents a dealership (a type of retailer, such as those in the motor industry) from 'switch-selling' more profitable and attractive competitor products to customers, thereby encouraging commitment and proper sales representation. Naturally, if a dealer agrees an exclusive dealing contract, this makes it more dependent upon its chosen manufacture, so it would expect compensatory benefits such as increased marketing support, interest-free stocking, and discounted corporate signage and showroom furniture.

Tying Agreements

Firms imposing exclusive dealing agreements will often also seek a tying agreement, in which they stipulate that the partner must take all of the firm's product range rather than simply cherry-picking the most profitable or popular products. To reinforce this, they would usually incentivise partners to sell a predetermined model mix.

GLOBAL MARKETING QUESTION

If you were tasked with advising Dyson (the manufacturer of vacuum cleaners, hand driers and air recirculation units) on how to enter the Russian market for the first time, what channel strategy would you advise them to adopt? In a simple table, show which type of intermediaries you would appoint in the first year and which intermediaries you would expect to have after 10 years, explaining your commercial rationale.

Logistical Considerations

All channel intermediaries must handle logistical issues surrounding the flow of products, payments, and information. The main tasks are as follows:

INVENTORY MANAGEMENT

- ▶ Ensure that they always have enough stock to fulfil customer orders
- ▶ Respond to more unusual customer orders by forwarding order to the manufacturer
- ▶ Pay their upstream supplier within agreed timescales
- ▶ Process payments swiftly from their own customers (Gallino et al., 2016)

WAREHOUSING

▶ Maximise the efficient use of available storage space

▶ Handle incoming and outgoing deliveries

▶ Manage financial costs tied up in stored goods

▶ Service the needs of the market

▶ Plan the transportation of products

▶ Absorb seasonality in supply and demand

▶ Accommodate the limitations of the premises to which stock must be delivered

MANAGEMENT OF LOGISTICAL INFORMATION

▶ Use data from previous sales periods to predict future order level

▶ Liaise with logistics companies over availability of vehicles and transport

▶ Ascertain the status of ordered stock being manufactured

Therefore, channel intermediaries undertake inbound logistical processes like order processing, monitoring, warehousing, inventory control, and handling goods, and outbound logistical processes like picking orders from stock and transporting products, plus large elements of the sales process and customer service.

NEW MEDIA QUESTION

If you were a marketing strategist for Chanel, the desirable perfume brand, how would you use social media and other digital technology to drive footfall into retailers selling your products and ensure that you provide retailers with the right stock at the right times to fulfil their needs? Consider three ways in which you would harness digital technology, discussing the advantages and disadvantages of each.

Retailing

Manufacturers of consumer products must decide what type of retail outlets they need considering the size and location of the market, regional variations in customer requirements, and the availability of suitable premises and channel partners. They must also consider the following:

Positioning: how it will position its retail network against those of the competition in terms of prestige, brand and corporate image, to differentiate it and add customer value (Raff & Schmitt, 2016).

Location: prestigious, high-value brands may operate retail outlets only in more affluent areas, whereas fast-moving consumer goods (FMCG) brands may require blanket coverage of a region or nation. Some manufacturers may require representation in locations specific to their core audience (e.g. ski manufacturers would need shops in ski resorts).

Pricing: pricing itself may be driven by the relative affluence of local customers, the strength of local competition, and the extent to which the resulting demand is elastic. It is also determined by marketing and business objectives (e.g. lower pricing if increasing market share is a priority, higher pricing if moving upmarket is more important).

Store characteristics: store image and atmospherics convey the firm's brand (Blazquez et al., 2019), so if a store location might tarnish the brand (e.g. by the presence of low-budget operators), the firm may consider the local profit opportunities cancelled out by the risk to brand prestige and sustainability.

Product mix and volumes: the product mix to be sold by a retailer and the anticipated sales volumes dictate the size of the store and its required capacity to display stock to customers.

Service levels: customers' service demands and expectations must be considered (e.g. the most desirable car brands have luxurious dedicated waiting suites for service customers).

Types of Retailer

Most people think of retailers as shops and stores, but there are several more common types, which are chosen to suit local customer needs, market potential, and product characteristics (Table 15.3).

Some organisations choose **multi-channel** or **omni-channel retailing** through a mixture of retailer types, believing that customers cannot be categorised into using only one retail outlet, but may use a variety according to their needs and expectations. Additionally, some trade door-to-door through **non-store retailing,** reducing overhead and building closer customer relationships (e.g. Avon cosmetics), and others conduct business digitally through **online retailing,** harnessing its responsiveness and low cost.

TABLE 15.3

Functions and characteristics of types of retailers.

Retailer type	Functions and Characteristics
Supermarkets and hypermarkets	• focus on perishable goods, especially groceries • large shops where customers can buy their weekly provisions in one place • ample parking, usually free to customers • low profit margins (under 5% are common) • large overall profits due to high sales volumes • major companies, few in number, often internationally owned (e.g. by Walmart in the US) • self-service and staffed checkouts • little customer product advice
Convenience stores	• like mini-supermarkets based in neighbourhoods • smaller than supermarkets, and stocking a much more limited range • focus on consumable goods, and perhaps newspapers and magazines • prices and profit per unit are higher than supermarkets • sell in much smaller quantities than supermarkets • limited private parking or street parking • often franchised • self-service or staffed check-outs • little customer product advice
Department stores	• prestigious multi-storey shops based in major centres of consumerism • focus mainly on housewares and fashion • sell reputed brands • relatively expensive • wide selection of high-quality products • areas of the store often leased to concessionaires (i.e. independent retailers who benefit from the footfall to sell their own products, such as perfumes and cosmetics) • plentiful customer product advice • high service levels
Speciality stores	• focus on one product category or purchase occasion (e.g. home improvements, gardening, car maintenance, furniture)
Variety stores	• stock a mixture of loosely connected products likely to appeal to the same shoppers
Discount stores	• entice customers with a promise of very cheap everyday products • often have a standard price (e.g. $1 or £1) and change product quantities

Retailer type	Functions and Characteristics
	• proliferate in less affluent centres of consumerism • low prestige • little care given to display and presentation • often poor product quality • business model sometimes called 'pile them high, sell them cheap' • little customer product advice; staff replenish stock or process purchases
Discount sheds	• large, out-of-town retailers (like discount stores, but bigger) • focus on a strong price offer • often located on retail estates with ample parking • little customer product advice; staff replenish stock or process purchases
Niche marketers	• usually found in smaller retail units in shopping malls and airports • focus on one specific product type (e.g. ties, handbags, whisky) • very wide choice within specialist product area • respected or prestigious reputation • expensive or mid-priced • good or excellent product knowledge, expertise, and service
Catalogue showrooms	• customers choose product from printed or digital catalogues, order at a counter, and have the product brought to them packaged without having seen it physically displayed • premises almost entirely dedicated to stock storage rather than accommodating customers • low store overhead

MARKETING DIRECTOR TASK

In Germany, France, and Italy, there are numerous dealers which commit insufficient resources to representing Zomotor, damaging sales volumes and revenue. Most of these underperforming dealerships have agreed to rescind the franchise, allowing Zomotor to appoint replacements. Lee is keen that newly recruited dealerships start strongly in their territories and that the manufacturer-dealer relationship is healthy. Lee realises the importance of working with channel partners on projects which are specific to their individual territories. For instance, they sometimes ask their regional managers to accompany dealership salesperson on high-potential corporate sales visits. Please help Lee to produce a list of additional actions which Zomotor and each newly appointed dealer could undertake collaboratively to build their relationship.

PHOTO 15.9
Many charities and not-for-profit organisations raise money from retail sales.

Chapter Summary

Channels to market comprise the partners and activities which get products or services from the originator (usually the manufacturer) to the customer or consumer. By working with intermediaries, value is added to the customer proposition, enabling each organisation to focus on their core activities. Partners help each other, not only in moving and storing products and sharing risk but also in marketing and selling the goods. Channel intermediaries include service providers like marketing agencies and transport companies, as they impact on customer satisfaction and service. Careful selection and management of partners is vital. Through training and incentivisation, firms can reduce channel conflict and nurture fruitful collaborations.

Key Learning Outcomes

▶ Organisations must design and maintain effective routes to market.

▶ Channel intermediaries undertake a variety of crucial roles.

▶ Power and conflict can undermine channel efficiency.

▶ Intermediary, customer, and firm requirements should underpin channel management decisions.

Recommended Reading

Croonen, E. P., & Broekhuizen, T. L. (2019). How do franchisees assess franchisor trustworthiness? *Journal of Small Business Management, 57*(3), 845–871.

Eshghi, K., & Ray, S. (2019). Managing channel conflict: Insights from the current literature. In *Handbook of research on distribution channels*. Edward Elgar Publishing.

Reimann, F., & Ketchen Jr, D. J. (2017). Power in supply chain management. *Journal of Supply Chain Management, 53*(2), 3–9.

References

Aykol, B., & Leonidou, L. C. (2018). Exporter-importer business relationships: Past empirical research and future directions. *International Business Review, 27*(5), 1007–1021.

Blazquez, M., Boardman, R., & Xu, L. (2019). International flagship stores: An exploration of store atmospherics and their influence on purchase behaviour. *International Journal of Business and Globalisation, 22*(1), 110–126.

Boyaci, T., & Gallego, G. (2004). Supply chain coordination in a market with customer service competition. *Production and Operations Management, 13*(1), 3–22.

Carson, S. J., & Ghosh, M. (2019). An integrated power and efficiency model of contractual channel governance: Theory and empirical evidence. *Journal of Marketing, 83*(4), 101–120.

Chen, I. J., & Popovich, K. (2003). Understanding customer relationship management (CRM) people, process and technology. *Business Process Management Journal, 9*(5), 672–688.

Claro, D. P., & Claro, P. B. O. (2010). Collaborative buyer – supplier relationships and downstream information in marketing channels. *Industrial Marketing Management, 39*(2), 221–228.

Cui, R., & Shin, H. (2017). Sharing aggregate inventory information with customers: Strategic cross-selling and shortage reduction. *Management Science, 64*(1), 381–400.

Dukes, A., & Geylani, T. (2016). *Dominant retailers and their impact on marketing channels* (pp. 137–56). Edward Elgar.

Emmett, S., & Crocker, B. (2016). *The relationship-driven supply chain: Creating a culture of collaboration throughout the chain*. Routledge.

Frazier, G. L. (1999). Organizing and managing channels of distribution. *Journal of the Academy of Marketing Science, 27*(2), 226–240.

Frazier, G. L., & Lassar, W. M. (1996). Determinants of distribution intensity. *Journal of Marketing, 60*(4), 39–51.

Gallino, S., Moreno, A., & Stamatopoulos, I. (2016). Channel integration, sales dispersion, and inventory management. *Management Science, 63*(9), 2813–2831.

Gilliland, D. I., & Kim, S. K. (2019). Building customer-centric marketing channel relationships: A model of reseller motivation and control. In *Handbook on customer centricity*. Edward Elgar Publishing.

Goering, G. E. (2012). Corporate social responsibility and marketing channel coordination. *Research in Economics, 66*(2), 142–148.

Iacobucci, E., & Winter, R. A. (2017). European Law on selective distribution and internet sales: An economic perspective. *Antitrust Law Journal, 81*, 47.

Mehta, R., Dubinsky, A. J., & Anderson, R. E. (2002). Marketing channel management and the sales manager. *Industrial Marketing Management, 31*(5), 429–439.

Mullin, R. (2018). *Promotional marketing*. Routledge.

Palmatier, R., Stern, L., & El-Ansary, A. (2016). *Marketing channel strategy: Instructor's review copy*. Routledge.

Porter, M. E. (1980). *Value chain analysis*. Oxford University Press.

Raff, H., & Schmitt, N. (2016). Manufacturers and retailers in the global economy. *Canadian Journal of Economics/Revue canadienne d'économique, 49*(2), 685–706.

Rosenbloom, B., & Andras, T. L. (2008). Wholesalers as global marketers. *Journal of Marketing Channels, 15*(4), 235–252.

Rosenbloom, B., Larsen, T., & Smith, B. (2004). The effectiveness of upstream influence attempts in high and low context export marketing channels. *Journal of Marketing Channels, 11*(4), 3–19.

Srivastava Dabas, C., Sternquist, B., & Mahi, H. (2012). Organized retailing in India: Upstream channel structure and management. *Journal of Business & Industrial Marketing, 27*(3), 176–195.

Takata, H. (2016). Channel integration: An explanation according to David Teece's theory of the boundaries of the firm. In *Looking forward, looking back: Drawing on the past to shape the future of marketing* (pp. 176–176). Springer.

Trivedi, M. (1998). Distribution channels: An extension of exclusive retailership. *Management Science, 44*(7), 896–909.

Zimmerman, A., & Blythe, J. (2017). *Business to business marketing management: A global perspective*. Routledge.

Glossary

Agent: a person or firm which finds customers for a manufacturer's product and takes a commission

Baby boomer: someone born between 1945 and 1965 (approximately)

Broker: see *agent*

Channel conflict: conflict between two or more channel partners, at interpersonal or inter-firm level

Coercive power: derived through force or threats

Co-marketing: two or more organisations collaborating to market their products/brands together

Digital immigrants: people who grew up before the internet and email became commonplace

Digital natives: people who grew up after the internet and email became commonplace

Downstream channel partner: a channel partner which is closer to the end user

Exclusive dealing: an agreement banning a partner from representing competitors

Exclusive distribution: carefully appointing just a few, strategic channel partners

Exclusive network: a network of very few, prestigious retailers in a given area

Expert power: derived through one's respected reputation as an expert

Footfall: potential customers entering retail premises

Franchisee: a firm (usually retailer/dealer) permitted to adopt the manufacturer's brand

Generation X: someone born between 1966 and 1980 (approximately)

Generation Y: see *millennials/Generation Y*

Generation Z: someone born after 1996 (approximately)

Horizontal integration: for example, one wholesaler buying other wholesalers

Intensive network: a network of very many retailers in a given area

Intermediary: a channel partner between the originator/manufacturer and end users

Key performance indicators (KPIs): targets against which performance is measured

Legitimate power: derived from seniority, authority, the law or a contract

Millennials/Generation Y: someone born between 1981 and 1995 (approximately)

Omni-channel retailing: selling through a mixture of retail channels and retailer types

Product mix: the mix of a firm's products to be sold

Referent power: derived from being emulated as a leader

Retailer: a firm (usually a shop or store) which sells products to end users

Reward power: derived through incentivising good behaviours or performances

Selective network: a network of an intermediate number of respected retailers in a given area

Stock inventory: the goods stored (often by a wholesaler)

Tariffs: charges and taxes imposed upon imports and sales by government authorities

Tying agreement: contract making a downstream partner represent a supplier's full product range

Upstream channel partner: a channel partner which is further away from the end user

Vertical integration: for example, where a manufacturer buys their wholesalers and/or retailers

Wholesaler: a firm which usually manages the flow of goods between manufacturers and retailers

Channel Management Case Study: Feragaia's Ambitious Spirit

Established in Scotland in 2019, Feragaia is a zero-alcohol, zero-sugar spirit distilled from 14 botanicals such as chamomile, seaweed, blackcurrant, and bay leaves. Whilst competitors in the emerging 'non-alcoholic spirit drinks' category distil alcohol off, Feragaia uses no alcohol during production. The Feragaia product, supplied in recyclable bottles and packaging, is complex and distinct in flavour. It is neither a whisky nor a gin, but is intended to be served neat, over ice, with a splash of water, with soda or tonic, or in 'mocktails' (alcohol-free cocktails). The production process takes inspiration from Scottish distillation techniques developed mainly in the whisky and gin spirit categories. By combining these techniques with a few of its own, Feragaia has achieved a completely alcohol free spirit. At £25 (approximately $34 or €28) for a 50cl bottle, it is priced closely to single malt whisky or premium gin.

Jamie Wild and Bill Garnock, who had been US-based executives for alcohol multinationals, founded Feragaia in their late twenties at a time when sales

continued

419

of alcohol-free and soft drinks in UK pubs, bars, and restaurants were soaring. Initiatives like 'Dry January' and 'Go Sober for October' have become popular amongst Brits seeking health benefits or ways to avoid falling foul of the country's strict drink-driving laws.

In January 2020, Feragaia won a supply contract with the prestigious, internationally renowned London department store, Harrod's. By the end of 2020, Feragaia had around 50 stockists in Northern Scotland, around 100 elsewhere in Scotland, one in Northern Ireland, one in Wales, two in the North of England, one in the English Midlands, 17 in London, and seven elsewhere in Southern England. Stockists include pubs, bars, hotels, guest houses, restaurants, whisky specialists, motorway services, department stores, and gift shops and are spread haphazardly throughout the UK, without overseas representation. The recruitment of a business development executive in early 2021 sees the brand seeking expansion both domestically and into selected foreign markets, including North America and the Middle East.

If Jamie and Bill hired you as their marketing consultant, what distribution strategy would you advise them to pursue in the UK and abroad? Which types of businesses should they try to recruit as retailers? What would be the commercial benefits of your suggested approach? How would you target and measure success? And how would you ensure that stockists represent your brand properly and drive forward your commercial performance? Prepare a comprehensive mind map so that you can present your recommendations to Jamie and Bill for ten minutes.

Sources

Feragaia website. Retrieved December 23, 2020, from www.feragaia.com

The Courier (Scotland). May 12, 2020 issue. Retrieved December 23, 2020, from https://www.thecourier.co.uk/fp/lifestyle/food-drink/1311406/a-sobering-time-why-scots-are-drinking-less-during-lockdown/

The Courier (Scotland). December 22, 2020 issue. Retrieved December 23, 2020, from https://www.thecourier.co.uk/fp/lifestyle/food-drink/1834534/feragaia-harrods-deal/

Edinburgh News. January 5, 2020. Retrieved December 23, 2020, from https://www.edinburghnews.scotsman.com/business/non-alcoholic-scottish-spirit-brings-pop-bar-edinburgh-1355114

The Herald (Scotland), December 21, 2020 issue. Retrieved December 23, 2020, from https://www.heraldscotland.com/business_hq/18959919.fife-alcohol-free-spirit-feragaia-hits-harrods-shelves-waterfront-site-bought-housing-butcher-hails-successful-christmas-36-years/

16 Digital Marketing

LEARNING OBJECTIVES

▶ To identify the media and tools used in digital marketing

▶ To explore the principles and ethics of interaction with audiences digitally

▶ To gauge the integration of digital and offline marketing

▶ To analyse good practice in creating user experience

Introduction to Digital Marketing

Digital media and online tools play an increasingly important role in marketing. We have embedded digital marketing throughout this book, as it is usually works in tandem with traditional, or offline, marketing. It adheres to broadly the same principles, but with online-specific considerations relating to privacy and ethics, and the mobile contexts in which customers use digital technology (Reyna et al., 2018). However, certain factors and issues are specific to digital marketing and worthy of separate consideration. Online and digital marketing now accounts for roughly 50% of global marketing spend. It experienced rapid growth during the first two decades of the 21st century due to the huge increase in internet usage amongst the general population, the explosion of social media engagement as a phenomenon, and the proliferation of smartphone ownership. It will never entirely replace traditional marketing methods, but it is emerging as the dominant partner due to its manifold benefits to suppliers and customers alike.

Online activities enable skilful marketers to create buzz – excitement amongst the public. This may result in online social contagion and electronic word of mouth (Filieri & McLeay, 2014), which spreads positive communications amongst consumers inexpensively and credibly. Market mavens – those consumers with expertise in certain product categories who disseminate this knowledge to others – can exert greater influence as

DOI: 10.4324/9781003170891-17

PHOTO 16.1
The domains of outdoor and digital advertising often overlap nowadays.

online opinion leaders (Clark et al., 2008; Sahelices-Pinto & Rodríguez-Santos, 2014), reaching a broader audience via blogs, vlogs, and online reviews. Organisations may also use digital technology to research and segment the market; a salient example is Tesco's collecting of customer data for targeted promotions via their Clubcard. Consumers benefit from digital marketing by being able to conduct information searches on comparative products quickly and remotely, to reduce in-store waiting by placing 'click-and-collect' orders, or by paying online for home-delivered goods. Just as importantly, they are able to interact spontaneously with their favourite brands, deriving enjoyment and a sense of involvement and community.

What Is Digital Marketing?

Digital marketing, or online marketing, is the promotion of brands, products, or services using the internet and other forms of digitally enabled communication. It facilitates customer interaction and involvement, often breaking down the barriers between a seller and a customer or blurring the boundaries between them. The days of passive marketing recipients are largely gone, as consumers seek to co-construct value alongside their favourite brands.

The main categories of digital marketing are (i) **digital advertising**; (ii) **content marketing**; (iii) **email marketing**; (iv) **marketing automation**; (v) **search engine marketing** (SEM); and (vi) **social media marketing** (SMM) – each of which we will explore in greater detail. Digital marketing can also provide a vehicle for other areas of marketing activity, such as relationship marketing and market research, or be intertwined with them (Benyon, 2019). For instance, organisations may elongate customer relationships and stimulate meaningful customer interactions (relationship marketing) by using digital technology and media. Indeed, digital applications enable new ways of employing the marketing communications mix, which can be designed to reflect customer segment needs and individuals' progress along the customer journey. The digital media used by marketers – the online places where they locate their marketing activities – are usually categorised as **owned media, paid media**, and **earned media**.

MARKETING ASSISTANT TASK

In Mexico, Tannya's boss wishes Zomotor to build a stronger online presence to create positive, brand-related discussions between customers. Some dealer salespeople and managers have com- plained that they find this inappropriate and an unnecessary change in what they perceive as a traditional industry and marketplace. The complaints invariably come from people who are nervous about change because they lack knowledge of the internet. However, other comments are from dealer contacts who use and understand the internet reasonably well but are less familiar with the potential efficacy of EWOM.

Tannya's manager has asked her to give a five-minute speech at Zomotor Mexico's annual dealer conference, and he would like to like to dedicate two or three minutes to addressing their concerns about this issue, defending the use of digital marketing and expounding its benefits. Please help her by recording a first draft speech on your smartphone.

Digital Disruption

Digital media have 'disrupted' marketing, forcing organisations to rethink their entire approach to marketing (Vieira et al., 2019). There are several themes, issues or phenomena within digital marketing which have produced this **digital disruption**:

▶   *User experience*: digital media enable unique user experiences which are tailored to their individual interests and needs rather than to those of a broader group

▶ *Free data*: readily available to marketers (although it is usually necessary to complement this with new data, which costs money to generate)

▶ *Subscription models*: 'memberships', which grant users access to online resources for a monthly fee (e.g. iFit fitness app, Netflix)

▶ *Usership over ownership*: being able to use something or have access to it has often become more important or desirable than owning it. For instance, increasing numbers of consumers prefer to access their favourite songs on Spotify than to own compact discs or physical copies of them. A side effect is **dematerialisation** – a reduced dependence upon physical resources.

▶ *On demand*: the purchasing, by consumers who may lack time or resources, of services from people who have time and those resources; perhaps the most salient example is Uber, the ride-sharing app

▶ *Freemium*: a pricing strategy which allows consumers to have free access to a basic service or, for a subscription fee, an improved (premium) service (Sato, 2019), such as language app Duolingo's advert-free version

Digital media have simultaneously redefined customer expectations and the ways in which brands market to, and trade with, their preferred market segments.

Types of Digital Marketing Media

Owned Media

Owned media are those online media which are the property of the organisation which is using them for its marketing. The most obvious example of owned media is the firm's own website or mobile site, but newsletters, blogs, and catalogues may also be owned media. Perhaps the major benefit of owned media is that the firm has absolute **control over content**: the message content, tone, graphics, and brand elements. The firm does not have to share screen space with rival brands or place itself at the mercy of a host media which will decide how prominently to display its content. Owned media can also accommodate **online sales**. For example, customers visiting the website of mattress manufacturer Dormeo can order their products for home delivery rather than entering a physical store where competitor product may be displayed (Ho et al., 2020). In this way, owned media can help brands to 'take their customers out of the market' by addressing their needs before they shop around.

Many firms have their own **social media accounts**. Whilst these are hosted by platforms such as Facebook and are therefore not entirely autonomous, they provide high levels of control and an ability to target audiences which might not necessarily visit the firm's website without prompting. Additionally, many have video channels hosted by video streaming platforms. Drinks manufacturer Red Bull maintains a powerful presence in part through its YouTube channel, on which it shows footage of motorsports and extreme sports which it has commissioned or sponsored. Their videos of wingsuit divers, base jumpers, and motorcycle stunt riders generate millions of visits and huge amounts of buzz amongst the general public. When Austrian skydiver Felix Baumgartner free-fell from a helium balloon 24 miles above New Mexico in 2012, millions of viewers tuned in to watch the live stream; the event was a major news item across the world and a common topic of conversation amongst friends and acquaintances globally. The enormous reach of the content significantly expanded recognition of Red Bull's brand and reinforced its bold values.

Paid Media

Paid media are those media which are not the property of the organisation being marketed but belong to third parties. Traditionally, these have included print and broadcast adverts and billboard posters, all of which are placed in spaces rented from others. In the context of digital marketing, paid media comprise social media adverts (rather than social media accounts), Google Ads, pay-per-click and display ads, retargeting, and the paying of influencers. **Social media adverts** represent a brand on Facebook, Pinterest, LinkedIn, or another social media site and typically appear on users' news feeds as sponsored ads, or as banner or skyscraper ads. These can be targeted by the platform to users who are a close match to the brand, by using their cookies (browsing history).

Google Ads is an online platform which displays adverts, product listings, and videos for firms which have successfully bid for the advertising space. These adverts may be placed in the search engine results or on other websites or apps. For instance, if a student in the North East of England has been searching on Google to help decide which universities to apply to, they are likely to find an advert for Northumbria University above or amongst their search engine results. Additionally, if they visit YouTube later that week to watch a music video or view a fashion show, they are also likely to see Northumbria University adverts – probably as pop-up ads in the bottom of the video screen. Pay-per-click advertising uses a similar principal, but the promoted company pays the platform owner only when a user clicks on the ad to find out more information. This usually redirects the user to a landing page which belongs to the brand (i.e. owned media) and is dedicated to the particular product or promotion in which the user has expressed an interest. This is intended to channel the user to the firm's website or even to make a purchase. The firm may set a spend limit so that, for instance, the adverts disappear when 50,000 clicks have been achieved, thereby assisting the budgeting process and ensuring an outcome from the spend. **Display ads** are visual ads placed on a third party's website for a fee (e.g. a betting company may display adverts on a football club's website).

Retargeting is the targeting of internet users who have already visited a firm's website but left without making a purchase. It is estimated that around 97% of website visitors fall into this category. The underlying principle is that people who were sufficiently motivated to visit a brand's website, either as the result of a search or motivated by an advert, are much more likely than others to buy from that brand. Naturally, they may have left the website due to finding the brand, product, or service unsuitable for them. But it is possible that they simply ran out of time, were interrupted, or needed some time to consider the potential purchase or to compare alternatives (Li et al., 2021). By retargeting these visitors, brands can offer an inducement to place an order, such as a timed discount, rather than wasting marketing spend on unnecessarily building initial brand awareness. In this way, conversion rates and profitability are improved.

Paid influencers are influential members of the public who are paid by brands to promote brands on social media. They may be paid money to do this, especially if they have a very large number of followers, such as leading Instagram and Twitter influencers (Wellman et al., 2020). However, they may be paid in free products or sponsorship. For example, a small number of people make YouTube videos and Facebook blogs about hillwalking and wild camping in the Scottish Highlands. The most popular of these are skilled and knowledgeable presenters who use drone photography and employ sophisticated production techniques to build a sizeable gathering; typical numbers are 6,000 subscribers, 20,000 views per video, and 5,000 views in the first week after posting. Clearly, these popular influencers have a loyal following of outdoor enthusiasts who are likely to be interested in buying tents, boots, waterproof clothing, walking poles, and many associated products. As a result, leading manufacturers of such products may provide the influencers with free gear to use and review. Influencers should declare that such an arrangement is in place (i.e. a declaration of interest) to ensure openness.

Earned Media

Earned media consists of any online content which has not been paid for by the brand being promoted. The most usual forms are **social media shares, likes, mentions** and **reposts, tweets and retweets, reviews**, and **unpaid endorsement by influencers**. It is often referred to as **electronic word of mouth (EWOM)**, as it is largely **peer to peer (P2P)**. Such communications enjoy a high level of credibility, as audience members trust each other to make more objective, reliable judgments about a brand than the brand would itself. They are usually also very inexpensive, take little or no management, may last much longer than other forms of online marketing, and can transcend geopolitical or cultural boundaries. However, the firm has little or no control over the message, so is dependent upon its brand being communicated in a supportive, positive manner. Negative EWOM can be extremely damaging.

Types of Digital Marketing

Digital Advertising

Digital or online advertising is any form of marketing communication which advertises or promotes a product, service, or brand on digital platforms or channels. It takes many forms; perhaps the most widespread is **display advertising**, in which text, videos, animations, logos, and other visual content are used to convey a brand within a website or on social media. Typically, third-party websites are used, such as a sportswear brand maintaining a presence through Facebook adverts or a car rental company advertising on an airline's website. However, marketers may also target display advertising at audiences in public spaces like airports, sports stadia, or hotels by using electronic advertising boards.

On third-party websites, adverts often appear as **banner ads** (wide and short) or **skyscraper ads** (tall and thin) around the edge of the website's core content. **Floating, expanding**, and **pop-up ads** are versions which change position, shape, or size to grab the attention. Some advertisers use 'clickbait', or provocative statements or questions to encourage audiences to click on the ad to access content. For instance, a banner may carry a photo of someone on a cliff edge and the text, 'These photos were taken seconds before disaster', to capitalise upon people's natural curiosity. **Sponsored stories** or **news feed ads** appear on social media sites and are targeted at individuals based upon the browsing history indicated by their cookies. For example, if you have recently visited package holiday websites, you are likely to see adverts from travel agencies on your next visit to Facebook.

Mobile advertising depends upon tablets and particularly smartphones to reach its targets. Often it takes the same forms as mentioned above but is tailored towards the limitations and advantages of these smaller devices. For this reason, content may need to be repositioned, condensed, and split across more pages to fit within the device screen and be legible. Likewise, content may be specific to the user's current geographical location so that, for instance, a Londoner visiting Edinburgh would see restaurant

427

deals and department store promotions taking place in Edinburgh, thereby increasingly the likelihood of stimulating unplanned, impulse purchases (Rafieian & Yoganarasim-han, 2021). This may be of real value to the user, not just the advertiser. **Chat advertising** may also benefit users as it allows them to type questions and receive instant responses from the advertising firm's customer service staff – or perhaps from automated **chatbots**. This may be welcome if the user is trying to decipher complicated information or product specifications, like comparing a motor dealership's used car offers.

Online advertising provides marketers with a number of key benefits. The **targetability** of adverts to potential customers based upon their profile, behavioural, and psychographic segment characteristics (i.e. who they are, what they do, and how they think) reduces wasted marketing and increases customer response rates. Modern, eye-catching, and **interactive** formats are more impactful than printed ads and more accessible than outdoor ads, driving **audience engagement**. Digital advertising is **fast and responsive**: a campaign or message can be launched within hours of a strategic marketing decision being made, which contrasts with, for instance, the many months it may take to have a billboard poster displayed. Moreover, online media provide an impressive **reach** which is not curtailed by national or regional boundaries but can travel internationally. As the adverts are replicable across a large target audience, the **cost per customer**, and even the **total cost**, is likely to be relatively low when compared with traditional media. Moreover, the success of an advert may be easily measured by the exhaustive **metrics** generated by software. Marketers can deduce which adverts or messages garnered the best responses from whom, when, and through which websites, thereby enabling them to hone their targeting decisions and improve their return on investment.

However, online advertising may be intrusive, like flashing pop-up ads when you are trying to access the information on the webpage underneath. They may also exacerbate some customers' problem behaviours, such as compulsive or addictive consumption, by constantly confronting them with offers for a specific product category. More broadly, it contributes to the unnecessary consumerism which can impoverish customers and exhaust the earth's resources. Advertisers themselves may also experience commercial disadvantages, such as 'banner blindness', in which repeated exposure to online advertising may fatigue consumers or make them impervious to adverts. Firms may also suffer from the use of ad-blocker software, and – on 'freemium' service sites such as Duolingo – users paying subscriptions to remove adverts, potentially leaving advertisers with the more price-conscious audience members.

Content Marketing

Content is the term for tailored marketing materials generated by a brand for distribution to a carefully selected audience which is intended to find the materials enjoyable and worthwhile, encouraging prospects to adopt the brand for the first time through trial purchase, and encouraging existing customers to become more loyal to the brand, resulting in more frequent and high-value purchases. **Content marketing** entails creating and distributing content online to targeted audiences to increase awareness and visibility, credibility, engagement, profitability, and sales. It uses a variety of formats, including **blogs, vlogs, podcasts**, photographs and videos, **infographics**, news items, articles, e-books, guides, and case studies. Before the advent of digital technology, content marketers relied on traditional means to reach their audiences. For example, in the early 20th century, the French tyre manufacturer Michelin distributed hard copies of their Michelin Guide about tourist destinations, hotels, and restaurants to stimulate consumers' desire to travel by car. Later in the century, content could be distributed via mass media (e.g. magazines, newspapers) or even within the packaging of goods. The online places most commonly used nowadays for content marketing are companies' own websites and platforms such as YouTube, LinkedIn, Tumblr, Yelp, or Pinterest.

Content marketing is not a separate entity within digital marketing, but a vital constituent part of all forms of digital marketing. For example, appropriate, relevant, and impactful content is necessary for a successful email marketing campaign or SMM strategy. It performs several important functions:

▶ Informs and educates the audience about the firm's brand, products, and services

▶ Demonstrates benefits of those products and services, rather than features

▶ Nurtures relationships between the firm and its customers (i.e. part of its relationship marketing strategy)

▶ Drives inbound traffic (i.e. people visiting the firm's website or physical stores), including pay-per-click traffic, and boosts conversion rates more generally (e.g. website visits to store visits/quotations to purchases)

▶ Addresses important public relations issues

▶ Enables quality input which search engines reward in an SEO strategy

▶ Builds a brand community

MARKETING MANAGER TASK

Dylan has been given substantial funds to implement a digital marketing and social media strategy. With Western social media platforms unavailable to him in China, he plans to use WeChat in place of Facebook, Sina Weibo instead of Twitter, Toudou Youku in lieu of YouTube, and the popular lifestyle discussion platform Douban. He cannot simply replicate what has been done in Europe, Australia, New Zealand, and North America, as the needs, expectations, and cultures of the target audience are different. Help Dylan by listing factors which he should take into consideration when designing the tone and content of his digital marketing in China.

Email Marketing

Email marketing is a firm's emails sent to its listed customers and prospects for the purposes of communicating new products, promotions, and discounts. It is much less expensive than sending printed materials, as it incurs no postage charges and fewer production costs. It is also a very fast and easy way to contact many recipients simultaneously without the need for an intermediary. The four main categories of marketing emails are as follows:

▶ **Acquisition emails**, which seek to encourage initial purchases from prospects who are not currently customers

▶ **Retention emails**, which seek to retain existing customers by maintaining the relationship and/or by encouraging repeat purchases

▶ **Promotional emails**, which give details of time-bound incentives to buy (e.g. a carpet warehouse offering 25% discount on all orders placed by the end of the month)

▶ **Email newsletters**, which provide current information about the brand, useful advice, and knowledge, broadening the extent of customer engagement with the brand

Despite its benefits, email marketing is often rather untargeted, sending a uniform message to a broad variety of people on the firm's database (Olson et al., 2021). It lacks interactivity and imagination, may be perceived as old-fashioned, can struggle to

PHOTO 16.2
By emailing store receipts to customers, firms can save paper and may also be able to keep in touch with customers via email for marketing purposes, with the customers' permission.

make itself heard against the background noise of everyday marketing communications, and some prospects and customers may find it an annoying and intrusive interruption, potentially alienating them from the brand.

Marketing Automation

Certain online activities, such as email marketing and posting social media content, can sometimes become unskilled, repetitive tasks which require no new human input to execute. Therefore, organisations may automate some or all of these functions to cut wage costs or to free up marketing staff for more sophisticated tasks. **Marketing automation** is often used when sending emails to relatively cold prospects with little potential, as the firm may consider it simply as a 'numbers game' which requires little skill or personalisation to produce a certain conversion rate. It is also employed for other activities which appertain to the collation and usage of customer data. Global spend on automated marketing is expected to reach $25 million by 2023.

Search Engine Marketing and Search Engine Optimisation

Search engine marketing (SEM) aims to increase the visibility of a brand within search engine results pages (SERPs). For example, a firm such as Parkdean Holidays – a major British holiday park owner – would wish for it to be the first result, or one of the first results, generated when consumers enter such terms into Google and other search engines as 'self-catering accommodation', 'family holidays', or 'static caravan parks'. Therefore, it may choose to use a **paid inclusion** approach, paying the search engine to include its brand prominently in results (although this is not allowed by Google or Ask). A more likely approach is to use **search engine optimisation (SEO),** in which website engineers design the structure and content of a firm's website to produce a more highly prioritised search result (Das, 2021). Many consumers only view the first page of search engine results when seeking a supplier of products, and many do not even scroll down to view the results on the bottom half of the page. Therefore, if a brand wishes to increase its market share and sales volumes, SEO is often central to this.

GLOBAL MARKETING TASK

If you were to market your university or company online to a new country, what sort of information do you think you might need to ensure that your web presence is appropriate and sufficient, and that the content and media choices meet the needs of your new audience? In a simple table, list six things you would need to know about the country and its population, and how you might research them.

Social Media Marketing

SMM uses platforms such as Facebook, Twitter, Snapchat, Instagram, LinkedIn, YouTube, Yelp, and Tumblr. Firms may adopt a **passive approach**, observing customers' comments about their products on social media to gain valuable yet inexpensive market insights, or may pursue an **active approach**, which is concerned more prominently with reaching out to their audience through public relations techniques, including the use of social media influencers.

SMM has a number of advantages. The media is modern and interactive, so firms can establish a dialogue with their audiences in real time and stimulate P2P communication. It is often relatively inexpensive and can be targeted efficiently, reducing wasted marketing (Li et al., 2021). Moreover, the success of an SMM strategy is easily measured, as platforms provide their customers (the organisations being promoted online) with comprehensive metrics. This in turn helps advertisers to fine tune their content.

STAKEHOLDER TASK

As a digital marketer for a supermarket, you are concerned that your online presence is geared exclusively towards your retail customers and that your employees are neglected. Produce a five-minute slide presentation on potential ways in which you undertake internal marketing (i.e. marketing to your workforce) digitally.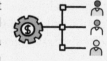

The Digital Customer Journey and Multiple Channels

A key strength of digital marketing is its capacity to take different approaches at different parts of the customer journey, and to do so as part of an IMC strategy. It is essential to consider the digital customer journey in the context of the entire journey – online and offline (Weber & Chatzopoulos, 2019). At the beginning of the customer journey (the **prospect phase**), audience members have little or no awareness of the brand, so marketing communications should address this. However, later in the customer journey (in the **acquisition phase**), users have much more awareness and information but need persuading to see the brand more favourably so that they buy product. Later still (in the **retention phase**) the firm must encourage customers to develop brand loyalty and make further purchases. In this way, digital marketing is an ideal way to conduct relationship marketing, establishing meaningful customer touchpoints. However, it is rarely used in isolation, instead working to complement other channels of marketing communication such as retail stores, printed materials, and broadcasts. When this occurs, it is part of a multichannel or omnichannel strategy.

A **multichannel strategy** centres around the organisation, using multiple channels to communicate to prospects and customers. At each stage of the customer journey, it is likely to target the customer with several types of communication. For example, during the prospect phase, it may use online forums and website content to complement broadcast and print advertising. The ways in which customers act at various stages of the journey are largely dictated by the resources provided by the firm.

An **omnichannel strategy** places customers, rather than the firm, at the centre of the process, providing information and selling to customers through multiple touchpoints. These include websites, smartphone apps, social media, retail stores, mail order, and freephone numbers. Unlike in multichannel, there is a very integrated approach which facilitates cross-selling across channels. An example of this is enabling customers to check in-store product stock availability via a website, and the **click-and-collect** process, which became so popular during COVID-19 lockdowns. Pricing across all channels is consistent to ensure credibility and avoid products from being 'distressed' (i.e. undercutting themselves on price), and customers are allowed to return product regardless of the channel through which they bought it. This gives customers peace of mind to purchase items such as clothes online without trying them first, although it has produced a logistical burden for selling firms.

Channels perform different roles which complement each other:

Stores and retail premises give customers an opportunity (i) to touch, feel, and try on products; (ii) to compare different items; (iii) to immediately obtain products and satisfy spontaneous needs (such as a soft drink to quench thirst); and (iv) to return products easily.

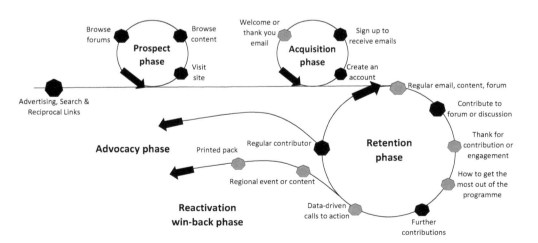

FIGURE 16.1
The Multichannel Customer Journey (adapted from Strahlberg & Maila, 2014)

Web-based resources provide (i) round-the-clock availability of product information, (ii) impartial customer reviews, (iii) latest pricing and promotion details, and (iv) some personalisation (e.g. recommending product based upon past purchases or browsing history).

Printed matter (i) conveys the appearance of products (i.e. with colour photographs) and (ii) constitutes a permanent object which the customer can keep close at hand – perhaps on their coffee table – whilst they contemplate a decision.

Prospects and customers often skip from one channel to another according to the evolution of their needs throughout the customer journey or purchase decision. This is perhaps most pronounced if the purchase is of a high value, infrequently bought, and carries a risk if the wrong decision is made. For example, a serious musician buying a piano may (i) recognise their need for a new piano when witnessing attractive new product in a store; (ii) search for product information on websites operated by the piano brand and by its competitors and retailers; (iii) seek the opinions of other users on social media; (iv) try different products in store; and (v) order a product and pay for it online.

When putting together a strategy to increase success at the touchpoints along the customer journey, digital marketers should at all times consider **user experience (UX)**. Laptops and even tablets are becoming a less preferred tool for accessing the internet, as more people consume web-based content on smartphones. This has broad implications: content must be designed to be legible on a smaller screen; firms may wish to introduce apps; marketers may track the locations of users (with their permission) to offer messages, information, or offers which are targeted at where they live, or where they are shopping at the time of engagement. As UX is subjective, users will experience web context within the contexts in which they view it – such as commuting on a train, before they get out of bed in the morning, or perhaps during university marketing lectures!

MARKETING DIRECTOR TASK

Lee wishes to harness the power of digital marketing by targeting opinion leaders – those influential and well-admired consumers whose recommendations are taken seriously by peers. Highly motivated by technology, they demand detailed specification lists and technical information. Lee realises that a successful digital marketing campaign will need to make special provision for opinion leaders. Help them by writing a short report describing the likely characteristics and interests of motor industry opinion leaders in Europe and North America, explaining how the campaign can be designed to cater to them without alienating the mass market.

Ethical Considerations

As with other forms of marketing, some audience members may not wish to be approached, considering it to be intrusive. Although users have a choice of whether to allow cookies when visiting a website and whether to unsubscribe from email distribution lists, they are not always aware of this or of the implications. **Permission marketing** is marketing to people who have volunteered personal data (especially contact details) and consented to being contacted for marketing purposes. Many people give data reluctantly to achieve a benefit, such as saving time or receiving useful product data. For example, they may give a great deal of information about themselves to an online insurance aggregator like GoCompare or CompareTheMarket to get instantaneous comparative quotes for car or home insurance but have concerns about the privacy of their data – how it is collected, used, archived, shared, and destroyed – and worry about being pestered. Digital marketers should adhere not just to legal regulations such as the EU General Data Protection Regulation (GDPR) but also to the principals of ethical practice.

The internet potentially provides minors and vulnerable adults to marketing produced by drinks companies, betting firms, tobacco goods manufacturers, and other producers of problematic goods. This necessitates a rigorous process to detect and discourage inappropriate user engagement. Contrastingly, a **digital divide** exists in all global regions, in which some people cannot access the internet due to poverty or lack of infrastructure or knowledge (Ragnedda & Ruiu, 2020). Marketers should consider how it prevents those people from being commercially excluded.

PHOTO 16.3
Junk email can be tiresome and intrusive.

ETHICS TASK

As a marketer for a supermarket, you are concerned that many of your poorer and more vulnerable customers are unreachable through online marketing due to the digital divide. This has brand and commercial implications for the supermarket, but it also means that the neediest customers may miss opportunities to save money through discounts and promotions. List three initiatives which the company could make to help reduce this social inequality, discussing the relative merits of each.

Measuring Digital Marketing Success

The measurability of digital marketing is one of its great strengths, and there is a huge number of metrics available to ascertain the success of a strategy, campaign, or action (Pandey et al., 2020). They fall into three categories:

- **Activity (input) metrics**: show what the firm has done (e.g. number of social media posts)
- **Interaction (response) metrics**: show how the audience responds to these inputs and materials (e.g. number of likes, comments, shares)
- **Performance (outcome) metrics**: show the outcomes of firms' activities (e.g. customer satisfaction, market share)

Some of the major metrics include the following:

- **Conversion rate**: any metrics which indicate the number of inputs to generate a desired output (e.g. social media likes per unit sold)
- **Cost per conversion**: a conversion rate specifically measuring how much it has cost to achieve a specific conversion or response (e.g. for each additional store visit generated)
- **Bounce rate**: the percentage of website visitors who leave after only one page
- **Dwell time**: the amount of time someone spends on the firm's website between arriving from and returning to the SERP
- **Average session duration**: the average time which a user spends on the firm's website
- **Click-through rate**: the percentage of times when a web-based advert is clicked on by a user, taking them to the firm's landing page
- **Average search depth**: the average number of different pages on the firm's site visited by a user in one session

436

▶ **Page views per session**: the average number of pages (including repeated ones) visited by a user in one session

▶ **Time on page**: the time which a user spends on one specific page

▶ **Ad clicks**: the total number of times a web-based advert has been clicked

▶ **Cost per click**: the number of clicks divided by the cost of displaying the web-based advert

▶ **Return on investment (ROI)**: as in other areas of marketing, this is an overarching metric which indicates what percentage of the total digital marketing spend was recouped in incremental profit or savings. For example, if a firm spends £1 million on a web campaign which produces £2 million of additional profit, the ROI is 200%. (Naturally, immediate benefits, such as additional income or higher customer satisfaction scores, may also be partially responsible for subsequent benefits, such as incremental repeat sales or increasingly positive word of mouth.)

An analysis of metrics should underpin any digital marketing strategy (Saura et al., 2017; Saura, 2021).

METRICS EXERCISE

You are providing consultancy services to Northumbria University as it rolls out a digital marketing campaign to increase the number of 17- and 18-year-olds attending its open days and applying for undergraduate study. Design a single-screen 'dashboard' showing the most important metrics in a user-friendly, intuitive way which will help the university's senior executives to understand the success of the campaign and where to make changes. Try to use a variety of data presentation techniques.

Chapter Summary

Digital marketing is not separate to other forms of marketing but integrated with it and inseparable from it. Most prospects and customers spend time online and expect to interact with their chosen brands there. The needs and demands of users vary throughout the customer journey, and marketers should design their online presences accordingly. Successful firms use all three categories of media (paid, unpaid, and earned) and realise the importance of mobile marketing due to users' increasing preference for accessing information on smartphones, often outside the home. The proliferation of online reviews, and the ability of users to express their opinions to huge digital audiences, means that firms should foster strong online relationships to prevent negative EWOM,

PHOTO 16.4
The use of digital tools for marketing is not confined to promoting brands or even goods – this one is a public service announcement", and should be inserted in chapter 16 immediately after the section "However, the digital domain constitutes not just an attractive location in which to undertake modern, interactive, measurable marketing, but an essential one..

which could be very damaging. Firms should also carefully consider the ethical issues associated with digital marketing, and especially those relating to children and vulnerable adults, data privacy and security, and the need not to be intrusive. However, the digital domain constitutes not just an attractive location in which to undertake modern, interactive, measurable marketing, but an essential one.

Key Learning Outcomes

▶   Digital marketing uses three main categories of media, according to who owns them, and a wide variety of tools.

▶   Digital marketing enables a high degree of user interaction.

▶   Digital and offline marketing should be integrated and ideally user-focused within an omnichannel strategy.

Recommended Further Reading

Li, F., Larimo, J., & Leonidou, L. C. (2021). Social media marketing strategy: Definition, conceptualization, taxonomy, validation, and future agenda. *Journal of the Academy of Marketing Science*, *49*(1), 51–70.

Olson, E. M., Olson, K. M., Czaplewski, A. J., & Key, T. M. (2021). Business strategy and the management of digital marketing. *Business Horizons*, *64*(2), 285–293.

Saura, J. R. (2021). Using data sciences in digital marketing: Framework, methods, and performance metrics. *Journal of Innovation & Knowledge*, *6*(2), 92–102.

Wellman, M. L., Stoldt, R., Tully, M., & Ekdale, B. (2020). Ethics of authenticity: Social media influencers and the production of sponsored content. *Journal of Media Ethics*, *35*(2), 68–82.

References

Benyon, D. (2019). *Designing user experience*. Pearson.

Clark, R. A., Goldsmith, R. E., & Goldsmith, E. B. (2008). Market mavenism and consumer self-confidence. *Journal of Consumer Behaviour: An International Research Review*, *7*(3), 239–248.

Das, S. (2021). *Search engine optimization and marketing: A recipe for success in digital marketing*. CRC Press.

Filieri, R., & McLeay, F. (2014). E-WOM and accommodation: An analysis of the factors that influence travelers' adoption of information from online reviews. *Journal of Travel Research*, *53*(1), 44–57.

Ho, J., Pang, C., & Choy, C. (2020). Content marketing capability building: A conceptual framework. *Journal of Research in Interactive Marketing*, *14*(1), 133–151.

Li, J., Luo, X., Lu, X., & Moriguchi, T. (2021). The double-edged effects of e-commerce cart retargeting: Does retargeting too early backfire? *Journal of Marketing*, *85*(4).

Pandey, N., Nayal, P., & Rathore, A. S. (2020). Digital marketing for B2B organizations: Structured literature review and future research directions. *Journal of Business & Industrial Marketing*, *35*(7), 1191–1204.

Rafieian, O., & Yoganarasimhan, H. (2021). Targeting and privacy in mobile advertising. *Marketing Science*, *40*(2), 193–218.

Ragnedda, M., & Ruiu, M. L. (2020). *Digital capital: A Bourdieusian perspective on the digital divide*. Emerald.

Reyna, J., Hanham, J., & Meier, P. (2018). The Internet explosion, digital media principles and implications to communicate effectively in the digital space. *E-learning and Digital Media*, *15*(1), 36–52.

Sahelices-Pinto, C., & Rodríguez-Santos, C. (2014). E-WOM and 2.0 opinion leaders. *Journal of Food Products Marketing*, *20*(3), 244–261.

Sato, S. (2019). Freemium as optimal menu pricing. *International Journal of Industrial Organization*, *63*, 480–510.

Saura, J. R., Palos-Sánchez, P., & Cerdá Suárez, L. M. (2017). Understanding the digital marketing environment with KPIs and web analytics. *Future Internet*, *9*(4), 76.

Vieira, V. A., de Almeida, M. I. S., Agnihotri, R., & Arunachalam, S. (2019). In pursuit of an effective B2B digital marketing strategy in an emerging market. *Journal of the Academy of Marketing Science*, *47*(6), 1085–1108.

Weber, M., & Chatzopoulos, C. G. (2019). Digital customer experience: The risk of ignoring the non-digital experience. *International Journal of Industrial Engineering Management*, *10*(3), 201–210.

Glossary

Buzz: excitement or a talking point amongst online audience members

Digital disruption: the internet's deep impact upon marketing and commerce in general

Earned media: unpaid online media in which others communicate the brand according to its merits

Electronic word of mouth (EWOM): online peer-to-peer (P2P) conversations

Omnichannel strategy: a user-focused marketing strategy integrating online and offline resources

Opinion leaders: influential peers who judge products and communicate their findings to audiences

Owned media: media owned and controlled by a firm

Paid media: media not owned by a firm but used for a fee

Permission marketing: marketing to users who have 'opted in' or chosen not to 'opt out'

Digital Marketing Case Study: Northumbria University

Northumbria University is located in the city centre of Newcastle-upon-Tyne in Northeast England. Previously a 'polytechnic' which focused overwhelmingly on teaching undergraduate students, it has since adopted a more balanced approach, significantly increasing the scale and prestige of its research and innovation activities. It is an anchor institution at the heart of the regional economy and society. Students' employability, learning experiences, and satisfaction are still of paramount importance, and students increasingly demand evidence of value for money, having paid tuition fees, rent, and living expenses. Many of Northumbria's students are drawn from the North East and North of England, but a significant number (especially at postgraduate level) come from elsewhere in the UK, the European Union, and more distant countries such as China, India, and Nigeria. The university considers itself a 'challenger institution' – no longer a former polytechnic but a true rival to more prestigious and research-rich universities. This is reflected by its growing international reputation within higher education. Whilst the main campuses are in the vibrant yet affordable city of Newcastle, the university also has campuses in Central London, Amsterdam, Qatar, and Sri Lanka

continued

and has strategic partnerships with other institutions in Hong Kong and Singapore, amongst many others.

Northumbria University is very active in all aspects of marketing communications but particularly in digital and online marketing. Its audiences, at home and abroad, include current and prospective students, alumni, parents and families, researchers, businesses, governments and public sector organisations, funding bodies, current and prospective staff, and student recruitment agents. It maintains a presence on Twitter, Facebook, and other social media platforms and uses email marketing to convey messages to target audiences. It projects a modern, inclusive image which draws upon a solid academic tradition whilst being forward-facing in its desire to empower students and other stakeholders.

Imagine you work in Northumbria University's central marketing department and have been tasked with overhauling its digital strategy to broaden awareness amongst prospective students from the South of England and from sub-Saharan Africa. Visit the university's current website and social media pages and draw a table to identify what you like and would retain, and what you would prefer to replace, explaining your rationale. Next, decide which digital communication media you would harness, indicating an approximate proportion of the total digital marketing spend which you would allocate to each. Then describe the messages, tone, and imagery which you would employ for each target audience, explaining the reasoning behind this and what you wish to achieve. Finally, choose four key metrics which you would use to ascertain the success of your strategy, saying why they are relevant and important.

Index

For Product Safety Concerns and Information please contact our EU
representative GPSR@taylorandfrancis.com
Taylor & Francis Verlag GmbH, Kaufingerstraße 24, 80331 München, Germany

www.ingramcontent.com/pod-product-compliance
Ingram Content Group UK Ltd.
Pitfield, Milton Keynes, MK11 3LW, UK
UKHW050109250425
457818UK00015B/354